Totalitarian Experience and Knowledge Production

Post-Western Social Sciences and Global Knowledge

The titles published in this series are listed at *brill.com/psgk*

Totalitarian Experience and Knowledge Production

Sociology in Central and Eastern Europe 1945–1989

By

Svetla Koleva

Translated by

Vladimir Vladov

BRILL

LEIDEN | BOSTON

Cover illustration: 'Ripple' by Boyan Montero. The image suggests the vague and diluted roles and positions that people – including sociologists – were obliged to hold in societies under a totalitarian regime. The two stones resemble human faces or masks. Their orientation towards the curved, rainbow-like line could be interpreted as a striving for knowledge, amidst all this blurriness. The title of the picture, Ripple, may remind us of the consecutive, and somewhat repetitive, waves of state policy towards sociology under the Communist regimes and their efforts to study and understand this society.

Library of Congress Cataloging-in-Publication Data

Names: Koleva, Svetla, author.
Title: Totalitarian experience and knowledge production : sociology in
    Central and Eastern Europe 1945-1989 / by Svetla Koleva ; translated by
    Vladimir Vladov.
Description: Leiden ; Boston : Brill, [2018] | Series: Totalitarian
    experience and knowledge production, ISSN 2352-5827 ; Volume 2 | Includes
    bibliographical references.
Identifiers: LCCN 2017041685 | ISBN 9789004322325 (hardback : alk. paper)
Subjects: LCSH: Sociology–Europe, Central–History–20th century. |
    Sociology–Europe, Eastern–History–20th century.
Classification: LCC HM477.E85 K65 2018 | DDC 301.0943–dc23
LC record available at https://lccn.loc.gov/2017041685

Typeface for the Latin, Greek, and Cyrillic scripts: "Brill". See and download: brill.com/brill-typeface.

ISSN 2352-5827
ISBN 978-90-04-32232-5 (hardback)
ISBN 978-90-04-33363-5 (e-book)

Beyond its declared choice of content (sociology as science, methodological study, knowledge controlled and organized in a conceptual system), every sociology is a very particular practice of scientific reason.

GIOVANNI BUSINO, *La sociologie sens dessus dessous/Sociology Turned Upside Down* (1992)

• • •

What is sociology? What is ethnology? It is foremost a complete questioning of the person devoting himself to it.

GERMAINE TILLION, *Fragments de vie/Fragments of Life* (2009)

• • •

In other words, perhaps someday we too will revisit everything in a different way –
we again, with a different view. That will be a frenetic desire to know, the passion of rediscovery, the contagious fever of erudition.
It will be a new perspective on everything,
a different another way of seeing and depicting the world.

ÉVELYNE DE LA CHENELIÈRE, *Les pieds des anges/The Feet of Angels* (2009)

• •
  •

Contents

Preface

Every book is written with particular intentions and ambitions, and involves specific challenges. The present book is no exception to this rule.

In *Totalitarian Experience and Knowledge Production*, we not only recognize the existence of totalitarianism and discuss the process of social cognition, but we support the idea of a possible connection between the two. Then, by adding the specification 'Sociology in Central and Eastern Europe 1945–1989', we narrow down the pursuit of knowledge about society to the time of totalitarian regimes within a concrete geo-political region and historical span. We thereby outline at once the intention, ambition, and challenges of this book.

In contrast to the normatively tinged assertion that sociology as a product of modernity can only exist under conditions of democracy and a free market, here we present the sociological rationalization of society—including society organized on totalitarian principles—as a "structuration of shared/common experience" (Gardani, 2013). We do not deny that sociology was born in specific societies and through a number of founding achievements (Fabiani, 1993, 1994), yet we cannot accept the idea there is only a single matrix for the development of this science, a matrix that must serve as an invariable yardstick for measuring the validity of any produced sociological knowledge. Assuming that cognition in social science represents a rational and methodical response to problems arising 'here and now', problems that coexisting individuals encounter in their personal and social experience, then the development of the science is inseparable from that specific experience and has the task of problematizing both the experience and the ways in which it is studied. Breaking from the democratic political traditions of society, totalitarianism as a social form of total domination is a product of the action (or inaction) of individuals and groups, including professional groups, but it also serves as a context of life-together and of its reflection. Hence, the practice of sociology under totalitarianism is part of the latter's specific organization; the challenge to researchers is to understand that practice in terms of its own measure rather than in terms of some previously given or presumed model.

Why is it that, 25 years after the collapse of Communism as a social-political system, we have chosen to revisit one of the forms of the rationalization of this system—sociology as practiced under the Communist regimes in Central and Eastern Europe? There may be various justifications of this interest, but I believe at least three reasons for it merit our special attention.

The past years since that collapse have shown that a change of labels is not in itself equal to a change of the cognitive attitudes and of the analytical approaches; that the designations functioning within a given social context may long conceal the realities and hamper the actual analysis of those realities (for instance, the societies in Central and Eastern European countries in the period 1945–1989 designated as 'socialist' at the time, were identified as 'totalitarian' after the collapse of the regime); that a change of conditions does not automatically lead to a change of cognitive practices; that the suppressed, pushed aside, forgotten past stands in the way of the present and delays the onset of a better future, desired by all.

Secondly, in the recently proliferating sociological and anthropological studies of the past influenced by Carlo Ginzburg's micro history paradigm, we remark that one element is persistently missing. Researchers seem to forget that the analysis of the past must start with what they themselves produced during that time, a time that was once the present in which they were living. In their initial enthusiasm about the historical change after 1989, social researchers were eager to study the unique transition from socialism to capitalism. Later they directed their attention to a dissection of the past socialism. In the last ten years, they have taken up the problems of globalization and the world crisis. Yet they have rarely looked back at the cognitive products of the Communist past or at themselves as authors of those products. It was as if, with the historical condemnation of the totalitarian past, all the experience acquired in that period, all the knowledge produced, all the traditions established had also disappeared into the past, and the economic and political transformation of the former Communist societies had transformed these scholars into qualitatively new agents of action and cognition.

Thirdly, in the period after 1989, we witnessed an interesting paradox. Beyond the strategic, politically aimed analyses which had continued throughout the whole Cold War period, Central and Eastern Europe became an object of interest for Western Europe only after ceasing to be a single geopolitical entity. Europe's division in two which had lasted more than forty years resulted in the West's consciously overlooking the other part of the continent, and in the coercively imposed mutual suspicion and lack of familiarity. But after 1989, this gave way to a brief, enthusiastic rediscovery, soon replaced with pragmatic relationships between leading and catching up countries in an expanding European Union. That year also put an end to the East-West divide in the field of social sciences, and sociology in particular, but not to the legacies of this divide. At the start of the changes, the basic form of exchange between Western and East European scholars was the one-way transfer of theories, methods, techniques, and practices from West to East. Guided by the cliché notion that their Eastern colleagues had pursued a highly ideologized professional practice under Communism, Western sociologists undertook the theoretical purification and methodological restructuring of the research field in the East of Europe. For their part, the sociologists of the former Communist countries who were under the stigma of a historical failure willingly accepted the transfer of knowledge and experience, without subjecting to reflection the epistemological foundation of this knowledge or its theoretical-methodological applicability. As for their own previous practice during the time of Communism, they simply turned their backs on it. Since it belonged to a past that had proven a failure, they felt this previous practice was more a burden that should be forgotten or rejected than a legacy worth studying and interpreting.

Without lingering on the specific modalities assumed by this distancing from the Communist experience (whether purposeful oblivion, unconscious suppression, embarrassed silence on the matter, firm denial, or a selective attitude to its various parts), we wish to point out that, very soon, sociologists in the East and the West alike realized that the past can neither be replaced nor changed, but can only be understood and assimilated in various ways. Early on, in the mid-1990s, attempts began at joint self-reflection on the preceding development of the discipline in different national contexts. The aim was to re-position it amid the growing internationalization and interdisciplinarity of scientific cognition. These collective efforts were manifest in two different research strategies with respect to the Socialist, Communist, or totalitarian[1] past of sociology. On the one hand, that past was integrated into the panoramas of contemporary sociology through the prism of its national variants (Genov, 1989; Genov, Becker, 2001; Kaase, Sparschuh, Wenninger, 2002; Keen, Mucha 1994, 2003; Kolaja, Das, 1990; Nedelmann, Sztompka, 1993; Patel, 2010). The practice of sociology under Communism was thought of in terms of broadly defined oppositions such as interruption-continuity, tradition-change, external-internal factors of development, East-West, Marxism–non-Marxist paradigms; it was presented as a negative experience that had developed in deviation from, or opposition to the world heritage and development of the discipline which was essentially Western in its origin, its sources of inspiration

---

1   The predicate would change depending on the theoretical paradigm through which the authors viewed the period under study. See the summary of debates on this issue in Deyanova (2008, 2010) and Kabakchieva (2016). Although linked to different theoretical paradigms, the adjectives 'socialist', 'communist', 'totalitarian' used by various authors are viewed here as conceptual identifiers of societies governed by the monopoly-holding and all-embracing power of the Communist Party (Kornai, 1992). As for the book's analytical model, it is based on the idea that the structural nature of the societies built after World War II in the countries of Central and Eastern Europe was gradually revealed in the course of dynamical interaction between the political, ideological, and sociological rationalizations of social reality (Part 1).

and its power of renewal. Thus, the Communist past of sociology in Central and Eastern Europe was included as an obligatory item in the periodically undertaken summing up of the discipline's history. The national specificities could introduce some local color to the general picture, but remained indiscernible and insignificant for the analysis of the major mission of sociology: the production of well-argued and objectively valid knowledge about the societies under study. On the other hand, an autonomous research field gradually emerged the basic object of which was the sociological practice from the time of Communism and the sum total of its theoretical, methodological, institutional, and deontological aspects. Various scholars in this discipline engaged in the search for explanations of what had happened *to*, and *in*, sociology in the societies under domination of the Communist party-state in Central and Eastern Europe. These researchers included both such as had actually taken part in the development of sociology in that period in those countries, and their disciples who had received their formation before or just after 1989; it also included Western sociologists who did not have their Eastern colleagues' direct personal experience of living and working under Communism. Depending on the traditions and specific conditions of reorganizing research in the different countries, the analysis of the recent past of sociology assumed different tempos and stresses, depths, and intensities. But in all cases, the focus of critical self-reflection was the practice of sociology in the Communist past *within a single country* most often viewed separately, and rarely compared with others in the same region and same period.[2]

But in both research strategies, the national sociologies of the former Communist countries of Central and Eastern Europe did not engage in dialogue with one another, did not see their work as part of a shared search for knowledge in which their specific cognitive and social experience—both similar to and different from the others—could question the very process per se of production of knowledge. This book was conceived with the intention precisely of placing in a *common framework* and in a *comparative perspective* the national

---

2 One of the rare exceptions is the project "Sociology in Eastern and Central Europe" initiated by the Department of Sociology in Toruń. This was a comparative study of Polish, Czech and Slovak sociology. Two conferences were held in the framework of the project: "Serving the Community or the Ruling Power? Polish Sociology in 1944–1989", Toruń, November 1995, and "For Continuity and Modernity: Preconditions, Possibilities, and Reality of the Development of Sociology in Slovakia", Bratislava, November 1996 (Turčan, Laiferová, 1997). See also Voříšek (2008). Even the book by Zinaida Golenkova and Nikolay Narbut (2010) on the history of sociological thought in Central and Eastern Europe discusses separately each national sociology (with its respective stages and trends of theoretical development).

sociologies that existed under Communism in Central and Eastern Europe. Underlying this intention is the belief that *comparative history* enables us not only to highlight the common and the specific in the development of a given phenomenon, but also to see how the distinguishing features contain, in an embryonic state, certain elements of convergence, while the shared features may conceal certain fundamental divergences.

The idea of conducting a comparative study of the national trajectories of sociology under the Communist regimes of Central and Eastern Europe was first tested through the research project "Sociology in Central and Eastern Europe from the Mid-1950s to 1989: The Road to the Challenges of the 1990s" conducted with the financial assistance of the Research Support Scheme of the Open Society Foundation, and implemented in the period July 1999—June 2001. Valuable incentives for this venture were provided by my meetings with some key figures of sociology in former Communist countries,[3] including Bulgarian sociologists Andrey Bundzulov, Stefan Donchev, Veska Kozhuharova (1938–2015), Chavdar Kyuranov (1921–2004), Stoyan Mihailov, Mihail Mirchev, Petar-Emil Mitev, Victor Samuilov, Mincho Semov (1935–2006), Zahari Staikov (1927–2001), Nikolai Tilkidjiev (1953–2012), Iordanka Tropolova, Kiril Vasilev (1918–2014), and statisticians Boris Chakalov, Anastas Totev (1906–2000), Venetz Tzonev (1917–2008), Yordan Venedikov (1933–2012); the Polish sociologists Jakub Karpiński (1940–2003), Hieronim Kubiak, Jolanta Kulpińska, Władysław Kwaśniewicz (1926–2004), Edmund Wnuk-Lipiński (1944–2015), Edmund Mokrzycki (1937–2001), Witold Morawski, Andrzej Rychard, Paweł Starosta, Antoni Sułek, Jerzy Szacki (1929–2016), Piotr Sztompka, Jerzy Wiatr, Krzysztof Zagórski; the Russian sociologists Andrey Alekseev, Albert Baranov, Gennady Batygin (1951–2003), Alexandre Boronoev, Alexandre Duka, Yurii Davidov, Boris Firsov, Alexandre Gofmann, Boris Grushin (1929–2007), Vladimir Kostyushev, Vladimir Kozlovskiy, Yurii Levada (1930–2006), Valery Mansurov, Marina Pugacheva, Vladimir Yadov (1929–2015); the Czech sociologists Jiří Buriánek, Pavel Kuchař, Miloš Havelka, Michal Illner, Pavel Machonin (1927–2008), Zdenka Mansfeldová, Ivo Možný (1932–2016), Jiří Večerník; the Slovak sociologists Dilbar Alijevová, Vladimír Krivý, Eva Laiferová, Ladislav Macháček (1942–2015), Soňa Szomolányi, Ľudovit Turčan; and the Hungarian sociologists Róbert Angelusz (1939–2010), Zsuzsa Ferge, Tamás Kolosi, Csaba Makó, Dénes Némedi (1942–2010), Péter Somlai, Julia Szalai, Ágnes Utasi. To them, and to all other colleagues who

---

3   The presentation of sociologists by countries follows the chronology of fieldwork in the frame of the research project.

accepted the challenge of conducting joint 'socio-analysis' of the Communist past of our discipline, I extend my heartfelt gratitude.

In the decade following that project, I fortunately had the professional opportunity to submit the project results to the pure curiosity of students (the kind of curiosity that comes before the interest of experienced scholars marked to various degrees by professional, political or national bias). These were students in the bachelor's, master's and doctoral programs in sociology at Sofia University St. Kliment Ohridsky (2010–2017), the University of Toulouse Jean Jaurès (2006), the University of Moncton, Edmundston campus (2006), and the University of Quebec in Montreal (2009, 2013, 2014, 2016). My work with these future specialists/professionals/sociologists was of decisive importance for the conception and development of the publication project. Decisive in two respects: first, the questions asked and interpretations offered by people who were biographically remote from the totalitarian reality in question, and who knew about the past and present of Eastern Europe mostly from literary sources rather than personal travel or contacts stimulated me to problematize what seemed self-evident in my life and professional experience, made me seek finer distinctions and more precise explanations. Secondly, in trying to understand the sociological practice under conditions of totalitarian regimes, the students often drew parallels with the current social reality and knowledge familiar to them. This sensitivity to any manifestation of monopolistic, undemocratic, opaque functioning in society affirmed my belief that knowledge is the most powerful weapon against totalitarian tendencies. Being very grateful to all my students, I would like to point out that their unconventional questions and original comments were some of the best incentives for my work on this book.

The book represents a token of gratitude to all the colleagues in different countries, of different generations and institutional background or circles with whom, on various occasions and in different ways, we have tried to understand that which has become our common heritage, even if not personally experienced by all of us. In expressing my respect and gratitude to all my colleagues, I would like to mention the much regretted Jean-Michel Berthelot who was director of the Center for Studies of Rationalities and Knowledge/ Centre d'études des rationalités et des savoirs and of the Institute for Doctoral Studies/Institut d'études doctorales at the University of Toulouse in the 1990s, and from 1998 to the end of his life in 2006, was professor in philosophy of the social sciences and sociology, and director of the Center for Sociological Studies/Centre d'études sociologiques at the University Paris-Sorbonne. Without his invitation to me to give a lecture course in the framework of the International Cooperation Competition Program of the French Ministry of Education and Research (1996–1998), and his conviction that the Communist past of sociology in Central and Eastern Europe is part of the collective history of this discipline and raises challenges to its contemporary development, the comparative study of national sociologies in former Communist Bloc countries would not have advanced from the stage of conception to the stage of completion. It is for the reader to decide whether this completed product has in fact fulfilled the initial ambitions and answered the defined challenge.

Acknowledgments

This book would not have been possible without the support and helpful care of colleagues and friends in Bulgaria, France, and Canada who were always reliable companions on the road to its completion.

I would like to extend my gratitude to all my colleagues from the Department of Knowledge Society: Science, Education, Innovations at the Institute for the Study of Societies and Knowledge of Bulgarian Academy of Sciences (ISSK/BAS); communicating with them brought constant confirmation of Kant's maxim that the '*correctness*' of our *thinking lies* in that we *think* in *community with others.*

I owe special thanks to Professors Pepka Boyadjieva, Liliana Deyanova, Georgi Fotev, Galin Gornev, Petar-Emil Mitev, Tanya Nedelcheva and Kristina Petkova for the scientific rigor and intellectual generosity with which they reviewed my dissertation "Sociology in Central and Eastern Europe, 1945–1989. Towards a Reflexive History of the Discipline" defended at the ISSK/BAS for the scientific degree Doctor of Science.

At various stages of my work, I have received stimulating remarks, ideas, suggestions, and comments from Associate Professor Patricia Vannier (University of Toulouse Jean Jaurès), Professor Jacques Boucher (University of Quebec in Outaouais), Professor Guy Ménard (University of Nancy). Professor Marie-Blanche Tahon at Ottawa University, Professor Shirley Roy at the University of Quebec in Montreal, and Claude Gauthier in Montreal created an atmosphere of intellectual care and empathy that enabled me to keep up my courage at the final, decisive stage of writing this book. To all of them I am deeply thankful.

The work would not have been more than a fond project without the invitation of Laurence Roulleau-Berger, Research Director at National Center of Scientific Research CNRS (France) and Series Editor at Brill; and without the professional skill and devoted efforts of the translator Vladimir Vladov, my colleague at the ISSK/BAS, it would not have reached the reading audience in English.

I want to thank my family and all my friends for their patience and their faith in me all along my professional path.

Introduction

Yesterday's sociology reviewed today, or, the past of sociology as it existed in the context of totalitarianism viewed today in the crossing perspectives of those who once practiced it in the countries of Central and Eastern Europe. This is the topic of the present book as well as the scope of its content. This is not an orderly and comprehensive history of East European sociology from the end of World War II and until the end of the Cold War, but an attempt at *reflexive history* of the discipline's development in the specific time and space situated between the establishment and the fall of the Communist regimes in Central and Eastern Europe. In this history, the past becomes an object of reflection for its own protagonists who strive to understand it—not in order to reject it or justify it, but to identify, on the basis of the scientific production and the lived experience, the inner resources, interiorized constraints, outward temptations, self-produced pitfalls which accompanied the practice of sociology in totalitarian organized social world.

Why was sociology able to exist and survive in the post-war non-democratic societies (under Communist/totalitarian/authoritarian regimes) in Central and Eastern Europe that lived under comparatively similar conditions of ideological, political, and social control, under the cognitive monopoly of the ideologized Marxist paradigm, and under various degrees (depending on the concrete country and period) of cognitive isolationism? This was the question that impelled my research efforts in the late 1990s in my capacity as a sociologist from a former Soviet Bloc country formed during the 1980s in two different scientific traditions—the Bulgarian and the French, and a researcher who practiced sociology from the early 1990s in a variety of academic and institutional contexts of production and reproduction of sociological knowledge. Without attaching to these biographical circumstances any greater meaning than that of a historical and social coincidence, I deem them worth mentioning as they may be relevant to the reader's vigilance regarding the analysis that follows. This analysis would not fulfill the requirements of scientific procedure, were it to remain enclosed in the biographical context that engendered it and seek to legitimize the cognitive results of this study on the basis of that context. However, recognizing the initial particularity of the author's position, this analysis could transcend it by subjecting the facts it deals with to the requirements of the pursuit of objectively valid knowledge. Even if it be partial and temporally situated (which would make it inevitably surpassable by other analyses), the scientific reliability of such knowledge

© KONINKLIJKE BRILL NV, LEIDEN, 2018 | DOI 10.1163/9789004333635_002

would stem not from the author's biographic background but from the way knowledge is attained, i.e., from its verifiability by the sociological community.

The question raised here derives from at least two paradoxes.[1] Firstly, the idea that sociology appeared within the family of sciences in the second half of the 19th century in response to new social problems posed by the emerging bourgeois society, and that it has developed to date in the form of a pluralist research program in politically democratic and economically free structures, is a view that excludes the possibility of the science of society developing in unfree societies which totalitarian societies generally are (Adorno, 1959; Geiger, 1949; Kelle, 1994; Lipset, 1959; Merton, 1973). On the other hand, before the demise of the totalitarian system, in all countries of the Communist camp there existed variously sized university and research structures working in the field of sociology, structures that had their own channels of dissemination of sociological literature and a system for the professional realization of sociologists.[2] The use of empirical social surveys gradually extended to nearly all spheres of social life; international studies were conducted in the framework of the Communist camp countries, and in some cases, collaboration extended to Western sociologists as well. This discrepancy between the theoretical principle and the empirical reality requires an explanation beyond the formal logical conclusion that the knowledge produced in undemocratic societies of Central and Eastern Europe was something other than sociology—or, at best, that the scientific and research practice figuring as sociology in these countries was of a particular (meaning non-Western) type. Secondly, in the first decade of the post-Communist period, there was an evident discrepancy between, on the one hand, the research experience accumulated by East European sociologists and, on the other hand, the way that experience was used and assessed by the international scientific community represented by the leading national

1   With regard to the present study, it is precisely these paradoxes that justify adopting a different starting point than the prevailing tradition where the initial question is commonly related to the conditions that make a given practice possible. The indicated paradoxes in fact point to the presence of a priori research attitudes that blur the practices in question to the point where they are excluded from the legitimate objects of research. The question *why* subverts and challenges the stereotypes; answering this question enables us to reach "the general question as to the conditions of the possibility of any scientific practice" (Bourdieu, Passeron, 1970: 64)—in this case, the sociological practice in totalitarian societies of Communist type.
2   What the contents of these structures and practices are, how they exist, and what is their cognitive and social importance, is a different matter. It is one of the questions dealt with in this book.

traditions of Western Europe and North America. The bi-polar way of thinking proved persistent even after the geo-political opening of borders, and continued to reproduce its own stereotypes. In applying their institutional mechanisms of selection, funding and management of joint research projects, and in using the more subtle mechanisms of division of intellectual labour, the cooperation programmes of the international foundations and the national governments (Great Britain, Germany, France, US) confirmed Central and Eastern Europe as a region synonymous with a specific profile of research practice. According to this view, the region carried the burden of its past and had to be assisted both at the theoretical-methodological and the organizational level. For their part, the sociologists from the former Communist countries—who felt marked by their inglorious past and had long awaited the opportunity to carry on free dialogue—were willing to accept the subordinate role relegated to them in this international division of labour. For both sides, the factor at stake was the legacies (in terms of theoretical and empirical research traditions, institutions, and staff) with which sociologists interacted in the new world without borders. This legacy, though rejected, passed over in silence, suppressed, or stigmatized, was nevertheless a common legacy and needed to be explained in the interest of sociology as a professional choice and vocation.

In this book, we think about the *past as a common history*, "even if that which is common is only the continuation of a controversy", as Daniel Innerarity notes (2009: 127). In attempting to capture that constantly questioned common past, we have privileged only a single, limited angle of view, that of the position of sociology facing its own history—more specifically, the attitude of national sociologies in Central and Eastern Europe to their own experience in communist-type totalitarian society. The justification of this choice of perspective is simple. Being the protagonists of this history, the sociological professional communities in these countries are the first to reveal or conceal, to value or devalue, various periods of their own development; they are also the first to bear the consequences of the verdict of history. Moreover, they are the first to know what it means to do sociology under the specific conditions of a Communist regime—simply because they themselves lived through and underwent Communism. As Germaine Tillion put it in her diary, "only in living can one become convinced that the *lived through* events are the key to the *observed* events" (2009). In other words, "to live through" a given reality, and "to observe" it are the two sides of the process of cognition; they mutually prove, reflect, amplify, question each other. Professional experience is inseparable from the experience its carriers have lived through, reflectively interpreted, and appropriated at various points of that experience including its emergence, repetition or rejection. Hence, every scientific discipline unfolds in this double movement of practicing scientific reason and then reflecting upon that practice. The discipline comprises what is done, produced, transmitted, and, concurrently, what is thought, said, discovered, confirmed or rejected about the results of its activity; in this way, a science legitimates the conditions of its practice, of its continuity in time.

This book is situated in the framework of this double movement which we attempt to encompass by dwelling on and interpreting historical facts, by outlining the perspectives and the drawn conclusions pertaining to various points of the event history, by observing the corrections made in the course of time, the personal self-disclosures, the painful process of coming to awareness, and the specialized analyses. Each of these elements of the book has a specific epistemological role; although the fact that they are discussed together may create the impression of a post-modern mix, they each have a separate role in the overall interpretation. They are mutually connected here within the theoretical framework of the analysis, presented in Part 1 of the book.

Thus, the object of analysis is the way in which sociology was constructed, developed and practiced under the specific conditions of a communist-type totalitarian society. In historical and geopolitical terms, the scope of study is limited to the sociological practice in six former Communist countries—Bulgaria, Czech Republic, Hungary, Poland, Slovakia, and the USSR—viewed as empirical examples of the realization of a new societal project in the framework of totalitarian structures and forms of governance. The justification of this historical and geopolitical limitation of the field of study derives from the common structural—scientific and non-scientific—context that these countries shared.[3] They were the countries best integrated within the cooperation structures during the period in question—in economic (Comecon), military-political (the Warsaw Pact) and scientific (the International Varna Sociological School/IVSS,[4] the Problem Committees for Multilateral Collaboration between the Academies

---

3 The context which, as indicated from the start, is fundamental to the comparative analysis that follows, itself needs to be explained before it is used for interpretative and explanatory purposes. This preliminary explanation will be given in the second chapter of Part 1.

4 Created by decision of the vice presidents of the Academies of Sciences of the Socialist countries in May 1980, the school is a "scientific initiative of the sociological institutes and sociological associations of the Socialist countries" (IVSS, *Statutes*, Art. 1); its work is effectuated by a Scientific Council, a director and scientific secretary whose functions and mandate are defined in Chapter 1 of the Statutes. Among the founding countries were Bulgaria, Vietnam (SR vietnam), GDR, Mongolia, Poland, USSR, Hungary, Czechoslovakia. The first session of the School was held on June 1–7, 1981 in Varna (Bulgaria). The sessions were organized to take place every two years and were hosted by the member states on a rotating basis. The last (fifth) session was held on September 4–8, 1989 in Seč (Czechoslovakia).

of Sciences of the Socialist Countries)[5] terms. Although the German Democratic Republic participated in these structures, the particularities of its historical formation in 1949 and of its post-Communist development after 1990 separate it from the others as a specific research case. As varying as may have been the post-war evolution of Rumania, Yugoslavia, and Albania,[6] these three East European Communist countries were also excluded from the analysis due to a common particularity of theirs. At different times before and after the death of Stalin, they took distance from the Soviet model of Socialism, and followed their separate paths of development until the collapse of the Communism.

Proceeding from the assumption that sociology is foremost a production of scientific knowledge about the social world—knowledge made valid with reference to models of rational critique adopted in the discipline (Berthelot, 2001)—the study of the forms and modalities of development of this science in the former Communist countries is focused on the particularities of socio-logical knowledge production in the one-dimensional socio-political, ideolog-ical and epistemic space of the Communist party-state. *What kind of knowledge was produced in* and *about* the Eastern European societies that implemented the political and social project of Socialism from the end of WWII until 1989, *how* was it produced, and *what cognitive and social value* did it have? Such is the research prism through which we attempt to capture and understand the development of *sociology under a totalitarian organization of the social world*. This development is viewed in terms of the *science's own measure of things*, i.e., as it itself constructed, grounded and applied knowledge about society—a society that though built as socialist was demystified in the course of its devel-opment and came to be seen as totalitarian. We believe that here lies the great-est challenge to the study of the sociology practiced in Central and Eastern Europe under the Communist regimes. The interdependence between science and context is accepted as an axiomatic truth, but it becomes problematic and gives rise to a series of questions regarding the relations between the *context* of practicing sociology, the *subject of sociology*, and the *practice of sociology per se*. What kind of society were sociologists in the former Communist coun-tries actually working in and studying? Was it the Socialist society proclaimed by the political project of the Communist party-state; or the Socialist society viewed today as a totalitarian society; or the delegitimized Socialist society; or the society of that time full of incipient totalitarian trends?

---

5   These commissions were created in the early 1970s and ceased to exist with the collapse of
    the Communist system.

6   For instance, unlike Yugoslavia and Albania, Rumania remained a Comecon and Warsaw
    Pact member to the end.

Posed in such a way, these questions imply an important assumption under-lying this analysis: that the development of sociology in Central and Eastern Europe in the period 1945–1989 was simultaneously part of specific histories and of a collective history. This refers to the perception of the history of the dis-cipline not in terms of the opposition of continuity vs. discontinuity, but as a complex and contradictory interplay between 'capturing' the problem (which is always situated in time and space) and interpreting the problem in a suitable theoretical perspective (which draws its legitimacy in the poly-paradigmatic field of sociology—whether a theoretical paradigm has already been estab-lished or is yet to be created in the course of research). Doing sociology in a definite place and time amounts, in fact, to its realization as a scientific proj-ect, i.e., "as a project of study [...] *with a scientific aim* (i.e., a study as rational, positive and objective as possible) of *the social facts as such*" (Simon, 2001: 2).[7] When this perspective is applied to the study of sociology as practiced in Cen-tral and Eastern Europe under the Communist regimes, it requires studying the topic through the prism of sociology's scientific tradition in order to un-derstand the trials and tribulations that the disciplinary identity of sociology had to undergo upon the emergence of new characteristics of the object and context of its scientific practice—that is, of the new Socialist society which, in the course of its development, came to be demystified as a non-democratic/unfree/authoritarian/totalitarian one.

In order to achieve the formulated objective, this analysis tests two hy-potheses which are a kind of concretization of the initial question as to the causes of the existence of sociology in a totalitarian-type society. If we may at all use the term sociology for the knowledge of society that was produced in the post-ww2 history of the Central and Eastern Europe countries, that is because the respective scholars working in this discipline managed to *build relatively autonomous institutional and cognitive zones*. In the course of perpet-ual recomposing of sociology's relations with the Communist party-state, the institutional structure of sociology in each of the discussed countries proved to be among the most important levers for the cognitive and social legitima-tion of the discipline. By means of comparative analysis of the institutional trajectories of the six national sociologies, we will reveal how sociology, in be-coming an institution *within* and *of* the structure of the totalitarian state, de-fended or failed to defend, developed or blocked its own disciplinary project. In tracing the sinuous relations between sociology and political power, we will

---

7   See also Coenen-Huther (2002), Fabiani (1994), Le Moigne (1995), Quéré (2002), Ragouet
      (1994).

distinguish the so-called *institutional cycles*, i.e., the recurring configurations of relations that led to the relatively uniform presence of sociology in the scientific field and outside it, in the respective societies during various periods of the development of sociology (Part 2).

As for cognitive autonomy, we find its manifestations in the ways East European sociologists practiced their science in the time of the Communist regimes as one of the forms of rationalization of the social world, alongside the political project of socialism and its ideological argumentation based on statist Marxism-Leninism. Across the frameworks of the separate institutional cycles, we trace the dialectical interaction between three types of rationalization of the societies of that time, and we demonstrate that each of these types *underwent the influence of, and exerted an impact on the others.* Such an analytic perspective focuses the research interest on transitions, interplay, and metamorphoses.[8] These, in turn, present a different picture of the empirical reality of society under Communism from the one depicted by the political and ideological rationalization of the regime; they also show that the sociology studying that reality was a multi-faceted discipline whose modalities of knowledge production were situated at various levels and at various distances from the politically endorsed and sanctioned model of scientific knowledge and the orthodox version of the dominant Marxist paradigm. That is why we may refer to different *modalities of sociology construction*—in each of these modalities, the components and stages of the cognitive process display different potentials for the defense of sociological knowledge from the dominant political-ideological schemas of perception and explanation of the world (Part 3). In a more concrete aspect, we assume that of all elements of the disciplinary project of sociology, the most sensitive and vulnerable is its model of scientificity. But this model is also an important source of change, inasmuch as the norms for producing scientific knowledge serve as the grounds for developing the other components of the discipline's project.

The revisiting of the sociological practice of the former Communist Bloc countries in the period 1945–1989 is invariably a risky venture whatever the chosen perspective or strategy of analysis. This period of the discipline's development was strongly charged with values, and was part of the personal and collective biography of the majority of sociologists active today in these countries.

---

8   Here we use the term "metamorphoses" in Robert Castel's sense: "'Metamorphoses', dialectics of the same and the different: to identify the historical transformations of this model, to stress the new and the permanent aspects that its main crystallizations comprise, even though in forms that might not be immediately recognizable" (Castel, 1995: 21).

They were formed as specialists within the intellectual climate, sociological practices, and educational and research structures characteristic of the period in question; some of them took part in the creation of the national institutions and traditions of sociology; and in their great majority, they were the teachers of the new generations of sociologists that came after 1989. Hence, from a purely epistemological aspect, the risk is great indeed. It lies in the danger of building a "discourse that legitimates science or a particular position in science", or that represents "a falsely neutral form of the dominant discourse of science about itself" (Bourdieu, 2001: 19). A possible means of escape from the trap of self-legitimation would be the reflexivity of what Bourdieu calls realist epistemology (Ibid.: 173-174).

> Understood as an effort whereby social science taking itself as object uses its own resources to comprehend and control itself, it [realist epistemology] is an especially efficacious means of increasing the chances of attaining the truth, [...] which makes it possible to control more carefully the factors that might distort the study. It is not a question of pursuing a new form of absolute knowledge, but of applying a specific form of epistemological vigilance—such as the vigilance in the course of fieldwork where the epistemological obstacles are primarily of a social kind.

In applying this reflexivity, let us point out at the start: the approach chosen here to the study of the sociology that existed in the countries under Communist regimes—an approach using various forms of self-description of sociological practice (academic production and personal testimonies of the participants)—has its limitations and blank spots. On the one hand, we have used the sociological analyses published before and after 1989 in separate countries; we examine these as being ways of presentation, defense, affirmation of sociology as a legitimate and autonomous activity for the study of society—ways applied in different periods of the development of the science and in specific national contexts. On the other hand, we have used the interviews conducted in 1999–2002 with 69 sociologists involved in the formation of their discipline in different periods of its post-war development in each country. These interviews are valuable because of the time they were made—they express the viewpoint of sociologists ten years after the Great Change. The two types of information sources placed here and now in mutual distance dialogue retain their epistemological value, but certainly undergo a change of meaning. However, precisely because of "the variability of meaning, depending on one's position in the chronotope" (Todorova, 2003: 16), they enable us to see the past through the kaleidoscope of contextualized analyses, assessments, commentaries as a key to understanding the past. If the reader, in turn, recognizes, questions, or puts in doubt the drawn conclusions regarding the development of sociology in the former Communist countries in the period 1945–1989, this would be convincing proof that the past of the discipline is part of the present and holds a perpetually renewed potential for problematizing its own practice.

PART 1

Methodological Notes

∵

CHAPTER 1

Following the Traces of the Past:
The Methodological Pitfalls of Time

> The world we live in at any moment is the world of the past.
>   HANNAH ARENDT (1961)

> If we are something, we are our past… Our past is our memory.
> That memory can be hidden or inaccurate—it doesn't matter. It's there, isn't it?
> It can be a lie but that lie becomes part of our memory, part of us.
>   JORGE LUIS BORGES (2014)

How to study the past of sociology in Central and Eastern Europe under the Communist regimes, both being part of it and knowing the end of the story? This question contains what is most importantly at stake in this study—to achieve valid knowledge about sociology under the specific conditions of a society that has passed into history, and to gain that knowledge with the assistance of people who practiced sociology in those past times. The task is even more complicated by the fact that this study was conceived and carried out more than 15 years ago, but presents its results today; this interval of time has inevitably led, in some degree and in some direction, to shifts of the conceptual framework of this analysis away from the theoretical model of the initial research project. Whatever its causes, the stretch of time of the research work is significant as regards how time is involved in cognitive activity, and as regards the methodological, epistemological, and deontological effect of time upon the knowledge production. Are we capable of controlling the time factor in the production of valid and verifiable knowledge, this supreme value of science?

Being an inherent element of all research, time poses what is perhaps the greatest challenge to historical study. Precisely because the actual reference point of studying the past is located in the present, the past proves to be the most mobile object of research. The present intervenes in the study of the past by raising its own questions, by referring to currently topical political and social issues, to accumulated knowledge, methodological achievements, etc. Since the present is therefore the inevitable "central element of every historical inquiry" (Chapoulie, 2005: 102), the basic methodological question is how, being situated in the present, we may study the past by its own measure, i.e., as an unfolding of events which 'happened-thus-and-not-otherwise'.

With regard to the history of social sciences, including sociology, these remarks are relevant to the ways we study the past of our particular discipline. The more than 40-year-old debate concerning the presentist vs. the historicist approach to the historical study of social sciences[1] has definitely favored historicism for its heuristic advantages in the thematic, theoretic, methodological, and deontological aspects. The principle of studying the past of any science in its own socio-historical context and in the logic of what happened 'then and there', enables us to study the past a) in the terms proper to it at a given stage of its development, and not in the categories and reference framework subsequent to that time; b) in view of the total set of conditions making its development possible 'then and there', and not in the perspective of the present-day institutional and cognitive development of science; c) by seeking the meaning and importance of scientific activity and cognitive results in and for that time, and not by ascribing values with reference to the present-day state of the discipline and its issues; d) using the specific tools of historical science (archives, testimonies, control for reliability) and going beyond the traditional focus on scientific works and their intellectual interrelatedness.

At the methodological level, the issue is to apply the "principle of non-reduction", formulated by Isabelle Stengers in connection with studying the "invention of modern sciences" (Stengers, 1993). The principle in question consists in the "refusal to reduce a situation to what the distance in time enables us to say about it today" (Ibid.: 52). This means that "before studying the products of a given situation, we must first of all identify the reference points that this situation itself has brought out" (Ibid.: 56). This is not a matter of rejecting the perspective that distance in time opens to the researcher of history of science, but of controlling the power resource that distance in time gives the researcher with respect to the "problems of the actors and their arguments [of that time]" (Ibid.: 58). Time sifts out the "winners" and "losers" at a given moment of the discipline's development, and filters the problems that are worthy or not worthy of the attention of researchers, that are resolved or important for the further development of a given science; it amplifies some arguments and devalues others (Ibid.: 52). Thus, there is a substantial risk that historical study might reproduce the trajectory of the discipline by 'piecing together' the

---

1   This discussion has drawn incentives and ideas from the epistemological debate in the history of science and in different specialties of history as a science (historiography, history of ideas, social history, micro history, etc.). A synthesis of the evolution from "conventional history" of the social sciences to a "full-fledged history" is made by Chapoulie (2005).

visible traces of the past, and not by analyzing the logic of the processes that have produced those traces.

To apply the "principle of irreducibility" to our object of research means to study the production of sociological knowledge in the time of the Communist regimes in Central and Eastern Europe not from the viewpoint of what we know today about the situation that engendered that knowledge, but in the perspective of the emergence of conditions that the situation created and that worked for the development or waning of that knowledge. This methodological requirement recalls Nietzsche's "genealogical" approach, which according to Szakolczai (1992: 93), specifically consists in

> raising the question not only about the origin and conditions of possibility, but of disappearance and breakdown as well. And the purpose of this is to identify the lasting effect beyond the visible purpose.

In other words, in studying the practice of sociology as a discipline in Central and Eastern Europe in the period 1945–1989, our task is to understand how sociology developed under the changing conditions of this new type of society which began with laying the foundations of socialism and passed through the construction of an integral socialist system until its breakdown, undergoing various crises along the way. We want to ascertain the effects of societal processes upon the particularities of sociology as a form of scientific rationalization of the respective social reality as well as the conditions for the emergence/ withering, the formation/non-formation of certain sociological practices as related to changes of the political, economic, and social framework of scientific activity.

The choice of doing a *reflexive history of sociology* in societies under Communist regimes, i.e., to study sociology with the aid of insiders on the basis of their experience and self-reflection, would require registering the effects of time upon the actors of this history. They appear in different positions with respect to the topic of research: as authors and analyzers of the disciplinary heritage, as initiators or followers of educational, institutional, editorial, research, etc. projects, as partners in international scientific collaboration, and as participants in changing partnerships with the political authorities, as critics or defenders of the discipline's past, etc. Moreover, these roles arise at different times in the development of sociology and at different times of the careers of the interviewed sociologists. "Who is speaking and in what situation is he/she speaking" (Stengers, 1997: 20), what categories of perception and assessment are in effect during the "transition from practical knowledge in a given area to reflective knowledge" (Chapoulie, 2005: 116), how do sociologists define themselves and identify themselves as a scientific community? All these questions are part of sociology's self-reflection, and they evolve in time and change their meaning and message. In that case, which is the valid picture of sociological practice in the time of the Communist regimes in Central and Eastern Europe: is it the picture that comes out of the texts published up to the end of 1989; is it the picture seen by the protagonists of history at the beginning of the 21st century, ten years after the great change; or is it the picture seen today based on the sociological heritage and its interpretation fifteen years ago? Any one-sided answer would be incorrect. The question is important primarily in that it points attention to the analytic instrument of the chronotope (the specific position in space-time) and the importance of taking into account the role of chronotope with respect to the sources of information (scientific articles, documents, interviews with sociologists) as well as taking into account the analysis offered here and the reception of this analysis. The chronotope should be viewed *not* as a factor that relativizes the scientific findings to a degree that we can say "anything goes", but as an element of the cognitive process itself, an element that illuminates the new "valence" for a given historical fact by raising new questions, revealing new, hitherto unsuspected connections, adding new viewpoints for knowledge of the past, or substituting, ousting, transcending the already existing viewpoints. Also, we should not forget that in the purely epistemological aspect, taking the chronotope into account is a measure that strengthens our critical vigilance at every stage of the cognitive process, inasmuch as spatial-temporal determination or contingency are characteristics both of the object and of the subject of knowledge. Viewed in the concrete contexts of the present (as changing configurations of actors, positions, challenges), the past of the discipline appears "richer, even more complex [...] perhaps not more 'objective' but certainly more interesting" (Stengers, 1997: 19), while the history of the discipline reveals itself as a path towards a possible "critical emancipation" (Boucheron, 2015).

The study of sociological practice in the time of Communist regimes through analyses, self-descriptions and self-reflection of the carriers of that historical experience also amounts to working with the memory of sociology as a discipline.[2] In that memory, it is possible to distinguish between contents related to the whole set of activities for building and developing the discipline, and

---

2   Here we borrow the distinction made by historical science between memory and history as forms of manifestation of the past in all social practices. The two are linked to different intentions and are not reducible to each other when we study the past of a given phenomenon. While memory is motivated by the need for legitimation and identity, history is an analytic activity of the historian guided by the interests of knowledge (Lavabre, 1994).

contents of a purely cognitive character, whether they be theoretical, methodological, or epistemological. Here we provisionally designate these two forms of memory as 'event-related' and 'cognitive'.

The former of the two refers to the retrospective interpretation of the discipline's past given by the participants themselves in that past. This interpretation may refer to the whole range of activities, actions, decisions, theoretical and institutional conflicts, events which make up the national practice of the discipline and legitimize and maintain its place in science and society. Expressed in memoirs, narratives, lived experience, this interpretation reconstructs not the past itself but the 'memory' of the past, and brings back to life not "the opinions of that time but the present-day opinions [...] regarding what happened 'then'" (Farrugia, 2000: 15). One of the basic sociological questions for contemporary social researchers of memory is how individual memories in the form of *autobiographical memory* intertwine, overlap, amalgamate in order to take part in the construction of *collective memory*, and how by that same movement, collective memory influences individual representations (Lavabre, 1994). However, both individual and collective memory are equally valuable for historical analysis, being always selective with regard to the past, calling it to life according to the imperative of the present and the current norms and values of society. They cross through the "'objective' history, including that of the discipline"[3] (Farrugia, 2000: 18), shift the emphases of the past, and illuminate the past under various angles in constant dialogue with the present. For its part, the present shows 'who' remembers and 'how', and thereby provides the researcher not with the 'truth of and/or the past' but with the variety of modes in which the past exists in the present. In other words, the memory carried by individual and collective participants in the events (in this case, participants in the cognitive and institutional construction and development of national sociologies in six Central and Eastern European countries in the period 1945–1989) reconstructs the course of those processes in a perspective that is at the borderline between objective and subjective, individual and collective, social and psychological. Thus, the individual and collective histories themselves become part of the topic of the rational history (in terms of historical study) which studies the past by means of scientific reflection and gives meaning to that past.

---

3 Farrugia writes about an 'objective' history of the discipline in the sense of Berger and Luckmann as an institutional reality whose existence both precedes and survives individuals. They 'enter' it and, through their interconnected actions and discourse, contribute to its stability and change.

As for the purely cognitive dimension of disciplinary memory, it includes the temporal relation of sociology to its own body of knowledge, methods, approaches, techniques, etc. To use the epistemological terminology of historical science, this refers to a "regime of historicity" in which the past recurs in the present, but only as knowledge (Hartog, 2003; Revel, 2001). From the viewpoint of the epistemological construction of the discipline, the problem of disciplinary memory concerns the modalities of cumulativity that characterize sociological knowledge. According to Jean-Michel Berthelot (1998: 33),

> The memory of disciplines functions in different ways depending on whether or not they are made up of mathematized theories [...]. When a certain concept is used, the natural language [of the human sciences] does not permit immediately recognizing the consecutive layers of its historical development. These sciences are not a result of slow purification [...] as in mathematics, but are a product of an indeterminate play of denotations and connotations. Thus, disciplinary memory manifests itself not directly and in an internally integrated way, but disjointedly, through reminders and references.

In other words, 'cognitive' disciplinary memory, or "conceptual memory" as Jean-Claude Passeron (1991: 106) calls it, exists objectivized in references, citations, or omissions of a theoretical, methodological and epistemological nature. Its function, similarly to historical memory in other spheres of social activity, is to legitimize, not analyze, the past of science. It is part of that past, but not part of the critical-analytic assimilation of the past that the history of the discipline provides.

Disciplinary memory has the particularity of being related to the product of cognitive activity and to the whole set of processes and relations that have made that product possible. Of course, this distinction is provisional and is meant to serve the purpose of analysis. In actual practice, the different aspects of the memory of the discipline exist as mutually linked and influence each other mutually, since they are always carried by the subject—the scientist, researcher, teacher or professional. These specialists may use different modes to express one and the same type of content (for instance, a given theory or method may be closely analyzed, critically employed in argumentation, cited in passing, permanently disregarded, or institutionally celebrated), or one and the same mode for expressing different contents (for instance, regardless of whether scholars use a given theory as a reference point or simply share the memory of the process of its creation, dissemination and application, they remain in the mode of selective reference to the past). Interwoven in the cognitive activity per se of the sociologist,[4] the forms, modes, and contents of the past of science form the tissue upon which the historians of a discipline focus in order to rationally analyze its legacy.

The important question for historical study is how to use disciplinary memory in such a way as to practice that discipline through critical self-reflection—and this, we believe, is the main purpose of occupying oneself with the history of science. Coming back to the carrier of the discipline's memory, we see that, regardless of whether they study, write, narrate or recall, the representatives of a given science are agents of an activity that is both specific—insofar as it is subordinated to the cognitive norms and rules of that discipline—and like every other social activity, insofar as it is guided by motives, intentions, goals, coercions, etc. (Bourdieu, 1980). As Giddens has pointed out (1995: 10):

> to be an 'author' of a text has a connection with being the author of an action. [...] to write something, just as to do anything, implies agency, reflexivity and the meshing of intentions with long-term projects.

In other words, if the discursive acts, written or verbal, are the empirical correlates of disciplinary memory, then apart from touching upon a certain topic or story, they are linked to the author's intentions, reflect the evolution of his/her theoretical stances and professional biases. Thus, any assertion, in the form of a scientific text or 'narrative' about science, may be viewed as a concentrated expression of the processes that have led to its formation. Such a perspective on the empirical material with which the history of science works provides several heuristic advantages for the analytical assimilation of the past of the discipline.

First, it overcomes the dilemma of the internalist vs. the externalist approaches to the discipline which puts epistemologists and historians of science in mutual opposition and divides sociologists into rationalists and relativists (Vinck, 1995: 83–138). The construction and development of disciplinary knowledge appear as a process of perpetual questioning of the formulations and assertions, their specification, updating, application, whereby the motors of this activity—the agents, resources and results—have a double, cognitive and social, identity. All these components operate concurrently and interconnectedly in scientific activity. Their joint action is objectified in a product the modes of existence of which (acceptance, rejection, oblivion, isolation,

---

4 Every cognitive act is ultimately an actualization of a scientific legacy (Fotev, 1993) regardless of whether or not the researcher's objective is concretely related to reconstruction of the discipline's past.

permanent presence) in turn depend on the coercions and influences coming both from science and from the surrounding world (Ibid.). To borrow Bourdieu's and Boltanski's terminology (Bourdieu, 1975; Boltanski, 1979), the scientist works at the borderline of different social fields—intellectual, political, cultural, industrial, etc.—which, moreover, interact with one another.

Secondly, the constructing of a discipline may be identified not only in terms of cognitive results viewed as scientific content, but also in terms of the conditions of production of those results which are always marked by the social relations existing within the scientific community and in a broader social context. At the operational level, this means that the study of a given science through its disciplinary memory follows the key events of its development viewed not in their immobility, as given once and for all, but in the perspective of the conditions and actions led to their appearance, their modeling and their change in the course of time.

Thirdly, the concept of disciplinary memory refers, albeit very selectively, to multiple actors and to the networks of relationships between actors that are invariably established in connection with contents claiming to be valid and to serve as supporting points in a discipline. Hence derives the advantage of the concept in question that it enables us to see how the discipline is shaped in the process of its own construction by the layering and interpenetration of different aspects of activity for the production of scientific knowledge.

• • •

So, in order to study sociology as it was practiced under the specific conditions of the Communist regimes of Central and Eastern Europe, we turn to its disciplinary memory in two provisionally distinct forms: 'event-related' memory and 'cognitive' memory. For the purpose of registering these forms in terms of empirical data, we use two basic sources of information which may be viewed as their empirical correlates. The 'cognitive' or 'intellectual' past of a discipline is captured by means of different texts such as scientific publications (books, articles, research projects), information about scientific events, government and political decisions, while the 'event-based' past is recorded through interviews with sociologists who were contemporaries and participants in the process of emancipation and consolidation of sociology in each of the countries under consideration. The match between the sources of empirical data and the types of disciplinary memory is, of course, relative. A text, whether scientific or referring to science, is a trace not only of the conceptual development and the institutional evolution of the discipline. It may also inform us about the configuration of relationships, the prevailing moods, preferences, expectation within and outside the sociological community. On the one hand, the conducted interviews with sociologists not only reconstruct the memory of some dramatic periods in the development of the respective national sociology, of the relations between researchers and Party functionaries, of the organization and implementation of research projects. They also comment on the role of Marxism in the conceptualization of the social problems of those times, on the gradual integration of other, non-Marxist, theoretical models, on the forms of ideologization of sociological interpretation, on the criteria of objectivity and validity of obtained results, etc. In other words, every information source contains layers of information related both to scientific knowledge itself and to the processes, events, dynamics of relations related to cognitive activity.

There is one other specificity of the empirical material used here that should not be overlooked in the course of analysis. The interviews with sociologists from different periods of the post-1945 development of East European sociology until 1989 put the respondent and researcher in a specific situation.[5] In their quality of sociologists, they turn the past of their discipline into an independent object of reflection. Thus their own professional practice, being a historical activity, is put to the test, since they take a stance regarding the discipline which they not only exercise but of which they are heirs (Stengers, 1993: 50, 80–83). In this sense, the interview combines elements of autobiographical narrative, of eye-witness commentary, and of a scientist's self-reflection. This specificity should be had in mind in the course of analysis, in order to avoid the reduction of the discipline's history to a retrospective interpretation by a group of participants, even though a representative one. Even when all the theoretical and methodological requirements for selection of respondents, interviewing, processing of results are properly observed, the interview situation nevertheless places the participants in a privileged position. It a) gives the interviewees the advantage of being the interpreters of events, episodes of the history shared by a given sociological community, and b) gives the interviewer the liberty (and the responsibility) of defining the framework of this interpretation and setting that framework within the project he/she has designed. Consequently, the past of the discipline as it has grown out of the joint actions of different actors appears reconstructed a first time by/in the narratives of eye-witnesses who remember, and a second time by/in the conceptual schema of the researcher him/herself (Farrugia, 2000: 47).

---

5 The situation of interviewing engenders specific on-going shifts and corrections because the representatives of the same professional community briefly enter the roles of interviewer and respondent. For more, see Berthelot (1996: 87–98).

Thus, through the act of reconstruction, both the respondent and the interviewer become participants in the act of turning the discipline's past into its history. This history is not comprehensive or definitive, because it has been 'written' by a limited number of its participants and also because it continues to be written through dialogue with the reader who, from the viewpoint of his/her present day, will put the past in a new perspective and under a new light. In other words, this analysis of the national sociologies in Central and Eastern Europe in the time of Communist regimes does not seek "to establish truth, but to describe the history of truth" (Topalov, 2004: 129) in the shifting layers of the past and present, in the interweaving trajectories of what was lived and done, in the 'socio-analyses' that the sociologists themselves perform at different moments of their own development and the development of sociology.

CHAPTER 2

The Object of Sociology vs. Sociology as an Object of Research: The Theoretical Pitfalls of the Conception of Totalitarianism

How to study a sociology whose research object no longer exists? How to study the sociological investigation of a society that came to frankly be viewed as totalitarian only after its demise? What should be the approach to the scientific experience of sociologists who were formed and practiced their discipline in a society that is not only past now but that was dethroned by its own course of development? These questions add a new methodological challenge to the study of sociology as it existed in countries that, from the end of World War II until 1989, were implementing the societal project of socialism whose realization led to its negation.

What kind of society was the sociology of that time really studying? Was it socialist (usually defined as 'administrative', 'state', 'developed' socialism), communist, authoritarian, totalitarian, left-totalitarian ...? Although all of these attributives refer to the same reality, each of them refers to a different theoretical perspective. But the search for an answer is situated beyond preliminary definitions and requires a research strategy that should show how society develops towards its manifestation as 'what it is'. According to the principles of irreducibility and chronotope discussed in the previous chapter (Part 1.1), this means that the ontological, phenomenological and axiological characteristics of the kind of society that was being built in Central and Eastern Europe in the period 1945–1989 are to be revealed gradually by focusing on the cognitive actions and/or inactions of the actors of sociological practice of that time. This methodological and epistemological orientation would be sufficient in itself, were not the object of sociology distinguished by particular features that present a challenge to the problematization of sociology as it existed in, and studied, that past society.

The society which for forty years cognitively and socially legitimated the existence of sociology in the former Soviet Bloc countries no longer exists either as an objective reality or as a conceptual entity or as an axiological perspective. Not only is it now part of the historical past, it figures in history by a different quality, under a different identity from what it once had (which does not imply that, despite defining itself as socialist, it did not produce totalitarian, authoritarian, unfree practices). The society that was the object of study and the context of the then-existing sociology proved to be not what it was—and this, not simply in the perspective of the general, fundamental sociological principle that "things are not what they seem" (Berger, 1963). The society that sociology studied and within which it developed, and that same society as seen from the present-day perspective are ontologically not two different societies, nor do they correspond to two different representations of one and the same society. It is a single society which, through the study of its history and the acquired knowledge of it, we may now perceive in its immanent identity and phenomenological evolution. This particularity of that past society has a value dimension as well. The 'socialist' ('communist', 'totalitarian') society has been discredited and rejected by historical development (although it continues to exist in several countries of the world). It has refuted itself by its own collapse; it has become the strongest indictment against the scientific practice built on its basis. For the first time in the history of sociology, we have a situation in which a sociology's own object of study (society) turns *against* that sociology not by representing a cognitive challenge to science, but by carrying a threat for the historical existence of that sociology (undermining the justification of its existence), and hence a threat to the very possibility of studying the sociology of that time as an independent research object.

How then to constitute that sociology as an object of study given that its own object of study is hard to pinpoint and lends itself to different interpretations? Here we may use the aid of two postulates, two well-known axiomatic rules from which, however, researchers rarely draw methodological orientation for their work. If we follow the postulate that sociology is part of its own object, being "the product and co-author of a certain social order" (Giza-Poleszczuk, 1989: 74), and also follow Hegel's thesis that the object is inseparable from its history, then it becomes essential for our analysis to clarify the *dynamic relationship* connecting sociology to the society that is both the object and context of sociological scientific activity, instead of defining beforehand the sociology's object and context of its practice.

An overview of relevant literature indicates that precisely the opposite research strategy has been applied and other research priorities have been chosen leading to an epistemological deadlock. It was only after 1989 that the kind of society in which sociology had been practiced in the time of Communist regimes was explicitly and by consensus defined as totalitarian in the East European countries themselves.[1] The conception of totalitarianism was first

---

1   In this assertion, there is no hint of reproach against the practice of sociologists in the society of that time and their forms of sociological reflexivity. Our interest here is foremost in the epistemological consequences that the *post factum* recognition of the nature of that society has for the analysis of the discipline that then studied it.

developed by Hannah Arendt in the 1940s in her comparative study of Hitler's Germany (1933–1945) and Stalinist Russia (1929–1941 and 1945–1953)[2] and was further developed in the 1950s and 60s by Carl J. Friedrich (1954, 1957), Carl J. Friedrich and Zbigniew K. Brzezinski (1956), Raymond Aron (1965), Herbert J. Spiro (1968), to mention only the classical authors and works in this field; after the collapse of the Communist regimes there, the concept of totalitarianism became a universal key to the explanation of the Communist past of the Central and Eastern European countries. Both in the East and in the West, 'totalitarianism' was unanimously adopted as a simple and brief designation of the social reality in Central and Eastern Europe in the period 1945–1989, thereby reducing the specific development and systemic logic of these societies to a few traits and dependencies. According to the 'totalitarian paradigm', during the whole 40-year period, the society that was being built in the Soviet Bloc countries was centered on the ruling political power embodied in a single party, and was implemented through the symbiosis of party and state structures. The Communist party-state covered all the spheres of society and penetrated all levels. The Communist ideology served to fortify the political-administrative symbiosis, presenting this new state formation as the result of a nation-wide revolution carried out under the leadership of the Communist Party. Hence, the foremost task of the party holding a monopoly on political power was to defend collective interests by occupying the whole space of 'life-in-society' and by appropriating the management of all modes of social life. Regardless of the evolution that the Central and Eastern European countries underwent over the years, the two fundamental characteristics of the societies they were building invariably remained the political-administrative power of the Communist party-state and Marxism applied as a state ideology. Out of these two, flowed all other, equally persistent characteristics of Communist societies, such as the full control of the Party-state over all spheres of public activity, including the production of scientific knowledge. It was the supreme right of the Party to define the problems of society and to sanction them as such; to impose its own vision of social development based on the social theories of Marx, Engels, and Lenin, taken as the only possible and valid axiological frame for reflection on society; to subordinate the activities of all social actors to the goals of the political project by redefining the direction, functions and purpose of every activity.

Several further characteristics of sociology—then assumed to be self-evident features—flowed out of this context, such as the dependence of

---

2   *The Origins of Totalitarianism* was first published in 1951, but the manuscript was completed in 1949.

26   CHAPTER 2

sociology on the key social agent (the Communist party-state), the status of
sociology as a science under party control, and the obligatory ideological load
carried by sociology. From here on, the modes of the cognitive and social existence of this science in totalitarian society derived from the varying ampli-
tude of party-state control and the specific inner resistance-capacities of the
scientific communities in each country. The problematization of the relationship between sociology and state power has become a central focus in relevant
literature. Regarding this relationship, the emphasis of scholars fell either on
the ubiquitous political power to which sociology was inevitably subordinate
in its scientific content and its institutional and professional aspects; or on
the development of sociology as a science despite the full political-ideological
control of the ruling power; or on the ambivalence and inner contradictions of
the sociologist's position in this situation (Bundzhulov, 2002; Dimitrov, 1995;
Koev, 1992; Lutyński, 1998; Nickolov, 1992; Petrusek, 1992; Szacki, 1998).
Even the attempts at building an 'internal' history of sociology as it existed in
totalitarian society, presenting it as a complex cognitive institution open to
different theoretical and methodological influences, and possessing a variety
of forms of scientific activity and different behavior models of scientists, are
centered on the holder of a monopoly on power (Mihailov, 2003).

This common present-day approach to the history of sociology as it was
then practiced in the former Communist countries has proven its heuristic
value in numerous studies; in this approach, the structure-defining features
of totalitarian society are taken as the basic support for a sociological explanation of the situation. Yet this approach is seen to have a troubling shortcoming. If the totalitarian character of society at that time was the invariable
characteristic of the social context in which sociology was done, the research
object of sociology then was always placed within the teleological perspective
of a socialist project for society. Paradoxically, sociology was being developed
within a totalitarian society as a *context*, but the society that was the *object of
sociological study* was intended to be a socialist one. This contradiction need
not be a problem if we assume we cannot today ascribe to the facts, events,
and phenomena of past times the meaning and significances they have for
us today, but did not have for the actors then, in that past context. There is
a more serious contradiction in the research approach we are discussing, a
contradiction that has inevitable consequences for further conceptualization
of the problem.

In previous reflections on the history of sociology as it existed in the former
Communist countries, the opposition between the context and research object of that sociology has been maintained. When we assign the features of totalitarian society only to the contextual conditions in which and against which

sociology had to develop at that time, we thereby exclude the research object of that sociology from the historical reality of the times, and substantialize that object. Hence, knowledge about society produced despite the social context of science assumes the characteristics of a monad, remains self-enclosed, or at best, appears as a counterpoint to the context. Thus, not only the mechanisms of the production of knowledge become opaque to us, but also the possible relationships between sociological cognition and social reality. The level at which the tension between context and cognition is retained proves to be precisely that of the opposition power vs. sociology, a perspective that logically leads to the image of sociology as 'victim', 'martyr', or else 'hero' in those times. Thus, we ultimately reach a familiar correlation that is true but limited in its theoretical scope—namely, that every society produces the kind of social science that it needs. Or, to paraphrase the historian Jean-Marie Fecteau, sociology measures up to the national space in which it exists, for good or for bad (2002). The circle closes in upon itself, leaving unexplained the tension between the almighty totalitarian state-party and the dependent sociology which has studied that society albeit in other terms; under this tension, sociology 'survives' while its research object passes irrevocably into the past.

If we postulate that in the former Communist countries the object of that sociology was likewise totalitarian in character—just like the social context—then even more insurmountable obstacles arise with even more serious theoretical and deontological consequences. In the cognitive aspect, the historical analysis would have as a starting point a static condition of society at a certain moment, and this would exclude from our conceptual framework the historicity that is proper to every phenomenon. It would then be impossible to understand the roots, manifestations, metamorphoses and collapse of totalitarianism in the separate countries. Being once born as totalitarian (why and how?), that society would seem invariably similar to itself in the course of decades (why and in what way?) until its breakdown (why and how?).[3] In a deontological aspect, postulating that society as totalitarian would lead to compromising, and also empirically false, conclusions. The sociology practiced in the former Communist countries would seem like an activity that, even then, recognized its own object of study as a totalitarian formation, but for some reason or other 'was hiding the truth' about that formation. In other words, Central and Eastern European sociology at that time was anything but scientific cognition. Yet, East-West scientific dialogue was maintained at the time

---

3   We must not forget that Arendt limited the historical scope of her conception of totalitarianism to Stalinist Soviet society which ended with the death of Stalin in 1953.

as evident by joint publications, joint projects, and collaboration in the International Sociological Association. It would then logically follow that Western sociologists were accomplices to a scientific hoax.

Hence, a preliminary definition of both the context and the research object of the sociology practiced in those countries in the period 1945–1989 as a totalitarian context and object does not provide an adequate theoretical basis for the study of that sociology. The causes are empirical, the consequences are theoretical. After World War II, it was foremost the social-political context of doing sociology that changed in the countries under Communist regimes. The context started to be radically different from the conditions in which sociology had originated in the second half of the 19th century, but it was also different from the conditions in Western democratic societies in post-war Western Europe and North America. Moreover, a qualitatively new, historically unprecedented society *began* to be built, whereby there also *began* the transformation of the very object of sociology, the object that for the previous century had generated, impelled and defined the discipline's identity.[4] In this sense, 'socialist' society was more than the space-time frame of the establishment and development of the discipline of sociology in the former Communist countries. That society put to the test the whole body of sociology, ranging from its theoretical-methodological instruments to the deontological code of its scientists, passing through the notion of what it means for knowledge to be scientific. In order to understand and explain the changes that took place in the production of sociological knowledge, the epistemological relation 'context—research object—sociology' must be rethought.

Though they are not identical or mutually reducible to each other, the context of social studies and their object cannot be viewed as separate realities, each with its own history and mutually influencing each other in some way in their interaction. Society as context and society as object of analysis are not external to each other either in the spatial, temporal, or ontological aspect, even though they do have a different epistemological status within the research process. There is a methodological principle, increasingly gaining ground in the social sciences, according to which "the context is immanent to the practices and cannot be a static structure" (Deyanova, 2001: 41). The application of this principle to the analysis of sociology as it existed in the time of the totalitarian Communist regimes entails, firstly, to put the context (the totalitarian state) and the study of 'socialist' society by sociology in a *mutual perspective,*

---

4   This refers to the qualitative identity of capitalist society over the whole course of its development regardless of its various forms and stages of transformation.

within a *common history* that can 'assimilate' (Fecteau, 2002)[5] both sides of this relationship and thereby show how society was headed towards its own demystification as being a non-socialist society by means of a double process: the objectifying of its principles into structures, institutions, and practices, and the objectification of those principles (in the sense of Bourdieu) through scientific knowledge production.

Secondly, it involves applying the principle of immanence which sees the context as incorporated in the cognitive process of sociology. But this requirement is not simple in meaning, and it may express different epistemological choices and solutions. Early on, Weber established the existence of a mutual dependency between social sciences and their objective context, "a context which builds their object and of which they are simultaneously a part" (Habermas, 1987: 26). This dependency may assume different forms in research strategies. It is often used as a declared precondition of that research approach in which the role of the context is postulated at the start and is then recalled at the end of the analysis, just enough to add some 'local color' to the established and confirmed generally valid tendencies and dependencies. With the evolution of sociology of science and sociology of knowledge, the importance of social determinants for the knowledge production was established as a methodological imperative valid for all elements of the cognitive process. In the broad sense of context, in terms of cultural preferences and patterns, political orientations, social interests and norms, the context may influence the knowledge production including the choice of research problem, the formulation of research goals and choice of techniques and methods, and the positioning of the problem in a specific theoretical framework. In most studies, however, the context remains an external factor with respect to the content of the produced scientific knowledge. This externalization of the context has been critiqued by the constructivist trend in sociology of science which argues that the context is always a part both of the internal organization of science and of the procedures for production and grounding of knowledge (Bruno Latour, Michel Callon, Karin Knorr Cetina). Every cognitive practice is a structured process of interaction between, on the one hand, the cognitive process comprising the total set of basic epistemic problems to be solved such as 'testing hypotheses',

---

5   We take the liberty of using this expression of Jean-Marie Fecteau, knowing that he used it in connection with an analysis of the role of the Catholic Church in 19th century Quebec. We use it because its figurative metaphorical form contains the important methodological requirement that we must seek the kind of frame for analysis in which the studied object can be seen not in itself but in its evolution interconnected with the social context.

'proof', 'grounding', etc., and on the other hand, 'social relations' in the framework of which solutions to those epistemic problems are sought (Knorr Cetina,
1995, 1998).

It is easy to see that the different views on the role of context in scientific
practice are related to different elements of the structure and process of cognition. When the context is formally taken into account, the research object is
viewed in some spatial-temporal framework, but this framework is not essential to the inner evolution of knowledge about the object. Here we see repro-
duced, to some degree, the familiar opposition between context and object of
sociological knowledge in post-totalitarian analyses of the sociology existed
under the totalitarian Communist regimes. The approach in which the context
is seen as having a determining, but external impact on the process of cognition looks for the projections of that context in elements such as the choice
of research themes, problems, goals, methods, schemas of interpretation and
explanation; but the autonomous content and internal constructing of these
elements is not touched upon. The new sociology of knowledge offers a completely sociological perspective on the context: this perspective considers impacts on the very core of the research process—its methodology, and sees the
context as an element that is incorporated in the method and that forms its
very tissue.

But underlying the different 'instrumental' value that these approaches
attach to the context, there is a more serious epistemological problem related to the claim of sociology to produce scientific knowledge, i.e., knowledge
the validity of which is not reducible to the conditions under which it was
produced (Berthelot, 1998). By expanding the determinative role of the context, do we not risk relativizing knowledge and contextualizing its validity to
a degree where science becomes a collection of precise, local, useful (insofar
as they serve a given context) but mutually incommensurable products of rational activity? Contrariwise, when narrowing the scope of action of the context, do we not expulse history from the development of science, including the
norms of science? And not least, in continuing to perceive the context in terms
of the opposition external vs. internal influence, do we not reproduce the old
dilemmas of universalism vs. particularism, rationalism vs. relativism without
overcoming them?

These warning questions bring us back to the principle according to which
the context is immanent both to social practice (which is the research object
of sociology) and to sociological practice. Applying this principle requires always viewing context, object, and sociology in their interdependence, their
mutual development. Every society—being both a context and an object of a
given sociological practice—is a reality that is built, changed, and developed

together with, and inseparably from the knowledge about that reality. It is within society that visions of that society (whether these be political, ideological, economic, esthetic, religious, scientific, etc.) are shaped, reformulated, transformed; and the task of reflexive sociology is to disclose how the discipline of sociology achieves, or fails to achieve, its cognitive project amidst the interweaving of different realities and discourses. In other words, being inseparable from its context as well as from its research object, sociology is part of both precisely as an activity transforming them through the knowledge it produces.

Specifically with regard to the study of sociology in the former Communist countries, this approach means we should view that sociology as a process of gradually advancing empirical investigation and theoretical identification of the contemporaneous society as a society that was gradually moving further and further away from its own project; with this approach, the sociology in question is not viewed as a practice inscribed within a predefined context and having for its object a reality likewise predefined by a set of pre-ascribed characteristics. Hence, the concept of 'totalitarianism' is used here as referring to a social form of 'total domination' and does not ascribe beforehand characteristics either to the context of sociology or to its research object at the time of the Communist regimes. The totalitarian dimensions and tendencies of the social reality of that time are disclosed in the course of research on the concrete historical interaction between sociologists and the society they were studying while being part of that society. In other words, here we approach the 'totalitarian experience' not as a tool for analysis but as part of the research object.

Thus, by placing the *research object* of the sociology practiced in the former Communist countries (i.e., the society of that time) in the perspective of its interconnectedness with the *context* in which that research object existed and with the *discipline* that studied it, we have better chances of understanding why the produced empirical data were not able to undermine the dominant Marxist paradigm; why the interpretations nearly always confirmed the formulated hypotheses, even if they had to be in contradiction with the empirical verification; why the ideological postulates became the organizing principle for explanations, while the theoretical premises quickly deteriorated into ideological generalizations; why the conscious deviations from the method made at the stage of data collection did not lead to falsification of that information at the stage of interpretation and analysis,[6] etc. Thus, the research object of that

---

6 Particularly indicative in this respect is was the sociological practice of illegal research centers of Solidarity at the time of martial law in Poland.

time, when viewed by us as a focus of the dynamically changing history both of the social context and of the sociology that studied that society, serves not as an occasion for 'accusing' the discipline of sociology as it was practiced at that time, but as a resource for understanding that past scientific practice and its paradoxes. In this kind of understanding, the social context is not demonized and sociology is not viewed as either victim or hero.

CHAPTER 3

Sociology Grappling With Itself: The Conceptual Pitfalls of the Single-variant Disciplinary Self-referentiality

How to view the sociology of European countries under Communist regimes in the period between 1945 and 1989? In the historical time and geo-political space of the Cold War, from the vantage point of Western Europe and North America, the sociology of these countries was behind the 'Wall', while from the vantage point of Moscow, the center of Communism, it was a sociology developing in the 'better' of the two societies. What does the geo-political position of this sociology indicate in terms of its context, its object of study, its type of sociological practice, and the knowledge it produced? What justifies our viewing together the several national sociologies in Central and Eastern Europe in the period 1945–1989? These questions take us to the core of the conceptualization of sociology as a scientific discipline.

Not surprisingly, during the whole period between the end of World War II and 1989, sociology existed in two separate worlds, similarly to and as a result of the division in two of political reality in general. Over the years, these two worlds displayed various degrees and varying intensity of mutual mistrust, disregard, and arrogance. On the one hand, there was the sociology of Western Europe and North America, the Western, non-Marxist, 'bourgeois', leading, developed sociology. On the other hand, there was the sociology of Eastern Europe, of the 'Socialist Camp' countries, a Marxist, Marxist-Leninist, 'pseudo-scientific' sociology. Each of these two definitions, ranging from the most politically-neutral to the most ideologically-charged, were rich in meaning for people at that time, regardless of the various degrees to which people on either side were respectively familiar with the 'other' sociology. In any case, there were two types of sociological practice built in diametrically opposite social-economic, political-ideological, and theoretical contexts. Beyond the particularities and specificity of separate national practices, Western and East European sociology followed forms of disciplinary development, discourse, social presence which were so different that the scientific knowledge they respectively produced about the two types of society often remained mutually untranslatable and inaudible.

This situation which continued for nearly four decades was such as to call in question the ways of disciplinary construction of sociology and the ways of interpreting this construction. From the viewpoint of history of sociology, at least several questions deserve attention. Given that sociology found a place among the family of sciences in the second half of the 19th century, and maintained this place thanks to its initial intention of producing knowledge about society that is objective and valid, and necessary for the development of society, then what is the meaning of this division into two hardly crossing trajectories of sociology in the West and East during the Cold War? Was the sociology practiced in Central and Eastern Europe under Communist regimes derived from the original disciplinary project, was it in opposition to it, or was it simply an "imported article"[1]? How was a bourgeois cognitive project able to break through into a non-bourgeois reality and assert itself there[2]? Additional questions arise at the epistemological level. Does sociology, like any scientific discipline, follow its own internal logic of development, or is it more susceptible than other sciences to social constraints that assume the form of logical constraints and vice versa (Bourdieu)? Does sociology remain hostage to the society that it studies, or does it succeed in devising a theoretical and methodological set of tools adequate to its research object, tools that lead to knowledge the validity of which is not reducible to the social conditions under which it was produced? What does it mean to study a society that had never before existed in human history, and to do so under conditions radically different from the context of sociology in its countries of origin? Did the relative cognitive isolation in which sociology developed in the former Communist countries until 1989 lead to the formation of 'pockets of knowledge', specific forms of rationality, singular discourses?

Sociological literature generally offers several answers which, despite their different overtones, all express essentially the same prevalent view of sociology under Communism. In cases when sociology is admitted to have existed in those countries, it is considered to represent either a break with the sociological tradition, or a deviation from it, or an 'error of history', or at best something so specific and unique as to make comparison impossible, not to say pointless. Regardless of "who is speaking and from where", the underlying reference frame of such conclusions is the sociological tradition in its first-born, Western version. It is also evident, and no less problematic, that the 'West European' measuring rod is being used without regard for its own principles.

---

1   As Jacques Coenen-Huther of the University of Geneva once shared in conversation.
2   We owe this formulation of the problem involved in the emergence and development of sociology under Communism in Central and East Europe to Galin Gornev of the Institute of Sociology at Bulgarian Academy of Sciences.

A look at the sociological tradition ranging from the classics to contemporary authors[3] would show that the sociological experience under the conditions of Communism was not a practice aside from, or beyond, or in spite of the sociological tradition, but was part of a history *both common and specific*. Thanks to Max Weber, we are reminded that, in order to study the post-war sociology in Central and Eastern Europe in an objective and sociologically relevant way, we must see it as a historical phenomenon that has both universal and singular disciplinary characteristics. Karl Marx's dialectical perspective invites us to see this sociology as a social process that can be understood in the historicity and dynamics of its own unfolding. Emile Durkheim, in turn, reminds us that we must emancipate ourselves from *prenotions* (a term he borrowed from Francis Bacon) and view the modality of sociological practice in the former Communist countries objectively and without bias as a "thing". Marcel Mauss expands our vision in showing that the study of a certain phenomenon as a "total social fact" signifies not only that everything we observe is part of the observation but also that we ourselves, as observers, are part of the thing observed. In other words, when viewed as "things", the sociological practices in the former Communist countries are related to representations, i.e., to the concepts, ideas, interpretations by means of which we study them. And not least, thanks to the demonstrated autonomy of the different value orders (the demonstration of which began in the modern age and was one of the preconditions for the birth and construction of sociology itself) and the transformations of those orders in the modern world, the whole sociological tradition provides guiding points for understanding East European sociology in the period 1945–1989 as a self-delimiting activity that was able to preserve its disciplinary identity by developing according to 'the rules of method'.

Thus, the way in which sociology views a given sociological practice is a test for sociology itself. If sociology were to forget or disregard its own principles and postulates, it would risk considering the respective practice not in accordance with those principles but with reference to the historical context of their formation and manifestation. That would be in complete disregard of the principle of immanence of context, with respect both to the research object and to sociology

---

3   Sociology which appeared as a result of the transition from 'traditional' to 'modern' society built its own disciplinary tradition as a set of epistemological, theoretical, methodological, and deontological principles and norms which allow defining the knowledge produced as sociological. The sociological tradition may be designated in the singular number only with reference to its specific cognitive practice as a discipline. Apart from that, only the plurality of its sociological practices in and through which it occurs ensure the possibility of its existence and vitality as a science.

per se, as discussed in Part 1.2., or of the requirement flowing from this principle that the role of the context must be taken into account at every stage of the research process. To the contrary, a research strategy that takes one specific context as an implicit reference frame for the analysis of sociological practices in other contexts runs a double risk. On the one hand, it finds itself at odds with the founding principles of its own scientific tradition, because it disregards the universality of those principles in the name of the exemplary status of a given disciplinary trajectory—in this case, the trajectory of West European sociology. What proves most at risk of violation here is the fundamental epistemological principle regarding the link between the object and the method of social cognition aiming to solve specific problems. On the other hand, such a strategy would be trapped in a the single-variant perspective on the discipline's development and would be deprived of the possibility of studying that development "with reference to the potential [it holds]", to paraphrase Lepenies's idea of the social sciences as "sciences of the possible" (1997). In the concrete case of East European sociology from 1945 to 1989, this would mean placing it and assigning meaning to its disciplinary development with reference to the West European version, instead of viewing it as one of the modalities of poly-variant historical processes which include the history of sociology, and as a key to understanding the specific reality of totalitarian-type societies.

The starting point of the analysis proposed here is to view post-war East European sociology as one of the many possible variants of disciplinary development, and that, regardless of its different temporality, it shapes the connected history of sociology jointly with other variants. In addition to the above-mentioned reasons, this choice of strategy is dictated by two more considerations. When seen as taking place in a multiplicity of variants, the sociological tradition becomes a lens through which we study each of its variants, and each of them, in turn, becomes a specific case relevant to explaining the practice and development of sociology in general. Precisely because it was part of the overall history of the discipline, *sociology under the Communist regimes raises questions about the scientific practice of sociology in general.* Secondly, when understood through the prism of universal founding principles of the discipline and the realization of those principles in multiple sociological practices, the history of sociology unfolds as a scientific analysis open to possible experiences, and not limiting itself to the territory of its historical roots and original sources. The analysis offered here views East European sociology under Communism as one of the variants in the disciplinary development of sociology, i.e., as a practice that has, and/or has not, developed with reference to the standards in effect in sociology. This analysis will try to reveal the possibilities (realized, missed, or frustrated) for production of a sociological knowledge

whose scientific value was dependent to a greater degree than in other societies and times on extra-scientific factors (political, ideological, geo-strategic,
etc.). Hence, the key issue for our study is: *what kind of conditions for its own
development did sociology manage to win in the societies ruled by the Communist
party-state, how and what kind of sociological knowledge was produced under
these conditions?*

Is it justified to speak of sociology as a whole in Central and Eastern Europe?
Can we examine all the different national sociologies under the Communist
regime together? At least two objections to this 'integrist' approach could be
pointed out. Firstly, because the development in each of the former Communist countries was very specific, the sociological communities in them underwent very different ordeals. Suffice it to mention some particular events that
marked the development of different national sociologies in particular ways. In
former Czechoslovakia, the social impetus of the Prague Spring, and the subsequent burden of "normalization" placed Czechoslovak sociologists during a
very brief period of time in two very different political contexts with inevitable
consequences for the institutional and disciplinary form of sociology in that
country. In Poland, the intense politicization of sociology after the creation of
Solidarity, the first independent trade union to be formed under a Communist
regime, had nothing in common with the ubiquitous ideologization, including
that of science, in societies ruled by Communist party-states. The revolution
that was crushed in Hungary in 1956, the reforms of Socialism begun in the
1960s and cut short after the intervention of the Warsaw Pact armies in Prague
in 1968 formed the backdrop against which Hungarian sociology moved toward professionalism and withdrew from ideological debates in order to guard
its research field from political meddling.

Secondly, during the first decade of the Great Change in 1989, the different
national sociologies considered and assessed their recent Communist past in
different ways. Overall, Polish and Hungarian sociologists, while not uncritical
of their own practice, acknowledged the achievements of their national sociologies under regimes that had not brooked criticism or individuals voicing
criticism. The Czech sociologists recognized the fact that they had been absent
from the international scene for at least 15 years after the Prague events and,
in their effort to make up for time lost after 1989, focused attention on themselves, forgetting the Slovak sociologists, their 'brothers in destiny'. The latter,
for their part, also forgot they had shared a common state with the Czechs
and undertook to excavate the past and highlight indigenous authors on the
national stage, thereby creating the image of a national sociological tradition
dating far back in time but long suppressed. As for Russian sociologists, having
been dethroned from their status of vectors of thought and action within the

former Soviet Bloc, and remaining outside the safe harbor of the European Union, yet convinced of their own uniqueness, they have fallen into a binge of reconstructing the history of ideas and of critical self-reflection, a trend that has had its ups and downs. Bulgarian sociologists are aware of their not particularly unblemished past, and have preferred to look to the present, hoping perhaps that the past is buried forever.

It would be mistaken to think that the attitude to the Communist past of sociology as described above is shared by all members of the national sociological communities and has found expression in a particular national spirit of those communities. The above description refers not so much to the actual state of these communities as to the fact that the national sociological writings in each country leave the reader with the sense of a prevailing post-Communist attitude to the past of the discipline.

Though they differed so much in their achievements and failures, and in their openness to, and presence in the international area of science, the national sociologies of Central and Eastern Europe under Communism are placed here in *a common frame of analysis* and are studied in *a comparative perspective*. This comparison, however, is focused not on the national particularities of disciplinary practice in the Communist spatial-temporal range but on how sociology was practiced in different national contexts united by the common denominator of the Communist social order. This distinction may seem at first glance negligibly slight, but it is definitive for the research approach applied here and its argumentation. In contrast with the periodically renewed debate about the contribution of national sociologies to world sociology, and about the cogency of taking the "nation-state as a meaningful framework for sociological theorization of the world",[4] our interest is focused on how sociology defended its scientific project within a political, economic and ideological context common to several national societies, and how sociologists in each national society dealt with the constraints of that context in order to produce relevant sociological knowledge about society.

The justification of this perspective of analysis comes from empirical reality itself. Having been placed by force of circumstances within a 'common history', the Eastern European countries in the post-war period—each in its own

---

4   See Nedelmann and Sztompka (1993), specifically the discussion between Jeffrey Alexander (1995), Richard Munch (1995) and Jacques Coenen-Huther (1996) published in *Swiss Journal of Sociology* and related to the article by Richard Münch in the same book. See also the special issue on "National Traditions in the Social Sciences" of *Revue d'histoire des sciences humaines* with a foreword by Heilbron (2008).

way—defied history. The convergences beyond the divergences, and the divergences despite the convergences in this shared historical experience will be studied here through the disciplinary history of sociology, while the national particularities of this experience will make the highlighted trends more salient. From an epistemological viewpoint, the disciplinary experience of sociology in Eastern Europe in the time of Communism is important for the production and argumentation of sociological knowledge. The national sociological practices in the former Communist countries faced a *common type of social reality* the study of which raised problems common to the sociologists of all these countries, and different from the problems faced by their colleagues during the same period of history in countries with a different social order. It is known that when solving problems raised by the sociological capture of a given specific reality, the universality of disciplinary principles meets with the particularity of their local practice, not in terms of a clash between the two aspects but as a concrete research (and hence social) situation to be mastered. This is the actual everyday situation of every sociologist whatever the place and time in which he/she practices sociology; a situation in which are simultaneously focused the epistemological norms of objectivity and relevance of obtained results, the methodological norms of scientific proof, the deontological norms of defending the validity of the produced knowledge before the public (and beyond the scientific community), and the multiple connections between different forms of power (scientific, political, financial, administrative, etc.). For the individual sociologist, this situation put to the test his/her knowledge and skills, theoretical and moral reference framework, and scientific and political convictions. Being heterogeneous and of different orders, these requirements are met in ways that undoubtedly vary in historical space and time, but just how they were met remains one of the most sensitive indicators for sociological practice, both in itself and in its relation to society. In studying the forms of sociological experience in the common and the specific conditions of Communist regimes in different countries, our task will be to reveal *the epistemological challenges that the context and object of sociology raised to its disciplinary construction and development.*

   In approaching this concrete sociological task, we find supporting points in two philosophers. Isabelle Stengers' methodological imperative is that (1997: 19–20)

> regarding each type of scientific practice, we should ask what 'being objective' means for it, in other words, what are the acceptable arguments, what serves as 'proof', what counts as a 'fact'.

More than any principle of a particular science, this imperative makes us sensitive to the totality of conditions that define objectivity and relevance in a given scientific practice. Moreover, Stengers takes the problem of justifying the objectivity and relevance of scientific cognition beyond narrow scientific definitions and sets it within the broader context of the relationship between 'sciences' and 'powers',[5] a relationship in which each side carries in itself the other. Hence, Stengers' outlined scope of reflection regarding scientific practice is the triad 'science—politics—ethics' in which each element would be impossible without the others, and also limits their potential power. Thus, scientific cognition is inseparably linked to the recognized and established, within that science, models for construction and verification of cognitive results, to political complicities in the production of knowledge and the reception of knowledge by the social actors to whom it is related and whom it affects (the political sphere), as well as to the possible perspectives for development it opens to society (the ethical sphere).

Thierry Hentsch is also philosophically sensitive to the epistemological complexity of scientific experience. His "ethics of the borderline" represents (2006: 14)

> an attempt to keep oneself at the limits. A way to touch what is missing. A domestication of the missing [...] To try to withstand that which effaces it. Not to lose track.

Here, the limits of scientific experience are seen as a movable distinction where the absent is not a lack or a shortcoming but a track of what has not yet been studied, not been noticed, and a sign for new investigation.

It is not hard to see that, in fact, Stengers' methodological imperative and Hentsch's idea about boundary as ethics reflect each other. Methodological precision is impossible without paying attention to, and respecting the things that fall outside, or are missing from the researcher's range of vision. Without an ethical attitude, the researcher's work becomes an extravagant, socially useless, supra-social claim to knowledge.

Guided by these principles, in our study of sociology in Communist Europe we will attempt to show and interpret two mutually connected processes

---

5   Inasmuch as Stengers emphasizes scientific knowledge from its production to its entry into society through interaction with those who are part of the researched problem, her understanding of power refers to a single identifying trait. Power can be recognized by "the fact of having the liberty to choose what you will hear and what you will remain deaf to" (1997: 29).

related to moving boundaries: 1) the process of theoretical, methodological, deontological shift, moving aside, positioning in the production of sociological knowledge which occurred in connection with the political-ideological changes in the context and the object of science, and 2) the process of undermining the social-historical boundary itself and shifting the horizons within society which occurred as scientists became aware of, and overcame the (self)limitations in sociological knowledge per se.

CHAPTER 4

Conceptual Framework of the Analysis

Sociology in Europe under Communism is, par excellence, an experience at the borderline (between two geo-political worlds, between two types of social reality, between one-dimensionality and pluralism as ways of thought and ways of action), hence, it is perhaps one of the most fruitful fields for studying the mobile boundaries between society and knowledge about society. However, can these movements and interferential effects be captured in a theoretical perspective, i.e., can they be anchored and fixed in an explanation that places its object within clear boundaries? With full awareness that the answer proposed here is one out of many possible, we will define two conceptual pillars of the conceptual framework in which we will study sociological knowledge in societies with a totalitarian experience. The concepts in question are 'disciplinary project of sociology' and 'project for a new society, or communist project for society' which are logically deduced through reflection on the methodological principles presented in the preceding chapters. Here we will discuss in greater detail their contents, way of conceptualization, and heuristic potential.[1]

In the research intention to study the East European sociology of the Communist period through the prism of its disciplinary tradition, the concept of disciplinary project is of central importance. This concept expresses the dynamic mutual connection between two fundamental principles of construction and functioning of modern scientific knowledge: *disciplinarity* as a social-historical principle of internal differentiation of sciences, and the *project* as a universal, historically established form of pursuing scientific knowledge[2]

---

1 For more details, see Koleva (2005) where the analytical potential of the two concepts has been used for the study of a single national disciplinary practice—sociology in Bulgaria during the period 1945–1989.

2 As far back as 1934, in his *The New Scientific Spirit*, Gaston Bachelard pointed out (1934: 15): "Above the subject, beyond the immediate object [of cognition—my addition], modern science is based on the project. In scientific thought, reflection about the object by the subject always assumes the form of a project". For Bachelard, "the direction of the epistemological vector undoubtedly goes from the rational to the real, and not reversely, from reality to the general, as all philosophers, from Aristotle to Bacon, have taught" (Ibid.: 4). This movement is effectuated through the project—consisting not in a formal procedure for arranging cognitive acts but representing an inner principle of the possibility for such arrangement to be made.

© KONINKLIJKE BRILL NV, LEIDEN, 2018 | DOI 10.1163/9789004333635_006

at the cognitive, institutional and social level simultaneously.[3] Viewed as an end product, the disciplinary project corresponds to an autonomous research field differentiated within the existing at a particular stage configuration of scientific knowledge. It refers to a body of knowledge that ensures the specific type of rational connection to the world that distinguishes each discipline. The constitution of an autonomous epistemic field is possible, however, only under certain cognitive, theoretical, methodological, and institutional conditions. These conditions, in turn, are a product of purposeful actions realized in various ways depending on the concrete socio-historical context. Thus viewed in the perspective of its realization, the disciplinary project mirrors the defining of goals and planning of action for differentiating an epistemic area that serves as a source of imperatives and requirements for a specific theoretical grasp of reality aimed at the practical assimilation of that reality. In this quality, the disciplinary project functions as a core of cognitive intentions, contents, and norms—a core that, in tracing the autonomous path of a given science, is made possible only by constant updating and development through the numerous acts of its representatives. In other words, the disciplinary project is the origin-based perspective of a given science; it is a projection not of its disciplinary past but of its disciplinary present (and future) as a continuation and renewal of its foundations. In the philosophical terms of Deleuze and Guattari, we may say that the disciplinary project is "the contingent new beginning of the same contingent process using other data" (Deleuze, Guattari, 1991: 94).

Paradoxically, the advantages the concept of disciplinary project provides for the analytical study of the scientific knowledge production and development are rooted in the limitations of the concept. Unlike the far more widely used concepts 'paradigm' (Kuhn, 1962), 'research program' (Lakatos, 1970), and 'research tradition' (Laudan, 1977), which are trans- and supra-disciplinary and cannot be tied to a single discipline, the concept of disciplinary project identifies the logical core (the specialized scientific cognition of reality) and the corresponding perspective of the separate discipline linked to that core. First, the disciplinary project of scientific knowledge orients and provides norms for the

---

3 Whatever the discipline, 'project' is the form that every aspect of research and educational activity assumes in modern organization and management of science. It is in 'project' form that scientists' communities and their members make, legitimate, argue, dispute their 'applications' for activity. The 'project' is a product and embodiment of instrumental rationality in the modern world, and it has become the level at which assessment and control of scientific cognition is effectuated, thereby being the form for professional recognition and a resource for a professional career, a condition for working in science, and an intermediary in the relations between science and society.

cognitive activity in a given science, but not as a pattern to be applied mechanically or a canon to be followed uncritically. Instead, it provides the researcher with the specific logical-theoretical world that, as the scientist encounters the infinitely multifarious empirical world, permits him/her to achieve what claims to be scientific knowledge about that world. In identifying the science norms of produced knowledge, the disciplinary project also makes it possible to analyze the grounds of those norms, their principles of functioning and the mechanisms for changing them. Thus, it is not a model created once and for all. Secondly, the disciplinary project implicitly contains the idea of initiality. If this idea is related to the principles and primal image of the discipline, then the attempt to describe these inevitably carries the risk of myth creation that Giddens writes about (Giddens, 1995). But perceived in another aspect—as a sign of the distinction that it marks, initiality makes the disciplinary project a clearer and more efficacious cognitive instrument. The disciplinary project is important for analysis not by the time and place it refers to but as an "event generating difference" (to use Stengers' expression) which, having once taken place, becomes a source of its own reproduction, continuation and development in new contexts and under new conditions. Hence, the initiality of the disciplinary project consists only in the difference it produces. In this respect, it is a generator of development rather than a pattern for duplication, and the task of an analytic study is to reveal the evolution of this initial difference in its concrete forms, modalities and manifestations.[4] That is why the plurality of paradigms, research programs, schools and currents created within the boundaries of the initial disciplinary difference does not correspond to a plurality of disciplinary projects in a given science, but characterizes the science's disciplinary project in its course of development.

With respect to the disciplinary project of sociology, the ambivalence of sociological knowledge should be emphasized. Claiming to be scientific and teleological, sociological knowledge remains divided between the imperative of being valid and the expectation of being useful. The categories of truth and utility are related, but not reducible to each other (Simmel, 1987), and prove to be the two interwoven registers of the validity of a given assertion. According to Max Weber, the objectively valid truth of the social sciences' knowledge

---

4 This interpretation of the disciplinary project is based on Stengers' views on the birth of modern sciences. She discusses their emergence "under the sign of the event" (Stengers, 1993: 84–101); here, 'event' is what creates a difference, without being a carrier of meanings. The latter are not attributive characteristics of the 'event' but are formed, defined and expressed through the manifestations which follow from, and continue the 'event' (Ibid.: 80–81).

is based on its logical coherence and objective correlatedness. However, the functioning of knowledge as 'practically true' expresses and confirms its social validity and is correlated not with its theoretical truthfulness but with its practical usefulness.[5]

This double link of the validity of knowledge to truth and usefulness is rooted in the very origin of the social sciences. They first appeared amidst the insecurity and confusion of transition from the traditional to the modern world, and they managed to claim and defend their right to existence both in the cognitive and social aspect only insofar as they "create their object in response to the expectation of the true, the just and the desirable" (Caillé, 1986: 33). According to Alain Caillé, this "demiurgic dimension" of the social sciences is a constitutive element of their epistemological and pragmatic specificity. From having been a pledge of their origination, this dimension quickly became a paradoxical aporia of their development because of "the inner indefiniteness and paradoxical, incomplete nature of the true and the just" (Ibid.: 38–39) which the social sciences themselves have revealed. "Their generic curse" of making the world comprehensible and manageable in the perspective of dynamically constructed meanings, i.e., of placing knowledge in a sort of perspectivism of meaning, remains the constant source of tension between *truth in science* and *truth in society*. As part of this rise of the social sciences, sociology has developed its disciplinary claims at the borderline between constructing scientific knowledge about the social and incorporating that knowledge within the body of society; between problematization and legitimacy; between interpretation and intervention; between explanation and its social uses that are always linked to a certain political-moral choice.

Insofar as the present study is situated at the crossroads of *reflexive sociology* and *reflexive history*, the specific research task here is to reveal the functioning of the disciplinary project of sociology in the historical space and time of the Communist regimes established after World War II through the reflexivity of memory. This explains the role of disciplinary memory as a component of the conceptual framework of the study. Regardless of whether it appears in an 'event-related' or 'cognitive' modality, disciplinary memory is a form of reflection of various aspects of the evolution of the disciplinary project, it is a crystallization of the stages of its growth, a concentrated expression of the state of the discipline at a given moment of its history. The artifacts of scientific memory are as much a means for studying the discipline's past as they are an element

---

5 Raymond Boudon sums up this dualism by citing Pareto: "As Pareto says, a theory may be *useful*, without being true" (Boudon, 2000: 348).

of its development amidst the infinite multiplicity of concrete situations and circumstances. The disciplinary project, for its part, being inseparable from the forms of scientific memory (always vacillating between personal and collective memory), places those forms in resonance with the history of the discipline.

The other significant component of the conceptual model of study (no less significant than the disciplinary project) is the political project of socialism in its ideological legitimation through Marxism. The post-war history of Central and Eastern Europe may be described as a process of the socialist project's reformulation, correction, and circumvention with the participation of different social actors. It may be assumed this process ends when the project-legitimating activities and the attempts at rational use of the structures and mechanism, levers and 'niches', chances and obstacles created by the socialist project over the years[6] prove practically invalid and socially useless, since they are blocking the development of all the actors involved, whatever their place and position in society. Simultaneously a hypothesis and an orientation of this study, the view of socialism as a project of a new society realizing *in* and *through* the activities of social actors rests on the understanding that the *agency* of social actors unfolds within certain structures and is at the same time constrained by those structures. On the one hand, this view emphasizes the autonomy, competence (in terms of knowledge and skills) and reflexivity of the social actor, without separating these qualities *from*, or opposing them *to* the institutional-organizational context of social action. On the other hand, this view takes into consideration the coercive and also permissive character of the institutional structures, whereby their characteristics are both a condition for, and a result of, the actions of the social actors. Moreover, as Giddens notes (1995: 213–214),

> action or agency implies the intervention (or refraining) of an individual in a course of events in the world, of which it would be true to say that 'he or she could have done otherwise'.

---

6 Examining the grey economy in Socialist Bulgaria, Roumen Avramov stresses that it encompasses not only actors operating at the margin of official economic life, but also legal and legitimate representatives—the enterprises. "They sought (and usually found) loopholes for bypassing the proclaimed rules. The economic actors had a remarkable imagination. The whole of Socialism may be told as the story of more or less successful attempts at bypassing these barriers" (Avramov, 2003: 132–133). In studying "the boundaries of dictatorshirp", Sandrine Kott also shows that the everyday functioning of Communism was effectuated through informal local overlaps, bricolage, and play with the limits of power (Kott, 2001). According to Liliana Deyanova, these were not 'informal' but rather 'non-public' ties existing as "objective structures of the field itself" (Deyanova, 2003: 308).

In the perspective of *agency*, socialist practice in the countries of Central and Eastern Europe appears as a result not of the autonomous action of a single monopoly structure which subordinates and guides all agents, but a product of the agency of all social actors. Through their "intervention (or refraining)", the social actors mobilize specific features of the structures and thereby both re-produce and transform their nature (Giddens, 1995: 195–215). In other words, they "make history under conditions independent of their will" (Marx); history not simply happens, but is done by the actions and interactions of a countless number of actors. As related to the project of building a new society, this view of socialism as an objectification of human agency entails two corollaries that are important for this analysis and must be specified.

Inasmuch as we are interested only in the conditions that make sociology possible and in the particularities of the development of sociology under the new historical context and with the discipline's new object, our attention is limited to their actual practical construction. That is why, here, 'socialism' is examined in the process of its formation or disintegration as an empirical and epistemic reality, a process occurring as a result of the action (or inaction) of social actors both in the sphere of politics, economy, law, education, etc., and in the sphere of science, particularly sociology.

The second specification is related to the term 'project' which defines the scope (and boundary) of the study of former Communist countries through the prism of the practically unfolding project of the new society. At a first approximation, at least three layers of the 'project of communism' may be distinguished: a) a basic core of ideas formed by the postulates of Marx and Engels,[7] which, later on, Lenin further developed in response to the immediate tasks of the proletarian revolution in a single country, under the conditions of Imperialism; b) the Soviet model of socialism, which was implemented for 28 years before the other Socialist countries appeared, passing through different stages ("military communism" and NEP under Lenin, forced industrialization and collectivization under Stalin) and establishing a monocentric and all-encompassing structure of the Communist party-state apparatus, a structure that would be applied in the other East European countries after World War II; and c) the national projects of socialism. Of course, this differentiation is provisional. It is not based on a

---

7   In this respect, a work of key importance is Engels' *The Principles of Communism* (1847), which was used in writing the *Manifesto of the Communist Party* by Marx and Engels (the first edition of which, from February 1848, continued to be added to and specified at publications in different languages until Engels' death in 1895), and *Critique of the Gotha Program* written by Marx in connection with the unifying congress of the German workers' movement in Go-tha (22–27 May 1875) and published by Engels in 1891.

formal temporal criterion, although the separate layers are linked to different chronologically consecutive periods in the history of socialism as idea and practice. The differentiation is also not of a purely substantial kind—where one quality in a layer would exclude all others and maintain that layer's specific (and pure) identity. The first differentiated layer is in fact the hard core of the communist project shaped by the ideology of the Communist party and defining the practice in the East European countries. The Leninist component here is as much pragmatic as it is ideological, inasmuch as all the texts written by Lenin around and after the October Revolution are variants of solutions to actual practical problems. The Soviet model of socialism was the first materialization of the project of a new society, and as such, it made the first break in the ideological construction of socialism: it was both a realization *of*, and a deviation *from*, the project. This contradictory movement is expressed in the "unique equation ('Soviet power +') expressing entirely new relations of political power, which ensure the goal-oriented process of [...] 'building' a new society" (Bundzhulov, 2003: 93). As for the national projects of socialism, they include both the hard ideological core and elements of the ideology and practice of the Soviet model reworked and adapted to the specific conditions in each country.[8]

Taken separately or together, the layers of the 'new society project' display an unbreakable connection to their ideological center—Marxism.[9] Recognizing that Marxism as ideology cannot be understood without the theoretical conception from which it grows and without the political doctrine that it grounds, here we emphasize the transitions by which the initial scientific content enters into the dynamic social space and becomes part of different forms of political use. These transitions make it possible to see the instituting of Marxism as state ideology in the building of 'socialist society', i.e., to reveal the social consequences of the institutionalization of Marx's theory of society, a theory that generated an ideological vision of the world.

---

8 For instance, the 'people's democracy'—a form of government established in the period 1944–1948 in countries in the Soviet sphere of influence—is an example of transition from capitalism to socialism that was different from the Soviet state model of dictatorship of the proletariat.

9 Here and further on we will refer to Marxism as a current of ideas and a theoretical orientation which, despite its different forms, varieties and historical developments, has preserved the fundamental value assumptions, basic cognitive principles and basic conceptual solutions derived from the intellectual legacy of Marx and Engels. Hence, the Marxism-Leninism that characterized the political discourse and vocabulary of sociologists under the Communist regimes is only one of the forms of this general tradition, although a very powerful and stable one.

While the *Manifesto of the Communist Party* (1848) of Marx and Engels is unanimously considered to be the first systematic exposition of the project for a communist society and of the political program for its implementation, its contents are rarely put in relation to earlier works, which set the cornerstones for a theory of society later to be called Marxist, as well as the methodology of that theory. *Economic and Philosophic Manuscripts* of 1844 and *The German Ideology* of 1845–1846 prepared the theoretical basis for the idea of a classless society that would transcend all historically transitional societies. The conclusions regarding the decisive role of the mode of production and alienated labour as characterizing the relations of production based on private ownership of the means of production are ideas that logically entail the prognosis that communism would eliminate alienation and be a triumph of liberty. This liberty would embody a qualitatively new type of organization of society based on public ownership. Marx's revelation of the social structure of capitalist society supported the idea that the class struggle of the proletariat is the only means for abolishing the forms of ownership and relations of production that generate the class division of society. Grounded in economic analysis, the idea of abolishing the capitalist system could be maintained only as a goal of political action for "the formation of the proletariat into a class, overthrow of the bourgeois supremacy, conquest of political power by the proletariat" (Marx, Engels, 1848: 22).

Linked to the fundamental principles of the scientific approach of Marx and Engels, i.e., the principle of the unity of theory and practice,[10] these results of their analyses entail that the model of a new society represents both a *logical conclusion* drawn from the economic and sociological conceptualization of the history of humankind and a *practical goal to be achieved.* In other words, the trajectory of their analysis, where scientific reasoning reveals the principles and mechanisms of functioning of capitalist society through the categories of historical materialism (relations of production, class relations, etc.), leads to the prophetic vision of a new mode of production which, by eliminating the restrictions of the preceding mode, proves to be simultaneously the most truthful, the most just and the most desirable. The logic of this theoretical

10   Starting from *German-French Yearbooks* (1843–1844), through the eleventh thesis on Feuerbach ("Philosophers have hitherto only *interpreted* the world in various ways; the point is to *change* it", *Theses on Feuerbach*, 1845), and up to his last works, Marx upheld the idea regarding the unbreakable connection between explaining the world and changing it. Social reality must be explained in order to be radically transformed, while the transformation itself is theoretically grounded as a fundamental change in the condition of the worker's world.

approach is to project a reality that does not exist at present but is claimed to be teleologically significant, and is therefore a practical mobilizing factor; this logic underlies the specific ethos of the sociology that has grown out of the Marxist tradition (Koleva, 2011). The particularities of this ethos will be presented in Part 3, in the analysis of the processes and modalities of disciplinary construction of East European sociology.

It is important here to emphasize the specific symbiosis between science and politics that characterizes the whole of Marx's work and the intellectual tradition that developed from it. This symbiosis flows from Marx's view on the overlap of the social purpose of philosophical-historical science and politics (science must explain the world in order to change it; in order to change the world, politics must understand it), and it explains to a considerable degree the origin and specific existence of Marxist ideology. The scientific hypotheses, theses and solutions proposed by Marx and Engels, combined with their social and political commitment and their belief in the socially transformative power of knowledge, form an amalgam of scientific knowledge and prospective social thought that becomes an ideological foundation of the project of a new society. In this sense, the ideology is not derived from Marx's theory of society but is an inseparable part of it, a building block, a defining component of the broad conceptual system.[11] Moreover, according to Petar-Emil Mitev (1984: 39), as early as the *Manuscripts* from 1844,

> The idea of communism is not only the crowning conclusion but, in a certain sense, is the preliminary condition for the whole conception. It is not a "premise" in the dogmatic sense, according to which Marx had a pre-assumed idea that he strove to ground at all costs, but in the scientific sense—only by going in a theoretical perspective outside the boundaries of the existing capitalist social order can the course of world history be understood at all.

In other words, communism already appears at the entry of the analysis defining its scope of ideas and axiological framework. Its functional differentiation into an ideology appears at the exit, after the theory has passed through

---

11   For Marxism, the mutual logical and substantial connection between theory, ideology and political doctrine asserted by Marx has proven to be a source of heuristic breakthroughs in the social thought of the time, but also a source of deep, irresolvable contradictions at the theoretical and practical level. In the following parts of this book, the analysis of the disciplinary practice of sociology and the practice of socialism in post-war Communist Europe will highlight these contradictions.

various stages of construction of its contents, as it seeks an outlet to social practice. In the light of Boudon's interpretation of ideologies, we may say that, once built, the theory provides arguments for the veracity of the ideological content, while practice is prepared to "use", instrumentalize, or transform it (Boudon, 1986).

True to Marx's principle of the unity of theory and practice, Lenin took the first step toward cognitive "emancipation" of Marxism's ideological content and its instrumentalization in political action. Lenin actually objectifies Marxism as an ideology and creates the ideological practice of the Communist Party and of the state ruled by it—the practice as we know it from the development of the former Communist countries. The grounding of the social role of ideology and of class organization, which is Lenin's basic task in *What Is To Be Done?* (1902), is carried out in view of the political goal and in the categories of political reason, i.e., in a 'regime of truth' typical for politics. Unlike Marx and Engels in *The German Ideology* where ideology is an element of the analysis of the social structure and is problematized as a product of the actual material relationships between people and of the "historical process of their life", Lenin is working (to put it in the vocabulary of constructivist sociology) with a politically pre-constructed concept of ideology. For him, ideologies are systems of ideas that participants in the class struggle use for their activity. This utilitarian understanding of ideology as a weapon of the class struggle underlies Lenin's conception of the organized class. Ideology not simply "imports" consciousness into the class,[12] it consolidates and guides it, turning it from a "class in itself" into a "class for itself", while the proletarian party provides the connection between "scientific ideology" and the "worker's movement". Lenin takes two important steps towards the instituting of Marxism as an ideology. First, through the combined term "scientific ideology", he explicitly indicates both the intention of ideological use of the scientific content of Marx's social theory and the fact that he has extracted the ideolo-genic (generating ideological conviction) content from the theory, such as the ideas of class structure and class struggle, of alienated labour and its abolishment through the destruction of the ownership form that has engendered it, etc. Second, he objectifies ideology in the political organization of the class. Thus, ideology embarks on the path of institutionalization which multiplies its power.

As a strategist of the revolution, or, to use Mannheim's expression, an intellectual-revolutionary, Lenin achieved the substantial and functional

---

12   This formulation occurs in Plekhanov (*Socialism and the Political Struggle*, 1883; *Our Differences*, 1885). For more details, see Mitev (1984).

synergy between science and ideology which, after the October Revolution, spilled beyond the party structures and penetrated into the state. In post-revolutionary Russia, Lenin turned from a "revolutionary intellectual into the official legitimator" of the new social and political order and of the vision that grounds it (Berger, Luckmann, 1966). He built the Soviet state in accordance with "the new definition of the world" given by Marxism, thereby making the state "more legitimate" (Ibid.). As the prototype of the socialist ideocratic state, the Soviet state was the first institutionalization of the Marxist ideology at the level of operative management of society, and this had inevitable consequences for all spheres of activity under its control.

Thus, during the whole period from 1945 to 1989, 'the project of a new so-ciety' represented a unity of idea and action, of discourse and practice—in Bourdieu's terms, of discursive and non-discursive practice—in Foucault's terminology. At every moment of its existence, the core of ideas provided the genetic connection between the on-going events and processes, while the ac-tions of social actors expressed the dynamics of the founding idea. Ideology, though renewed over the years, remained the matrix of the historical realiza-tion of the project, drawing new impulses from the sphere of practice. For their part, the actions of social actors were constantly measured against the 'project of socialism', even when it had long-ceased to be a moral imperative, a source of motivation, or a basis of societal integration. This paradox is certainly one of the greatest challenges to researchers seeking an explanation for the vitality of Socialism over more than four decades in Central and Eastern Europe, and for the unpredictable and relatively easy way in which it reached its histori-cal end (Možný, 2003). Our own attempt at interpreting this paradox is made in the perspective of a study on the realization of the new society project *in*, and *through*, the actions of actors, part of who are the sociologists themselves. We seek to understand what it is that is constantly fueling tension—and how—between the idea and action, so that reality gradually drifts away from the ideological blueprint of society and becomes aware of being different from that image. In particular, we are interested in how sociology 'contributed' to maintaining and subverting the 'project of socialism in action', i.e., how sociol-ogy showed (or did not show) society as it is, and thereby made society visible (non-visible) to the intervention of various social actors.

• • •

Are the two projects representing the basic components of the conceptual model of this study identical? The possible mutual similarities and differences implicit in the two concepts point to the historical grounds and the genealogical link of the project of scientific cognition of society and of the project of socialism to "modernity as an unfinished project" (Habermas, 1980).[13] The emergence and development of sociology as a science are inseparable from the project of modernity, whose ideas of rationality and progress presuppose and postulate the ideal of knowledge that permits predicting and controlling man's natural and social environment. On another plane, that of practical action, the Communist ideology radicalizes the ideas of rational and successful management of individual and collective activities by objectifying them in a social project postulated as the purpose of every action. Thus, while sociology legitimates itself by producing and providing a (future) action-oriented knowledge about society, the communist project is imposed by the planning of action in accordance with knowledge about the better future condition of society. This is where the similarity ends between the 'project-based character' of sociology as a scientific discipline and of communism as a form of realization of modernity; this similarity had found expression in the linking of the rationality of knowledge with that of action, a link of which modernity is both a source and a carrier.

The differences are also rooted in modernity, more specifically, in the existing tension, pointed out by Habermas, between, on the one hand, the autonomous spheres of science, morality, and art (the differentiation of which characterizes cultural modernity according to Weber) and on the other hand, the "specialized forms of practice" in which "the knowledge accumulated in science, morality, and art" (Habermas, 1980) is expressed and institutionally objectified. This "sublating" of expert cultures (Ibid.), i.e., sublating of the tension between theory and practice, whatever its concrete forms, may serve to express the history of modernity since the Enlightenment and until now; it also helps to clarify the specificity of sociology as a project for scientific grasp of the social, and the specificity of communism as an all-embracing project for radical social transformation. Belonging to different value orders, sociology and the communist project differ with regard to the status and role of knowledge and the social-practical action related to the latter. In the scientific project of sociology, knowledge is guided by the requirement for an objectively valid and verifiable search for truth, and, in this sense, it is hence a constantly

13   Here, I would like to specially thank Kolyo Koev, now a professor at the New Bulgarian University, who pointed out to me the need to lend greater precision to these two concepts, which have proven to be slippery—he made this remark long ago, when I was working on my book *Sociology as a Project* (Koleva, 2005). Despite their common historical roots, the 'scientific project of sociology' and the 'Communist project' have had very different cognitive and social characteristics.

renewed process of self-construction according to historically established and developed rational rules and procedures. Conversely, knowledge in the communist project exists as an already discovered truth from which the rational actions required for its practical implementation may only be deduced.

As forms of rationalization of socialist society viewed in the course of their own construction and development, the political project of socialism, the Marxist ideology, and the sociological practice under the Communist regimes lead us to focus on a) identifying what is general and specific in them, so as to find a bridge between explanation and action, this bridge proving to be one of the most basic grounds for the existence of all three forms; and on b) delimiting the levels at which the substantial and formal interactions and mutual influences between them take place. Analyzed in their dynamic interaction, the political, ideological, and sociological forms of rationalization of society at that time show that society in its contradictory evolution, in which forms of social mobilization and political repression, of personal antipathy and collective resignation, of adaptation and escape, of support and rejection coexist, follow one after the other, or replace one another. Thus, we see before us a society that, despite the proclaimed socialist ideal, produces totalitarian (in form and content) practices and thereby poses a challenge to the whole disciplinary apparatus of the sociology studying it; we also see a sociology that, in expanding its own theoretical, axiological and epistemological horizon, undertakes to show that empirical reality is moving away from the tenaciously upheld political and ideological image of the 'better', 'more just', 'more equitable' society which is superior to capitalism. We have yet to see the concrete forms of these interactions and mutual influences.

PART 2

Institutional Cycles of Sociology in Central and Eastern Europe, 1945–1989

∵

CHAPTER 5

From Historical Chronology to Institutional Cyclicity

As regards the study of a discipline's development, there can hardly be a more fruitful field, but also more mined with risks, than the history of its institutionalization. Scientific institutions—ranging from research and educational units to professional organizations and communication networks, and passing through norms, principles, rules—seem deceptively easy to study. As objectified instances of the activity for differentiation, organization, justification, and control over the collective scientific enterprise, they are comparatively easy to identify. At the same time, being an accumulated past and a mobile present, they concentrate within themselves both the discipline's chronology of cognitive and social legitimation in a given social-historical context and the inner dynamics of scientific activity. The layers they contain, and the movements to which the scientists themselves subject these layers (burying them, moving them aside, uncovering them, digging them up, etc.), establish that frail connection between past and present that makes the discipline exist in multiple concrete historical forms. As a product of scientific institutionalization, consisting in a constant updating of the activity for asserting and defending a given discipline, these mobile layers are hard to capture and even harder to interpret. When the layers in question are situated in scientific institutions, which are places of effective scientific activity, they make of these institutions places of memory and of oblivion, lifesaver belts and pressuring instruments, zones of freedom and of non-freedom. In this complexity, scientific institutions can be one of the possible keys to understanding the way in which scientists perform their professional duty to produce objectively valid knowledge about reality.

The institutional history, of which sociology in the former Communist countries is the product and the carrier, is studied here from the perspective of a single question: how does sociology construct the cognitive and social chances of its own development, turning itself into an institutionalized activity in an environment where all institutions were socially forced to follow the proclaimed goals of the Communist party-state and were controlled by the pyramidal and tentacled structure of this power? In other words, how does sociology defend and develop its disciplinary project, given that it has become

© KONINKLIJKE BRILL NV, LEIDEN, 2018 | DOI 10.1163/9789004333635_007

an institution *in*, and *of*, the political-administrative structure of society at that time?

This reduction of the research focus does not cancel the question as to how institutionalization is viewed as a process in time, or vice versa, how the historical chronology, typical for every process, tailors the object and shapes the avenues to the study of the process. At the same time, this reduction leads to certain choices. A chronologically exhaustive and detailed description of the sociological institutions for research, education, publication, expertise provision, etc. in each country would *not* be the solution to the problem. It would provide a relatively full picture of the institutions but could not reveal how they assisted or hindered the production of scientifically objective knowledge about the society of that time. Neither would the division of the period 1945–1989 into sub-periods be a solution: this, for several reasons. First, every simple, one-dimensional criterion of periodization would be more or less arbitrary. Second, any attempt to define a composite criterion capable of integrating the intellectual, social, and political histories in the course of which a given science developed, would violate their fundamental irreducibility, as well as the "principle of irreducibility" in studying the past. Third, this would require explicating the notion of period, lacking which, the analytical procedure would be unfounded.

Turning to the interpretation offered by historians whose discipline seems to hold a methodological monopoly on matters of periodization, we find an additional argument for avoiding periodization as a tool for interpreting historical phenomena.[1] In his introductory lecture on "History of Powers in Western Europe, 13th–16th centuries" at the Collège de France, Patrick Boucheron (2015) defines 'period' as "a time given by us which we can use at our discretion, exceeding it, transferring it". That is why, "we have no the duty—[and, we would add, the right]—to transform it into something that exists through itself, a delimited thing living a life of its own". According to Boucheron, since it is "an accumulated past", the time of a period is significant for the layers of present-day reality, which "archeology regards as always active, useful to understand". The refusal of the privilege and power of the scientist to designate periods does not, however, amount to a refusal to describe the historical period of the phenomenon under study.

---

1   This is an additional, but very pertinent argument, since the idea of understanding the institutional history of sociology in Central and Eastern Europe in the period 1945–1989 in terms of institutional cycles, not institutional periods, was first argued and applied in Koleva (2002a).

It would not be correct with respect to the course of this research to claim that the study of the institutional history of sociology under the Communist regimes does not lean on historical chronology. To the contrary, chronology helps us see the facts, it makes salient the events, enables noticing the recurrences, coincidences, and differences. However, in order to understand the *logic* behind what happened, we need to go beyond the chronology of facts, or more precisely, to enter within it. The concept of 'institutional cycle' is an instrument we use to identify and analyze the activity of East European researchers for institutionalizing sociology as a legitimate approach to the scientific study of society under the specific conditions established by the Communist party-state. Through it, we designate not periods but the periodically recurring configurations of social-political, intellectual, organizational, etc. relations that lead to a relatively identical status of sociology within the scientific and social space of a given society at different points of a segment of the discipline's history. The concept is constructed by tracing the historical chronology of three spheres differentiated as components of the conceptual model of the study: politics, ideology, and sociology. The rationale for such an approach lies in the hypothesis that the developments of the three are interrelated; this hypothesis is tested through the study of the institutional cycles in the development of post-war East European sociology. Through the prism of institutional cycles, we also test the hypothesis regarding the construction of zones of institutionalized professional activity that regulate (in regimes of permission, defense, restriction, hampering) the upholding and application of the principles of sociology's disciplinary project.

Insofar as the historical canvas of Communist Europe in the period 1945–1989 was defined by the politics and ideology of a monopoly power—the Communist party-state, important reference points for the study are some key events in the political history of the former Communist countries considered together. The 'shared destiny' of the Communist countries of Central and Eastern Europe was charted at the Teheran Conference (November-December 1943), then reconfirmed at Churchill's visit to Moscow (October 1944) and firmly asserted at the Yalta (February 1945) and Potsdam (July 1945) conferences. This destiny began to effectively unfold after the end of World War II, when the agreements made between the Great Powers of the anti-Hitler coalition to give over Eastern Europe to the Soviet sphere of influence came into effect. Regardless of the varying positions of the countries during the war (Bulgaria, Hungary, Slovakia were satellites of Germany, while Poland and Bohemia were occupied by Hitler's forces), they all started on the road to socialism, with the Soviet state as their model. Although the Soviet model was implemented in all these countries by coalition governments (in which the proportion of Communist and non-Communist parties was different in each country) under the form of 'people's democracies', it was imposed as the matrix of social and political development everywhere as early as the first post-war years, 1945–1949. Hence, it is not surprising that, having completely gained political control in the early 1950s, the Communist leaders would diligently and unswervingly carry out in their own countries the purges and repressions familiar from Stalinist practice.

Stalin's death (5 March 1953) and the famous 20th Congress of the CPSU (February 1956) at which Nikita Khrushchev read his report "On the Cult of Personality and Its Consequences", better known as the 'secret report': these are the two marking events of the first important change to take place in the vision on socialism in course of construction, and in the style of Communist governance.[2] Of course, this was a process whose high points not only assumed different forms but had different results for the subsequent evolution of society in each of the countries under study. In Poland and Hungary, the revision of the socialist project expressed itself respectively in manifestations (against the arrest of Cardinal Wyszyński and of workers' protests in June 1956, during the international fair in Poznan) and revolts (the Hungarian uprising of October 1956). These developments were resolved peacefully in Poland (without Soviet intervention) and ended in Hungary with bloody suppression by the Soviet Army. In Czechoslovakia, the course of de-Stalinization and liberalization of socialism culminated in the Prague Spring of 1968 whose concept of "socialism with a human face"[3] deviated so drastically from the Soviet-model of reforms of socialism that it brought about the intervention of the Warsaw Pact armies in August of that year. In Bulgaria and the USSR, the political changes initiated from the top were not marked by any mass outbursts of popular energy, despite the liberating effect they had on the minds of people and on the public moods.

Even this short list of events indicates that the time between February 1956 and August 1968, which came to be known in historical literature and everyday

---

2   The events had a different significance for East and West at the time. Here we only note their nature as a line of demarcation in 20th century history.

3   That is how the large-scale reform was defined in the "Action Programme of the Czechoslovak Communist Party", published on 10 April 1968 in the party newspaper *Rudé právo/Red Justice*. That same month, the program was translated into English and disseminated abroad by the Czechoslovak Telegraph Agency (in Baeva, 2010: 190–208). For details, see Remington (1969).

speech as the "thaw",[4] comprises contradictory trends. The movement away from the typical Stalinist modes of governance by means of repression and terror, defined by Hannah Arendt as one of the fundamental elements of the totalitarian regimes, did not revoke the use of violence as an instrument of Communist rule in the name of the unity of the Socialist system. The beginning of reform of Socialism through disclosure of the truth about the past was at the same time the beginning of a crisis, both in the East and in the West, of the Communist idea and of faith in its implementation. If Khrushchev's 'secret report' in 1956 "put an end to Socialism (Communism) as a spiritual challenge", as the historian Iskra Baeva points out (2010: 154), with the dramatic events in Czechoslovakia in 1968, "Communism ceased to be an intellectual problem and turned into a problem of power", according to the philosopher Leszek Kołakowski (cited from Baeva, 2010: 154). Soviet Socialism as a societal system, and the Cold War as an international system entered a new phase.

The next decade and the early 1980s were a time of building 'the developed socialist society' as a historically determined and necessary stage of the first phase of the communist formation, foreseen early on by Lenin. In the documents of the Central Committee of CPSU related to the 60th anniversary of the October Revolution, it was reported that the developed socialist society was already a fact in the USSR; the political goal now was to build it in the other socialist countries as well. The new ideological formulation of the political project of socialism confirmed by the leadership of the fraternal Communist parties became a common emblem of the Soviet Camp in the 1970s. The implementation of this political directive, however, was carried out through different courses in each of the countries: there was a hardening of the regime in Czechoslovakia after 1968, a consolidation of the party nomenklatura and political stagnation in the Soviet Union under Leonid Brezhnev, continuing liberalization and less fixation on ideology in the Hungary of János Kádár, political destabilization in Poland under the impact of periodical outbursts of students' and workers' protests (March 1968, December 1970, June 1976, August 1980-December 1981), a dexterous balancing between internal directives and external imperatives in Bulgaria under Todor Zhivkov (the only Communist leader who was able to hold on to his position in power for 35 years—from March 1954 to November 1989).

Thus, each of the countries under study entered the 1980s with differing political liabilities and assets, both of the regime and the citizens. Poland was

---

4   The expression was taken from the title of Ilya Ehrenburg's novel *The Thaw* published in 1956.

the first country of the Communist Bloc to establish a free trade union, entirely independent of the Communist Party and the state, and officially recognized by the state authorities.[5] This was the first breakthrough in the monocentric and pyramidal structure of political-administrative power. This case of institutional recognition of the right to free association undermined the founding principle of the Communist party-state—its total control. As an autonomous political actor, the trade union Solidarity would define the political development of Polish society during the whole decade of the 1980s, the culmination of which would be the democratic elections in June 1989, which were won by the opposition and led to the first government in Eastern Europe with a non-Communist prime minister (Tadeusz Mazowiecki). The Polish experience was echoed with various degrees of intensity and speed in all the other Communist countries, but it was Mikhail Gorbachev's[6] political program, gaining world renown under the name of "perestroika",[7] that gave the real impetus to political change and civic revival in the East European societies. The attempt initiated by Moscow to overcome the crisis of Socialism and save it through radical economic and political reforms, quickly spread throughout the Communist Camp, to be met with various degrees of reservation by the national Communist parties and with widespread enthusiasm by the population. Assuming different forms and dimensions depending on the national traditions and specificities of the political context in the separate countries, perestroika led to a common ultimate result: the "delegitimation of the whole system of Soviet-type state Socialism" (Baeva, 2010: 273). The fall of the Berlin Wall in October 1989 marked the symbolic end of the Communist regimes in Central and Eastern Europe, while the breakdown of the USSR in December 1991 signaled the end of the Soviet Bloc as a political and social system as well as the end of the Cold War as a world geo-political order.

---

5   Born as a strike committee heading the strike at the Gdansk Shipyard in July-August 1980, the trade union Solidarity was recognized by the Supreme Court of Poland and officially registered on 10 November 1980.

6   A Soviet leader of a new generation, Mikhail Gorbachev (1931-) was elected secretary general of the CPSU in March 1985 after the death of the three general secretaries Brezhnev, Andropov, and Chernenko who were all born in the first decade of the 20th century and were part of the party-state gerontocracy in USSR.

7   The new Soviet doctrine was formulated in Gorbachev's book *Perestroika: New Thinking for Our Country and the World* published in 1986 in Russian and immediately translated into 18 languages. It referred to the renewal and acceleration of the Soviet economy, "glasnost" (transparency and public candor in political and social life) and the democratization of party and state governance.

The political chronology of the Communist regimes in Central and Eastern Europe, given in various degrees of detail, with an emphasis on various national events, figures in publications and in interviews with sociologists as a very general historical framework for discussions on the respective national sociologies. Most of the interviewed sociologists examine the periods of sociology's development in their countries in relation to the evolution of the political regime there, viewed over the decades and in terms of key international and national events. Nearly all of them point out how hard it is to draw a clear and strict dividing line between the purely cognitive, internal scientific criteria and the socio-political criteria for periodization of the discipline's Communist past. They are unanimous that the degree of liberalization of the political regime was a factor of the development of sociology.

In this study, the overlap in descriptions of the evolution of separate national sociologies in terms of their relations with political power has enabled us to go beyond the dependency indicated by interviewees and to see it as a dynamic relationship between sociology and power in which these elements interact and do not remain self-enclosed. The periods in the development of sociology marked by the historical turning points, in fact, display relatively similar conditions of cognitive and social presence of sociology under relatively identical modes of political governance within chronologically distant segments of time. At first glance, this seems to confirm the determining role of the Communist party-state as holder of a monopoly on political power for the development of sociology in these countries. However, a comparison of historically recurring modes of sociological practice shows how the set of relations in which sociology is involved outgrows the politically modeled society, and how sociologists, without entering into open conflict with their normative and institutional framework of activity, were able to unfold conceptual, theoretical, and methodological creativity by applying various strategies of going about their professional activity despite the extra-scientific criteria imposed upon their research field.

This is the path that led us from the *historical chronology of institutions* to the *institutional cyclicity* in the development of sociology in post-war European Communist countries. By arranging and jointly presenting simultaneous and consecutive events in different social spheres, the chronological description gives a density to historical facts, thanks to which we may pass on to the next stage of the search for connections between the evolution of heterogeneous phenomena. Here the historical connection between the chronology of sociology and that of the ruling power, respectively, that of society, is captured and analyzed through the concept of institutional cycle. Institutional cycles are based on empirically observable, recurring characteristics in the cognitive and social existence of sociology, and they do not coincide with chronological periods of political history, although they are linked to them. Moreover, the same institutional cycles may occur in different segments of time for the separate national sociologies. By tracing the dynamics of institutionalization of sociological activity in the countries under study (which is inseparable from other dynamics, such as political, of ideas, interdisciplinary, etc.), we have distinguished three periodically recurring cycles of institutional development in these sociologies in the period from 1945 to 1989: *institutional reanimation, institutional mimicry*, and *institutional expansion.* The subsequent analysis will examine their manifestations in a chronological order.

CHAPTER 6

Institutional Reanimation of Sociology: 1944–1948/49

The attention devoted by historiography of sociology to the second half of the 1940s is inconsiderable compared with its attention to the interwar years and the early 1950s. This is even truer as concerns the sociology in the countries that found themselves in the Soviet zone of influence after the war. Historical analyses of sociology under the Communist regimes usually take as its starting point the year of the definitive takeover of political power by the Communist party in the respective country: 1948 or 1949. However, there is also a conceptual approach to this sociology that situates its beginning later on, in 1956, based on the hypothesis that the liberalization of the Communist regimes, which began that year, gave impetus to the revival of national sociologies and led to an increasing heterogeneity in their development despite the common social-political conditions (Keen, Mucha, 1994: IX–XII, 1–10). Historical studies on Russian/Soviet sociology have presented a case that, while special, confirms the general tendency. In publications on the history of sociology in USSR, which had a boom in the 1990s, the prevailing opinion is that the 1930s, a time of the 'totalitarian Soviet state', cut short the cognitive and institutional development of sociology which was to be revived only after 1956 (*History of the Development…*, 1989; *History of the Emergence…*, 1989; Golosenko, Kozlovskiy, 1995; Novikova, 1996; *Sociology and Power*, 1997; *Sociology in Russia*, 1998). Here the post-war period 1945–1949 falls within the large historical hiatus for Soviet sociology.

The claim that an interval of four or five years was too short to have had a serious influence on the further development of society and of sociology is true only from the retrospective viewpoint of what we know today about the history that followed. If we place ourselves in the stream of events at that time as described and interpreted by historians and sociologists, we would see some facts that testify to the relatively swift restoration of sociological structures and activities interrupted by the war, and in some cases, of the beginning of institutions of education and research activity in sociology.[1]

---

[1]   The overview, presented below, of sociological activities and institutions in the first post-war years in the Communist countries is based on Batygin (1998), Batygin, Deviatko (1994), Becskehazi, Kuczi (1994), Boyadjieva (2010), Genov (1994, 2002), Illner (2002), Kolosi, Szelényi

© KONINKLIJKE BRILL NV, LEIDEN, 2018 | DOI 10.1163/9789004333635_008

Of the various forms of sociological activity that existed before the war, lecture courses were the easiest to recommence or to initiate. In Poland, lectures in sociology were resumed in Warsaw, Poznań, and Kraków; courses in sociology were introduced at the newly opened universities in Łódź and Toruń, as well as at the university in Wrocław which was now within the boundaries of Poland after the addition of the Western territories to the country; strong interest was shown in the teaching of sociology in colleges (Kraśko, 1998: 178–181). The universities of Prague, Bratislava and Sofia also resumed their pre-war lecture courses in sociology. The activity of Inocenc Arnošt Bláha's seminar in Brno, and the Sociological Seminar at Comenius University in Bratislava recommenced. Teaching of sociology began at the University of Budapest, where a department of sociology was created in 1946, headed by Sándor Szalai, a student of the Frankfurt School. In 1945, a department of sociology was established at Matica Slovenská, the national cultural association, in Martin. Among the countries under study, the exception was USSR, where since the 1930s, Stalin's vulgate of Marxism had been in force and universities taught historical materialism and the Marxist science of society.

Publication activity returned to its pre-war pace as regards books with the word 'sociology' in the title and periodicals related to sociology. In 1946, publication was resumed of the first Polish specialized journal in sociology, *Przegląd Socjologiczny/The Sociological Review* (established in 1931); in the same year, in Czechoslovakia, publication resumed of the journal *The Sociological Review* (founded in 1930 as an edition of the Sociological Seminar at Masaryk University in Brno, and which was the official printed organ of the Masaryk sociological community in Prague since 1931). Also in 1946, the Sociological Department at Matica Slovenská began publishing Slovak Quarterly, *Sociologicky Zbornik*, which continued until 1948.

As for research work, it was revived above all in Poland, where sociologists who had survived the war undertook to study the social changes taking place in Polish society. According to Nina Kraśko (1998: 179), of particular interest to them were

> the problems of the Western and Northern territories. [...] Stanisław Ossowski and his colleagues studied the sense of national and regional cohesion and the determinants of identification with Polish nationality in

(1993), Kraśko (1998), Kusá et al. (2002), Kwasniewicz (1993, 1994), Mucha, Załęcki (2002), Macků (1996), Markiewicz (1970), Možný (1996), Némedi (2010), Némedi, Róbert (2002), Pasiak, Machacek (1994), Szomolányi (1995, 2009), Turčan (2000). With a few exceptions, bibliographic references are indicated only in footnotes, so as not to burden the main text.

the rural inhabitants of Opole Silesia. Integration of vernacular people and immigrants was also the focus of study for participants of Kazimierz Dobrowolski's sociological seminar at the Jagiellonian University. [...] The students of Paweł Rybicki from the University of Wrocław [...] also studied this problem.

In the other countries, scholars were primarily laying the foundation of organized collective research activity by building the infrastructure of sociology. In Hungary, an Institute for Social Research was established at Budapest University, which conducted a few social studies in the period 1946–1949. An Institute of Sociology at the Bulgarian Academy of Sciences was established for the first time in Bulgaria; its director was Iliya Yanulov, a specialist in social legislation and labour relations, who was a member of the Belgian Solvay Institute of Sociology. At the Institute of Philosophy of the Academy of Sciences of USSR, 'something like a sociological section' was created under the leadership of Mark Baski; its main task was 'to study and criticize foreign sociological theories'. According to Gennady Batygin, this unit had "an exceptionally great importance for the formation of the genre 'criticism of bourgeois sociology' in Soviet social science" (Batygin, 1998: 31).

The post-war (re)start of sociology varies from country to country depending on the pre-war intellectual traditions and the institutional, organizational and human resources potential that survived the war. Poland and Czechoslovakia had a considerably advantage, because there the organizational and cognitive institutionalization of sociology had begun in the 1920s and 1930s, initiated and impelled by figures well-known even today, like Florian Znaniecki, Stefan Czarnowski, Ludwik Krzywicki, Tomáš Masaryk, Edvard Beneš, Inocenc Arnošt Bláha, Anton Štefánek, Alexander Hirner, Peter Gula. Their students in Poland[2] and Czechoslovakia, as well as Bláha, Štefánek, Hirner and Gula themselves, undertook the post-war revival of the sociological legacy from between the two wars and the expansion of its institutional basis.

---

2 Of the generation of Polish sociologists formed before WWII, those with the greatest contribution to the institutional revival of sociology in the first post-war years were: two of Znaniecki's students—Józef Chałasiński (nominated the vice rector and then rector of the University of Łódź) and Jan Szczepański (who replaced Chałasiński as dean, and then as rector), the younger collaborator of Znaniecki, Tadeusz Szczurkiewicz (who taught in Poznań and Toruń), Czarnowski's two assistants Nina Assorodobraj and Stanisław Ossowski (dean of the Department of Humanities at the University of Łódź at its beginning), and Maria Ossowska and Kazimierz Dobrowolski in Kraków.

The situation was different in Bulgaria and Hungary. The sociological interpretation of social reality had some significant national figures in these countries, such as Ivan Hadjiyski, Venelin Ganev, Ferenc Erdei, Imre Kovács, among others; efforts at studying the economic and social backwardness of the two societies were made through empirical surveys on the labour conditions of workers and rural household budgets (Bulgaria) and in sociographic works on the situation of the agrarian population (Hungary), but these did not lead to the formation of an autonomous research field, distinguishable within the national scientific traditions. These particularities of the two countries highlight both the success and the subsequent rapid failure of the first attempts to institutionalize the already existent but unorganized efforts at social scientific study of their societies. In the first post-war years of social enthusiasm and political pluralism, there was a favorable configuration of local social actors for realizing the idea of institutionalizing the research (in both countries) and educational (only in Hungary) activity of sociology. The newly created institutional units, however, were still 'young' and frail when the radical change of the social order set in, and a single party not simply came to power but imposed its societal model upon the whole society. The closing down in 1948–1949 of the Department of Sociology and the Institute for Social Research at Budapest University, and of the Institute of Sociology in Sofia was one of the first materializations of the new model, which was based upon total domination of a single vision of the world, on a total lack of distinction between spheres, levels, manifestations of life-in-society, and which eliminated all differences and differentiations. These acts were solid proof that it was impossible to defend positions won, but still unfortified, in science and society.

As for USSR, it cannot be said that the creation of a group for the study of foreign sociological theories at the Soviet Academy of Sciences represented a breakthrough in the disciplinary structure of Stalinist Marxism, inherited from the 1930s. Although created within an academic structure, this unit had service functions (to provide information that might be useful for developing personal ideas among scholars holding high positions in the Party and state structures) and remained under the control of those scholars (Batygin, Deviatko, 1994).

Inasmuch as data and analyses related to the first post-war years of sociology in East European countries are scarce both in the literature familiar to us,[3] and in the interviews, our reflexive assessment of this short period in the

---

3   The author's lack of knowledge of the national languages of the countries under study (with the exception of Bulgarian and Russian) is certainly a handicap that has restricted the use of available literature. A lack of awareness or consideration of this fact would certainly be damaging to this study. However, as any other handicap, when integrated into the author's own approach to reality, it simply becomes another, different way of access to it.

discipline's history must assume the form of a hypothetic interpretation. The latter, of course, is based on the reflections that sociologists in these countries have made on various occasions, at various times during the post-totalitarian development of the discipline. This hypothetic perspective is related to the fact that we strive to overcome the problem of our limited information by logically constructing a possible explanation valid for all countries under study. It goes without saying that the rational structuring of facts proposed here is open to the 'Popperian' risk of proving invalid if new empirical data eventually appear.

"Historical intermezzo" (Jiří Musil), "sociology's peaceful coexistence with Communism" (Szacki), "hopes for development" (Kraśko), "society-oriented sociology" (Lutyński)—these are some of the different definitions of this short chapter in the discipline's history in post-war Central and Eastern Europe. Each definition has a different stress depending on the viewpoint of the researcher. Their common element is *the return of sociology to its pre-war occupations and institutional forms under the new social-political conditions.* Even in cases where lecture courses in sociology or new institutional units were opening for the first time in a country, the connection to what had been done before the war, and to the people who had done it was maintained. The changed conditions had no influence on the university curriculum for sociology or on the scientific organization and research tools; only the thematic priorities changed (the focus was placed on the new society as an alternative to the pre-war one) and the research tasks (it was important to provide information for the successful construction of the new society). At that stage, the sphere of higher education and science was not a priority for the coalition governments. They were absorbed foremost in the economic and material restoration of their countries and in political rivalries related to building the new state system. The system had to be rid of the persons who had directly or indirectly collaborated with the local pro-Hitler governments or the occupiers,[4] and to be based on new organs and new official positions. The anti-fascist coalitions' intervention in

---

4   The process of "defascization or denazification", which was common to all of post-war Europe, had two aspects: punishment (dismissal) of the former political elite, and replacement of the state administration. Already in the *Declaration on Liberated Europe,* approved and signed at the Yalta Conference (February 1945), it was noted that "[...] the establishment of order in Europe and the new structuring of national economic life must be achieved in ways that will allow the liberated peoples to destroy the last traces of Nazism and Fascism and to create democratic institutions of their own choice". These were also the primary goals of all new governments, established on the basis of the anti-fascist fronts and their programs (Manifesto of the Polish Committee for National Liberation, 22 July 1944; Proclamation of

education and science was limited to purging the teaching staff of fascist elements, and to purging the libraries of works of fascist leanings and supplying Marxist-Leninist literature as a means of ousting the reactionary ideology and shaping a new political consciousness among the population. At this stage, the biggest change in the university curriculum was the introduction of dialectical and historical materialism as a new discipline, which was very quickly institutionalized in the form of special university departments. Starting from 1947, the reform would touch on the other elements of education and scientific activity—curriculum, organizational structures and methods of university education, the regulations and institutional structure of scientific research, enrolment of students, etc. (Koleva, 2005; Kraśko, 1998).

On the other hand, sociologists, most of them with leftist convictions, shared the new political vision and the related hopes for a 'new' democracy,[5] different both from the regimes of the pre-war bourgeoisie (authoritarian, dictatorial, collaborationist, fascist—depending on the concrete country) and from the Soviet model of state socialism. Publications and interviews with Polish sociologists who received their university education in the post-war period confirm the civic sympathy and commitment of sociologists to the beginning

---

the Fatherland Front Government to the Bulgarian People, 9 September 1944, and Program of the Fatherland Front Government, 17 September 1944; Declaration of the Provisional Hungarian National Government, 22 December 1944; Program of the New Czechoslovak Government of the National Front of Czechs and Slovaks, 5 April 1945). In the Central and Eastern European countries, the removal of the wartime ruling elite was effected through extraordinary legislation and by new judicial organs—the so-called People's Court and extraordinary courts which issued thousands of death sentences or at least condemned the sentenced individuals to permanent removal from the political and public life of the countries. The formation of the new powers' state apparatus was achieved through so-called administrative purges (removal of the former wartime administration) carried out under the control, but also with the support, of the Allied Commission of Control—an international organ in the former German satellite countries whose mission was to supervise the implementation of the peace treaties signed on 10 February 1947 in Paris. For more details, see Volokitina et al. (2002: 63–98).

5   While immediately after the war the expression 'new democracy' was used, with the rapidly growing ideological confrontation between East and West, the term 'people's democracy' (which literally means "people's rule of the people") became prevalent. It was also used to designate the official form of government adopted in all the East European countries (including Albania, Rumania, and Yugoslavia) after the war. The term served a double purpose: to indicate the difference from the bourgeois model of Western democracy, and to show the people's democratic model was tolerated by the USSR. Present-day historiography views this form as a poly-variant transition, which ended in 1948 with the establishment of the Communist parties' monopoly on power (Volokitina et al., 1993).

social transformation. In describing the political and intellectual situation in the country immediately after the end of the war, Jerzy Wiatr points out (interview with Jerzy Wiatr conducted on 29 March 2000, Warsaw, personal archive),

> these first four years were marked by the very active involvement of sociologists in the transformation. [...] They were enthusiastic, that is enthusiastic doesn't mean non critical. They were critical of the political situation, lack of freedom and so one. But they were enthusiastic about the changes of the society. They symphatize with social transformation.

Jerzy Szacki, also a university graduate from the post-war period and one of the important researchers of the history of sociology, including Polish sociology, points out two coexistent tendencies in the attitudes of Polish sociologists directly after the War (1998: 119):

> [...] on the one hand, sociologists wanted to continue, in new conditions, the work begun in pre-war years; on the other hand, they demonstrated considerable willingness to coexist peacefully with the official regime. There is no indication that it was impossible to reconcile these two motives at the time. This is because the majority of Polish sociologists who survived the war and had not left the country showed leftist inclinations. They also harboured the strong illusory faith that the new political system would not be a simple replica of the classical Soviet system but would instead, at least to some extent, develop into something better and more original. The cultural policy of the communist regime undoubtedly supported this illusion. All political opposition was treated absolutely ruthlessly whereas the communists were more flexible in their approach to the so-called old intelligentsia whom they wanted to win over in order to reconstruct the pre-war academics institutions.

Analysis of administrative documents and publications dating from the first decade of Poland under Communism lead Nina Kraśko to conclude (1998: 181):

> All in all, the expectations of the sociologists and the new regime concerning the future of sociology in post-war Poland seemed to converge, whereas the fact that the majority of sociologists who were in charge of scientific institutions understood and supported the social and economic

changes taking place in the country seemed to insure a good climate of the development of the discipline.

We should make a brief remark here before drawing a general conclusion. Citing the testimonies and publications of Polish sociologists does not indicate we are extrapolating the national situations of sociology from the country with the most developed pre-war tradition (in respect to scientific activity and institutions) and to the other East European countries. This period of the development of sociology has been the object of sociological self-reflection most of all in Poland, and the facts and assessments presented here are illustrations, not arguments. As for the cogency of the interpretation they offer, as pointed out earlier, these views should be compared with broader empirical information and may be tested by any researcher.

In pursuing the logic of this study, we may assert that, in the post-war years, amid the beginning political reorientation of social development, in an atmosphere of widely shared and socially mobilizing belief in a new perspective, *sociology in these countries was returning to its institutional home, abandoned during the war, and starting to restore it.* The reanimation of institutions did not involve a change in the content of their activity, or the structure of their organization, or the body of theoretical knowledge and research tools used before the war. These developments went on concurrently with sociology's recommenced function of being useful to society (pointed out early on by the classics of this science). But what would that new society turn out to be?

We see there was a sort of continuity in the theoretical status, and the place and role of sociology within the scientific and social sphere during the first years after the war, despite the commenced political transformation of society. In the terms of the conceptualization proposed here, the *disciplinary project of sociology in these countries remained unchanged.* Perhaps this is one of the reasons why Polish and Czech sociologists (Chałasiński, 1948; Illner, 2002) have viewed the time from 1918 until 1948 as a single, continuous period or as a sociology that had re-emerged in "direct continuation of the pre-1939 sociological experience" (Szacki, 1993: 168).

The subsequent history will show that the brief interval from 1945 to 1948/49 was in fact an interlude in the disciplinary development of sociology. This does not deny its nature as an institutional revival of the sociological activity that existed, to various degrees and on various scales, before the war in each of the countries under study. Seen in a historical perspective, this nature shows the revival of sociological practice to have been a cycle, not an intermediate period. The return of sociology to the "family of legitimate sciences" after 1956 was certainly an institutional rebirth. But more than that, it was a real renaissance which enlarged the horizons, and involved the institutional expansion of the discipline. The institutional development of sociology in fact entered a new cycle. However, before that, history would carry sociology through the first cycle of institutional mimicry.

CHAPTER 7

Institutional Mimicry I: 1948/49–1956

Between 1948/49 and 1956, sociology in the countries under Soviet influence found itself in a period of timelessness when, as scholars unanimously agree, its institutional practice was eliminated. The motives and the initiators of this development came from outside sociology; its executors were social actors both outside and inside scientific circles. In all the countries in question, the change was abrupt, and the result—strikingly uniform.

The courses in sociology, resumed or newly opened immediately after the end of the war, were abolished in all universities. Suddenly, without warning or debate, starting from the academic year 1949–1950, the specialty of sociology in all Polish universities was replaced with the specialty 'social sciences'. As Nina Kraśko notes (1998: 186), in October 1949,

> when the freshmen of the humanities, including sociology, turned up for their first day of term, they were told that they would be studying social sciences according to the new curriculum.

In the other countries, the existing departments of sociology and the newly formed research units were shut down. Some of the teachers of the pre-war generation, as well as their students, were driven out of the chairs of sociology or the universities; others emigrated, and still others, such as Sándor Szalai (the first head of the Department of Sociology at the University of Budapest), were put in jail. Publications with a sociological content were stopped.

What was happening in East European people's democracies that led to such a turnabout in the development of sociology? And what did this turnabout express? The brief answer is that a totalitarian organization of the 'socialist'-type state and society was being built. The expanded answer would involve tracing the pre-history of the process and seeing the turnabout as the result of connected actions of people from the political and scientific spheres.

Towards 1948–1949, the ruling coalitions established on a broad anti-fascist base were completely taken over by the representatives of the Communist party within them. Their electoral victories led to the definitive elimination of post-war political pluralism and to imposition of the Communist project of the new society as the only possible variant of social development. However, the preconditions and resources for the implementation of this project had already been established thanks to the radical changes initiated

© KONINKLIJKE BRILL NV, LEIDEN, 2018 | DOI 10.1163/9789004333635_009

with the collaboration of those who had until then been coalition partners[1] and with the support of other, still autonomous, economic, professional and institutional actors.

First of all, the coalition governments, although provisional organs, had initiated important legislative changes in various spheres of public life (in industry, transport, trade, agriculture, science, education, culture, the arts) which centralized the activity in all of these and gradually asserted the state's monopoly of control over their development. New organs of governance were created as sub-divisions of the national fronts; their main mission in the first post-war years was to establish political control over the work of government institutions. However, in many spheres there was an interweaving, and at times merging, of the functions of these sub-divisions and the state organs. Formed by delegated representatives of the coalition parties, and elected by the population, these national councils gradually turned from organs of self-governance into organs of state government (Baeva, 1995, 1998; Chichovska, 1981; Isusov, 1978; Kołomejczyk, Koseski, 1977; Migev, 1981). Administrative structures of state regulation and control were built, which replaced the autonomous public law institutions in the respective spheres, enforced political considerations in the management of activities in the respective areas, and duplicated the functions of the high state structures. Moreover, their leaders held important positions in the leading organs of the coalition parties. Of the numerous examples, here we will point out a few from the sphere of education, science and culture. In Bulgaria, a Committee for Science, Art and Culture began functioning on 1 January 1948, replacing the Chamber of National Culture established by Regents' Decree on 15 May 1945 as "an institute in which the creative person takes part freely through his organization" and not as an administrative unit of state governance (Chichovska, 1981: 466–467). In Poland, besides the Central Council for Science and Higher Education, created in 1947 and responsible for the development of new curricula, there was also a Council of Higher Educational Establishments in Poland, the president of which, Włodzimierz Sokorski, was concurrently a member of the Politburo of the Polish United Workers' Party (PUWP) (Kraśko, 1998: 184).

---

1 It must not be forgotten that the Communist parties played a role in two aspects: they prepared the programs of the anti-fascist fronts at the end of the war which would become the programs of the first governments; then they imposed the view that the first post-war governments must not only deal with reviving the economy and administration in the respective country (a stance shared by the other political parties as well) but also undertake significant transformations in all spheres of society (Baeva, 1998).

Secondly, the legislatures (at first the provisional national assemblies or councils, and later, the elected parliaments) adopted laws that launched radical reforms in industry (laws for nationalization of private enterprises, whereby private ownership in industry was restricted or completely abolished; these were passed, respectively, on 24 October 1945 in Czechoslovakia, 3 January 1946 in Poland, 23 December 1947 in Bulgaria), in agriculture (laws or decrees on agrarian reform adopted on 6 September 1944 in Poland, 17 March 1945 in Hungary, 13 March 1945 and 12 March 1946 in Bulgaria),[2] and in the state administration (in accordance with the policy for building a new, politically reliable state apparatus). In 1947–1948 were adopted the new constitutions of Bulgaria, Czechoslovakia, and Hungary, designed after the model of the Constitution of USSR of 1936. Poland was an exception. While the first, so-called "little" constitution of 1947 made no reference to the Soviet model, the Constitution of People's Republic of Poland adopted in July 1952 was a faithful copy of the Soviet Constitution. In any case, all these constitutions turned the economic, political, and ideological principles of the new social order of the 'people's democracy' into laws. The leading role of the Communist parties would be asserted in the new constitutions adopted in the 1970s.

Third, the anti-fascist measures declared by the coalition governments regarding the removal from all public spheres of cadres who had fascist activity in their past were carried out diligently not only by various government and national front structures but also by ordinary citizens and rank and file members of the political parties. In this activity, the professional unions in various areas of culture, science, and education displayed not only efficiency and radicalness in preparing lists and proposing punishments but also a desire to assume powers of an administrative kind. Especially telling in this respect was the activity of the Union of Education Workers in Bulgaria (Chichovska, 1981: 462–471).

Hence, in the perspective of the idea that the political project of socialism was a reality constructed with the participation (or non-participation) of various social actors, we may say that, by the end of 1948, in all the countries under study, the first radical acts were carried out for the transformation of the organization of state and society in the name of the new society. These actions, though political and legislative in nature, affected all spheres and levels of society. The changes taking place were marked by *"the dynamics of politics and the stabilizing functions of law"* (Yotov, 2001: 14). Acting jointly in coalition governments, the

---

2 Of course, the restructuring of the economy and the state on a socialist basis was a gradual process carried out through a series of laws. Here we have pointed out only the first legislative acts that came into force under the administration of the coalition governments, opening the way to the new economic and political order.

political parties and formations covered different roads in their opposition to the Communist party in the respective country until they were ultimately eliminated or 'melted into' that party. The struggle against fascism and for a more just society, waged under the banners of different ideological currents during and immediately after the Second World War, gradually proved dominated by the Communist vision of a socialist society, with its economic foundations, class relationships, and morals. This vision was endorsed through legislation in the first years of 'people's democracy'. Public ownership of the means of production, state monopoly over banking and insurance, industry and trade, the cooperative principle in agriculture, Marxist-Leninist education for all strata of the population, were no longer elements of the political program of a party but features that structured the new relationships in public life.

Thus, in the early post-war years, the first step was taken which would be of fundamental importance for the future historical destiny of the new social project. *This project was legitimated through law; once fixed in legislation, it became legal.* Later, at the end of the 1940s and early 1950s, when the field for political action was permanently restructured from one with multiple parties, pluralism of ideas, and differentiation of powers, into one with a single party, monolithic in ideology, and homogeneous in power, the juridical legitimation of socialism as a historical goal of social development would prove to be one of the strong power resources for the subject of governance. This resource would enable the Communist party-state to permanently substitute the legal code with an ideological code, i.e., to separate legitimacy from legality, and to tie legitimacy only to the ideological project in the name of which radical changes were being made in the legal foundations of the old capitalist society. Thus, two of the characteristics of the ideal type of totalitarian state would acquire completeness in the functioning states of East European countries, namely, the radical elimination of the differentiation between the legal and the legitimate (Arendt) and the identification of ideology as the 'supreme source of legitimacy' in society (Bundzhulov, 1995). Nevertheless, it is necessary to point out that this came about only after the political project of the new society had received legal endorsement.[3] This is not to deny that ideology was the supreme

---

3   At first glance, there appears to be some contradiction between this interpretation and Arendt's thesis about the facade legislation and the complete disregard for legality by totalitarian regimes (Arendt, 1979). The examples she gives of the Weimar Constitution (which was never revoked but was completely ignored by the Nazi state) and the 1936 Soviet Constitution (adopted but not abided by) actually illustrate that the total subordination of the juridical sphere to ideology is one of the fundamental characteristics of totalitarianism.

legitimating instance under Communist rule, nor do we attempt to find some other initial source of legitimacy in the new society; we are merely stressing on the conditions that made it possible for ideology to acquire such an 'exceptional' status. Having been proclaimed and anchored in the constitution, Communist ideology became the invariable support of state governance, although the daily functioning of government had no need for legal sanction, given the total expansion of the political power of the Communist party and the concentration in it of all kinds of particular powers. In fact, the Communist Party would revert to the sanctioning force of law whenever it had to 'legalize' some new ideological or political course.[4] This fact points attention to an essential particularity of modern society. Regardless of the concrete type of a society, the juridical legitimation of its ideology is as much a formal as a deeply substantial act constitutive of social reality. In fact, the law sanctioned the idea and the future practice that would implement that idea, but it also sanctioned the role of the idea as a source of legitimacy for social practice.

And so, towards the years 1948–1949, the laying of the foundations—material, normative, institutional, and staff-related—of the new social relationships was completed. The new social classes were constituted, in terms of discourse and in practice, through acts of expropriation, nationalization, formation of cooperatives; the new professional groups were formed as the state took over, and acquired a monopoly on enterprises, administrative functions, professional and branch organizations. The new political subjects were arranged in a hierarchy and subordinated according to the degree to which they embodied the historical goal of development. With the coming to power of the Communist Stalinist governments, there began what Baeva (1998) has called the "uniformed" years of building the state and society following the Soviet model as an accomplished form of totalitarian organization of the Communist-type state and society.

Since the party and state archives of the former USSR and the former Communist countries were opened, modern historiography has had at its disposal a new documentary basis that permits it to describe the concrete details of the historical process of constructing the state and society as totalitarian. Since the events occurring between 1948/49 and 1953/56 in this region are of interest to us only in their connection with what happened *with* and *to* sociology, here we will undertake to reveal the *internal logic of this process* which led to the dismissal of sociology not only from the scientific but also from the social space in the countries in question. Using an ideal-type approach, and combining the

---

4   The adoption of new constitutions (Czechoslovakia, 1960 and 1968; Bulgaria, 1971; Hungary, 1972; Poland, 1976) is an indicative example in this respect.

results of philosophical, political, sociological, and historical research, we will try to reveal the bi-lateral process of, on the one hand, objectification of to-talitarian principles, norms, and mechanisms in the structures, institutions, and practices, and on the other hand, the transformation of these practices into guarantees, carriers, and implementers of the totalitarian regime in these countries.

Having conclusively eliminated its political opponents by the late 1940s, the Communist parties in all East European countries declared themselves "the leading force in the state and the public organizations", and set themselves the strategic goal of "building socialism".[5] In the course of a few years, the party-state leadership in each country restructured the political, state and civic spheres according to the principles of the Soviet political regime. The monopoly and concentration of all power in a single party made possible the building of a symbiotic political-state structure of a monocentric, pyramidal and tentacled type. In the practice of the Communist party in all of these countries, we discern the *characteristics of the totalitarian regime*: merging of party and state functions, multiplication of state services and organs, effaced distinction between legislative, executive and judicial power, between the functions of governance and of control,[6] "the transformation of classes into masses" and of the individual citizen into "a never-changing identity of reactions" (Arendt, 1979: 438), the substitution of ideology for the principle of action. We also find the instruments of totalitarian power in action: the political trials against the "enemy with a party card",[7] unreliable people being sent to labor camps not for any real violation but for potential ones, systematic selection of MPs according to party criteria, party-based cadre policy in all spheres and at all levels of society, the formation of a "professional party bureaucracy" (Ðilas, 1957).

---

5   See the documents and declarations of the congresses of Communist parties after, or around the time of, the formation of the first single-party governments.

6   These practices are described and documented in detail in Volokitina et al. (2002).

7   In accordance with Stalin's postulate regarding the intensification of class struggle during the transition from capitalism to socialism, and with the assistance of Soviet advisors sent to each country, political purges were conducted at the end of the 1940s and early 1950s within the Communist parties, and show trials against high-ranking Communist leaders were held in separate countries. Some of the most important trials, ending with death sentences, were that of László Rajk (minister of internal affairs, and later of foreign affairs in Hungary), who was executed on 15 October 1949; that of Traycho Kostov (vice prime minister of Bulgaria) who was executed in December 1949; the trial, in November 1952, of the "leadership of the anti-state conspiratorial center" headed by Rudolf Slánský (former secretary general of the Czech Communist Party) where eleven high-ranking party functionaries were sentenced to death by hanging, and three, to imprisonment for life.

Seen even in this brief summary, these elements of governance of the Communist parties in the countries in question in the period 1948/49–1953/56 leave no doubt that the state and society acquired the features of a totalitarian organization in which:

- all political (mostly the agrarian parties were preserved from the period of coalition government) and mass organizations (of the popular fronts, of youth, of trade unions, etc.), all state and social institutions were in direct dependence on, and under constant control by, the Communist party (a *monocentric structure*);
- the Central Committee of each Communist party with its two main organs—the Secretariat and Politburo—were the supreme source of direct vertical power for all party organizations at all levels (local, regional, in enterprises, in administrations, in educational institutions, etc.) and for all other forms of organization of the economic, social, cultural, etc., life of society (a *pyramidal structure* as opposed to hierarchic structures which have subordinated levels, each with its own prerogatives, and vertically co-subordinated);
- a Communist party that builds party organizations in all spheres of society and at all levels of organization of life-in-society (a *tentacled structure*);
- ideology was the supreme and universal normative, axiological, interpretative measure for any action.

How did the totalitarian state organization manifest itself in the sphere of higher education, respectively in sociology; or how did education and science become part of this organization, and objectify and maintain its basic principles of functioning? The key to understanding this logic, which points to a *homology between the political-state and the academic sphere*, is ideology as the highest legitimating principle in totalitarian society. What happened was in fact an institutionalization of Marxism as state ideology in all countries under Communist governance. The process was gradual, beginning under the coalition governments, and it acquired a complete form under the single-party Communist governments at the end of the 1940s and beginning of the 1950s. Its implementation may be examined with the aid of the distinction drawn by legal science between 'institutions-organs' and 'institutions-mechanisms' (*Dictionnaire...*, 1990: 167).

The basic 'institution-organ' was the department of propaganda and agitation at the Central Committee of the Communist party. Whatever their specific designation and renaming in the separate countries, their main function everywhere was to assist the CC of the Party in "competent and complex elaboration of ideological issues, agitation-propaganda and cultural-educational work". Every department was structured into sectors, the most important of which were related to public propaganda of Marxism-Leninism, agitation, party education, science and education, art and culture, the press, cultural-educational work in the mass organizations. This structure enabled the Communist parties to organize and control the dissemination and assimilation of Marxism-Leninism not only among the party cadres and membership but also throughout society, by means of a) specific party resources (propaganda, agitation, schools and courses); b) specialized spheres of professional activity (science and education, culture and art); c) the institutions of mass information and mass access to culture (the press, libraries); d) the mass organization structures.

The role of the propaganda and agitation departments at the Central Committees of the Communist parties as the head ideological authorities is made particularly evident by their relations with departments and units of the Ministry of Education (for instance, the Supreme Council for Education in Bulgaria,[8] the Central Council for Science and Higher Education and the Council of Higher Educational Establishments in Poland). These units were initially established upon a broad social basis, but their structure was constantly subjected to analysis and discussion in the propaganda and agitation departments of the Communist parties. Moreover, changes were made in the organizational structure, ideological platform, staff, forms and target groups of activity on the basis of proposals submitted by the party departments to the Central Committees (according to data from the Central Party Archive of the Bulgarian Communist Party and from *Eastern Europe in Russian Archives' Documents*, 1998). The broad ideological program of the coalition governments, upon which the activity of these councils was initially based, was substituted with the postulates of Marxist-Leninist ideology, and state power was asserted as the supreme principle of governance.

In a broad sense, the state-controlled enterprises, schools, and newly established agricultural cooperatives may also be viewed as forms of institutionalization of Communist ideology insofar as their structures were founded on the ideological principles regarding public (and/or cooperative) ownership, the right to labour and education for all, protection provided to all citizens by the state of the proletarian revolution, predominance of public and collective interests over individual and private interests, etc.

---

8   The Supreme Council for Education was "established as a consultative organ at the Ministry of Science and Education which will deal with changes in the structure and orientation of ideas of the educational system and the contents of the curricula" (Chichovska, 1981: 469). The council began work on 28 May 1945 under the chairmanship of Todor Samodumov (a Communist).

As for 'institutions-mechanisms', viewed as a set of rules regulating a given activity or situation, here the modalities by which the ideological principles of Marxism-Leninism expanded their range of impact, and the degree of penetration of their regulating functions proved inexhaustible. In this respect as well, the Communist Parties' propaganda and agitation departments were the organizers and regulators of the whole activity for devising forms and mechanisms of Marxist-Leninist ideological influence. These departments examined the school curricula for all educational levels with respect to content and teaching methods, they overviewed the criteria for assessment of works of art and science, and the criteria for purging the libraries of fascist and reactionary literature (especially in the period 1945–1948/49), the requirements for staff selection in all spheres of activity, especially in higher education, and prepared these for approval by the Central Committee through proposals for decisions. In fact, it was through the institutions-mechanisms that the Communist parties, in the first post-war years, *took the first steps towards 'exporting' the ideological contents outside the sphere of direct political action.* After the complete takeover of power, these institutions ensured the practically unlimited scope of impact of Communist ideology as a regulating and legitimating authority.

Of course, the Central Committees' propaganda and agitation departments would seem to be nothing more than ordinary units of the Communist party structure if we overlook the fact that they were not simply an element of the whole but a source of relatively independent activity, separated into an autonomous sphere. The transformation of ideological activity into an independent sphere of professional occupation with its own agents (agitators, propagandists, lecturers), its own products (plans, programs, syllabi, methodical guidance, literature for party educational work, reports on the condition of party education and propaganda of Marxism-Leninism), its hierarchy (agitprop departments in the regional, district and municipal committees of the Communist party, party committees in the state enterprises and administrations, etc.), and its institutions (the Higher Party Schools), is one of the strongest empirical proofs that ideology was institutionalized in the framework of the party structures. However, the sphere of ideological activity under the monopolistic governance of the Communist parties had two other particularities. First, it was the only sphere whose structures did not duplicate some other state or non-state structures,[9] and second, as indicated above, it not only interacted

---

9   All other sectors of public activity that were subject to the governance of the executive power, such as economy, agriculture, healthcare, science, education, culture, etc., had their corresponding departments in the Communist parties at all levels, from central to local.

with the other areas of professional activity but gradually began to regulate and control the process of their construction and development by means of the institutions-mechanisms. Thus, ideology, as a legitimating principle of every form of political action, spilled beyond the framework of that action and expanded its scope to the degree that politics subordinated all other activities. From that moment on, we may say *Marxism-Leninism was an ideological institution not only of the Communist party but also of the state* that party was building. The state-controlled ideology guaranteed the total domination of the Communist party as expressing and carrying the political project for the new society and as generator of the one-dimensional and indistinguishable character of the social world, since any gesture, thought, action, intention were possible only if conforming to ideological prescription.

Under the established party-state structure's monopoly of power, based on the ideology of Marxism in its 1930s Stalinist interpretation, the declaring of sociology as a "bourgeois pseudo-science" by the Stalinist East European governments was a politically legitimate act, and a logical one from the viewpoint of governance. Insofar as sociology did not correspond to the Soviet canon of the Marxist-Leninist doctrine,[10] there was no place for it in the politically endorsed area of legitimate sciences. Paradoxically, in the course of large-scale social changes, the science whose task was to provide objectively valid answers to the problems posed by social development was substituted with an abstract philosophical doctrine. Political expediency and scientific paradox were in fact the two sides of one process. The elimination of sociology from society through political acts and ideological arguments, the taboo on sociology and its ousting from the sphere of science expressed the beginning radical transformation of

---

10   The dogmatization of Marxism was completed in the Soviet Union in the late 1930s when a series of discussions concluded with Stalin's essay "On Dialectical and Historical Materialism" (1938). According to this version of the doctrine, the composite parts of Marxism-Leninism are: *dialectical materialism* (the most general conception regarding the world based on the belief in the objective and causally determined nature of all phenomena, the primacy of matter over mind, and the principle of the unity and struggle of opposites as the motor of development), *historical materialism* (the conception that social development is determined by scientific laws, its main principles being historicity, dialectics, material determination of the forms of social life, and class struggle as the motor of human history), and *scientific communism* (which studies the emergence and development of communist society, the main stages of which are the proletarian revolution headed by the Communist party and aimed to abolish private ownership and the power of capital, and to seize political power by the working class, the construction of an economic and political system of an intermediate, socialist type, and ultimately, the complete victory of communism).

the social where the autonomy and distinctive specificity of the various spheres and their value orders were effaced and subsumed under the super-valorized and unconditionally asserted political sphere with its ideological order. While the initiator and motor of this change was the Communist Party, its actors were the representatives of the other spheres—in our case, the academic circles.

The immediate and usual explanation of the situation in which sociology found itself after 1948–1949 as due only to the monopoly of power held by the Communist parties (Becskehazi, Kuczi, 1994; Genov, 1994; Kolosi, Szelényi 1993; Kwasniewicz, 1993, 1994; Pasiak, Machacek, 1994; Urbanek, 1994) is partially true with regard to the historical facts and partially satisfactory with regard to the research task of revealing the genesis of the conditions that led to certain results in the development of sociology. Before receiving an institutional blow based on ideological arguments from the subject of political power, sociology and most of its representatives had already opened and turned to the political project of the new society and to its scientific argumentation in Marxism. Even in the first post-war years, discussions were held in the main relevant journals in each country (*Voprosui Philosophii/Questions of Philosophy* in the USSR, *Philosophska Misyl/Philosophical Thought* in Bulgaria, *Myśl Współczesna/Contemporary Thought* in Poland, *Sociologický revii/Sociological Review* in Czechoslovakia) regarding the tasks and functions of science in the new social-political reality, and regarding the need to study Marxist theory in order to provide an adequate rationalization of the social changes. The cognitive situation in the social sciences and the restructuring of their epistemic field until 1953–1956 would depend on which interpretation of Marxism would get the upper hand: the instrumental, related to the practical goals of the sole holder of political power, or the scientific interpretation, the aim of which was to obtain empirically verifiable explanations outside of any ideological functions. Hence, sociology's deprivation of its institutional name reflected the already beginning cognitive and axiological reorientation of the social sciences.

Another question is why social researchers in East European countries in the 1950s accepted the version of Marxism that was politically instrumentalized by the Communist parties, why they sought legitimation of their own professional occupation in the politically conceptualized knowledge of society? From the viewpoint of the modalities of disciplinary construction of sociology, this question will be specially discussed in Part 3. Here we will only give a summary of the logic of the trends, before demonstrating that their concrete historical manifestation points our attention to the existence of different variants of development, or rather to another interpretation of the point in the development of sociology at which the discipline was deprived of its institutional identity and social legitimacy.

And so, what certainly played a role in the constituting of an area of 'Marxist-Leninist' science from which sociology would be excluded, was the nature of Marxism as a theory, political doctrine, and ideology. In turn, the instrumentalization of Marxism by a single political subject, using the doctrine to impose and spread its power over the entire society, effaced the boundaries between the separate forms of Marxism and turned this doctrine into a monistic whole. The institutionalization of Marxism-Leninism in the different state-public (scientific, educational, cultural, etc.) and party structures put an end to pluralism in society and set the beginning of the functioning of society as a united, unarticulated whole, with a single and all-encompassing center of governance and coordination. Under such a configuration, we could hardly expect that social science might have slipped out of the scope and pressure of the new institutions and norms.

However, certain historical facts contradict this summary logic of trends and compel us to correct the assertion that sociology was completely eliminated in the former Communist Camp from the end of the 1940s to the middle of the 1950s. The heated debate on the pages of *Myśl Współczesna/Contemporary Thought* in 1948 between Stanisław Ossowski on one side and Adam Schaff and Julian Hochfeld on the other, regarding the functions of Marxism, was conducted in the field of science by researchers of a Marxist theoretical orientation who defended contrary viewpoints. Ossowski argued for the need of theoretical renewal of Marxism and for a firm demarcation from the serving of party goals, so that the doctrine might not become a "religious prophecy", while his opponents upheld the view that Marxism had a double—scientific and ideological—function.[11]

In Bulgaria, the journal *Philosophska Misyl/Philosophical Thought* began to efface the boundaries of scientific competence of the social sciences as early as the beginning of 1945, and to pass sociology over in silence in interpreting the new social realities while asserting the central cognitive role of Marxist-Leninist philosophy. Interestingly, sociology had found a place in the Marxist current of Bulgarian science as far back as 1936, when Todor Pavlov, in the first edition of his *Theory of Reflection* published in Russian, developed the idea that sociology was a particular science different from Historical Materialism as a philosophical science. This fact from the evolutionary history of the Marxist conception of the nature and character of sociology is most often pointed out by historians of Bulgarian sociology as a point of departure for arguing sociology is an independent, particular science, an argument used nearly twenty years later

---

11   The discussion is analyzed by Kraśko (1998: 181–184).

in Zhivko Oshavkov's book *Historical Materialism and Sociology* (1958). Why did Todor Pavlov's formulation developed within the framework of Marxism fail to play any role for restructuring Bulgarian epistemic space during the first ten years of Communism in this country? How to explain that its author, who held key positions in political power and the management of science after the Communist takeover of power, did not strive to defend and realize his own conceptual stance? Is it enough to point to contextual coercion as the decisive factor of this? Generally speaking, if 'bourgeois' sociology has no right to exist in the new social-political context, why was a Marxist alternative of the science not immediately constructed in order to respond to the new worldview and cognitive and ideological orientation of the socialist society? Why did it have to wait approximately ten more years?

And not least, as contemporary Russian historians of sociology in the former USSR have pointed out, there is no official or semi-official document explicitly prohibiting sociology as a science in the Soviet Union—the country that was exporting the socialist project (*The Russian Sociological Tradition...*, 1994: 18). "Even in the most Stalinist possible dictionary, that of the late 1930s, the term 'sociology' is present as a basic concept of Marxism" (Ibid.). Stalin used the term in the positive sense (Stalin, 1928) unlike the derisive marginal notes written by Lenin in May 1920 on the pages of Bukharin's *The Politics and Economics of the Transition Period.*[12]

It was precisely these particularities of the cognitive presence of sociology (as a name, a theoretical and intellectual stance, and a field in epistemic space) that led us to the assumption that the external intervention in the institutional structure of sociology may be effective providing it corresponds to the science's own dynamics at a given stage of its development. In other words, if the institutional destiny of the forms of sociological activity depends on how developed these forms are, the institutional elimination of sociology cannot be a general and undifferentiated indicator of the state of sociology in the countries under study even under common conditions and contextual trends in all these countries.

---

12   Batygin explains Lenin's ironic attitude by the fact that, in Bukharin's book, Lenin detected the influence of Bogdanov's "organizational-sociological ideas" which he rejected. Lenin's notes were known to only a narrow circle of people from the Socialist Academy who later used them to oppose "Lenin's 'party principle' to Bukharin's sociology (and 'scientific' approach in general)" (Batygin, 1998: 29), as Bukharin had developed it in *Theory of Historical Materialism. A Popular Textbook on Marxist Sociology* (1921). Ironically, it was precisely Lenin's "scientific sociological definitions" from his work *The Friends of the People* (1894) that became standard texts in the fight against the Bukharinist 'heresy' which ended with Stalin's victory in 1929.

The following facts confirm the idea that, in this period, sociological knowledge was not completely effaced from the sphere of knowledge in the various countries, i.e., that *this was more a case of institutional mimicry than of complete institutional liquidation.*[13] Lectures on general and particular sociology were replaced by historical and dialectical materialism, but under the designation 'history of social ideas' sociological knowledge continued to be taught in the universities of Warsaw, Kraków, Łódź, Wrocław. In Czechoslovakia, the sociological perspective was preserved, though with great difficulty, in the proximate disciplines demography, urbanism, social demography, and healthcare (Linhart et al., 1996). Some departments of sociology existing until then were substituted with departments of General Ethnography or of Marxism-Leninism, others were transformed into chairs of History of Philosophy and Social Ideas (Musil, 2004). Some of the sociology teachers transferred to them; the same happened in the universities of Kraków, Warsaw and Poznań.

Research activity was not completely stopped. In Poland, it continued in the newly formed institutes, laboratories and departments of philosophy. In 1952, in Poland, the first Marxist-oriented Scientific Resources Training Institute was established, affiliated with the Politburo (later re-labeled Institute of Social Sciences); its Historical Materialism Laboratory, headed by the sociologist Julian Hochfeld,[14] studied social and economic problems on the basis of diary material (Kraśko, 1998). In the same year, the Minister of Higher Education opened two chairs of philosophy at the University of Warsaw, each of which housed a laboratory dealing, respectively, with social (not sociological) ideas and with historical materialism. One year later, the chairs were incorporated into the Institute of Philosophy of which Maria and Stanisław Ossowski (people with leftist convictions but not members of the PUWP) became senior faculty members. In the University of Łódź, the newly created Laboratory on

---

13   The basic sources of information are Kraśko (1998), Linhart et al. (1996), Musil (2004).

14   Julian Hochfeld—a holder of doctoral degrees from the Jagiellonian University in Kraków and the Sorbonne in Paris—was a leading member of the Polish Socialist Party even before the War, spent time in the circle of Polish emigrés, returned to Poland in 1945, and became a member of the Political Commission (equivalent to the Politburo) of the Polish Socialist Party after the WWII. When he opposed the merging of the Polish Worker's Party and the left wing of the Polish Socialist Party into Polish United Workers Party/PUWP (December 1948), he was deprived of all his political positions and moved to academic life. The example of Hochfeld's two careers, political and academic, which intertwined but were mutually discrepant and also discrepant with the changing political trends after the first years of the war, serves to guard us from hasty conclusions about the determining role of political power for scientific development.

History of the Press in the 19th Century—headed by Chałasiński, a student of Znaniecki—trained the first post-war sociological researchers. Moreover, although in just one place, sociology was designated under its own name, and the problems of sociological methods (direct observation, official statistics, interviews, personal documents) were openly discussed. This was the journal *Myśl Filozoficzna/Philosophical Thought* founded after the First Congress of Polish Science held in Warsaw in 1952 that was strongly critical of sociology. In Prague, the Masaryk Society for social research was preserved as a small, closed circle, far from the attention of the party-state organs.

These forms of concealed or veiled presence of sociology can be observed primarily in Poland and Czechoslovakia where the institutional, intellectual and cadre legacy of pre-war sociology was strongest and the institutional reanimation directly after the war was carried on at a faster pace. There, the carriers of sociological knowledge placed sociology in a sort of hibernation, waiting for better times for public legitimation of the science. In the countries that had no institutionalized research and education practice in sociology between the two wars, such as Bulgaria, Hungary, the USSR, the restored or newly created elements of sociological activity after the war were easily abolished under the new scientific policy of the governments. But even there, possibilities for development were not completely closed. The researchers who would later become the restorers or 'pioneers' of sociology after 1956 continued to work even though within the straitjacket of triumphant Marxist-Leninist philosophy.

The post-war years 1948/49–1953/56 reveal to us what was perhaps one of the first paradoxes in the development of sociology under the Communist regimes: *without being officially banned, sociology did not exist officially; though not officially, it did in fact exist*. It had no institutional home, but sociological knowledge continued to be taught and produced, though not designated by its disciplinary name. Various interpretations may be given of this paradox. Some explanations affirm the totalitarian character of the regime with respect to its arbitrary quality and the supremacy of ideology; others point out the lack of professionalization in the sphere of sociology; still others argue that the system was irrational ... But there was something else, perhaps more important that this paradox makes visible to us, something related to the actors in their variety of professional, ideological and moral stances, motivations, and strategies. It was on those actors that the chances of sociology—as a collective enterprise and professional vocation—depended, even at times when the roads seemed to be inalterably prescribed.

CHAPTER 8

Institutional Expansion I: 1956–1968

8.1 Sociology and Politics: Limits of (In)Compatibility

The temporal boundaries of the first cycle of institutional expansion of sociology in Central and Eastern Europe are set provisionally in the discipline's institutional history in each country, but, certainly, with reference to political history. The years 1956 and 1968 mark two turning points in post-war social-political history in all of Europe, which both opened and closed various possibilities for development. For the Soviet Bloc countries, both years were high points of the commenced and interrupted trends of democratization of state socialism, times of breakthroughs and stopping of holes, times of hope that a change of the System was possible, and of disappointment that the change failed to come about. Both years were turning points, since for victors and vanquished alike, the society in which they lived would no longer be the same.

Key political events in 1956 were the 20th Congress of the Communist Party of the Soviet Union with its official condemnation of Stalin, the June and October revolts in Poland ending with the peaceful return (of course negotiated with the Soviet Union) to the post-war concept of "Polish road to socialism", and the Hungarian Revolution with its rise and bloody suppression by the Soviet Army. If the roots of these events lay in the totalitarian practice of the Communist party-states, systematically constructed after 1948 in all countries within the Soviet zone of influence, their immediate preconditions arose from the course undertaken by Moscow after the death of Stalin in March 1953 to soften the conduct and consequences of totalitarian governance. The change of the Soviet political leadership and the launching of a new policy (extensive amnesty, collective exercise of power, separation of party from state functions) were the first signs of de-Stalinization, deciphered with varying speed and willingness by the party-state leaders and social groups and strata in the other countries. The East European Communist parties, who were building the totalitarian structures of state and society in their own countries, were obliged to revise the blatant Stalinism of their governance. "The mode of use of relative freedom" (Baeva, 1995: 31) varied in the different countries and led to different results. By the time of the famous February Congress of CC of CPSU in 1956,

© KONINKLIJKE BRILL NV, LEIDEN, 2018 | DOI 10.1163/9789004333635_010

- Hungary had moved from the "new political line" of Imre Nagy's government (July 1953)[1] to the new "dogmatic renaissance" (in early 1955), and in the course of events Nagy was removed from the position of prime minister, expelled from the Hungarian Communist Party and from the Parliament, deprived of the right to lecture in the university; Khrushchev's "new course" was taken up by the old political player, the Stalinist Mátyás Rákosi. While Nagy's new policy gave rise to hopes for the de-politicization of education and culture, the return to 'strongman' politics signaled that deviation from the ideological canon would be punished.

- In Poland, the Polish United Workers Party (PUWP) restructured the positions in the party structure following the Soviet example, but preserved the persons holding those positions.[2] The Party freed from prison the former first secretary of the PUWP Władysław Gomułka and many other political prisoners, closed down the notorious Ministry of Public Security—the chief perpetrator of political repression and violence—but remained silent about its own responsibility for the governance of the country until then. In only three years, the intellectual sphere was transformed in Poland. New forms of debate appeared (the first discussion clubs such as the "Crooked Circle Club",[3] the Interschool Discussion Club of Contradiction Seekers, the Political Discussion Club at Warsaw University) but also new topics of debate. Writers, painters, philosophers, social scientists, historians, began to openly discuss the Marxist-Leninist principles of art and culture, the ideological party control over science, the politically based assessments of Polish history.

- Party leaders in Czechoslovakia had made a reorganization of state and party positions, undertaken changes in industry and agriculture, but

---

1 The program of the Imre Nagy government envisaged changes in the economy (decreased rates of industrialization, more investments in light industry, abolition of normative restrictions on the development of crafts) and in agriculture (the right to dismantle the cooperative farms at the explicit request of more than half the members, decreased duties of farmers towards the state). It aimed to raise the living standard of the population, to restore the trust of the intelligentsia, and to achieve national unity.

2 The position of chairman of the party was substituted with that of first secretary, but the man holding it was Bolesław Bierut, one of Stalin's best disciples.

3 Among the participants in the club were the sociologists and philosophers Julian Hochfeld, Maria Ossowska, Józef Chałasiński, Tadeusz Kotarbiński, Leszek Kołakowski, and Adam Schaff.

had disregarded the question of political rehabilitation of the victims of the 1951–1952 trials. As in Poland, intellectuals here had responded fastest of all to the new ideological course, declaring themselves against dogmatism in the social sciences and in support of freedom of expression and the creative development of Marxism. As in Hungary, the disciplined response of the ruling power against 'erroneous' interpretation of political intentions was soon to come.

- In Bulgaria, the party and state leadership declared its support for the new political course of Moscow, made shifts of personnel and formal restructuring of party positions, but maintained continuity in governance and made no significant change in the methods of centralized management of industry and agriculture. Critical voices were heard among writers.

After the 20th Congress of the CPSU, the differences of response to the directives coming from Moscow continued and even grew deeper to the point where, at the end of 1956, the first cleavages and quasi-cleavages in the totalitarian order of the 'socialist' system became visible. Reform was possible, but only within the limits set and controlled by the Center. Any attempt at crossing the boundaries was ended either with compromises (as in Poland) or with a radical return within limits (as in Hungary). Quasi-reforms in Bulgaria and Czechoslovakia, together with these countries' support for Soviet policies (including the Soviet military intervention in Hungary, which represented a violation of all international and moral norms), safeguarded them against excessive internal and external political pressure but deprived them of the collective experience of independent development. The system was preserved at the international level, but its integrity was dearly paid for in victims and in strongly shaken faith in its ideological messages. The matrix of societal development remained the same: the leading role and monopoly on power of the Communist party, the unconditional domination of Marxism-Leninism as state ideology, the primacy of political-ideological expediency over all other forms of rationality, with less use of physical, but no less use of symbolic violence towards interpretations and gestures considered "counter-revolutionary", "reactionary", and ideologically unorthodox. In other words, the matrix preserved its sanctions and coercions, but the ways in which it was applied became increasingly different.

It was in this context of *universal normative validity* of the political-ideological model and of the different *effective* application of this normativity in the different countries, that sociology returned to the scientific and social space after 1956. The important sociological question is not so much *how this return came*

about as *why it was at all possible*, given that the structural and functional principles of the system remained the same.

The widespread opinion that the political "thaw" was a favorable factor for
the revival of East European sociology after 1956 is empirically precise but
analytically limited. It simply repeats the deterministic explanations regarding
the objective impact of the context, the one-way and all-encompassing dependency of the social on political power in totalitarian states. We find a heuristi-
cally promising perspective for explanation in Danilo Martuccelli (2016) who
considers the relation between reality and action through the prism of the
following question: "how [...] did reality become a regulative idea capable of
drawing a borderline between the possible and the impossible" (2006: 111).
He seeks an answer to this question in the dynamics—we would even say, the
dialectics—of the constraints of the environment and the imaginary limits
of reality.[4] Acknowledging the sanctioning role of reality, Martuccelli makes a
deeper analysis of the function of the perception of limit of action. This perception "defines the 'impassable' limits of reality, despite multiple practical
openings" (Ibid.: 102) and models action even before the concrete penalty can
come into effect. In other words, the individual's belief in a possible resistance
(penalty) coming from reality is effective *before* an eventual act, not *after* it is
performed. An activity "encounters and always thwarts the constraints, but as
for the limit, that is something of a strictly imaginary order of things" (Ibid.:
107). In the aspect of society, this refers to the ways by which societies in history set the limits and constraints of reality, or to the so-called "regimes of reality" which express the sphere of privileged activity and around which the limit
of reality—the limit of the possible and the impossible—is constructed.[5]

It would not be mistaken to say that East European societies, during
the whole time of Communist governance, were in a political, or politico-
ideological, "regime of reality". In Part 2.7 of this text, we have shown how
the Communist parties imposed the political-ideological project of the new
society as an axiological horizon and normative framework for any activity.
From here on, our attention will be focused on the role of sociology in the
concurrent process of instituting and overcoming of the political limits of
possible–impossible action, as well as the consequences of this role for its own
development.

---

4 Though in a different analytic perspective, the study of socialist enterprises in GDR conducted by Sandrine Kott shows the effectiveness of Communist norms of conduct insofar as these
   norms are integrated by individuals (2001).
5 According to Danilo Martuccelli, the history of societies passes through four major "regimes
   of reality": religion, politics, economy, and ecology (2014).

The political year 1956, with its contradictory events, was a Rubicon that sociologists, or future sociologists (who were then students in philosophy, history, law, economics, philology, etc.) in the separate countries would cross in the coming years in various ways and at various tempos, but with the same result for all. By the end of the 1960s, sociology in all the countries under study would acquire its institutional structures, personnel, and research results which would assert its legitimacy as a specific disciplinary approach to social reality.

> In the 1950s, the institutional system was already welded together by an ideology that pursued a super-goal. 'The things in life' were subordinated to a super-idea; social space was super-ideologized.

That is how Petar-Emil Mitev, one of the 'pioneers' of the revival of sociology in Bulgaria in the 1960s, and a key figure in its development throughout the whole Communist period, summarized the structure and spirit of the system in the countries of Central and Eastern Europe (*Sociology in Bulgaria...*, 2012: 98). It was this system that the new political course of Moscow undertook to reform *without de-ideologizing it*. Pragmatic orientation, eradication of errors and distortions from the past, condemnation of repressions: these were the new ideological messages along the road to the invariable target—building socialism. It was in this environment of new political tasks, and an unchanged supreme goal of social development, that sociology returned to the "family of sciences" in publicly claiming its intellectual commitment to the processes of renewal, critical interpretation of the existing Communist practice and readiness to exercise its professional competence in the service of the reformed political project of Communism. At this stage, the political vision of society and of society's perspectives was a generally shared bounding horizon of scientific though and social expectations.

The new possibility for cognitive and institutional legitimation of sociology in East European countries after 1956 is usually explained by the sociologists themselves in terms of the historical coincidence of the power-holder's political interests and the cognitive interests of the sociologists or of the newly emerging academic community which preferred the empirical study of society to the repetition of postulates of the state ideology. They point out the mutual instrumentalization and legitimation of sociology and power (Koleva, 1998; Kolosi, Szelényi, 1993, Kwasniewicz, 1993). The researchers took advantage of the declared goal of scientifically-based management, while the ruling leaders took advantage of the possibility to make use of the produced sociological information. Still, why was the function of an *instrument of legitimation* of the new political order, in Berger and Luckmann's sense (1966), assumed precisely by sociology, and not by the then authoritative and recognized disciplines of

Marxism-Leninism such as historical materialism, scientific communism or political economy of socialism?

There are other views, especially among Soviet sociologists. Vladimir Shub-kin, one of the eminent members of the "sixties generation" in Soviet sociology[6] tells the story without any pretensions to theorizing, but only so that "the future theorist may imagine the conditions under which we lived and worked". He recalls (*Russian Sociology of the 1960s...*, 1999: 69)

> The appearance of sociology, of 'concrete social surveys', after the death of Stalin and the 20th Congress of CPSU, were unexpected. [...] it did not come about at the will of those *above*, as happened in the case of scientific communism, the history of the party, historical materialism, but [it came] from *below*. The revival of sociology was a surprise to Western political scientists, Sovietologists, and sociologists as well.

Igor Kon, an important figure from the same generation of sociologists, adds (*Russian Sociology of the 1960s...*, 1999: 127)

> Soviet sociology [...] arose on the wave of Khrushchev's reforms and its officially proclaimed function represented their informational provision. But even in this most narrow, technocratic sense, sociology carried a powerful social-critical principle. After all, it implied the study of reality, which inevitably, no matter how timid a conformist the researcher might be—and there were many such among Soviet sociologists, demonstrated the lie and inconsistency of the dominant ideology. And the party mandarins unerringly sensed this danger. The Institute for Concrete Social Studies (ICSS) was created out of inertia at a time when the party had no need for it at all. [...] In the meantime, 'mature socialism' asserted itself as unproblematic. The Soviet society, having attained a degree of maturity at which essence and phenomenon coincide, made science superfluous.

---

6   In post-1989 sociological literature in Russia, the "emerged sociology was identified with the 'generation of the sixties'; they had wished to build "socialism with a human face". This generation experienced the negative consequences generated by the Second World War. Many of them belonged to the families that suffered political repressions during Stalin's regime and were anti-totalitarian in their political attitudes" (Zdravomyslova, 2010: 142). According to some representatives of this generation, and some analyzers of Soviet sociology, this first generation of Soviet sociologists brought about "sociology's second birth in the sixties" (Ibid.; Novikova, 1996).

Gennady Osipov, a supporter of sociology as an independent science, and the leading promoter of the building of research units that preceded ICSS, as well as of that institute, presents an interpretation that is seemingly different from Kon's and that sheds additional light on the mutual relations between sociology and power in the post-1956 period (*Russian Sociology of the 1960s...*, 1999: 101–102).

> Of course, the Institute would never have been created if our partocracy had not had a personal interest in this: the emerging sociological movement had to be put under control. This was the main thing, since the movement was proving to be, as they say, out of party control. The open intervention in the work of scientists would be a complicated thing—this could be done more easily through the existence of institutional forms. And secondly, they hoped to use sociology for factual support of the party course, the congress decisions. Plus, grounding the slogans that were raised and composed in CC. [...] My report[7] at that time was built on the claim that sociology could serve society, reveal the shortcomings, be used by the party for solving many issues. If I had not said that, the decision would not have been made.

The common feature of the various types of interpretations of the post-1956 revival of sociology is the view of power and sociology as separate spheres that enter into certain configurations. The testimonies of Soviet sociologists, however, direct attention at that *borderline zone* in which the *effective* action of each of the two spheres springs from that sphere itself, being something more than a simple reaction to the other, while both remain inscribed within the context of the whole society. After several years of nameless existence or institutional absence from East European countries, sociology returned to the "family of legitimate sciences", having been permitted to return by the new political leadership in each of the countries. This inevitable act was concurrently a logical result and an empirical confirmation of the fundamental principles of totalitarian governance of society, even in its softened forms. However, the political 'midwifery' performed in the rebirth of sociology was possible not only because new political elites had appeared but also because now there were people carrying a new, non-ideological, not based on historical materialism, but sociological, way of thinking about society. While preserving the fundamental

---

7   This was a report on the need to create an academic institute for sociological studies which Osipov presented to the Department of Science of CC of CPSU.

principles of political structuring and functioning, the liberalization of society raised "[politically tabooed] questions that could not be formulated otherwise than as scientific questions" (Ferge).[8] We are far from accepting the mutually pragmatic attitude of the two protagonists (power and sociology) as a dominant explanation of the revival of sociology in the Communist Bloc after 1956. Society evolved in a way that confirmed Durkheim's most important methodological lessons about the dialectical relation between knowledge of society and the possibility of the existence of society. Under a totalitarian Communist regime, politics (the supreme regulator) defines the limits of possible, or impossible, development, including those of sociology, and the Communist party (supreme agent of sanctioning action) controls those limits; but the findings of sociology, and the idea about the eventual impact of those findings upon society define the limits of permissible, or impermissible, political action. The institutional and cognitive development of sociology before 1989 in each of the countries under study is in fact a specific historical example of these mutual relations.

8.2   Toward Institutional Expansion: The General and the Specific

After 1956, the institutional structures of sociology were built first, and most quickly, in Poland; last and most slowly in Hungary; and at a relatively equal pace in Bulgaria, Czechoslovakia and USSR.[9] The two opposite ends with regard to institutional development, Poland and Hungary, display most clearly

---

8   Zsuzsa Ferge refers to questions of social inequalities and poverty, which being in contradiction with the official ideological doctrine of a classless, just, and equal society, did not figure in political discourse (interview with Zsuzsa Ferge conducted on 28 March 2001, Budapest, personal archive).

9   Here and further on in this book, the explanation of the characteristics, aspects, and tendencies in the institutional and cognitive development of East European sociology emphasizes one national sociology or another. The choice of this perspective is closely linked to the conducted study and the initial analysis of the collected empirical data. Here, we will only recall some basic postulates assumed in the study: a) the national trajectories of sociology are specific and unique to each country in question, but they also have a shared history; b) this history evolved under the relatively identical conditions of the sociopolitical, ideological and scientific space of the Communist state-party, but did not lead to a uniform model of development. The common trends were manifest through specific modalities; c) at certain moments of the development of a given national sociology, there were 'events' focalizing and demonstrating particular modalities that remained invisible in the other national configurations of circumstances.

the weight of politics and the importance of the situation in science for the revival of sociological activity. In Poland, there existed both the current political conditions (achieved general agreement on the democratization of Polish society within the framework of the Socialist Camp) and the pre-existing scientific conditions (preserved teaching and research activity, though under a different name, and preserved and further developed intellectual resources) for a rapid re-institutionalization of sociology. By contrast, in Hungary none of these favorable conditions was present: there was a deep political fissure, repressive action after 1956, a scattering of the intellectual potential after 1948 and 1956; moreover, institutional units had been destroyed in the previous period.

Only in Bulgaria, USSR, and partially, later, in Hungary, was the new institutionalization of sociology preceded by a wide theoretical debate on the problem field of this science. This particularity was not coincidental. In all three countries, for different reasons, the attempts made between the two wars to legitimate sociology as an research activity and through its institutions were either cut short (in the USSR, orthodox Marxism was imposed in the 1930s) or lacking. Even if they did study and analyze social reality, the Bulgarian and Hungarian researchers of the 1930s and 1940s did not succeed in separating their work as an independent field possessing its own professional, organizational, educational, etc., resources. After World War II, the results in these two countries were weak and short-lasting, as we have shown in Parts 2.6; 2.7. This particularity confirms the important sociological regularity valid for the development of any specialized activity, including sociology itself. The social legitimation of a scientific discipline by means of the establishment of its organizational forms is possible only if cognitive legitimation has already been undertaken and relatively completed, while its institutional legitimation provides the possibilities for further development as a science.

Both in the USSR and in Bulgaria, the fight for asserting sociology as an independent discipline was fought on the field of, and with respect to, the cognitive structure of Marxist-Leninist social science and its corresponding organizational and staff infrastructure. In all of the countries under study, historical materialism was the officially recognized, most general theory of society, and after 1948, this philosophical status it had was institutionally established through lecture courses, university staff, departments in institutes of philosophy, specialists, publications. Hence, the efforts of sociologically oriented Soviet and Bulgarian researchers were aimed at drawing disciplinary boundaries between historical materialism and sociology. The way this problem was resolved is what primarily determined the modalities of development of sociology in both countries (to be discussed in Part 3). Here we will outline most generally the cognitive solution of the matter offered by Soviet and Bulgarian scholars, and we will do this in terms of the repercussions this solution had for the institutional structure of sociology.

In the reforming Soviet social sciences of the mid-1950s and early 1960s, the theoretical debate on the epistemic relations between sociology and historical materialism, reinitiated by Jürgen Kuczynski's article "The Sociological Laws" (1957) in the journal *Voprosui Philosophii/Questions of Philosophy* ascribed theoretical and methodological superiority to historical materialism as a general sociological theory, while associating sociology with 'concrete surveys' of society. Before that, however, in 1955, the authoritative economist and statistician V. S. Nemchinov had formulated in the ideologically neutral terminology of statistics the *differentia specifica* of sociology as a science studying "mass processes", while leaving the speculative concern with the "general principles" of social development to historical materialism. Gradually, the conception as to the existence of three levels of social knowledge took shape in Soviet Marxism; these were the most abstract philosophical level—dialectical materialism; an intermediate level—historical materialism as the most general theory of society; and the level of concrete social studies of society (Glezerman, Kelle, Pilipenko, 1972). Consequently, the whole 1960s would be characterized by the creation of new structural units and organizational forms for 'concrete sociological surveys' on different social problems, conducted within the academic, university, Communist party or Komsomol[10] structures (Mespoulet, 2007b; Novikova, 1996).

Unlike their Soviet colleagues, Bulgarian sociologically oriented researchers were able to already assert the name 'sociology' in the epistemic area of the social sciences at the end of the 1950s. The major merit for this belongs to Zhivko Oshavkov.[11] After a discussion on the object of Marxist-Leninist

---

10   Komsomol, a syllabic abbreviation in Russian, is the briefer designation of the All-Union Leninist Communist League of Youth. The Communist youth unions in other Communist countries were also referred to as Komsomol.

11   Until 1989, the sociological establishment in Bulgaria usually associated the birth of modern Bulgarian sociology and the creation of a Bulgarian school of sociology with Zhivko Oshavkov (1913–1982). He was the founder of the Bulgarian Sociological Society (1959), the creator of the first sociological research group established in the Bulgarian Academy of Sciences (1962), the founder and first director of the Institute of Sociology at BAS (1968–1972), initiator and organizer of the first large-scale sociological surveys in Bulgaria ("Religiosity in Bulgaria", 1962; "Town and Village", 1968), and vice president of ISA (1970–1974). After 1989, critical reflection on his role in sociology included even his scientific works in the scope of a general reassessment of the national sociological tradition (Dimitrov, 1995; Draganov, 1993; Koleva, 2002c; Kostov, 1993).

philosophy,[12] he argued the disciplinary distinction between historical materialism and sociology in a series of publications (1956, 1957, 1958).[13] He sought arguments in support of the autonomy of sociology within the system of Marxist cognition, without impairing the integrity of the system or the links between its separate parts. Historical materialism—the main obstacle in the Soviet concept of social sciences dating from the 1930s—was examined in its epistemological status of a philosophical conceptualization of society that provides the particular discipline of sociology with a common vision of the social and methodological principles of the study of society. As regards the cognitive boundaries between scientific communism and sociology, the dialectics of their relationship was argued through a speculative logical procedure. As an integral part of Marxism, scientific communism studies the essence, ways of attaining, and mechanisms of functioning of communist society. Precisely as a theory treating the problems of the socialist society's future, scientific communism was seen as an internal horizon of sociology, an autonomous science of society. The integrity of Marxism was thereby preserved, while sociology was emancipated within the limits of Marxism, preserving its relations of 'kinship by line and degree' within the latter's components. We are inclined to think that this astute way of cognitive legitimation of sociology as a particular empirical science played a specific role for the institutionalization of sociology in Bulgaria in the 1960s. This view is justified by the fact that given similar favorable circumstances both in the USSR and in Bulgaria (a positive attitude and professional interest in sociology among scholars holding high positions in the scientific and party hierarchy, a growing number of new generation researchers oriented to sociology, weakening positions of the conservative philosophical circles) the institutional structures of sociology bore the name of the science in Bulgaria but not in the USSR.

The Hungarian defenders of sociology as an independent science employed an even more ingenious stratagem. According to Julia Szalai, "the first major argument of sociologists was that Marx talked about a classless society, while 'socialist' society was still a class society" (interview conducted on 27 March 2001 in Budapest, personal archive). Thus, without denying historical materialism as a theoretical basis of Marxist social knowledge, they justified the need

---

12   The discussion was organized in late March and early April 1956 at the initiative of the Department of Marxism-Leninism at the Ministry of Culture and the Institute of Philosophy at BAS.

13   This refers to the articles "The Process of Differentiation of Philosophy and the Non-philosophic Sciences as Specific Forms of Cognition" (1956) and "On the Object of Philosophy and the Non-philosophic Sciences" (1957) which later appeared as parts of the monograph *Historical Materialism and Sociology* published in 1958.

for sociology as an empirical science that studies socialist society as the first phase of communism. According to Kolosi and Szelényi's analysis (1993: 147),

> The advocates of sociology wanted to show that sociology is not a 'bourgeois', thus, anti-Marxist science. The creation of a "Marxist sociology" [...] would not replace, but complement historical materialism. According to their definition, historical materialism was the philosophy of Marxism, and sociology a special field of social investigation dealing with 'concrete social reality' from a Marxist perspective.

Except for Poland, which had the largest number of graduate sociologists or specialists in the social sciences formed before and after the war, in the countries under study the process of institutional legitimation of sociology after 1956 was carried out by actors with different status, professional background and political past. A special study of the personal trajectories of concrete participants in this process might show not only the complex relations that existed between scientists and power but also the contradictory building and stabilization of the limits of Communist political reality with the aid of sociology as well as the ambivalent development of sociology as part, and limit, of this reality. Here, based on the conducted interviews and archive documents, will will note only some specific features and give a few examples.

Most generally, two social positions played a crucial role in the institutionalization of sociology in the countries under study during the 1960s—the social position of lecturers in Marxist-Leninist philosophy, historical materialism or scientific communism who were employed within the Communist party's system of educational institutions (e.g. Włodzimierz Wesołowski in Poland, Jaroslav Klofáč and V. Tlustý in Czechoslovakia), and the social position of scholars in the upper echelons of the state-party and Komsomol apparatus or in the administrative structures of science (e.g. Yurii Pavlovich Frantsev and Petr Nikolaevich Fedosseyev in the Soviet Union, Niko Yahiel and Mincho Semov in Bulgaria, Ferenc Erdei and András Hegedüs in Hungary, Antonín Vaněk in Czechoslovakia).[14]

---

14   Gennady Batygin refers to a specific category of specialists who contributed to the revival of Soviet sociology in the 1960s and to building its positive international image. The people who had graduated from the prestigious Moscow State Institute of International Relations and "who did not go to work in the diplomatic corps came into sociology and brought with them the spirit of diplomacy and a certain diplomatic courtesy. They were amiable, good-looking, imported, they spoke foreign languages" (interview with Batygin conducted on 15 May 2000, Moscow, personal archive). Of course, these people assumed one of the above-mentioned roles.

In some cases, promotors of sociology combined positions of power both in the political and in the scientific-organizational structures of their country. Over the years, this double status would prove to be a means of defense of sociology against political power, and of provision of financial resources for large-scale research projects, but it would also be an instrument for carrying through party policy, for sacrificing scientific goals to higher political-state interests, for ideological tailoring of the sociological findings. The hybrid position of the sociologist-political functionary, in its concrete manifestations, confirms the hypothesis regarding the mobile boundary between sociology and power within a social reality that is, after all, delimited by the holders of political power.

Seen from the side of actors, the post-1956 institutionalization of sociology in these countries makes salient two other particularities of the System. It was able to accept and assimilate the political metamorphoses of a person, but it marginalized and expelled those who failed in political adaptiveness. The professional biographies of András Hegedüs and Alexander Hirner are particularly telling in this respect.

Hegedüs was the head of various ministries under the Rákosi regime in the 1950s, chairman of the Council of Ministers of Hungary (1955–1956); he signed the document asking Soviet troops for assistance during the revolution of 24 October. He fled to Moscow after the Soviet intervention, returned to Hungary after 1958, and subsequently held numerous academic posts, created the first sociological research group in 1963 which grew into the Institute of Sociology at the Hungarian Academy of Sciences in 1971. However, in 1968 he was opposed to the Soviet intervention in Czechoslovakia (1968), whereupon he was dismissed from his position of director of the Institute of Sociology and expelled from the Hungarian Communist Party in 1973 for his political and ideological views.

Alexander Hirner graduated in philosophy from the Faculty of Arts of Comenius University in Bratislava in 1940 and specialized in Rome (1941) and Paris (1948–1949). In 1944, he initiated the creation of the Sociological Department at Matica Slovenská, and was an active participant in the Slovak National Uprising of that year. In 1958, he became the victim of a politically arranged trial (having been accused of bourgeois deviation and sabotage) and was sentenced to 13 years of prison. Conditionally released from prison in 1966 and fully rehabilitated in 1969, until the end of his life (1987) Hirner worked in various places, mostly under definite term contract, studied problems related to factories, labour, living standard, wrote works that Slovak and Czech sociologists assess as fundamental theoretical and methodological contributions

(Macháček, 2000; Nešpor, 2013; Turčan, 2000). Some of these works have not been published to date.[15]

8.3   Paradoxes in Institutional Expansion

8.3.1   *Professional Associations Without Sociologists*
The sociological associations were one of the first forms of institutionalization in the countries under study. They were established in the following chronological order: in USSR in 1958 *de jure* (the Soviet Sociological Association began to function *de facto* after 1961), in Bulgaria in 1959 as the Bulgarian Sociological Society transformed into Association in 1969, in Czechoslovakia in 1964 (Slovak Sociological Association) and 1966 (Czechoslovak Sociological Association).[16] The Polish Sociological Association, founded as a Scientific Society by Florian Znaniecki in 1931, revived its activity in 1957 (Sułek, Kraśko, 2002).

With the exception of Poland, we see an obvious paradox in these countries: there were no professional sociologists, but there were associations of sociologists. There was no sociological activity properly speaking, not even any structures educating sociologists, but there were professional organizations whose members self-identified as sociologists. The creation of a public non-governmental organization in societies under the strict control of Communist parties was an act with important consequences for the self-construction of the discipline in each of these countries. In their desire to demarcate themselves from the still powerful dogmatic wing in Marxist-Leninist philosophy, the founders of these associations actually provided themselves with a double opportunity: to engage researchers interested in the empirical study of society to sociology and to connect the association members to world sociology. This double function was particularly clearly displayed in USSR. Given the absence of a center with

---

15   In the perspective of the history of sociology, it would be of interest to note the destiny of Hirner's book *Česka a slovenská sociológia do roku 1948/Czech and Slovak Sociology until 1948*. The manuscript of the book was completed in 1970, but for many years was available only as a cyclostyle edition at the Institute of Sociology in Bratislava. It was first published as late as 2014, in an electronic version under the editorship of Juraj Schenk (Alexander Hirner. *Česká a slovenská sociológia do roku 1948*, Bratislava, Stimul, 387 p., http://stella.uniba.sk/texty/AH_sociologia.pdf).

16   See Pasiak and Machachek (1994: 91). However, at the opening of the roundtable "Czech Sociology 1965–1989", held on 27 May 2003 in Prague, Oto Sedláček talked about the creation of a sociological association in the country in 1964, with Jaroslav Klofáč as its first president; this was at a time when nearly all professional sociologists of the preceding period had emigrated (*Sociologický časopis*, 2004: 697).

a genuinely sociological disciplinary project, the Soviet Sociological Association gradually assumed the role of coordinator of sociological research in the country, and initiated (at its General Assembly in February 1966) a discussion on matters related to the construction of the infrastructure of sociology as an autonomous science—from the teaching of the discipline and training of sociological cadres to diversification of the types of sociological research and organization of the life of the growing academic community. Through the mediation of the association, seminars and discussions including the participation of Western sociologists were organized (Batygin, 1998; Koleva, 2002b). Having become collective members of the International Sociological Association, the national associations became a sort of guarantor of the profession's disciplinary field in their countries, and contacts between West and East began in these fields starting from the 1950s. Not that these associations were oases lying outside the scope of the political power holder or the secret services[17]; but they did provide professional reference frames in which political intrusion could not be direct or unavoidable.

Historical chronology shows an interesting detail. Even before the appearance of these national sociological associations, the International Sociological Association (ISA), created in 1949, sought contact with Eastern Europe. In 1953, it sent an invitation to the Academy of Sciences of USSR for participation of Soviet scholars in the Second Congress of ISA at Liège, Belgium. The report by the Chief Scientific Secretary of the Presidium of the Soviet Academy to the head of the Department of Science and Culture at the CC of CPSU states (*Sociology and Power*, 1997: 15–16),

> The program of the Congress examines questions that present no interest to Soviet scientists: results of the survey on the social origin of separate professional groups, such as teachers, employees, etc., projects for empirical surveys on the social composition of the population, on social status and social changes, on the juridical ways for resolving conflicts, etc. [...] The themes of the Congress are not of topical interest, because it is not connected to the important problems of modern life and the fight for peace throughout the whole world. Moreover, the Congress is convened by ISA which is a creation of UNESCO; in whose activity, as is known, USSR[18] does not take part. [...] Consequently, the Presidium of the AS of

---

17   Most of the interviewed sociologists adduced facts and events from the history of the national associations, or from participations of their members in world congresses of sociology involving the presence of colleagues who were known by everyone to be collaborators of the secret services.

18   USSR became a member of UNESCO on 21 April 1954.

USSR considers inexpedient our participation in the Second World Congress of Sociologists.

In its report to the secretary of CC of CPSU, the department of Science and Culture repeats the arguments of the Presidium of the AS of USSR and succinctly concludes, "We judge the decision to be correct" (Ibid.).

Three years later, the political situation had changed but not the institutional situation of sociology. Despite the continuing lack of a sociological institution, a Soviet delegation of eleven people took part at the ISA Congress in Amsterdam in 1956,[19] headed by Petr Fedosseyev, then director of the Institute of Philosophy at the AS of USSR. Polish sociologists also attended, and only Zhivko Oshavkov from Bulgaria; according to recollections of some of the interviewed sociologists, representatives from the other Communist countries were also present. The number of participants from Eastern Europe increased at the following congress in 1959, in Stresa, Italy, and eventually, at the congress in Evian in 1966, the Bulgarian delegation then numbering 32 participants, with the support of the Soviet delegation of 80 persons, proposed that the 7th Congress of ISA be conducted in Varna, Bulgaria, in 1970.

On the basis of archival material from the Russian Academy of Sciences, Gennady Batygin (1998: 33–34) concludes that, thanks to Georges Balandier, then head of its International Social Science Council, UNESCO undertook to establish contacts with the Soviet Academy of Sciences as early as 1956. As a result, the first international meeting of sociologists was organized under the aegis of UNESCO in Moscow in 1958 at which the then chairman of ISA, Georges Friedmann, was invited, whose sympathies for the new Soviet society dated from long before

---

19   The sociologists very rightly use the word 'delegation' in their publications and memoirs. The Central Committee of the Communist Party (via the department responsible for science) approved the lists of participants and the heads of the groups attending scientific events abroad (congresses, conferences, symposiums); these were not visits of independent individual scientists but of organized and controlled groups. The three volumes of collected documents *Sociology and Power* (1997, 2001, 2008) present the pedantic correspondence between the Presidium of the AS of USSR, the Department of Science at CC of CPSU (which changed its name over the years, while its basic function of control over science and higher education remained the same), the Secretariat of CC of CPSU, and the Presidium of CC of CPSU, related to determining who would be the Soviet delegates to ISA congresses.

the war.[20] "From 1957 to 1961, the Institute of Philosophy alone was visited by 217 foreign philosophers and sociologists" (Batygin, 1998: 34), including Alvin Gouldner, Charles Wright Mills, Talcott Parsons, Robert Merton, Thomas Bottomore, and Raymond Aron.[21] Regardless of whether the Communist party-state used these international contacts for the purpose of 'export of ideological influence', it is a fact that *scientific contacts between Western sociologists and their East European colleagues began before the discipline of sociology was institutionalized and professionalized in the countries under study.* With regard to the development of sociology, these first contacts contributed, especially in the Soviet Union, to the social legitimation of the discipline, making a breakthrough not so much in the political thinking at that time but in the political language, which gradually began to accept the terms 'sociology' and 'sociological research' (Koleva, 2002b).

Seen from the Western side of the 'Iron Curtain', the international collaboration between West and East also fitted into a political project. It was part of an "intellectual Marshall Plan", as Michael Pollak refers to the Ford Foundation Program (Pollak, 1993). The strategic goal of this program in post-war Europe was to strengthen political pragmatism, to weaken Marxism and the national intellectual traditions through the construction of applied social sciences and the production of empirical knowledge oriented to solving social problems. Paul Lazarsfeld played a key role in implementing this scientific policy.[22] His

---

20   Between 1932 and 1936, Friedmann visited the Soviet Union three times and published two books about the country. In the first one, *La Crise du progrès* (1936), he expressed support for the regime and for Marxism as a more humane vision of the world, but was critical in the second, *De la Sainte Russie à l'U.R.S.S.* (1938), where he expressed his rejection of the cult of Stalin and the political trials of 1936, interpreted by him as remnants of the czarist regime.

21   It is not coincidental that we are pointing out only the international contacts of Soviet scholars. The rapid revival of international cooperation after 1956 with the most isolated and most strictly controlled country of the Communist Bloc, and with the sociological tradition that had suffered the most from political intervention and repression, highlights much more clearly the role of the international community for the national development of sociology in an undemocratic social-political context. The resuming of international contacts of Polish sociology—given this country's strong pre-war tradition and the role of Znaniecki who was the 44th President of the American Sociological Association (for the year 1954)—seems to have been an almost natural development.

22   Lazarsfeld was an intermediary between the Ford Foundation and UNESCO; he consulted the Norwegian government in the creation of the Institute for Social Research (1948), gave lectures in Poland, chaired the conference on public opinion research methods held in Warsaw (1958), prepared the program for exchange of social researchers between

empiricist conception of sociology as a discipline based on techniques and oriented to the market and clients fully corresponded to the international strategies of the large American foundations (Ford, Rockefeller), as well as to the needs of post-war Europe (Ibid.).

8.3.2   *Research Structures Without Educational Structures*

The process of institutionalization of the discipline was gradual, polycentric and oriented to research rather than education. Poland was an exception in this respect. It was the only country in which university courses in sociology were restored as early as 1957, along with the institutionalization of research.

The first research groups, laboratories and units of sociology were created in different places. First of all, this happened in the existing institutes of philosophy at the national academies of sciences where the research groups created in the early 1960s grew into academic institutes of sociology. Thus, the sociological group created by Zhivko Oshavkov at the Institute of Philosophy of the Bulgarian Academy of Sciences in 1962 would become the basis for the Institute of Sociology, established in 1968. In 1962, a department of sociology headed by Ján Pašiak was created within the Philosophical Institute of the Slovak Academy of Sciences; in 1965, this department evolved into an independent sociological institute within the Academy.[23] A similar course led to the establishment of the Institute of Sociology in Prague in 1965 and of the Institute of Public Opinion Research at the Czechoslovak Academy of Sciences. Despite "personal rivalries and mutual antipathy between the three protagonists"—Szalai, Erdei and Hegedüs—and "the real conflict between the

---

Yugoslavia and USA (1959), worked actively on the creation of the Central Europe Center for Research and Documentation in Social Sciences in Vienna together with Adam Schaff and Jean Stoetzel (the mission of the Center was to stimulate comparative research between East and West Europe (1958–1964)). In the context of the Cold War, the creation of this center in Vienna would have been impossible without the support of the Soviet Union. In an interview from January 1987, Jean Stoetzel points out: "Adam Schaff had the backing of the Russians. They always played the game of cooperation, because they liked places where one could talk, discuss, without serious consequences" (*L'Autre Europe*, 1987: 4). Regarding Lazarsfeld's influence on Polish sociology, see Sułek (1998).

23   Unlike other countries, where the initiator and head of the first established sociological group usually became the first director of the academic sociological institute (for instance, Zhivko Oshavkov in Sofia, Gennady Osipov in Moscow, András Hegedüs in Budapest), in Bratislava, the first to be appointed director of the Institute of Sociology was Andrej Sirácky whose "almost Stalinist past definitely served as a guarantee for the party bureaucracy at that time that Slovak sociology would continue in the direction expected by the regime" (Roško, 1995: 156).

would-be sociologists and some ideologists" (Nemedi, 2010: 155), in 1960 a small sociologically oriented research group was created at the Institute of Philosophy of the Hungarian Academy of Sciences. It became independent under the directorship of Hegedüs in 1963 and evolved into an Institute of Sociology in 1971. In 1966, sociological sectors were created in the already existing structure of the Soviet Academy of Sciences and its regional branches: first, a department of concrete social studies headed by Gennady Osipov was established at the Institute of Philosophy, which two years later became an independent Institute for Concrete Social Studies at the AS of USSR (1968); after that, two sociological sectors (on sociological problems of management and on culture) were created in Sverdlovsk (now Yekaterinburg) at the Department of economic studies of the Ural Branch of the Soviet Academy. Between 1965 and 1967, in Novosibirsk, the economist Abel Agambegyan, then director of the Institute of Economy and Organization of Industrial Production at the Siberian branch of the AS of USSR, succeeded in building a sociological department headed by Tatyana Zaslavskaya, which would become one of the powerful such centers outside of Moscow during the remaining years of the Soviet period of sociology in Russia. Only in Poland was academic sociology institutionalized at the same time as philosophy. Adam Schaff, the first director of the Polish Academy of Sciences' Institute of Philosophy and Sociology, established in 1957, explains this Polish 'exception' as "a way of 'smuggling' sociology into institutional academic structures along with philosophy."

Together with research units in the framework of academies of sciences, research groups and laboratories were created in universities—for instance, Stefan Nowak's group at the University of Warsaw, the Laboratory at Leningrad State University, the main promoters of which were Vladimir Yadov and Andrey Zdravomyslov, and which would later evolve into the Institute for Complex Social Studies at Leningrad State University.

The third type of institutional structures with sociological orientation was established outside academies, in strictly political or specifically professional frameworks. Such units were created, for instance, at the publishing or organizational structures of the Komsomol (in Bulgaria, Russia, the GDR), at the Communist party's educational structures (Bulgaria, the GDR, Poland, Czechoslovakia, Hungary), at the international Communist press (e.g. the Prague-based international monthly *Problemi na mira i sotsializma/Problems of Peace and Socialism*),[24] at national statistical services (Hungary), or at ministries or government

---

24   A monthly theoretical international journal of the Communist and worker's parties published in 28 languages in Prague from 1958 until 1990.

institutions (like committees of culture, committee for television and radio, etc.). As the interviewed sociologists pointed out, in many of these units empirical surveys on social problems began spontaneously, at the initiative of some individual or several people who succeeded in uniting some other enthusiasts around themselves. Only after obtaining visible results did this type of research activity acquire an organizational form. This was particularly typical for surveys on youth and public opinion which were organized at the national printed organs of the Komsomol (for instance, at the newspaper *Komsomolskaya Pravda/Truth of the Komsomol* in USSR, the newspaper *Narodna Mladezh/People's Youth* in Bulgaria), before becoming separated into independent specialized structures.[25]

Here are some of the most important institutions oriented to sociological surveying, and situated outside academies to be established in the period 1956–1968 in the countries under study; they are the ones most frequently referred to in publications and interviews:

1957: Center for Media Research at the Workers' Publishing Cooperative PRASA in Krakow

1958: Centers for Public Opinion Research at the Committee on Radio and Television and at the Academy of Social Sciences of Polish United Workers Party in Warsaw

1960: Institute for Public Opinion Research at the newspaper *Komsomolskaya Pravda/Truth of the Komsomol* headed by Boris Grushin; it conducted eight nation-wide surveys in just the first two years of its existence.

1964: The Group for Sociological Surveys, under the leadership of V. G. Vasilyev at the Central Committee of the All-Union Leninist Young Communist League. Similar groups were later created in more than 40 districts, regional and republican committees of the Komsomol.

1966: Social Science Research Institute at the CC of the Hungarian Communist Party in Budapest.

---

25   In fact, the very first sociologically oriented institutes for youth research were created in Germany: the Deutsches Jugendinstitut in Munich, FRG (1963) and Zentralinstitut für Jugendforschung in Leipzig, GDR (1966). As pointed out by Petar-Emil Mitev—director of the Scientific Research Institute on Youth in Bulgaria (1972–1988) and president of RC34 "Sociology of Youth" at ISA (1982–1986)—"of importance [for this] was the awareness of the need to invest in the new generation in order to overcome the crisis brought about by the war and the 'brown plague'" (Mitev, 2016: 127).

1968: In Bulgaria, the Center for Sociological Research on Youth at the Central Committee of the Dimitrov Communist Youth Union[26] headed by Mincho Semov and based on youth research that had begun in the newspaper *Narodna Mladezh/People's Youth* and the magazine *Mladezh/Youth* since the early 1960s.

1962–1970: In Slovenia, ten sociological centers on problems of labour, culture, law, healthcare, radio, agriculture, ethnic relations, etc. were created. They conducted a total of 118 surveys of which 24 are considered fundamental.

In all these cases, the groups in question conducted research activities outside the established academic practice, and political and scientific interests clashed in connection with them. Created with the 'blessings' of the ruling political power, planned by that power to carry out political orders and as a place for direct political control that would serve as a kind of alternative to the academic milieu, in each of the respective countries, these research centers and units became some of the most authoritative sociological survey institutions outside the academies. The post-1989 assessments of their activities coming from all sociologists—whether they had worked in them or not—remarkably coincide. Regarding the Social Science Research Institute of the Hungarian Communist Party, Tamás Kolosi, who started his professional career at that institute in 1968, says: "It was a Party Institute but very strongly connected with the reform-oriented Party leaders. ... [the staff] were deeply open-minded. It was an interdisciplinary institute" (interview with Tamás Kolosi conducted on 28 March 2001, Budapest, personal archive). In his analysis of Hungarian sociology, Dénes Némedi, whose university career was entirely connected to the Department of Sociology of the University of Budapest, points out: "The party created its own Social Science Institute as a counterweight to the Institute of Sociology, but in fact it became just another center of social research" (Némedi, 2010: 157).

These institutes were headed by researchers who have made a mark on the development of their national sociology, and whose important contribution is unanimously recognized. Several generations of sociologists were formed in them, who, thanks to the rich professional experience acquired there, ensured the post-totalitarian development of sociology in their respective countries after 1989. These non-academic research centers are one of the strongest proofs of the power of resistance of professionalism in a society whose predetermined

---

26   It was transformed first into the Center for Scientific Research on Youth in 1974 and then into the Scientific Research Institute on Youth in 1979.

model of development was guarded and controlled by the whole political-administrative structure. The history of their creation, however, indicates that the *agency of the researchers* themselves was based on their being able to see the post-1956 thaw as an opportunity opening new horizons. In many cases, the political decision that endorsed the creation of these structures outside the academies came only after the researchers had achieved results. I will give one example—the creation of the Institute for Public Opinion Research at the newspaper *Komsomolskaya Pravda/Truth of the Komsomol* in Moscow. This example is worth considering because, on the one hand, it gives some notion of how an accidental conjunction of circumstances combined with efforts to prepare the event could bring about the desired result; on the other hand, it shatters the notion that public opinion could not exist in an unfree society, let alone be surveyed. Boris Grushin recalls (*Russian Sociology of the 1960s*, 1999: 208–209):

> I don't remember when the idea of creating the Institute for Public Opinion was first born. [...] it came as the result of the collective efforts of several people, not only mine [...]. The first survey was conducted on 10 to 14 May 1960. We knew we could not conduct an all-Union survey and we took the 30th meridian, we carefully selected the topic. The scandal with the American pilot Powers was going on at that time,[27] [...], some tension appeared, and together with this, Khrushchev assumed the role of pacifier. That is why the topic 'Does Mankind Have a Chance to Prevent a World War?' sounded very timely? [...] We conducted an operatively quick survey on this question, we processed the results in a single day and on 19 May 1960, *Komsomolskaya Pravda* came out with a beautiful title: "Yes!—answers the 30th Meridian".
>
> I remember we spent all night in the office of the editor in chief, waiting to see how the news would be viewed by CC of CPSU. Early in the morning, they called Voronov [the editor in chief] from the telephone of the "first man" and they announced: "Nikita Sergeyevich [...] says 'Wonderful'! We congratulate you on your great success!" On the next

27   Francis Gary Powers was an American pilot whose Central Intelligence Agency U-2 spy plane was shot down on May 1st 1960 while flying a reconnaissance mission in Soviet Union airspace. Powers tried to save himself by bailing out with his parachute, but he was arrested in the outskirts of Sverdlovsk. On 19 August 1960, he was sentenced by the Military Collegium of the Supreme Court of USSR to ten years of prison, but on February 10, 1962, was exchanged for the Soviet KGB Colonel William Fisher known as "Rudolf Abel", at the Glienicke Bridge in Berlin.

day, the newspaper *Pravda/Truth* [organ of the CC of CPSU], from which it was perfectly impossible to get praise, in a brief rubric—"The latest mail"—expressed its full support, and we exulted at our victory. This victory became even greater when an outright hysteria started up in the Western press that a public opinion institute had been opened in the Soviet Union.

No doubt, the people in power had a political interest, but in this case as in many others, also of importance was the anticipatory work of the initiators of forms that would be confirmed by the rulers.

As to the training of experts in sociology, it started only after some research experience had been accumulated and the research program of sociology had been expanded. This happened in the second half of the 1960s—initially within the structures of Communist party schools as an incomplete degree (Bulgaria, Hungary, Russia); and, in the 1970s, as a specialization course or as separate degrees at universities. The lack of an educational tradition in sociology was certainly one of the factors for the belated formation of an educational structure of the discipline in most East European countries. However, the Polish scientific policy in this period points our attention to certain subtle elements of the management of the educational and research spheres of science. In the early 1960s, a law was passed that regulated the educational and research activities of scientists drawing a dividing line between them.[28] Teaching and research were differentiated. University teachers could not head or take part in research groups created in academic institutes. The scientist could choose which sphere of professional activities to work in. Thus, Maria and Stanisław Ossowski chose the University over the Academy of Sciences.

This disbalance between the educational and research structures of science affected sociology in the country with the strongest tradition in both spheres, and was long maintained in other countries as well, through formal and informal means.[29] It is one of the expressions of political fear of the possibility that sociology might have a social influence on young people. In fact, the administrative dismissals of teachers-researchers in sociology, occurring at various

28 Jakub Karpiński refers to this law as representing one of the changes in the development of sociology after 1956. According to him, the effective application of the law did not affect sociologists – Communist Party members (interview with Karpiński conducted on 25–26 March 2000, Warsaw, personal archive).

29 In the interviews, some of the Hungarian and Czech sociologists pointed out that the criterion of party membership was an informal requirement—not explicitly formulated anywhere—for being appointed to work in the university.

times during Communist rule in the countries under study, confirm this type of political behavior.

8.3.3   *Conducting Sociological Research Without Professional Experience*

In all the countries in question, the restart of sociology after 1956 began with a large number of social surveys. Paradoxically—with the exception of the Polish sociologists, and a few Czech and Slovak sociologists—the researchers oriented to sociology in these countries were novices in the field. They were primarily educated as philosophers, historians, philologists, jurists, and were taking their first steps in sociology in the late 1950s and early 1960s, learning their craft on the job. Vladimir Yadov's description of Soviet sociologists of the 1960s as "self-made professionals" starting from scratch (Yadov, 1999: 42–63) may be rightfully applied to their Bulgarian and Hungarian colleagues of the same generation as well, and to some of the Slovak researchers (Pasiak, Machacek, 1994). Conducting social surveys proved to be the first school in professional training for the people who would build the national sociologies and would train the following generation of sociologists in their countries.

Here are some of the important social surveys conducted in the countries under study in the period 1956–1968:

National social surveys

Bulgaria: Survey on the time budget (1959) conducted by the Central Statistical Office; *Religiosity of Bulgarians* (1962) and *The Town and the Village in Bulgaria* (1968) under the direction of Zhivko Ochavkov; *Potential Migration of Rural Youth to Cities* (1967) conducted at the initiative of the newspaper *Narodna Mladezh/People's Youth* and with the support of the Ministry of Agriculture and the Central Committee of the Communist Youth League, and carried out by Center for Sociological Research on Youth, an independent unit at the Youth League, specially created for this survey; the leaders of the study were Anastas Iliev and Mincho Semov;

Czechoslovakia: a representative research on social stratification directed by Pavel Machonin (1967);

Hungary: a social survey on time budget, and several stratification surveys, under the direction of Zsuzsa Ferge and István Kemény at the Hungarian Central Statistical Office (during the first half of the 1960s); a survey on the factors of differentiation in socialist society in the sphere of labor under the leadership of András Hegedüs (1964);

Poland: *The Students of Warsaw* (1958) and *Social Structure and Class Consciousness* (1961) under the direction of Stefan Nowak and Stanisław Ossowski;

USSR: a study on work collectives in factories in Moscow and Gorky conducted
by the Research Group "New Forms of Labor and Lifestyle" formed within the Section on Historical Materialism at the Institute of Philosophy
(1959); the first public opinion polls conducted by the newspaper *Komsomolskaya Pravda/Truth of the Komsomol* (1960); a study on the time
budget of workers from the Kirov Plant; and a survey on attitudes and value orientations of Soviet workers, entitled *Man and His Work*, directed by
Vladimir Yadov (1966–67); the Taganrog survey of mass consciousness
conducted by Boris Grushin (1966–1974); 'concrete surveys' of industrial
enterprises in Sverdlovsk and the cultural-technological development of
the working class (Ural).

Comparative international surveys:

- *Topical Problems of Leisure Time*—the first ever comparative survey
  in the Socialist countries under the leadership of Boris Grushin at
  Komsomolskaya Pravda//Truth of the Komsomol with the participation of
  Bulgaria, Poland, USSR, and Hungary (1964);
- *Time Budget*—the first international East-West survey under the leadership of Alexander Szalai, funded by the European Coordination Centre
  for Research and Documentation in Social Sciences at UNESCO, with the
  participation of Belgium, Bulgaria, Czechoslovakia, France, FRG, GDR,
  Hungary, Peru, Poland, USA, USSR (1965);
- *Social Problems of Labor and Production*—a Soviet-Polish survey headed
  by Gennady Osipov and Jan Szczepański (a book containing the survey
  results came out under the same title in Russian in 1969).

As a whole, these surveys showed the clearly empirical orientation of the
reviving sociology in all the countries under study after 1956, as well as the
international comparative perspective in which this revival was taking place.
In the analyses and testimonies of sociologists after 1989, both these features
were assessed as being ways to legitimate sociology as a scientific discipline
producing empirically verifiable knowledge about society according to inter-
nationally recognized standards and procedures. The social surveys proved to
be the main spearhead with which the researchers proved that the *differentia
specifica* of sociology consists in the production of objective empirical information about the state and functioning of society, in contrast with the general
and abstract postulates of historical materialism. A second paradox is evident
here, related to the quality of the first social surveys. People without degrees in

sociology, together with statisticians and mathematicians, conducted studies that were unanimously recognized to be exemplary in their methodological rigor and research precision.

Going back to the time of the first social surveys, Venetz Tzonev—a statistician who had designed the samples for both of Zhivko Oshavkov's surveys—summed up (interview with Tzonev conducted on 28 October 1999, Sofia, personal archive):

> Initially, we started out with great ambitions, and overall, in the spirit of these ambitions, we achieved some original results at methodological level. This is true for the Youth Center and the migration study as well. Never afterwards was the level of *The Town and the Village in Bulgaria* attained. [...] This is also true as concerns Oshavkov's survey of religiosity.

According to Mincho Semov (*Sociology in Bulgaria...*, 2012: 94), among the survey achievements of Bulgarian sociology,

> the survey on religiosity and the survey on the migration of rural youth are at the highest level. [...] I think we achieved a peak at the very start. I don't know what the colleagues think about it, but I am convinced that we started out from a very high level, an international level of the methods for that period.

Talking about the Novosibirsk sociological "school", Tatyana Zaslavskaya pointed out that the distinctive feature of the school was (*Russian Sociology of the 1960s*, 1999: 146)

> the scientific level and methodological requirements for the surveys. We did not allow hackwork, there was a very serious attitude to what we were doing, starting from the courses and the diploma theses of the students. The requirements were in the air, people couldn't imagine it could be otherwise. [...] In this sense, we had a normal spirit.

This assessment was confirmed by Vladimir Yadov (interview with Yadov conducted on 17 May 2000, Moscow, personal archive):

> Zaslavskaya's school was absolutely professional, objective, later subjected to serious repressions... Her associates studied the village and were the first to raise the issue that the basic problem of the village is not so much economic as social, that the social infrastructure of the village is

absolutely undeveloped, that youths' leaving the village is due not so much to their dislike for rural labor but to the utter cultural emptiness of the village—the absence of libraries, movie theatres, there isn't even electricity. They applied strong methodological techniques—factor analysis, taxonomies—and they typologized the villages on the basis of empirical data. They designed schemas, maps with which they showed the causes for migration from the village and, finally, what can be done about it.

We have no reason not to accept the assessments of the participants in these surveys and of their colleagues, especially as it is a sort of self-assessment of the whole activity of people who were among the active 'builders of contemporary sociology' in each of the countries under study during the whole period of its development under Communism. From the viewpoint of the disciplinary construction of sociology in a changed, but invariably ideologized, society, these surveys had a double cognitive value. First, they confirmed that the construction of sociology as a scientific discipline was impossible without the articulation and mutual verification of theory and empirical data, independently of the social context of the practice of sociology; and second, they showed that the surest means for sociology to distance and demarcate itself from ideology was to look at ideas through the prism of facts.[30] Thus, through scientific partnership with statistics and mathematics in the renewing but still unstable atmosphere of the 1960s, East European sociology embarked on the road of professionalism, aiming to build each survey upon the connection between problematization of social phenomena and adequate methods for their study and measurement; this legitimated sociology as an independent science and characterized its disciplinary specificity.

8.3.4   The Self-Constructing Sociological Public: Inside and Outside the Official Space

While immediately after 1956, the debates on sociology were conducted on the pages of specialized philosophical, economic, juridical periodicals or in the party, Komsomol, or trade union press, the 1960s witnessed the appearance of the first academic journals of sociology in the countries under study. In Poland, the *Przegląd Socjologiczny/The Sociological Review*, which had been stopped in 1949, started to come out again in 1958. New journals on sociological problems

---

30   Nina Naumova says: "Empirical reality is a grand thing. You can say all sorts of things, but it will show you that the situation is exactly the opposite" (*Russian Sociology of the 1960s...*, 1999: 310).

appeared: *Studia Socjologiczne/Sociological Studies* published by the Institute of Philosophy and Sociology at the Polish Academy of Sciences and the Committee on Sociology of the Polish Academy of Sciences (1960); *Ruch Prawniczy, Ekonomiczny i Socjologiczny/Juridical, Economic and Sociological Movement* published by Adam Mickiewicz University and Poznan University of Economics (1960); *Roczniki Socjologii Wsi/Annals of Rural Sociology* (1962); *The Polish Sociological Bulletin* published by the Polish Sociological Association (1962). In Czechoslovakia, *Sociologický časopis/Czech Sociological Review* was established in 1965 as an organ of the Collegium on Philosophy and Sociology at the Czechoslovak Academy of Sciences, and in 1969, the Slovak journal *Sociológia* began to appear published by the Institute of Sociology of the Slovak Academy of Sciences. The first Bulgarian academic journal in this field—*Sotziologicheski problemi/Sociological Problems*—started coming out in the beginning of 1969 as a joint organ of the Institute of Sociology at the Bulgarian Academy of Sciences and the Bulgarian Sociological Association; this journal inherited the bulletin *Sociological Research* which came out in 1968. In Hungary and USSR, academic journals in sociology appeared later (the Hungarian *Szociológia/Sociology* started publishing in 1972, and the Soviet *Sotziologicheskie issledovaniya/Sociological Studies* in 1974) in a different political and institutional context.

In any case, after 1956, the scientific periodicals in sociology were one of the factors that began the structuring of the scientific and professional environment in East European countries, and they may be viewed as an element and a mark of the institutional expansion of the discipline. The fact must not be overlooked that the growing but still small group of sociologists in each country represented a public for its own publications and created the official space of its own publicity. Inasmuch as this form of institutionalization of sociology was also officially endorsed by the holder of political power, this too can be considered a *co-construction of the space of scientific publicity*. Over the years, this publication space would become the field of internal scientific and politico-scientific clashes which would mark the temporary victory of one side or the other.

However, another space appeared early on, in the 1960s, which, though situated in scientific institutions, was not an element of their official organizational structure. These were the scientific seminars,[31] some of which were

---

31   Here I would like to express my special gratitude to Marina Pugacheva from the Institute of Sociology at the Russian Academy of Sciences. In an interview conducted in Moscow in May 2000, she brought to my attention the role of the methodological seminars in developing a solid theoretical culture among Soviet sociologists. She kindly gave me the report on her research project "The Adversities of the Soviet Sociology: A Study of Archives and Oral History" (RSS No 1310/1996, Soros Foundation), and some of her unpublished manuscripts.

usual, regular, "not shady" (Levada in *Russian Sociology of the 1960s...*, 1999), while others were in the "grey", "intermediate zone between the permitted and the prohibited" (Tabatchnikova, 2007). "Scientific life is seminar life"—Yurii Levada stated, thus making a brilliant summary of this specific sociological phenomenon of Soviet science. Levada's methodological seminar, Grushin's 47 Friday Seminar, organized in connection with the preparation of the Taganrog Project, Bestuzhev-Lada's prognostic seminar in Moscow, Yadov's seminar in Leningrad, the Novosibirsk seminar conducted by Shubkin and Shlyapentokh were among those that offer what is probably the most incontestable proof of the vitality of scientific knowledge and the internal logic of its development in a socially, institutionally and culturally inadequate context. As forms of informal scientific exchange, a "second science" and as alternatives to historical materialism, these seminars became a *sui generis* school of sociological culture. Though not creating unique scientific products, they contributed to the formation of the theoretical resources of Soviet sociology by adopting the latest achievements in Western sociology, and to the development of a cognitive sensitivity to the other sciences by recruiting experts from different disciplines (economists, logicians, mathematicians, statisticians, psychologists, historians, lawyers); they also helped cultivate a professional ethic of high academic standards, freedom of thought and critical reflexivity (Koleva, 2002b).

"Seminar" science, in the form of sociological study circles or thematic seminars, were characteristic of the other countries as well in the 1970s and 1980s as an alternative to the scientific environment with respect to initiating young people to sociology or debating certain problems under the cover of designations acceptable to the political and administrative power. The fact that these seminar forms existed during the second cycle of institutional mimicry as well, and in the second cycle of institutional expansion, make them an interesting phenomenon in terms of the transmission, assimilation, and production of sociological knowledge under the conditions of the Communist regimes.

8.4   Intermediate Recapitulation

In all the countries in question, the post-1956 institutionalization of sociology started from the sphere of research, then expanded across that space, and marked a boom in the late 1960s. The research institutions, professional associations, periodicals were the main instrument by which sociology differentiated itself and defended its disciplinary identity in the cognitive and social space of each country. Its educational institutions made their way into the university structures much more slowly and to a more limited extent. Sociological publications on the matter and the conducted interviews highlight a reason for this which recurs in all the countries: to the Communist regime, the university departments were felt to be much more dangerous than the research field. It seems young people and the possibility of influencing them proved the limit of politically admissible intellectual freedom (Koudelka, 2004; Kraśko, 1998; Némedi, Róbert, 2002; Petrusek, 2004; Szacki, 1993, 1998).

The lack of professional experience of the supporters and promoters of sociology in the countries under study was compensated for by their enthusiasm and will to prove the heuristic potential of the discipline (which were common features of that generation according to the recollections of its representatives), and also by consistent work for assimilating the sociological methods and methodological vigilance at every stage of research. The professional breakthrough made by sociology novices in each of the countries was assisted to a considerable extent by the beginning international collaboration amid the otherwise continuing Cold War between East and West. The first specializations of Polish sociologists in the US after World War II,[32] the first, though rare, specializations of Soviet researchers in Great Britain, the scientific trips to foreign countries, the first international conferences of ISA (Moscow, Warsaw), the scientific exchange between the Communist countries are the few but solid elements of the growth of sociological professionalism in the 1960s.

---

32   For Polish sociologists, this possibility was due to a "historical accident", as Hieronim
      Kubiak called it. Some of the aid (goods, food, medicine, tools and other basic necessities) that Poland received directly from the American National Committee for International League and from the Federal Government of the USA during and after the war, had to be paid in Polish zloty "which was non-convertible currency at that time. And what did Americans do with this Polish non convertible money? They used a part of it for constructing the American Embassy in Warsaw [...] and a part for establishing the Fund for helping Polish scholars. It was the Marie Curie Fund, it had an acronym, but I don't remember exactly [...]. And immediately the program of exchange of Polish scholars was established between America and Poland. For that purpose, from the very beginning, we used grants of the Fulbright Foundation. And now what happened? Due to [the favorable circumstances] that Polish sociology had a good reputation from pre-war time, that there was money available and due to Polish scholars living abroad, including Polish political émigrés, gradually Polish scholars began to leave Poland for studying and post-graduate training in the USA and participated in the exchange program" (interview with Hieronim Kubiak conducted on 5 April 2000, Krakow, personal archive; see also Kubiak, 1996). Added to this was the financial aid coming from the Ford Foundation in the form of "travel grants for Polish social scientists, books for Polish libraries, and visits of foreign scholars to Polish research centers". The aid amounted to over half a million dollars in 1957, according to Antoni Sułek (1998), and 270,000 dollars in 1958, according to Pollak (1993).

In the following decades, this professionalism would be put to the test and would prove to be what the discipline's development was staked on during the series of political turnabouts in Communist governance. The year 1968, with the intervention of the Warsaw Pact in Czechoslovakia would close the partial de-Stalinization that had begun in 1956 and would open a new stage in the 'straightening out' of the political course. As concerns sociology, 1968 would place it in a new cycle of institutional mimicry, the start and manifestations of which would prove to be different in the different countries.

CHAPTER 9

Institutional Mimicry II: 1968–1980

The year 1968 was the *annus mirabilis*—the year of wonders for the entire world, or at least for the mutually confronted Eastern and Western blocs. It was the year of escalation of the war in Vietnam (which had begun in 1956) and the anti-war movement in the US; of the "Cultural Revolution" in China which had begun in 1966 and now reached a peak; of powerful workers' revolts followed by even more powerful student revolts in France and Germany; of the Prague Spring and the military intervention of five Warsaw Pact countries in Czechoslovakia. Though taking place in separate countries, these events had international repercussions and transnational impacts. Their 'revolutionizing' impulse turned their messages into universal references for political activity, as well as for scientific reflection, in the following decades.

Apart from that, each of the Communist countries experienced the year 1968 in its own specific way, according to its own preceding history; and each reacted differently to the large-scale reform program of the Czechoslovak Communist Party headed by Alexander Dubček,[1] and to the August events in Prague which put a dramatic end to the model of "socialism with a human face".[2] The result was the same for all: the end of the liberalization of the Communist regime that had commenced after 1956 and a return to ideological 'hardening' and intensified political control over all spheres of society.

---

1 The Slovak Alexander Dubček, elected chairman of the Czechoslovak Communist Party (CZCP) on 5 January 1968, immediately undertook modernizing Czechoslovak society. In the course of eight months, he carried out reforms that deviated so far from the Soviet model of state socialism strictly imposed and followed in the countries within the Soviet zone of influence, that this led to the military intervention of the Warsaw Pact armies aiming to preserve the integrity and structural principles of the Communist system. The most important aspects of Dubček's reform program concerned politics (separation of party from government functions, abolishing the accumulation of several positions by one person), constitutional structure (federalization of the country), economics (liberalization of the economy, giving a more important place to the market), culture (freedom of expression, abolishment of censorship over the media).

2 The entry of the Warsaw Pact armies into Czechoslovakia on 21 August 1968 was preceded by events indicating the growing economic and political crisis in the separate countries and the whole Communist bloc, and by attempts to manage this crisis: a session of the Political Consultative Committee of the Warsaw Pact in Sofia (6–7 March 1968); student riots in

Against the backdrop of the conservative turnabout in the political course, the new borderline drawn between permissible and punishable activities in the Communist bloc, and the new blow dealt to the beliefs and hopes for a just and free socialist society, we now turn to what was happening to the institutional development of East European sociology. Various publications, personal assessments and testimonies in interviews, and archival documents, indicate there was some ambiguity in the institutional status of sociology in the decade following the critical year 1968. On the one hand, there was an evident trend of political-administrative coercive measures taken against the organizational forms of sociological activity, similar to coercion exercised during the first cycle of institutional mimicry in 1948/49–1956. On the other hand, the state gave financial support to the discipline's official research and educational institutions. In both cases, the situation of sociology was due to a specific constellation of positions and roles in science and politics, and to the professional 'philosophy' and personal characteristics of the people occupying those positions in each country. Behind the variety of cases and forms of institutional wandering, dissolving or transformation of institutions, the same phenomenon

---

Poland (from 8 March to the end of April of that year); a meeting of Communist party leaders in Dresden (23 March 1968) devoted to problems of economic cooperation and the international situation, and focused on the beginning changes in Czechoslovakia and their eventual consequences for the country and the whole Communist bloc; a session convened by Leonid Brezhnev in Moscow (8 May 1968), with the participation of Todor Zhivkov, Walter Ulbricht, Władysław Gomułka, János Kádár—the four Communist party leaders most loyal to the Soviet leadership—at which the plan for operation X was prepared (aiming to solve the "Czechoslovak" problem, including by eventual military action); "The Letter of Five Communist and Workers' Parties to the CC of CZCP" (from CPSU, PUWP, GUSP, HSWP, and BCP) drafted at their meeting in Warsaw (12–14 July 1968) in which two contrary theses were expressed: "We had, and have, no intentions of interfering in matters that are purely internal affairs of your party and state, of violating the principles of respect for independence and equality in the relations between communist parties and socialist countries" as opposed to "Together with this, we cannot agree that hostile forces should push your country away from the socialist path and create the danger of separating Czechoslovakia from the socialist community. That is no longer your own affair" (cited from Baeva, 2010: 203). While during this whole period of attempts at 'saving' Czechoslovakia and the Communist bloc, the strongest opponents of Dubček's reform policy were Bulgaria, Poland, USSR, and GDR, by contrast, Hungary, in the person of its leader János Kádár, was a moderate defender. The reasons for Hungary's attitude may be found in the fact that economic reforms begun in that country in 1967 fully matched the Czechoslovak reforms, as well as in the history of the preceding period: the severe crisis of Hungarian society after the revolution of 1956 was abated slowly, but in the long term led to greater civic and political liberties and to the government's consideration of public attitudes.

is visible: *the relative shrinkage, in each country, of the scientific autonomy of sociology, of its presence in the scientific and social space, of its scope of activity.* This gives us reason to talk about a second cycle of institutional mimicry in the post-war development of sociology in the countries under study.

9.1   It All Began With Czechoslovak Sociology ...

It would not be contrary to the facts to say that the second cycle of institutional mimicry began in Czechoslovak sociology. Moreover, of all the countries under study, only in Czechoslovakia did the political blow dealt to sociology come as a direct result of the tragic end of the Prague Spring. The new party leadership headed by Gustáv Husák started the so-called "normalization" in order to restore the 'socialist authenticity' of Czechoslovak society and its governance. This practically meant removal of the reforms and reformers (1969–1971) and preservation of the status quo (1971–1987).[3] It was the political measures taken in the first period of "normalization" that would return Czechoslovak society to the totalitarian practices of the Communist party-state typical for the late 1940s and early 1950s. The Czechoslovak Communist Party (CZCP) purged all professional groups according to its own criteria of political loyalty, and once again subjected activities in all spheres of society to its own political purposes through violence, humiliation, and accusations. "Screening committees",[4] "replacement of Party ID cards", political "purges" composed the reality of totalitarian experience that Czechs and Slovaks experienced for a second time after World War II. The only thing lacking was the physical elimination of people in the Stalinist period of governance by the CZCP—but the totalitarian methods of Husák had a no less devastating effect on the professional ethos and moral atmosphere in all spheres of society.

The assessment of "normalization" of Czech and Slovak society, and of the national sociology in particular, began after 1989 (Havlová, Sedláček, 2004;

---

3   The entire period of Gustáv Husák's governance (1969–1987) is defined as "normalization" insofar as the restored political and police control and the repressions against dissidents became a continuing characteristic of this regime, even though they assumed more moderate forms in the 1980s. "Normalization" began under the slogan "Oppose the right-wing time-servers in Marxist sociology" (Roško, 1995).

4   As Eduard Urbanek decribed it, "the screening process was a method used by officials of universities and other educational institutions to evaluate, through personal interviews, the political orientation and attitudinal disposition of individuals toward the Party and ruling regime" (1994: 86).

Macháček, 2004; Machonin, 2004; Možný, 2004; Petrusek, 1992, 2004; Šiklová, 2004; *Sociológia*, 1998; *Sociologický časopis*, 2004; Žatkuliak, 1998). Before examining the objective dimensions of the 'devastation' in sociology, it is important to see how "normalization" was carried out. Considering the personal experience of the victims is one of the possible ways to see, without passing judgment, the dividing line between possible and impossible action faced by every generation at critical historical moments, and to feel the moral dilemmas involved which we too often ignore in the name of objective and unbiased knowledge. Moreover, this experience illuminates the role of ideas with respect to what is permitted/prohibited at the level of everyday life, ideas that make of reality an authority that regulates and sanctions conduct.

The study on *Self-censorship and "Text coding" of Academic Texts in Czech Republic during Normalization, 1968–1989* (2001–2004) by Libora Oates-Indruchová contains valuable testimonies and confessions about this period. Here we will cite her account of a conversation she had with one of her respondents. In answer to her question (Oates-Indruchová, 2007: 299–300)

> "So, what was the vetting like? ... People were called up one by one and they had to sign something, or what?", the teacher in Professor Gladiolus prevailed and he began to explain patiently:
>
> "The exchange of the IDs meant that, as a self-disciplined Party member, you had to present yourself in front of a committee at such and such time. The committee consisted of representatives of our workplace, and then there were two workers, you know, the working-class cadres." [...] "But I ... if you threatened me with life ... but this is a psychoanalytical repression, I cannot recall what they asked me."
>
> "They asked questions?"
>
> "Of course. The basic question was about one's opinion on the entry of the armies. The question number two was: 'Comrade, how do you see your further participation?' Meaning, active participation, right? 'How would you like to participate in the consolidation process?' Basically: 'What is your idea of what you could do from now on?' We were all prepared in one way or another: blah-blah. But I saw the piece of paper then. It was a coincidence that I saw it. He had these marks there: zero, cross, one. That could not have meant anything else than a decision about our doom. Which means the struggle for self-preservation was decided in advance."
>
> [...] "Those whose Party membership was cancelled simply did not get a new ID. That was the lower punishment: 'Comrade, you are not ours any more.' But if you were expelled: 'We kicked your ass.'"

All was much clearer now, but I pushed the matter further still: "Did they invite to the questioning also those whom the Party expelled? You know, I cannot find out about it anywhere."

"Because it's not written anywhere! Of course they invited everybody. Look, those who now play heroes and say: 'I didn't even bother to go,'—there were only a few of those. Those were the people who really knew that the battle was lost. Those really did not bother. They knew. [...] By the way, some already left the country. But the majority did go, although ... listen, it was so incredibly humiliating ..."

"I can imagine."

"And yet, we went."

"Why did one do those things ... the various things that one cannot even explain to oneself now?"

"Because then, if we had known the end of the story, we would have faced them bravely and said: 'Kiss my ass! We are not going to humiliate ourselves in this way!' But it was not like that. We were meeting each other, inventing various strategies, trying to think what to say at the committee. It was not that simple. We were, of course, trying to solve the problem of what to say, so that we did not make complete fools out of ourselves. Some even cried and begged the comrades. There were some like that, but not many. But there were. They debased themselves, stooping to the lowest level"

Libora Oates-Indruchová adds her analysis (Ibid.: 300):

One can only try and stretch the limits of one's imaginative capabilities to get the feel of the atmosphere of suspense, thwarted hopes and vague threats. One can even argue that the creation of such atmosphere was the greatest 'achievement' of Normalization. The powerful suggestion seeping through all interaction and all *language* at one's workplace that something *might* happen to one, and one did not know what, proved to be perhaps the most efficient tool of control, paralyzing people of above-average intelligence and accomplishments into inaction—and self-abasement. Most of "my" researchers who were old enough to remember the vetting and its aftermath agreed that the blacklisting of people from jobs, professions and publishing gradually subsided by 1973–74. Then it became possible even for those who were fired as politically undesirable to find some form of professional existence, although they could hardly expect any formalized rehabilitation. Yet, as is apparent from their stories, the Party maintained a grip on their consciousness and the general consciousness of the academic community.

The Czech and Slovak sociologists who had undergone "normalization" primarily emphasized the objective dimensions of "normalizing practices" in sociology rather than their psychological effects (Macháček, 2000, 2004; Machacek, 2006; Petrusek, 1992, 2004; Pasiak, Machacek, 1994; Roško, 1995). Their analyses and testimonies outline the following picture of Czechoslovak sociology in the early 1970s.

First, sociology was deprived of the researchers who had contributed to the revival of the discipline and the building of its academic institutions after 1956. Expelled from czcp and dismissed from their institutional positions on the grounds of political 'unreliability', some of them were deprived of the possibility of exercising the profession of sociologist (Jaroslav Klofáč was forced to work in a shoe factory, Pavel Machonin—in the sphere of sports and in pottery industry, Miloslav Petrusek as a librarian), others continued to work in research institutes under part-time work contracts and "with an appropriate 'tutor' who had an excellent Party reputation and was trusted by the higher-ranking Party leaders" (Machacek, 2006: 78; interview with Ladislav Macháček condected on 30 November 2000, Bratislava, personal archive), still others continued their research activity in non-academic, non-sociological institutions and units (Anton Štefánek, Alexander Hirner, Ján Pašiak, Josef Alan, Jiří Musil). At the same time, politically reliable persons were appointed, their work contracts were for terms of four years, unlike the three or five-month contracts of the other employees (Pasiak, Machacek, 1994: 94). Later, "some opportunities were offered to sociology graduates from Cracow, Poland, and Bratislava and Brno" (Ibid.).

Second, the educational structures of sociology were changed. The Czechs were hit much harder in this respect than the Slovaks (interview with Vladimír Krivý conducted on 30 November 2000, Bratislava, personal archive). Departments of sociology were shut down in Prague and Brno; later on, departments of Marxism-Leninism, scientific communism or concrete social studies were created, and teachers from the Institute of Marxism-Leninism at the Higher Party School were appointed there. The enrolment of students in sociology was discontinued in Charles University in Prague, and when enrolment was renewed in 1974, the permitted number of students was nine persons a year (Linhart et al., 1996; Urbanek, 1994). Being further away from the center of power,[5] Bratislava was spared the liquidation wave in education. In ten years of its existence (1964–1974), the Department of Sociology in Bratislava trained

---

5   Distance from the national centers of political power (Moscow, Prague, Warsaw) as a possibility for relatively greater academic freedom is referred to in interviews with Vladimir Yadov, Ladislav Macháček, Pavel Machonin, Yolanta Kulpińska (personal archive), and Tatyana Zaslavskaya (*Russian Sociology of the 1960s...*, 1999: 132–155).

115 sociology graduates in a five-year curriculum in the discipline, and "in 1974 the Ministry of Industry announced that it would request approximately 15 to 20 [sociology] graduates in the following years for enterprise and personnel work" (Pasiak, Machacek, 1994: 95).

Third, the least affected seems to have been the research structure of sociology. The Institute for the Study of Public Opinion at the Czechoslovak Academy of Sciences discontinued its activity. The Academic Institute of Sociology in Prague was included in the newly formed Institute of Philosophy and Sociology,[6] and the one in Bratislava remained independent until the end of 1974.[7] Scientific functionaries loyal to the party were appointed as directors: Radovan Richta in Prague and Joseph Hrabina in Bratislava. The sociological journals *Sociologický časopis/Czech Sociological Review* and *Sociológia/Slovak Sociological Review* continued to come out, but their boards of editors were replaced (Klobucký, 2009). Non-academic institutes and research units with a sociological orientation were preserved under strict regard for the staff's party loyalty and centralized planning of the research programs.

This context—in which institutes were more or less formally preserved, but their activity was reoriented and modulated with reference to the "normalizing" policy of CZCP—had the strongest transformative impact on sociologists as a community. According to Miloslav Petrusek (1992), after 1970, the sociological community was divided into three groups.[8] On the basis of his analysis, it is possible to distinguish three internally contradictory trajectories of

---

6   The closing down of the independent Institute of Sociology in Prague, and the transference of its structure to a merged institute of philosophy and sociology is viewed by Oto Sedláček (chairperson of the round table on "Czech Sociology 1965–1989" held on 27 May 2003 in Prague) as the liquidation of the Institute. People who took part in this measure were scholars loyal to the CZCP—Svoboda, Hodek, Hrůza, Hrzal, Richta (*Sociologický časopis/Czech Sociological Review*, 2004: 698). According to Miloslav Petrusek, a participant in the round table, the institutional unification of sociology with philosophy from which sociology had separated with difficulty in the 1960s, represented a step backwards. It led to the thematic and organizational restructuring of sociology's field of study and to the shameful practice of criticizing not only Western sociology (an occupation that some people "lived on professionally"), but living sociologists as well (Ibid.: 705).

7   The Institute of Sociology in Bratislava was united to the newly created Institute of Philosophy and Sociology at the Slovak Academy of Sciences on 1 January 1975. Andrej Sirácky, a professor from the party-science nomenklatura, was appointed as its director. In 1990, it again became an independent Institute of Sociology (Falt'an, 1995).

8   Such groups are differentiated in the interviews with Michal Illner (22 November 2000, Prague, personal archive) and Ľudovít Turčan (28 November 2000, Bratislava, personal archive).

professional development of sociologists. The first type is the trajectory of marginal professional development characterizing the small group of people excluded from the discipline of sociology. The larger part of these people "completely stopped working in sociology, and some, in the late 1970s and in the 1980s began to appear mostly as political figures" (Ibid.: 11). The second trajectory was that of "internal migration" which characterized the way most sociologists left working at low positions in sociological institutions exercised their professions: formally, they had accepted the "rules of the game" but in fact tried to bypass the rules in various ways. The third trajectory was that of conformist behavior adopted by a small group of sociologists who were "normalizers" of their discipline. This group "normalized" sociology in accordance with the new principles, thereby weakening it in the scientific aspect but preserving it as an institution. The benefit accruing from such vegetation were the privileges and high positions these sociologists received from the Communist authorities.

We are inclined to believe that the reversal to classic totalitarian principles of political governance of Czechoslovak society dealt the heaviest blow specifically to the scientific ethos of sociology. The professional principles and norms could not be applied or protected; instead they were replaced with political considerations and ideological arguments, and the latter were imposed as the criterion of admissible and acceptable knowledge about society, politically certified as 'scientific' knowledge. From a present-day viewpoint, we can define this condition of sociology as the 'compromising' of the profession, or even more strongly, as its 'political corruption'. In any case, this process would not have been possible without the collaboration of part of the sociologists themselves.

But still, since "there was no chopping off of heads but, rather, the cutting off of hands" (Pasiak, Machacek, 1994: 94), the possibility of preserving the professional ethos of sociology remained, and Czech and Slovak sociologists managed to guard the spirit of the discipline within the marginal space of activity that they created or in which they found themselves (Havlová, Sedláček, 2004; Machacek, 2006; Purkrábek 1995; Šiklová, 2004; Spalová, 2006). Perhaps that is why, in Martin Potůček's book *The Normalization in the Social Sciences. My Life in Normalization* (1995), some of the interviewed Czechs, such as Boguslaw Blažek and Alena Hromádková, view "normalization" from another perspective: "I have no reason to sort of complain too much about normalization. Thanks to it, I overcame the administratively defined normality, so that in my views, I reached a stance that I would hardly have reached under the conditions of real normality".[9]

---

9   The citation is from Miloslav Petrusek's commentary on the jubilee assembly of Czech sociologists held on 17 May 1995 at the Faculty of Social Sciences of Prague University (Petrusek,

9.2   .... And then the National Sociologies of Poland and USSR Followed

The institutional blows and personal losses undergone by the sociological communities of Poland and the Soviet Union in the 1970s began with the 1968 crisis in the Communist bloc. It would be overhasty, however, to view them as a direct result of the crisis. As everywhere in society, here too, the chronological sequence of different orders of events makes visible the effect of historical circumstances without proving whether they are the cause or only the condition enabling the effect of other causes (Matalon, 1994: 128). The military intervention of the Warsaw Pact armies in Czechoslovakia was a key event in the history of the Communist bloc by its drastic and uncompromising aggressiveness which brought about an irrevocable fissure in relations between allies and deep cleavages within each country. In this sense, the post-1968 development of national sociologies was inevitably connected to the events, but depended both on the way in which the ruling party and society reacted to the crisis and on the internal political dynamics in each country.

In Poland, the stimulus for changes in sociology came from the March student strikes and the anti-Semite campaign that preceded the August rout of the Prague Spring. Paradoxically, the country that had had the most liberal regime of governance after 1956, began to restrict the freedom of expression in the early 1960s[10] and eventually, to come to repressions against students, writers, university teachers, high-ranking party officials and state employees of Jewish origin in May 1968.[11] This unleashed one of the biggest emigration waves in the post-war history of the country. Nearly 20 thousand Poles of Jewish origin left their native land. As elsewhere, in the scientific and university circles the ones most affected were individuals. The now world-renowned Zygmunt Bauman, Maria Hirszowicz and Leszek Kołakowski (who

1995). As for Potůček's book, Petrusek notes that only nine of the 40 interviews conducted by the author in February 1989 were included in it. Before its publication in 1995, the interviewees were given the opportunity to edit the initial version of the text.

10 From February 1961 to October 1963 were abolished the "Crooked Circle Club", the Interschool Discussion Club of Contradiction Seekers, and the Political Discussion Club at Warsaw University. In 1964–1966, court trials were held against intellectuals charged with participating in discussion clubs or possession of anti-socialist literature (Baeva, 2010: 384–385).

11 The student protests in March 1968 were sparked by the Ministry of Culture's announcing the last performance of Adam Mickiewicz's play *Forefathers' Eve* (inspired by the Polish national liberation movement against Czarist Russia) would be on 30 January 1968. Immediately after the performance, a youth procession was formed chanting slogans "We want more performances!", "Free theater, free art!" More than 50 youths were arrested on

was not of Jewish origin) were forced to leave their country; a number of scholars, including sociologists, were thrown out of the universities, others were accused of liberalism and revisionism. The sociological institutions were preserved as organizations, but the spirit in them changed. Contemporaries of this period share:

> I would say, the period 1968–1979 was the period of corruption in sociology. Many sociologists got corrupted by the same liberal communist regime. [...] After the political pressure over sociology, the political control was not very tight, and so we could produce all kind of works, theoretical, methodological and empirical. [...] But there was very little spirit of criticism of the system or whatever. This was a kind of communist positivist period. (interview with Edmund Mokrzycki conducted on 23 March 2000, Warsaw, personal archive)

> The 1970s period was a very quiet period and nothing particularly interesting happened because sociology was depressed by the 1968 events. (interview with Antoni Sułek conducted on 24 March 2000, Warsaw, personal archive)

Even the work of the Polish Sociological Association, the sociological institution freest of political control, was disrupted after the political repressions of 1968. At the opening of the Fourth Congress of the Association in 1969, Antoni Sułek recalls (quoted interview),

> A leading official PUWP (Party) sociologist criticized in his official address the fact that Polish sociologists have to study social problems, the bad sides of social reality. And then Stefan Nowak said that in his opinion,

---

that occasion, predominantly of Jewish origin (according to the Polish press). The events that followed include: an extraordinary meeting of the Union of Polish Writers on 29 February 1968; a student demonstration on 8 March which evolved into mass student protests in all large university cities in Poland; party meetings throughout the whole state administration at which hundreds of people of Jewish origin were criticized, expelled from the party, and later dismissed from work; arrests and convictions of students and assistant professors in Warsaw, Kraków, Gdansk. According to Iskra Baeva, underlying these events was an internal party conflict between the old generation of internationalist party functionaries headed by Władysław Gomułka, and the new generation of party nationalist apparatchiks united around the Resistance veteran Mieczysław Moczar (Baeva, 2010: 382–395).

studying social problems is the most useful thing for society that sociology can do.

The fact that after the Third Congress of the Association in 1965, only two congresses were held until 1980[12] shows "that the authorities were afraid of, not of the contents of sociology, but they just were afraid of something unexpected, that something could happen" (Ibid.). Jerzy Szacki, president of the Association in the period 1972–1976,

> recalls his presidency as 'continually picking one's way between the wish to act and the demands of the authorities, continually steering a middle course between what one would like to do and what one was able to achieve' (Kraśko, 1997). The PTS [Polish Sociological Association] was continually being accused of 'political willfulness'" (Sułek, Kraśko, 2002: 222).

At the same time, in the years of "permissive authoritarianism", as Jadwiga Staniszkis defines the period of Edward Gierek's leadership (1970–1980),[13] there was visible a kind of peaceful coexistence and "mutually advantageous cooperation"[14] between sociology and the holders of power. The majority of sociologists responded to the political demand for modernization of management based on scientific information about society. In 1971, a new system was put in place for state support of research based on funding research programs, not institutions. "The System of Values and Aspirations in Socialist Economic Development" was one of the priority national programs in the government's new science policy, and many sociologists were engaged in its

---

12   The Fourth Congress of the Polish Sociological Association devoted to the topic "Sociological theory and research and societal practice" was held in 1969 in Poznań, and the Fifth Congress on "The development of Polish society and sociology" was in 1977 in Kraków.

13   This refers to a type of governance where the state continues to be dominant but tolerates the creation of small opposition groups. According to Staniszkis, since Poland relied on Western credits and had assumed the role of intermediary between East and West, the country's political leadership was forced to display a minimal degree of tolerance. Staniszkis developed this view at the Sixth Congress of the Polish Sociological Association (Łódź, 9–12 September 1981). See Mink (1982: 157–164).

14   The expression "mutually advantageous cooperation" was one of the euphemistic formulations describing relations between Communist countries in all Comecon and Warsaw Pact documents. In this case too, as in regards to relations between countries, historical experience refuted the political phraseology.

implementation.[15] In these favorable circumstances, sociologists succeeded in winning important recognition for their institutions. In the mid-1970s, the category of 'sociologist' was included in the Code of socio-professional categories (Mink, 1987: 16). The tension between sociology and power became visible when the sociological data and analyses showed the deterioration of the economic and social situation of the country. Party-state restrictions on the publication of results deemed unfavorable for the ruling authorities and on the funding of sociological research gave birth to two contrary phenomena, or rather a single phenomenon with two faces. This metaphor of the 'two-faced Janus' refers to the production of information for two zones in both of which access to that information was restricted and outside the public domain. The political authorities relied on institutes attached to the party structures (such as the Institute for Research on Fundamental Problems of Marxism-Leninism at CC of PUWP) to conduct public opinion surveys for "internal use". The sociologists who had withdrawn from state support moved to the field of Samizdat which had emerged after the workers' protests in 1976. A game of hide-and-seek began in which there would be no winners, and all would prove to be losers.

In the Soviet Union, the institutional reorganization of sociological activity, the staff changes in the leadership of sociological institutions, and the dismissal of well-established sociologists came as a result of the interweaving of specific circumstances in the scientific and political spheres after 1968. An emblematic event for Soviet sociology which caused institutional trauma and disrupted the development of sociology revived after 1956 was the very vocal discussion—initiated by the scientific-political nomenklatura—of Yurii Levada's *Lectures on Sociology*. He had read them at the Faculty of Journalism of Moscow State University and had published with the support of the ICSS in 1969.[16] In recalling the atmosphere surrounding the scandal, Levada points out (*Russian Sociology of the 1960s...*, 1999: 86)

> In itself, there was no justification for all that fuss, I had never attached particular attention [to those lectures]. The fuss came about because

---

15   The first director of this program was Jan Szczepański (1971–1975); after him, its leadership was entrusted for 15 years to Jerzy Wiatr. In the framework of the program, 26 research projects were carried out.

16   *Lectures on Sociology* was published in the "Methodical Guides" series of the *Information Bulletin*, issues 20–21, March–May 1969, with a print run of 1000 copies (Levada, 1969). The bulletin at that time was an edition of the Institute for Concrete Social Studies and the Soviet Sociological Association.

in the course of three or four years [...] there was an interregnum in
the country, a kind of free interval [...]—the one (Khrushchev) was
gone, the other (Brezhnev) was not yet settled in power; and in 1969,
after Czechoslovakia, the ruling power became defined and a series of
tightening ups began in various fields, [...], the wave reached ICSS [In-
stitute for Concrete Social Studies] as well. They were not at all pleased
that the chief liberal of that time, Rumyantsev, was head of this institute and that one could work, argue, think there. [...] 'They' needed to
tie up even the least liberal thought and to attach ICSS, [an institute]
that our official philosophers did not like at all. It was really thought
that there is no sociology different from philosophy; philosophy was
Istmat [historical materialism] and Diamat [dialectical materialism],
and there could and should be nothing else, [anything else] would be
a distortion.

Once sparked, the scandal evolved in the way customary for totalitarian power:
discussions in scientific units (joint session of the Departments of Philosophy
of the Academy of Social Sciences at CC of CPSU and the Higher Party School
at CC of CPSU on 20–24 November 1969; in ICSS; in the Department of
Philosophy of the humanities faculties of Moscow State University/MSU);
discussions in the committees of the local party organizations of ICSS and
MSU; party punishments (Levada was dismissed from the position of 'secretary
of the party organization at ICSS and from membership in the party bureau',
the editor in chief of *Informatzionnui byulleten*/*Information Bulletin* received
a severe reprimand, noted on his party card); a prohibition on the publication
of texts by Levada[17]; official party decisions for "raising the ideological-political
level" of scientific production of the members of ICSS, and for "purity of

---

17   The fact that Levada's texts in the following years remained unpublished is one of the many
      examples of how political pressure was made effective not by those exercising it but by
      those upon whom it was exercised. Asked whether there had been an official or tacit order
      that his works should not be published, Levada responds: "I have never heard of such an
      order. [People] were simply afraid. In *Questions of Philosophy*, a journal that had a friendly
      attitude to us, the editor in chief at that time was Ivan Frolov, a young man who consid-
      ered himself progressive. He had said he would not print a single line against Levada, but
      also Levada must not be published. He fulfilled both promises" (*Russian Sociology of the
      1960s...*, 1999: 88). However, the published *Lectures* were not seized by the authorities, and
      copies of them could be found in the public libraries: Vladimir Kostyushev came across
      Levada's book in the Saltykov-Shchedrin Library in Leningrad in the 1970s. (interview with
      Vladimir Kostyushev conducted on 20 May 2000, Saint Petersburg, personal archive).

Marxist-Leninist theory and abidance by the party principles of development of sociological science".[18]

The long-term consequences of the scandal were more devastating: in 1971, Alexey Rumyantsev was dismissed from the positions of vice president of the AS of USSR and director of ICSS; Mikhail Rutkevich was appointed director of ICSS, the man who was considered the "chief destructor" of the Institute and of the sociology that was being developed there; closing down of units in ICSS (one of which was the Center for Public Opinion Research created in 1970 and headed by Boris Grushin); "dismissal" of research associates or their voluntary resignation (for example, Levada). The researchers who in the 1960s, in the "wonderful liberal atmosphere under Rumyantsev" (Yadov), were able to push forward the reviving Soviet sociology, were now scattered and, until the mid-1980s, worked in other academic or non-academic institutes.[19] The institutional wanderings of individual sociologists dramatically marked their personal professional trajectories. However, all this certainly had a no less negative impact on the whole sociological community. *It eliminated the institutional possibilities for transmitting research experience, for training the following generation of sociologists, for scientific debate and the publication of sociological texts.*

But sociologists with their already accumulated professional experience were able to find alternatives and spaces where they could develop their scientific discipline according to its own measure and oppose 'official science', while also "adapting to some degree in order to preserve their 'Self' and their science" (Osipov in *Russian Sociology of the 1960s...*, 1999: 109). Far from Moscow, the

---

18   This phraseology occurs in all documents on the Levada case published in *Russian Sociology of the 1960s* (1999: 485–507), except for Levada's statement at the above-mentioned session on 20–24 November 1969. Levada draws a clear distinction between "qualified", content-related criticism and ideological accusations regarding insufficient class and party perspective (Ibid.: 485–481).

19   Here are a few examples of researchers whose professional career in ICSS was cut short in the late 1960s and early 1970s. Yurii Levada went to work in the Central Economic-Mathematical Institute of the Soviet Academy of Sciences (1972–1988); Nina Naumova went to work in the Institute on Management Problems at the Soviet Academy (1973–1976); from 1974 to 1987, Boris Grushin worked for terms of several years each in the Central Economic-Mathematical Institute of the Soviet Academy of Sciences, at the All union Scientific Research Institute on Systemic Studies, and at the Institute of Philosophy of the Soviet Academy of Sciences; starting from 1975, Igor Kon was a research associate at the Institute of Ethnography of the Soviet Academy of Sciences; after 1975, Andrey Zdravomyslov worked at the Institute of Marxism-Leninsm of CC of CPSU; Lev Karpinsky worked in the publishing house Progress (1973–1975), and after being expelled from CPSU in 1975, was unemployed for a long time (*Russian Sociology of the 1960s...*, 1999).

sociological research units in Leningrad and Novosibirsk were no less the target of ideological pressure. The seminars formed in the 1960s—these "unofficial or semi-official forms of intellectual communication"[20]—continued their activity in Moscow, Leningrad, Novosibirsk, and several other cities. As institutions of their time, "a time of aging of the social-political system, of liberal hopes, of first attempts at direct resistance, of breakdown of official social science", they attracted many scholars by their "non-traditional themes, interdisciplinarity, openness to discussion" (Levada in *Russian Sociology of the 1960s...*, 1991: 89–94). Without exaggerating the role of the seminar that he led for more than 20 years, Levada clarifies (Ibid.: 91)

> I think we gathered all those who were trying to think independently, to be in touch with what was happening in the social sciences. There were also some people who came simply out of curiosity. [...] I look upon this skeptically [...], because nothing original or serious was created. And the whole circle of ideas—they were basically educational ideas in the field of sociology, culturology. I believe it was interesting not as a discovery but as a movement, as a way of social contact, of organization, as a source of inspiration. Viewed from the perspective of the present, there was a great deal of naivety as well, and insufficient educatedness, as nobody had really seriously trained our generation.

This form of existence of Soviet sociology in the 1970s and 1980s resembles Michal Illner's description of the state of Czechoslovak sociology after 1968 (2002: 406)

> Sociological research continued, but mostly outside the Academy and universities. No new concepts and thoughts incompatible with Marxist political orthodoxy could be publicly presented. Gradually, however, an informal sociology developed in the form of discussion groups, applied research team, etc., often under odd institutional roofs, where more open discussions could take place. Semi-legal sociology.

Formal preservation of ICSS or organizational restructurings of research units on the one hand, and on the other hand, institutional destruction of the community of those researchers who continued to be guided by scientific criteria

---

20   As Levada calls them in an interview conducted on May 18, 2000 in Moscow (personal archive).

in their professional activity; transference and harboring of sociologists in institutions with non-sociological fields of study and semi-concealed intellectual exchange in the framework of seminars; control over science—including sociology—by scientific 'agents' of the party apparatus and intellectual life in the half-forbidden, half-permitted zones of social organization of the totalitarian state—these are the two faces of the institutional mimicry in which Soviet sociology would reside until the beginning of Gorbachev's perestroika.

9.3   Atypical Cases: Bulgarian and Hungarian Sociology

Post-1968 Bulgarian and Hungarian sociologies represent atypical cases of institutional mimicry as compared with the other national sociologies of the countries under study, as well as with the preceding cycles of institutional expansion and mimicry.

At first glance, after the critical year 1968, the development of sociology in these two countries did not pass through any serious crisis situations and continued its institutional growth. A successful breakthrough was made in education. The first university programs in sociology were begun in 1972 at Budapest University (ELTE/Eötvös Loránd University) and in 1976 at Sofia University. The research activity which was a condition and guarantee for the first institutional expansion now extended its scope. In Hungary, research on social structure and social inequalities continued to be done by different institutional teams (Zsuzsa Ferge and Rudolf Andorka in the Central Office of Statistics, Tamás Kolosi in the Institute for Social Sciences of the Communist Party, István Kemény and Iván Szelényi at the Institute of Sociology, Hungarian Academy of Sciences); rapid development began in the fields of sociology of education (Ferge), urban sociology (Szelényi), and industrial sociology (Héthy, Makó). The state invested considerable financial resources in sociological research (Becskehazi, Kuczi, 1994; Némedi, Róbert, 2002; Némedi, 2010).

The situation was similar in Bulgaria. Here, sociologists succeeded not only in convincing the party-state leadership, headed invariably since 1956 by Todor Zhivkov, of the social importance of sociology, but to penetrate the high levels of the party hierarchy as counselors, secretaries of the party's Central Committee, heads of cabinets and departments.[21] This ensured them financial

---

21   Niko Yahiel—head of the Department of Sociology of Science and Technological Progress at the Institute of Sociology of BAS (1968–1989), editor in chief of the journal *Sotziologicheski problemi/Sociological Problems* (1979–1983)—was an associate in chief at

comfort, a comparative degree of protection for their professional occupation, and the possibility to resolve tensions more or less favorably to themselves in cases when the findings of social surveys were not to the liking of the people in power. Sociology's whole institutional, academic, and extra-academic structure in the country (the Institute of Sociology at BAS, the Center for Sociological Research on Youth,[22] the Labour Institute, the Trade Union Institute, the publication units at the ministries and administrations)[23] expanded its research activity.

Moreover, Bulgarian sociologists managed to win credit among the international sociological community. In September 1970, the Seventh World Congress of ISA was held in Varna, Bulgaria, despite the crisis in international relations after the military aggression against the Prague Spring and the Czechoslovak Sociological Association's initial boycott in objection to Bulgaria's hosting the event. The then president of ISA, the Polish sociologist Jan Szczepański, displayed remarkable diplomatic talent, professional responsibility,

---

the CC of BCP (1949–1988). Stoyan Mihailov—deputy director of the Institute of Sociology at the time of its foundation in 1968, and its director (1973–1976)—was deputy director and director of the Department of Propaganda and Agitation at CC of BCP (1973–1978) and secretary on ideological affairs at CC of BCP (1978–1988). Velichko Dobriyanov—director of the Institute of Sociology (1976–1986), editor in chief of the journal *Sotziologicheski problemi/Sociological Problems* (1974–1978)—was deputy head of the Department of Science and Education at CC of BCP (1970). Mincho Semov—the founder and first director of the Center for Sociological Studies at the Central Committee of the Communist Youth Union (1968–1972), the initiator of the creation of the specialty of political science at Sofia University/SU (1985–1986), rector of SU (1985–1989)—was an associate of the CC of BCP (1977–1982). Lyuben Nikolov—founder and head of the Department of Sociology at Sofia University (1976–1991), was an adviser to the Secretary of CC of BCP responsible for ideology (1973–1983); after this secretary lost his position, Nikolov was advisor at the cabinet of the President of the State Council. Mincho Draganov—head of the Department of Social Psychology at the Institute of Sociology of BAS (1972–1994) and editor in chief of *Sotziologicheski problemi/Sociological Problems* (1987–1994)—was an associate at the cabinet of one of the secretaries of the CC of BCP during the 1980s. Chavdar Kyuranov—head of the Department of Sociology of Work at the Institute of Sociology of BAS—had been an adviser at the State Council (specifically, at the Council on Human Resources) in the 1970s and in the late 1970s became part of the team of advisers to Alexander Lilov, CC of BCP Secretary on ideological affairs. In that same period, this team included Ivan Stefanov, senior research fellow at the Institute of Sociology of BAS (1970–1983).

22   See footnote 26 in Part 2.8.

23   An almost complete list of the sociological units created in a number of institutions and public organizations after 1963 in Sofia is given in Vasilev et al. (1990: 48).

and civic courage in resolving the problem. In a letter of 7 May 1969 to Josef Solař, president of the Czechoslovak Sociological Association, Szczepański wrote (*Russian Sociology of the 1960s...*, 1999: 612)

> After the political events of August 1968, proposals arrived at the Executive Committee of ISA regarding the transference of the congress to another country. However, the Committee upholds its view that these events in no way change the goals of the organization. For many, these events were a heavy and painful blow. But we do not believe that these events, as well as other cases of political turmoil, such as the current wars in Vietnam, the Near East, Nigeria, should change the fundamental goals of ISA. For us, the duty of sociologists consists not in deepening the differences ensuing from the contradictions between separate countries, but in the search for means of increasing intellectual rapprochement of scholars of all states, regardless of the differences of their political regimes. [...] our association may contribute to the creation of a 'world' sociology and a theory of a planetary human society if it stands by the principle of connections and cooperation between sociologists from all continents, countries, political organizations, from all types of economies and cultures.

The tension was overcome[24] and the congress took place with the participation of 3,201 sociologists from 49 countries on five continents (Africa, North and South America, Asia, Europe) of which 1,596 participants were from 'capitalist countries', 1,466 from 'socialist' countries, and 139 from developing countries. Czechoslovakia had 131 participants (Mihailov, 2003: 69–70; *Transactions of the Seventh World Congress of Sociology*, 1973: 173–292).

Setting aside the ideological confrontation and political utilization of the congress, typical of those times, and the present-day opposed assessments of the events,[25] the Seventh Congress of ISA was the first great 'face-to-face'

---

24   The documents published in *Russian Sociology of the 1960s* show that besides the Executive Committee of ISA, institutions and individuals who took part in resolving the conflict were the Congress's Bulgarian Organization Committee headed by Zhivko Oshavkov, the president of the Soviet Sociological Association Gennady Osipov, the Soviet Academy of Sciences, and the CC of CPSU (1999: 610–613).

25   While the assessment by Bulgarian sociologists who had taken part in preparing and organizing the Congress is entirely positive (Mihailov, 2003, 2010), sociologists from Eastern Europe (Jerzy Szacki in an interview conducted on 23 March 2000, Warsaw, personal archive) and the West (Birnbaum, 1993) describe it as a "circus".

meeting of East and West on the territory of a Communist country. Sociologists from the Communist bloc countries were able to hear their Western colleagues among whom were some authoritative figures and names gaining world renown, such as Daniel Bell, Daniel Bertaux, Peter Blau, Luc Boltanski, Raymond Boudon, Pierre Bourdieu, Theodore Caplow, Fernando Henrique Cardoso, Robert Castel, Manuel Castells, Paul-Henry Chombart de Lauwe, Terry Clark, Lewis A. Coser, Michel Crozier, Monique De Saint-Martin, Joffre Dumazedier, Claude Durand, Shmuel Eisenstadt, Norbert Elias, Amitai Etzioni, Franco Ferrarotti, John Goldthorpe, Alex Inkeles, Claude Javeau, Raymond Ledrut, Seymour Lipset, Helena Lopata-Znaniecki, Thomas Luckmann, Alberto Martinelli, Robert Merton, Helga Nowotny, Talcott Parsons, Tamotsu Shibutani, Neil Smelser, Jean Stoetzel, Alain Touraine, Immanuel Wallerstein. Most of the Western sociologists there were meeting for the first time with real researchers from Eastern Europe, not scientific propagandists, and were acquiring their first direct, though limited, experience of 'socialist' reality. Were this the only benefit of the Congress amid the continuing Cold War, sociology would still prove to profit by it in the short and long term. We may suppose that this event had an influence, however slowly exerted and mediated, on the mutual knowledge of the two politically divided worlds.

Let us return to the national contexts of sociology in Hungary and Bulgaria in the period 1968–1980. The fact that the discipline was continuing to develop does not mean it was spared political blows. As in the other countries, such blows fell primarily on individual researchers—the institutions in which they worked were preserved, though with some minor restructurings in some cases. In addition to receiving party penalties, some of the Hungarian philosophers and sociologists who had criticized the Warsaw Pact intervention in Czechoslovakia were forced to leave the country (Ágnes Heller, Ferenc Fehér). Others (András Hegedüs) were obliged to leave their positions of leadership in the scientific institutions. Over the years, people were periodically accused on political grounds (István Kemény in 1973, who emigrated to France in 1977) or expelled from the country (György Márkus, and other members of Lukács's Budapest School in 1973, Iván Szelényi in 1976).

In the memory of Bulgarian intellectuals, two philosophers, Assen Ignatow and Zhelyo Zhelev,[26] are emblematic of the Bulgarian Communist Party's repression on science. The punishments administered to these individuals at

---

26   Assen Ignatow, an assistant of formal logic at Sofia University (su), was accused of revisionism for a sociological article he had published in Austria, advancing the thesis regarding the growing importance of technocracy staff, dismissed from su, and forbidden to teach and publish. Having gone to attend a scientific conference in Brussels in 1972,

different times of Bulgaria's political history, indicate the constant ideological vigilance of the Communist regime, but also show there was no more intense mass-scale repression on the Bulgarian intelligentsia after the political purges of the late 1940s and early 1950s. Political pressure was constant but dispersed; it fell effectively on a separate person but it had a potential 'disciplining' effect on the whole professional community and thus effectively eliminated the possibility for collective resistance.

The development of sociology in Bulgaria and Hungary in the 1970s permits us to capture the specific particularities of the System. Under János Kádár's liberal regime and Todor Zhivkov's avoidance of repressive excesses, the structural principles of totalitarian power were maintained but their forms were softened or their scope of action was periodically reduced. In this situation, there becomes distinct the specific atmosphere of 'playing with the System', typical of the Communist countries after the historical failure of the Czechoslovak attempt at democratization of socialism, and after the small, day-to-day failures of attempted action against the shortcomings of the System. The declarative respect for principles and their actual bypassing in concrete behavior represented two parallel worlds under Communism which ensured its long duration until the time when the second of these worlds openly declared that it wanted to "live within the truth" (Havel). The contents of this ambiguity of social reality and the way in which sociologists overcame it in their publications and research activity will be discussed in Part Three. Here, we would like to consider the specific mode of scientific communication devised in response to, and as an expression of, this ambiguity by the sociological communities in the separate countries during the decade following the Prague Spring. The intentional avoidance of discussions within the discipline (for instance, between Marxists and non-Marxists in Poland, or between different research groups on social stratification in Hungary) was one of the characteristic features of the scientific atmosphere in the 1970s, as often pointed out by the interviewed sociologists

---

he remained in Belgium and then settled in Germany, where he worked until his death in 2003. Zhelyo Zhelev, a PhD student at the Department of Dialectical and Historical Materialism at the Philosophy Faculty of SU (1961–1964), was expelled from BCP in 1965 for his criticism of Lenin's definition of matter presented in his doctoral dissertation. After that, he was dismissed from SU and banished from Sofia. In 1967, he completed his book *The Totalitarian State* published in 1982 under the title *Fascism*. New punishments followed, and he was dismissed from the Institute of Culture (1975–1982). He was one of the founders of the Club for Support of Glasnost and Restructuring (November 1988), leader of the democratic opposition, and President of Bulgaria from 1 August 1990 to 22 January 1997.

who were contemporaries of this period (Zsuzsa Ferge, Dénes Némedi, Tamás Kolosi, Ladislav Macháček, Edmund Mokrzycki), and in publications (Becskehazi, Kuczi, 1994; Némedi, Róbert, 2002; Némedi, 2010). Whether motivated by an instinct for self-preservation, by professional solidarity, or by clear awareness of the relationships between sociology and power, the result was the same.

We did not agree with one another, we had different theoretical frameworks, but under the conditions of this dictatorship, it was practically impossible to carry on scientific discussions because every debate would at once degenerate into political reports. (interview with Zsuzsa Ferge conducted on 28 March 2001, Budapest, personal archive)

Sociologists avoided academic criticism of each other's work because they did not want any dissension in the intellectual ranks to be exploited by the authorities for political ends. (Becskehazi, Kuczi, 1994: 49)

The prevailing mode of behavior was to avoid the conflict between Marxists and non-Marxists. Both sides were trying to go away [...] because the prestige was on the side of non-Marxists, and the power was on the side of Marxists. And since those Marxists in the country—but genuine scholars, they wanted to stay genuine scholars, wanted to become even more genuine scholars and wanted to become friends to those who were not Party members—they avoided conflict ... (interview with Edmund Mokrzycki conducted on 23 March 2000, Warsaw, personal archive)

After Wiatr's attack against Malewski in the end of the 1950s, and Schaff's against Nowak in the early 1960s,[27] there were no debates between Marxists and non-Marxists. The inclination of non-Marxists was to let the Marxists handle the phraseology. It was not our duty to intervene. Doing so, we might burn our fingers. [...] In general, sociologists did not emphasize that there was a Marxist and non-Marxist sociology, they coexisted

---

27   This refers to the criticism against the article "Empirical Interpretation of Historical Materialism" by the non-Marxist Andrzej Malewski published in *Studia Filozoficzne* in 1957 in which the author subjected the validity of certain Marxist formulations to empirical verification. The main argument of the Marxist Jerzy Wiatr was that Marxism is an integral system, hence it is not correct to take separate phrases or make separate verifications with regard to it. The second debate initiated by Adam Schaff was aimed against the so-called "survey mania" which he assessed to be a research trend marked by idealism and subjectivism, the exponent of which, in his view, was Stefan Nowak.

without giving it a name. We did not say there were two camps, because that was a bit dangerous, we did not want to wake up the evil spirits. (interview with Jakub Karpiński conducted on 25–26 March 2000, Warsaw, personal archive)

Defined as a "gentleman's agreement" (Kolosi, quoted interview), "unwritten pact" (Szacki, 1998), an "acceptance game" (Petrusek, 1992), "negative solidarity" (Bad, 1986), this mode of existence of sociology clearly shows the behavior aspect of institutional mimicry. In assuming a behavior that does not question the principles of the institutional structure, sociologists provided themselves the material conditions to work and safeguard their occupation from political utilization. This mimetic behavior did not cross the permitted lines of the system. However, compromise came at a price: scientific dialogue was blocked within and between institutions. Still, there was an alternative—dialogue was transferred to the semi-official zone of "seminar science".

9.4   Intermediate Recapitulation

For the second time in post-war history, with the conservative turnabout in Communist governance, East European sociology entered a cycle of institutional mimicry. Unlike the first such cycle (1949–1956) which had been preceded by relatively weak sociological activity and took place amid complete political rejection, social de-legitimation, and institutional absence, of sociology, the second cycle came at a time when, in all the countries in question, the discipline had achieved a relatively complete institutional structure, intensive research activity, a community of sociologists identifying themselves as such, and regular academic publications. No doubt, this new institutional milieu would prove a determining factor for different forms of professional self-defense of sociologists. The types of pressure exerted by the political regime would continue to determine the force of the institutional blow and the drama of the experience undergone by the sociological community. That is why, amid the already constructed institutional environment of sociology, destabilized as it was by political intrusion and renewed ideological control, sociologists would develop two basic organizational forms of professional self-preservation.

First, sociologists continued to work within the official institutional framework with tacit acceptance of its structures, of the socio-political *status quo* that maintained, and of the theoretical Marxist profile that characterized it. Some of them, however, consciously distanced themselves, without making it salient, from the professional model of ideologized knowledge and Communist party commitment imposed by this framework, and concentrated their efforts on the production of knowledge in accordance with world standards of science. Thus, through their work these sociologists created that "grey zone" Miloslav Petrusek refers to, in which people consciously committed "moral and scientific, specialized dishonesty" against the institutional structures of their own discipline (1992: 11).

Second, sociologists applied their acquired professional experience outside the institutions authorized to carry out research and educational activity in the discipline. This category of activity includes: what Antoni Sułek defines as "oral sociology" in Poland; the similar in form theoretical seminars in the Soviet Union which gained ground as early as the 1960s as a sort of "parallel science" shaping free-thinking and informed researchers, even if it did not create unique cognitive products; the nascent underground press; the surveys that Czech sociologists succeeded in conducting after losing their jobs and finding employment in new non-sociological institutions. Similar to the first organizational form, this type of sociological activity was also marked by respect for the norms of scientific truth.

As in "any long-played game with vague and undefined rules" (Petrusek), there were undesirable results here: compromises regarding the content of research, shying away from public debate (to the extent there was such at all), and avoidance of initiating such debate. It is also important to note that these organizational forms of sociological practice existed in two different—even diametrically opposite by their degree of political freedom and ideological tolerance—contexts. If in the period under consideration (the 1970s included) Poland was the country with the broadest range of admissible differences, the area in which non-conformism could go unpunished was the most limited in the Soviet Union and Czechoslovakia[28] in the decade after the Prague Spring.

---

28   One of the strongest testimonies of the critical situation in Czechoslovakia arising from "normalization" was Charter 77—a civic manifesto against the Czechoslovak state's violating of democratic rights and liberties, despite having signed the International Pact on Civil and Political Rights and the International Pact on Economic, Social, and Cultural Rights in 1968, and having ratified the Concluding Act of the Conference on Security and Co-operation in Europe (Helsinki, 1975). Charter 77 was published on 1 January 1977, together with the first 242 signatures of people supporting the declaration. The sentencing of ten of the Charter's most active supporters, including the three spokesmen Jan Patočka, Václav Havel, and Jiří Hájek, to prison terms of up to five years in October 1979, was a particularly vivid demonstration of the absence of political freedom, and the persecution of dissidents, in Czechoslovakia. Although it did not provoke a mass opposition movement, nearly 40,000 citizens had signed it before the downfall of the regime in November.

There was also a third type of sociological activity which, like the first type, continued to be practiced within the existing institutional structure of the discipline, but unlike the first, remained bound to the ideologically decreed image of communist society and to the doctrine of the superiority of socialism over capitalism as a formation. In this case, it was mostly a political, not an institutional mimicry of sociology.

That is why only the first two organizational forms preserved the professional experience of sociologists and permitted them to carry it into the dynamically changing context of the 1980s.

CHAPTER 10

Institutional Expansion II: 1980–1989

In a comparative chronological perspective, the 1980s was the most heterogeneous and diverse period of developments in sociology in Communist Europe. The development, recognition of, and reaction to, the economic, political and social crisis through organized social actions and political programs went at a different pace in separate countries, so that, within the same period of time, the situation was different in each country. Hence, the sociological communities in the countries faced identical problems related to the scientific study of the society of 'real socialism', but at more or less different times.

For the Communist countries of Central and Eastern Europe, the 1980s began with a political crisis coming, once again, from Poland. A wave of strikes—a customary phenomenon for Poland—began in protest against the government decision on 1 July 1980 to raise meat prices, and then evolved into a wide social crisis after the V. I. Lenin Shipyard in Gdansk went on strike on 14 August 1980. These strikes proved to be the trigger for what would ultimately happen at the end of that decade—the historically unprecedented transition from 'communism' to 'capitalism'[1]. The founding of the independent and self-governing trade union Solidarity, and its official recognition by the ruling Communist party represented a breakthrough in the principles of the system of 'socialist' society. This was the first, and irreversible, step from Communist party monopoly to political pluralism. Hence, the whole decade of the 1980s passed, on the one hand, in attempts by the political leaderships in all East European Communist countries to patch this breach, and on the other hand, in efforts on the part of civic associations and initiatives to widen it even more.

The political, economic and social metamorphoses of the Communist system were accelerated by another emblematic event of that decade: the election of Mikhail Gorbachev as head of the Politburo of the Communist Party of the Soviet Union in March 1985. His policy of perestroika gave impetus to the processes

---

1　Of course, this process includes the transition from totalitarian to democratic organization of society. Unlike the West European countries that had passed through totalitarian or authoritarian forms of government before and after World War II (Italy, Germany, Spain, Portugal) but had preserved the principles of capitalist economy, the countries of Central and Eastern Europe had been building a 'new' society according to the Soviet model of state socialism. That is why, after 1989, the very type of society was radically transformed, not just some separate spheres in it. In this sense, the transformation here was systemic.

© KONINKLIJKE BRILL NV, LEIDEN, 2018 | DOI 10.1163/9789004333635_012

of transformation of the political foundations of 'socialist' society, forcing the leaders of the national Communist parties to take measures for reforming the system in their own countries, and stimulating the kind of authentic political activity among citizens that had been periodically quelled, or long forgotten, in the separate countries. Depending on the respective political constellation, the dexterity with which party leaders managed the crisis, and the force and scale of social resistance to the ruling party, the countries all came to the same result—the end of one epoch and the beginning of another—but in different ways, at a different tempo and with different repercussions along the way.

Sociology at that time was in its second cycle of institutional mimicry and functioned in the form of official, unofficial, and semi-official structures within, and outside, the sphere of sociology. However, in the context of deepening economic crisis, and political crisis managed with variable success, we will look at what was happening in the institutional development of sociology. What were the developments of these forms of exercising the profession of sociologist? Were there any organizational innovations in sociological activity, and if so, what were the new aspects, and how did they arise? Not least importantly, can we say there were some common trends of development in the 1980s, inasmuch as the national sociologies in the region entered the new decade with different institutional heritages from the 1970s whose moral and psychological burden had engendered fissures of varying depth in the national sociological communities, with different configurations of relations between sociologists within vs. those outside the politically recognized zone of professional occupation, and with different relations between the various groups of sociologists and the still monolithic political nomenklatura.

Given the different points of development reached by the countries, and their specific national contexts, it would be logical to expect that their differences, if not increase, would at least not diminish. But a comparison of histories shows a similarity in the ways and means by which sociologists not only defended and upheld their professional vocation but even expanded the presence of their discipline during the whole 1980s. Institutional mimicry was replaced with a *new cycle of institutional expansion*. It would be more precise to say that the forms of professional experience in the second cycle of mimicry evolved in such a way that the zones of legal vs. non-legal presence, and legitimate vs. non-legitimate absence of sociology expanded the size and influence of those zones to the extent where they came to mutually interpenetrate and mutually publicize each other. In this way, a general, strongly differentiated space of sociology was formed which defines the discipline's development in the 1980s as a second cycle of institutional expansion. How did this happen, and why?

10.1   It Started With Polish Sociology

The Sixth Congress of the Polish Sociological Association held in Łódź from 9 to 12 September 1981—at the same time as the First Congress of Solidarity—not only took stock for the first time of sociology's performance in studying Polish society before and after the appearance of the trade union, but also became the first public stage of the divisions and oppositions in the institutional attachments of Polish sociologists which had started since the mid-1970s. History was moving at an accelerated pace after the appearance of the independent trade union, and illuminated and enhanced these differences. Nevertheless, changes had taken place.

The major dividing line—that between official and unofficial levels of sociological activity—was still there, but moves from one to the other were no longer concealed. Sociologists engaged in the building of the trade union Solidarity freely declared their stance and were among the first to analyze societal changes using the method of participant observation. At the congress's first plenary session, Jadwiga Staniszkis, a teacher at Warsaw University, defined and explained what was taking place in the country as an "institutional revolution". By contrast, a number of important figures of the sociological establishment who were in favor with the "old regime" (Mink, 1982) were not present at the congress. This withdrawal from the most representative stage of the national sociological community was a clear indication of the change that had taken place in the ratio between different institutional authorities in Polish sociology.

The shifting of layers, and opening and closing of specific spaces of professional sociological activity increased after martial law was declared (13 December 1981– 22 July 1983), and the trends continued to the end of the 1980s. The extraordinary situation during the rule of Wojciech Jaruzelski engendered two new dividing lines—between public vs. concealed sociological information, and between legal vs. non-legal structures producing sociological information, creating at the same time possibilities of slipping from one side to the other of this line of demarcation. Before martial law was imposed, the clandestine press (*Krytyca*, *21*, *Vacat*, *Polityka Polska*, *Przyjaciel Nauk*, etc.) often succeeded in publishing *legal* surveys *conducted by state institutions, but kept in secret.* After 13 December 1981, this press published *illegal* surveys conducted by social research centers of Solidarity (OBS) *which were not authorized by the state.* Based on the archives of the trade union's Coordinating Bureau in Paris, Marek Tabin presented 12 non-legal surveys, the earliest of which had been conducted at the end of December 1981, and the latest, in 1985. The survey questions ranged from Poles' attitude to martial law and to the acts of the now illegal trade union, to the economic situation of households and the attitudes towards the legal system, the Church, the police, and the current political events. The aim of these surveys was "to gather objective information about the problems that were being distorted and falsified by the official media" (Tabin, 1987: 72). In terms of production of sociological knowledge, the question of drawing a contrast between truth and lies in Polish society at that time was

> a question of opposing knowledge about society obtained by scientific means and thanks to the efforts of researchers, and science (?) about the society constructed for the purpose of propaganda and, in one way or another, deceitful (Ibid.: 71).

At the same time, the official authorities created their own Center for Social Opinion Research (CBOS) by one of the first decrees of military legislation in 1982, and appointed the sociologist-colonel S. Kwiatkowski as its director.

Although their material and technological facilities were not equal, the legal and non-legal survey centers faced the same difficulties in terms of access to respondents and the respondents' trust in the survey interviewers (Tabin, 1987; Sułek, 1992). The dividing line between official and illegal sociology was overcome in the mid-1980s when illegal surveys were practically discontinued and institutionalized state-endorsed sociology succeeded in proving its professional quality. While in 1987, Georges Mink, a Polish sociologist working in France, believed that "in the joint march of Polish society and Polish sociologists toward their respective emancipations, sociology profited more by the social changes than society did by the activities of sociologists" (Mink, 1987: 17), around ten years after the collapse of Communism, the Polish sociologists who had been involved in the events on the side of Solidarity assessed as rather positive the contribution of sociologists to the political solution of social problems.

In any case, the 1980s were a time of visible polarization between the *sociology of the establishment* and *opposition sociology*; the beginning of this polarization can be seen as far back as the time following the March events of 1968 when the university teachers' and researchers' support for the student protests did not go without political repression and administrative punishments. Though few in number, the texts written in jail and left unpublished—according to Karpiński's account—were among the first signs of the 'two-faced Janus' of sociology. This contrast would continue to exist in the 1970s as a contrast between publishable sociology and "oral" sociology, "in other words, [as] what was officially tolerated and what constituted opposition" (Kubiak, 1996: 22).

As paradoxical as it may seem, these two faces of Polish sociology, divided in terms of location and organization, and with different social presence in Polish society, first came out into the open simultaneously after the imposition of martial law in December 1981. During the following decade, however contrasting they may have been in content and political orientation, they displayed the same feature of Polish sociology—"its engagement in public affairs" (Kubiak, 1996: 28).[2] The divided Polish sociology was united with regard to the deontological model of the sociological profession, and the question was not whether the sociologist was committed to values, but to which values he/she dedicated his/her professional capacity. An even more important question arises here: how did the political-moral choice of the sociologist influence the production of sociological knowledge, and did sociologists reflect on their choice, and on the effect of that choice on scientific results?

Considering how specific its development was in the 1980s, are we justified in including the Polish case in the common history of sociology of the countries under study? Here we refer once again to one of the principles underlying our analysis: in certain periods of history, a given national sociology is able to concentrate within itself the ongoing transformations so intensely that its development makes salient certain trends that are hard to capture in the development of the other sociologies sharing similar histories.

10.2   "Seedbeds of Experience" in Other National Sociologies

The common denominator in the 1980s between Polish sociology and the national sociologies of the other countries under study was the existence of "seedbeds of experience/foyers d'expérience" as Foucault would have called them. Some of these were newly formed, others were continuing from earlier periods. During the last decade of Communism, the discussion clubs formed in the framework of Solidarity, the seminars, the new illegal journals were forms of sociological activity in which knowledge and norms of behavior, social and individual time were not only connected but in harmony. By the experience acquired through these forms, sociologists were able to fit in the trends of the

---

2   Hieronim Kubiak explains "the principle of engagement" in the social sciences in Poland as rooted in the country's past history. Since the disappearance of the Polish state in the late 18th century, passing through Communism, and until the transition to democracy and a market economy at the end of the 20th and beginning of the 21st century, social expectations in the country had always been for "the social sciences and their practitioners to provide not only knowledge, but also instruments for changing reality" (Kubiak, 1996: 28).

times and shifted the horizon of possible reflection on society beyond the politically imposed limits.

These "seedbeds of experience" had various institutional homes. They arose within academic space or outside it; as part of the official institutions of knowledge, or outside them, or at their margins; their participants might belong simultaneously to the official intellectual circles and to the newly created groups. The various structures of Solidarity (discussion clubs, social survey centers, etc.) engaged the larger part of those Polish sociologists who were employed in state institutions of sociology—without leaving their jobs as teachers or researchers, they worked as experts for the independent trade union. When Solidarity became illegal under martial law, they continued to work for it, now illegally, without stopping their work in academic institutes, in universities or in the Polish Sociological Association. In the internal dynamics of the scientific community, certain processes are visible that indirectly confirm the sustainability and force of their professional ethos. On the one hand, the collaborators of the secret police in research institutes and departments "were able to report what we were doing, but they were not able to stop our activities" (interview with Edmund Wnuk-Lipiński conducted on 30 March 2000, Warsaw, personal archive). On the other hand, a considerable number of sociologists who were Communist Party members left the party after the appearance of Solidarity, and especially after martial law was imposed. But even those who remained in the establishment, "knew that to be a sociologist in Poland means that you have to comply with standards of the occupational milieu, and you have to comply with certain basic universal standards of performing sociology" (Ibid.).

The "seedbeds of experience" in other countries emerged in a different social-political context than the Polish one, and had the following particularities. Some of these focal points carried on into the 1980s the organizational forms and thematic orientations of the discussion clubs, the study circles and groups that we saw emerging in the late 1960s and first half of the 1970s. In addition to the already discussed seminars in the Soviet Union, there had been seminars in Czechoslovakia as well which continued to be active in the 1980s. They were created by sociologists in non-academic institutions and formations in which they had found jobs after being obliged to leave the academic circles during the "normalization" (Spalová, 2006). There were also seminars conducted in the framework of official institutional structures, on topics that formally corresponded to the socially important priorities as defined by the government. The seminar on "Socialist Way of Life as a Social Reality" headed by Ivo Možný in Brno, and the collections published under the same ideologically correct title are recognized by Czech sociologists as places where high quality sociology was done amid a strongly ideological environment (Možný, 2004; Petrusek, 1992; Spalová, 2006).

In the 1980s, however, new seminars were established by a new generation of sociologists formed in the 1970s by the generation that had paved the way for sociology in the reforming Communist society of the 1960s. These were informal communication groups that, without entering into institutional conflict with the official structures, served as a space for thinking outside the dominant canon and as reference groups for some of the young researchers at that time. On the basis of two examples taken from different social-political contexts, we will try to show not so much the common and the specific in these forms of activity but their multifaceted character. The Marx seminar in Bulgaria and the "Islands of Positive Deviation" in Slovakia were established and existed at the same time under contrasting conditions of weakened (Bulgaria) and of sustained (Slovakia) political pressure. The Marx seminar—created in the framework of Sofia University in 1979—was as much an element of the restructuring scientific space in Bulgarian social science and the humanities,[3] as it was a unique form of scientific communication in its conception and its practice. Both fitting within, and deviating from, the official canon of discourse (it was designated "Marx" seminar, not "Marxist-Leninist"), the seminar functioned as[4]

> a united dialogue subject [consisting of] people of the same mind who do not think the same things but know how to think together (Deyan Deyanov: 281);
> a field for dialogue between different authors and intellectual traditions (Andrey Bundzhulov: 297);
> a possibility for constructing a niche of free scientific movement of which there was a shortage at that time (Kolyo Koev: 261);
> a scientific program (Andrey Raychev: 309);
> an attempt to understand a different Marx. Not the official, not the one of Marxist-Leninist ideology (Liliana Deyanova: 322).

---

3 Active concurrently with the Marx seminar were: the informal group Synthesis from which the future postmodernists of Bulgarian science and culture would come, the Philosophical Salon around Nikolay Vasilev, a teacher of philosophy at Sofia University, the group of medievalist philosophers, the Plato Seminar, the Wittgenstein Seminar, the seminar "Face and Mask" (*Sociology in Bulgaria...*, 2012; *Piron*, 2013–2014).

4 All quotations are from *Sociology in Bulgaria through the Eyes of the Generations* (*Interviews with Bulgarian Sociologists*) (2012).

The Seminar was an informal group that had publicly established itself as an institution in the highly emblematic Auditorium 65 of Sofia University; it declared it was disbanding in 1986, having regularly held throughout the whole time of its existence public conferences (1983, 1984, 1986) that we may today rightly define as interdisciplinary.[5] Even though it included some "political actionists" (in the words of Deyan Deyanov), the seminar remained entirely within the field of science and did not cross the line to political engagement.

The "Islands of Positive Deviation" had a different basis and form of existence. This phenomenon was so named for the first time in September 1989 by three sociologists—Martin Buturá, Vladimír Krivý, and Soňa Szomolányi. They thereby designated certain isolated forms of alternative thinking that had been visible since the mid-1980s, the participants in which did not accept the politically imposed norms and strove for a change of the existing conditions. People from different social strata and of different institutional positions took part in them, but the trend could become a force only if there were "a network of communication among individual islands to create 'the appearance of an entire archipelago of positive deviations'" (Doellinger, 2013: 185). The accelerated political activity in the autumn of 1989 contributed to the rapid materialization of this idea by the Slovak civic and political movement *Public Against Violence* established in Bratislava in November 1989. The three sociologists mentioned above were co-founders and active members of this movement.

While the former, Bulgarian case was a scientific forum with no political pretensions, the latter may be said to have been an emerging public forum nourished by sociological reflection. In both cases, however, there was an expansion of sociology into the territory of science and society; this expansion represented an attempt to maintain the independence of science from politics (the Marx seminar) or an attempt for sociology to assert itself as a resource for changing the system by "the powerless", according to Havel's expression (the "Islands of Positive Deviation"). Regardless of their differing goals and history, the two formats of sociological activity were the product of *autonomous activity* of sociologists themselves, carried out within the System but independently of the principle, then in effect, that any collective action must be coordinated with, and approved by, the ruling party. Things certainly had changed in the 1980s, including the generations. However, the fact that under the system's unchanging principles of functioning sociologists were creating new organizational forms that did not seek the government's political 'blessing', but turned

---

5   The representatives of the informal scientific groups mentioned in footnote 3 gathered at these conferences.

their back to the system or even openly attacked it, testifies to the attainment of a degree of autonomy of sociological action (in its cognitive and social form) that was appearing for the first time in the discipline's history under the Communist regime.

Apart from that, the underground press which had appeared in the 1970s continued to publish sociological analyses. A new addition to this press was the entirely sociological journal *Sociologický obzor/Sociological Horizon* published from 1987 to 1989 as samizdat in Czechoslovakia. Similar to the Polish sociologists at the time of martial law (according to Wnuk-Lipiński's account), in this journal, Miloslav Petrusek, Josef Alan and others published articles under pseudonyms (Spalová, 2006), a fact that clearly indicated the continuing danger of state repression. Samizdat publications offered translations of works by Alexis de Tocqueville, Raymond Aron, Roger Scruton, David J. Levy, Freidrich von Hayek, Karl Popper, Jacques Monod which were first published in Czech thanks to the secret financial support of Lord Dahrendorf (Spalová, 2006). "For the first time, Weber was published extensively in a clandestine way in Poland" (interview with Edmund Wnuk-Lipiński conducted on 30 March 2000, Warsaw, personal archive).

10.3   Official Institutional Structures, Old and New, and Their Strategies

The increasingly dynamic social and political developments of the 1980s led to changes of the institutional strategies of the official actors in the field of sociology. This was done against the background of continuing vacillation between restrictive and permissive action on the part of the holder of a monopoly on political power. Despite Gorbachev's course of reforms, each national Communist party (increasingly differentiated internally) attempted until the very end of its rule to contain the tension between the empowered and the powerless through typical measures against criticism of the system. Punishments and threats became more severe and grew in direct proportion to the spread of civic movements in the separate countries in the late 1980s.[6] There

---

6   The year 1988 marked the start of intense civic mobilization. Some important events in that year were the manifestation in Hungary celebrating the anniversary of the Revolution of 1848, and proclaiming slogans demanding freedom of the press, freedom of association, and free elections (March); manifestations in Prague marking the 20th anniversary of the Prague Spring (August), or in honor of the 70th anniversary of the creation of the Czechoslovak state (October), or in honor of the 40th anniversary of the UN General Declaration of Human Rights, a manifestation that took place during the visit of French president François

was a visible increase of engagement of sociologists in these movements, and this trend had repercussions on the way official sociological institutions functioned. Both the ruling authorities and the sociological community had long ceased to be homogenous, having undergone intellectual, institutional and professional differentiation over the years; hence, only by concretely retracing the dynamics of the relationships between the different strata within these groups can we depict the complex and ambivalent change of balance in favor of the extended field for free action. Here we will confine ourselves to showing the main political and scientific strategies applied in the 1980s; though their effect on possibilities for developing sociology in the already existing institutions were felt at different times, they ultimately led to a common result. *On the threshold of the Great Change, sociologists were constituted as an autonomous, internally differentiated subject within the scientific and social-political space in each country.*

While in Poland the imposing of martial law did not affect the content of university curricula or the teaching staff (according to accounts of the interviewed sociologists), in Slovakia there was a temporary stop of enrolment in the discipline of sociology in the period 1980–1982 (Pasiak, Machacek, 1994; Macháček, 2004; Eva Laiferová in interview conducted on 29 November 2000, Bratislava, personal archive). Sociologists have accounted for these two contrary situations in university education in sociology by different political authorities' strategies implemented in the universities through the party-controlled scientific nomenklatura. In Poland, Wojciech Jaruzelski's government was busy pacifying relations with the workers and the trade union Solidarity, while in Slovakia, where the Department of sociology at the University of Bratislava had never been closed and had continued to train students in sociology after 1968 (unlike the respective departments in Prague and Brno), the number of sociology graduates by the start of the 1980s had begun to seem menacingly large to the rulers.[7] The official argument, of course, was a declining interest in sociology.

In the Soviet Union, only toward the end of the perestroika was sociology finally separated from philosophy as a recognized autonomous scientific

---

Mitterrand (December); the creation of Democratic Forum comprising over 350 Hungarian intellectuals, writers, artists, and sociologists (September); the establishment of several civic associations in Bulgaria including the independent trade union Podkrepa/Support (11 February 1988) and the Club for Support of Glasnost and Perestroika (3 November 1988).

7   According to Macháček, "ten years after the normalization, there were about 300 sociology graduates in Slovakia, working in enterprises, institutes, as journalists (interview with Ladislav Macháček conducted on 30 November 2000, Bratislava, personal archive).

discipline in universities; and only then did the training of specialists in a full university cycle begin.

The institutional trends in the research sphere were different from those in education. In 1982, a new Center for Public Opinion Research (CBOS) was created in Poland as a result of a government concept and in response to the government's need for objective information about public attitudes in a society that was highly polarized following the imposition of martial law. In 1985, in Hungary, TÁRKI, the first private social research institute in the Communist bloc was created. According to Tamás Kolosi, its founder, it worked "with absolutely Western sociological standards" (interview conducted on 28 March 2001, Budapest, personal archive). From the start, the institute joined the international network for comparative studies, becoming a member of the International Social Survey Project (ISSP); in 1986, it also became a member of the International Federation of Data Organizations and of the European Organization of Data Archives.

In 1988, after nearly twenty years of organizational eclipse and periodical administrative purges in the second half of the 1960s, the Institute for Concrete Social Studies, one of the most liberal institutes in the Soviet Academy, returned to the stage of science under the straightforward name Institute of Sociology (Mandeville, 1989; Mespoulet, 2007b).

At first glance, these institution-related events in the three countries seem so different that it might be thought methodologically incorrect to juxtapose them. But if we put the institutional history of each national sociology in the general perspective of institutional cycles, we would see these as similar processes of upholding professionalism in sociology and asserting the discipline's social role, a trend that passed through contradictory modes of interaction with the political power. Having been created as an instrument of the ruling power, CBOS proved its competence and was recognized even by the opponents of the government, because its researchers were formed according to professional principles and not in the political tradition. In Hungary—the most economically liberal Communist country—the breakthrough made by sociologists was as logical as it was opportunistic. Between the intensely politicized community of Polish sociologists on the one hand and Hungarian sociologists on the other hand whose accumulated research practice and social experience in the 1970s had made them choose professionalism over political activism, the Western partners in applied comparative research (on social stratification, inequalities, lifestyle patterns and attitudes) were inclined to work with the latter.

The institutional odyssey of academic sociologists in Moscow which ended favorably for them in 1988 confirms once again that a government tends to endorse already existing activity. The specific feature here is that, under totalitarian governance, the holder of power has unlimited authority to legitimate or not legitimate a certain activity as a social fact, thereby switching the places of cause and effect in the course of the emergence of that fact. In all cases, the Communist party was the initial source of the decision, even if the latter were generated by on-going processes. The Institute of Sociology at the Soviet Academy of Sciences was not the product of the June 1988 decree of the Central Committee of the CPSU "On Increasing the Role of Marxist-Leninist Sociology in Solving the Crucial Problems of Soviet Society" (*Sotziologicheskie issledovaniya*/*Sociological Studies*, 1988), but the Central Committee's decree came in response to the degree of development and presence of sociologists in the life of Soviet society over the preceding two decades.

In fact, during the last decade of the Communist regimes, the field on which the conditions for the increasingly autonomous development of sociology were established and upheld was that of the official public sociological institutions themselves. Their professionalization was the most potent "weapon" in the ongoing battle against the agents of power (party apparatchiks, science functionaries, secret service agents). Unlike the preceding cycles of the first institutional expansion (1956–1968) and the second institutional mimicry (1968–1980), in the 1980s sociology had established and expanded its professional guild to the point where the battle was transferred to sociology's own ground. The opened archives of the state security services, the archives of the Central Committees of Communist parties, the history of sociological institutions as told by their members all confirm the continuance of familiar practice, such as sending 'political observers', secret service agents, ideologically loyal scholars to international and national forums, and to every scientific event at home or abroad; the practice of coordinating the list of participants in ISA congresses with the science departments of the Central Committees of the Communist parties; censorship and self-censorship; intrusion in the editorial policy of journals, etc. Though neither the structure of power nor its principles of functioning had changed, their effects on the professional field of sociology and on sociologists were no longer the same. Even in the case of the Conferences of Editors of Philosophical and Sociological Journals of the Socialist Countries—held since the mid-1970s to transmit the political directives of Moscow to scientists in the satellite countries—the political functions of the conferences was gradually replaced with scientific purposes (Tilkidjiev in *Sociology in Bulgaria...*, 2012: 238–239, 242).

Moreover, the correlation of forces had changed. *Sociologists had created zones of autonomy within their institutionalized activity.* Polish sociologists had negotiated the right to publish works in print runs of up to 100 copies without going through the state censorship procedures; this practically deprived ideological control of its power (a fact pointed out by all the interviewed Polish sociologists; see also Kwasniewicz, 1994: 38). This right combined with the technological possibilities of photocopying enabled the unchecked dissemination of non-censored sociological literature.

Starting from its first 1984 issue, the Bulgarian academic journal *Sotziologicheski problemi/Sociological Problems* introduced the rubric "Sociological Texts with Critical Commentary" at the initiative of Lyuben Nikolov, then editor in chief of the journal. This rubric not only replaced the previous rubric "Critique of Bourgeois Sociology" but also changed the intellectual standards of dialogue with the sociological tradition. There was also a change in the International Varna Sociological School (IVSS) created in May 1980 in Prague at the Conference of Vice Presidents of the Academies of Sciences of the Socialist Countries.[8] Though the School was certainly a product of coordinated party policy of the Communist countries, in the course of its work it deviated from the initial conception of its creators and from the envisaged forms of control. While the School's first sessions only accepted sociologists from the 'fraternal socialist countries', they gradually came to include Western participants as well. This trend which took place in the context of Gorbachev's detente policy toward the West and the policy's corresponding ideological discourse is reflected in the amendments to the Statutes of the School adopted at its session in September 1989 in Seč (Czechoslovakia). As a matter of fact, this proved to be the last session. Here are some examples illustrating the trend (my italics):

Statutes of the IVSS adopted on 5 June 1980, amended on 5 June 1981	Statutes of the IVSS adopted in September 1989
4. Aims and goals of IVSS:	4. Aims and goals of IVSS:
4.1. To further the development of *Marxist-Leninist* sociological theory, history of sociology, and methodology of social studies.	4.1. To further the development of *sociological science in its quality of* theory, history of sociology, methodology and methodic of empirical surveys.
4.2. To promote the modern defining and effective discussion of *topical problems of the development of socialist society*, the study in a sociological perspective of *significant social processes in the capitalist and developing countries.*	4.2. To promote the modern defining and effective *sociological study of the processes of renewal of socialist society.*

8   See footnote 4 in Introduction.

4.4. To promote the expansion and improvement *of cooperation between sociologists and sociological institutes of the socialist countries* and the expansion and deepening of cooperation with *the progressive sociologists from non-social-ist countries.*

4.6. To contribute to *popularizing Marxist-Leninist sociology.*

8. Members of the School may be so-ciological institutes and organizations of *the other socialist countries* [besides the founders and already admitted members—my note].

21.1. Keynote readers at the scientific sessions may only be sociologists who have sent the final texts of their reports at least six months prior to the consecu-tive session.

22.2. The scientific council and the commission confirmed by it accept only reports and lectures corresponding to the tasks and theme of the session, and of high scientific quality.

4.4. To promote the expansion and improvement *of international sociological cooperation.*

4.6. To contribute to *popularizing sociological knowledge and socio-logical culture in society.*

8. The Scientific Council may de-cide to accept as members of the School sociological institutes and organizations of *other countries.*

Revoked

Revoked

Ironically, the School's new Statutes adopted in September 1989 would never be applied. In laying down the changes, the Statutes, as every such document, aimed to organize the 'future' in accordance with the present. But though the present might carry the seeds and signs of incipient change, the future is open and cannot be laid down in a document. The accelerated political develop-ments in the autumn of 1989 in East Europe, preceded by a hot political sum-mer in Poland and Hungary,[9] proved this point. Unexpectedly both for the East

---

9 Appointed as a result of Solidarity's decisive victory at the elections for the Sejm and the Senate in the summer of 1989, the Catholic thinker Tadeusz Mazowiecki became the first non-Communist prime minister in the country's history as a Communist state (and the first in the whole Soviet Bloc) and formed the first non-Communist government. These events, a sure sign of the start of the transition, had been preceded in Poland by a strong wave of

and the West, the Communist regimes fell one after the other, and Communism as a social-political system ceased to exist on the international scene. The Great Change began, and with it, the inevitable reassessments of the past. But the stakes involved in the ongoing present, as well as new knowledge of the past would change those reassessments in the following years.

10.4   Intermediate Recapitulation

Within the historical chronology of the separate national sociologies, the second cycle of institutional expansion had different starting points but a common finishing point in time; it was carried out at a different pace in different countries but had the same final result. In the 1980s, institutional expansion was evidenced not only by a growing number of forms of sociological activity, the proliferation of sociological surveys, the creation of new institutes *but also* by the specific combination of old and new institutional forms, the interweaving of scientific, political and civic commitments, the transition from clandestine to open activity, and the rivalry between the sociology of the establishment and alternative sociology. Unlike the first cycle of institutional expansion (1956–1968), where there was a closer correspondence between the political intentions of party reformers and the scientific goals of the upholders of cognitive and institutional emancipation of sociology, during the second institutional expansion there were deeper divisions both between sociology and the ruling power, and within the sociological community itself. These differences were evident in the specific modes of institutional expansion in these two chronological periods in the countries under Communism.

First, the most distinctive feature of the first institutional expansion had been the formation of institutions permitted and endorsed by the Communist party-state. In the second institutional expansion, the generators of institutional forms of sociological activity were likewise the state, but also the researchers themselves and civic movements. While in the late 1950s and the

---

strikes in the spring and summer of 1988 which led to the first in Eastern Europe round table between government and opposition. Although the distinction between government and opposition was not so clear in Hungary, a round table was organized there as well (starting on 13 June 1989) which decided parliamentary elections would be held in the spring of 1990. On 27 June 1989, the barbed wire fence at the Hungarian-Austrian border was symbolically cut by the foreign ministers of the two countries. With this initiative, the Hungarian foreign minister Gyula Horn made the first breach in the 'Iron Curtain'; many East Germans would soon pass through it to reach West Germany.

first half of the 1960s the legal and legitimate forms of sociology were built by official institutions, in the 1980s sociology had many faces—it inherited from previous decades, and expanded the official, semi-official, and illegal places of doing sociology and of applying sociological knowledge.

Secondly, while in the first period of institutional expansion the sociologists themselves sought to obtain from the Communist party a political umbrella for their work (indicative of this were the strategies, common to all the countries, of building national sociological associations whose first presidents—in most cases formal ones—were scholars enjoying the trust of the ruling power), in the second institutional expansion, they rejected such protection and even turned their own institutions into places of opposition to the ruling power (for instance, the Polish Sociological Association in the period of martial law, or the Institute of Sociology at the Bulgarian Academy of Sciences, which hosted the unofficial meetings of the Club for Support of Glasnost and Perestroika).

Thirdly, over a period of twenty years, the relatively homogenous sociological communities in all these countries changed into a heterogeneous professional category whose component groups established and developed different places of scientific and social (political and civic) practice. Besides the factor of growing specialization—an element of the professionalization and generational renewal that normally accompanies the development of any professional community—the differentiation here additionally followed the lines of adopted strategies in response to the attitudes of the Communist parties. While in the 1960s, the national sociological communities integrated themselves within the System by their united public support for the project of a new society and a generally shared commitment to the production of scientific knowledge that would further the project's implementation, the 1980s witnessed internal divisions in the profession based on sociologists' differing attitude towards the System and towards relations with the ruling party. Depending on the concrete political situation and the specific modes of construction of each national sociological community, sociologists had different forms of professional and civic behavior expressing their attitude toward the society of "crisis socialism", and there were different combinations of these forms. The professionalism of sociologists was combined with their open political engagement—for the cause of Solidarity in the case of Poland, and in support of Gorbachev's perestroika in the case of the Soviet Union, or in social activism among the Czechs and Slovaks in the late 1980s. An alternative form was scientific independence and a distancing from politics adopted by a large portion of Hungarian sociologists, or the consciously adopted apolitical attitude among the young generation in Bulgarian sociology at that time. Some Czech and Slovak sociologists continued to practice their profession outside sociological, official political, and informal civic institutions. The attempts to humanize the System from within continued on the part of sociologists serving as buffers between the political and academic fields.

These different forms of sociology's scientific and social presence freely chosen by the sociologists themselves indicate at least two changes had taken place in the discipline's development. On the eve of the Great Change, the practice of sociology in the European Communist countries was *institutionally diverse in terms of scientific vocation and civic engagement.* The formal and informal borderlines between the permitted and the prohibited had changed, and sociology could now study society without political restraints.

CHAPTER 11

Institutional Cycles: General Conclusion

In the post-war Communist countries of Central and Eastern Europe, the sociological practice began with a paradox. In order to provide for its own need to pursue the scientific study of society, the discipline sought cognitive and institutional legitimation in an environment where every sphere of activity was subordinated to the principles deriving from a supreme source—the Communist party-state and its Marxist-Leninist ideology. Insofar as these two pillars of Communist society—regardless of the evolution of social processes—remained unchanged, the development of sociology throughout the whole Communist history of the region consisted in the effort to resolve this paradox. Theoretically, in the institutional aspect, this would mean winning the right of autonomy for its own institutions with respect to other sciences, and building an institutional environment that protects the specific principles and norms of the discipline. The great challenge was how to do this in a sustained context of Marxist-Leninist science institutionalized and controlled by the Communist party-state. In view of the fact that the holder of a monopoly on state power was omnipresent through its institution-organs (the local party organizations, funding, etc.) and its institution-mechanisms (criteria for assessment, for professional growth, etc.), was it possible for institutional autonomy to guarantee the independent development of the discipline and its scientific project? Could sociology's educational, research, and publication institutions provide a defense for the scientific ethos against the Marxism-Leninism that had become a state ideology? Was there any place at all for a zone of freedom from the total institutional pressure of the System?

It is precisely the concept of institutional cycles used here that enables us to reveal sociology's complex and ambivalent connection with the System, and also to identify the internal paradoxes of the institutional construction of the discipline. The pattern of institutional cycles designates the specific spatial-temporal modes of scientific and social presence of sociology resulting from the specific constellation of sociology-power relationships in historically distant periods of time; hence, its use as an analytical instrument has highlighted the following particularities in the development of sociology between the establishment and the collapse of Communist regimes in the countries under study.

Regardless of the cycles in which it happened to be (those of institutional reanimation, institutional mimicry, or institutional expansion), sociology

© KONINKLIJKE BRILL NV, LEIDEN, 2018 | DOI 10.1163/9789004333635_013

existed and developed not only in relation to, despite, in harmony, or in conflict with the institutional model of society. Its development was also a constant conquest and defense of territory from the holder of a monopoly of power and from the dominant Marxist-Leninist paradigm for the world. The people who took part in these efforts through the years were the initiators and 'builders' of the discipline's first post-war research and educational institutions, as well as their followers and disciples. While the former were, for the most part, novices in sociology coming from various other fields (philosophy, economics, history, law, philology) and received their training through the first lecture courses on sociology organized at the study centers of the Communist parties (?!), the following generations moved toward specialization in the discipline and entered the profession as graduates in sociology. Apart from that, in every generation, sociology is done simultaneously by ordinary members of the scientific institutions and by people marginal to the institutions, by scientists dressed in power and by scientific functionaries, by sociologists intermediating between the academic and the political spheres, by conformist sociologists and by rebel sociologists. These different categories are certainly to be seen everywhere and in all historical circumstances. What is particular about East European sociology under the Communist regimes is the *evident discrepancy between position and role*, a discrepancy that might either safeguard or put at risk the development of sociology. Each national sociology had its defenders and guardians in the person of scholars engaged in political power, but also its executioners in the person of high-ranking sociologist administrators in the scientific organizations. There were sociologists in each country who kept their high positions in the scientific institutions by offering their political self-criticism, while others preferred professional rather than institutional recognition; this professional status would seem paradoxical, were it not for the fact that upward professional mobility in a Communist society was linked to the requirement of loyalty to the party. Beyond the concrete cases, these paradoxes are also important in the ethical aspect, as they indicate that *moral integrity and alternative ways of acting are possible even in a totalitarian-type society*.

Sociology in course of institutionalization and sociology that has become an institution in the broad sense (as a regulating authority) was practiced in various organizational forms—both legitimate and illegal, official and nonofficial, formal and informal, within sociological institutions and outside them. In fact, these forms existed throughout the whole post-war history of sociology in the countries under study—though with varying relative importance for the discipline's autonomous development. Depending on the concrete political situation and on the configuration of relations within the sociological community, the official institutions could prove to be factors of defense and protection or of pressure and repression. Outside the administrative shelter provided by an officially recognized institution, unofficial (illegal, semi-legal, informal) modes of sociological activity continued to exist quietly or in the shade of non-sociological institutions, preserving and reproducing their professional experience. In some cases, they put that experience at the service of social and political causes opposed to the status quo, in other cases, they hedged themselves from politics, confining themselves to scientific communication. Jointly, simultaneously, in various combinations or separately, passing from one cycle into another, at times overlapping in the person of the sociologists working in them, all these forms served to multiply the places for doing sociology, ramified sociological activity and units, and built a communication network. What kind of sociology was done and what knowledge was produced by these forms during the various cycles of the discipline's institutional development is another matter. The modalities of cognitive construction of East European sociology during the various institutional cycles of its development will be the topic of analysis in the next part of this book.

PART 3

*Disciplinary Construction of Sociology:
Processes and Modalities*

∵

CHAPTER 12

A New Context, a New Object of Research: What Kind of Sociology?

The establishing of Communism as a social-political system in Central and Eastern Europe after World War II placed world sociology in an unprecedented situation. Alongside the conditions of economic freedom and political pluralism which had accompanied the development of this discipline from the middle of the 19th century and until that moment, the sociology now had one more economic, political and ideological context made uniform and controlled by the Communist party-state. The bourgeois, capitalist, democratic society that had engendered sociology, and had also constituted its disciplinary object of study, now entered into competition with the Communist society that was being built.[1] The quickly begun Cold War divided humankind into two geopolitical worlds whose borderline crossed all spheres of society, including the sociological study of society. However, both worlds continued to exist in the framework of modernity, although they were implementing two diametrically opposed projects for the rational, i.e. scientific, organization of society.

How did this new situation in human history affect the cognitive development of sociology? Without seeking, or being able to make, a global assessment of this process, we formulate the question thus in order to outline the perspective of our analysis. Only if viewed as part of a common, collective disciplinary history can sociology in the countries of Central and East Europe in the time of Communist regimes shed light on the ways the discipline was constructed *amid a new context and with a new research object*. On the other hand, only if viewed in their respective historical specificities can the different national sociologies in the Communist countries display the theoretical, methodological, epistemological, deontological challenges they faced in upholding their identity as a scientific discipline. In other words, as regards the cognitive development of the discipline, the case of 'sociology under conditions of a Communist

---

1   The establishment of Communist regimes in the CEE countries that fell under the Soviet zone of influence after World War II changed the ratio of forces and turned Communism into an international system. Apart from this, as early as the 1920s, democratic bourgeois society had been put to the test by totalitarian or authoritarian regimes, which ended with the end of the war in the case of Italy and Germany, but continued until the 1970s in Portugal and Spain.

social order' permits studying the problems that the social-historical distinctions in the discipline's context and object raise for sociology's construction as a scientific and social practice.

In its practice, Communism demonstrates several persistent characteristics that invariably recur regardless of the evolution of its political tasks and of the strategies corresponding to those tasks, and regardless of the national particularities in the implementation of the project for a new society. The building of a communist society is based on the hegemony of a single political subject and of that subject's vision of the world. The political monopolism of the Communist party ensures its *total domination over society* and permits it to assert itself as the supreme source of legitimacy in all spheres of society. Having been institutionalized as a state ideology, Marxism-Leninism became the ideological foundation of political power, and hence, a dominant reference framework for all activities in society. Such a structuring of society influenced the functioning of that society.

First, the autonomy of, and distinction between the separate social spheres were effaced. The principles and norms specific to each sphere were absorbed by the axioms of the new society's political project as ideologically rationalized by the Communist party. The project for a new, more just and equitable social order was taken over by a single political agent and 'embodied' in structures and images that, in their mutual determination, buttressed the monopoly position of the Communist party and its vision of social development. On the one hand, the public image of the society constructed by the various social agents living in that society, was so invariable, so much the same in all cases, that the 'material' reality underlying it began to appear fully identical with the image. On the other hand, all spheres of society were constructed to correspond to the project's imperatives, so that they became 'impregnated' with the vision of a society moving unswervingly towards the supreme goal—communism. A kind of symbiosis was established between the politically organized social reality, the ideologically legitimated and legally sanctioned social project,[2] and the different forms of presentation (political, ideological, scientific, cultural, etc.) and implementation (economic, educational, legislative, state-organizational) of that project.

Secondly, a kind of monotheism of values was established in society. Presenting communist values as superior and universal, and declaring itself their bearer and guarantor, the Communist party did not tolerate the existence of any other values. Moreover, holding a monopoly on power, the party imposed

---

2   We recall that the building of communism as a goal of social development was made law in
    each country by the constitutions adopted after the final takeover of power by the Commu-
    nist parties at the end of the 1940s.

the axiological model of communism as the only measure of any action or thought, and thereby destroyed the possibility for the existence of any value 'polytheism' or of any groups that might carry values other than the communist ones. The cause of this lies in the nature of the supreme values (truth, good, beauty). As Perelman and Olbrechts-Tyteca have indicated, these "are universal only to the extent that they are undefined" (1970: 101–102). When specified in their content, they only reflect "the aspirations of specific groups" united around them (Ibid.). Thus, the Communist regime's value reductionism creates a 'screen society' homogenous with respect both to values and to stratification which screens the study of the actual functioning society.

Thirdly, the society dominated by the Communist party-state functions without allowing any teleological, pragmatic or interpretative alternative. The project traces a single goal of social development (communism); moreover, it points to a single matrix for attaining it (the leadership of the Communist party) and a single theoretical 'algorithm' for justifying and explaining everything that happens on the road to that goal (Marxism-Leninism as the most general theory of society and methodology for the study of society).

Given the lack of distinction in Communist society between various social orders (political, economic, religious, public vs. private) and between various spheres of activity, is there any place here for sociology as an autonomous activity producing objective and valid knowledge of society? Under conditions of institutionalized value monotheism where all people follow the same model of values and, moreover, have no possibility to openly uphold a different one, what kind of society would sociology be studying? Can society be studied scientifically when there is only one permissible paradigm of the world whose political endorsement and institutionalization excludes the possibility of alternative conceptions and models? Can sociology legitimate itself as a scientific cognition of society given that ideology operates as the supreme source of legitimacy in Communist society?

Considering the logic underlying the historical development of sociology *before* the appearance of totalitarian-type societies (Communist or non-Communist), these questions should be answered negatively. Sociology is made possible as a product and condition for the development of modern democratic society; hence, it seems its existence would be impossible in an undemocratic society. However, when these questions are considered in the light of the cognitive development of sociology as a scientific project, and viewed through sociology's own theoretical principles and achievements, they problematize the very construction of the discipline in case a new project appears, one different from the heritage of the Enlightenment, but also 'a fully modern project' intending to organize society in a scientific way (Ionin, 2007; Michéa, 2007).

   Like any scientific discipline, sociology is simultaneously "a social space for legitimation of knowledge" and "a logical space for the construction of argumentations" (Berthelot, 1996: 100). The analysis of the post-war institutional history of sociology in European Communist countries through the prism of institutional cycles (Part 2) revealed the specific logic of the discipline's organizational emancipation and development in societies constructed and dominated by the Communist party-state. In those societies, the stake involved in the autonomous development of sociology is not only to achieve organizational institutionalization of the discipline, but to safeguard the places where sociology is done (official, semi-official, and unofficial) from the intrusion of the holder of power, and to protect professional standards in the course of the various political- moral choices that sociologists must make. In Part 3, the emphasis will be on the sphere of analytical activity of sociology in East European Communist countries; here, sociology is viewed *as a scientific study of an essentially new type of society which serves as both context and object of the disciplinary practice.* How did sociology conceptually grasp, and theoretically explain a society that, in the course of more than four decades, was building the Communist societal project under conditions that evolved from the total domination of the holder of political power to a situation of varying in strength and intensity forms of political and ideological control, still under the invariable monopoly of Marxism-Leninism as the horizon of ideas and values? What is the sociological knowledge produced under such circumstances, what is the cognitive value of that knowledge, and its social significance?

   Two assumptions derived from the traditions of sociology of knowledge and sociology of science underlie the rethinking of the cognitive construction of sociology in societies marked by various forms of totalitarian governance. On the one hand, sociologists undergo the influence of ideas and values predominant in the political, ideological, and cultural space of the society which they are studying, and in whose context they are practicing their discipline (Barbano, 1961). On the other hand, they produce the type of knowledge that can be assimilated by the respective social environment (Merton, Wolfe, 1995). This double "cultural and social incorporation of sociological knowledge" as "a part of what that science is" (Merton, Wolfe, 1995) in fact provides the theoretical possibility for achieving sociological knowledge, regardless of whether the context is favorable or not to the production of this knowledge.

   The study of the cognitive development of sociology in European Communist countries reveals how this theoretical possibility was realized in practice, and shows the deontological, epistemological and theoretical-methodological challenges that faced its disciplinary construction. Using the idea of cycles in the institutional development of sociology as a frame of reference, the analysis of the cognitive legitimation of the discipline and of its processes of knowledge production proceeds in three main directions. First is presented the deontological model of 'Marxist-Leninist' science and its epistemological projections for the study of the new society. After that are analyzed the forms of sociological practice and the modalities of sociological knowledge under the conditions of the new epistemological deontology; here, we show the influence of this deontology on the thematic structure, way of problematization, and model of argumentation during the different institutional cycles. The concrete specifics of the modalities of disciplinary construction prove to be determined not so much by the cycles as by the organizational forms of sociological practice. While the organizational forms provide the conditions for production of a specific type of knowledge, the cycles amplify or weaken the effect of those conditions, hamper or are conducive to that effect. Finally, special attention is devoted to the ways and strategies by which sociologists defended day after day the scientific ethos of their discipline under the various social functions they assumed, or regardless of those functions. Unlike their colleagues in democratic, non-totalitarian societies, sociologists in the Communist countries not only worked at the borderline between different social fields—intellectual, political, cultural, industrial, etc. (Bourdieu, 1975; Boltanski, 1979), but acted in a context where the professional field might at any moment be taken over by the political field and subordinated to the goals and principles of the political and ideological rationalization of the world.

Thus, by identifying and analyzing the cognitive modalities of sociological practice during the different institutional cycles, we expand the grounds for arguing that the *formation of zones of relative institutional and cognitive autonomy* was the most important condition for the possibility of sociology as a scientific discipline under conditions that were unfavorable to, or threatened, its own development as objective and verifiable knowledge of society. Viewing the cognitive development of sociology under Communist regimes in connection with its institutional development permits seeing how sociology sought, and found, and used possibilities for scientific activity; it permits identifying the mutual relations that existed between institution and production of sociological knowledge; identifying which institutions, and to what degree, permitted subversive research activity and achieved a breakthrough in the social-political context, or, to the contrary, imposed norms that positioned sociology to correspond to the general context; it permits ascertaining when deviations from the institutional program began and what their consequences were for the cognitive development of sociology.

CHAPTER 13

From a New Deontological to a New Epistemological Model of Social Science Cognition

Having fallen in the Soviet zone of influence after World War II, the countries of Central and Eastern Europe cut away from their past of bourgeois political regimes and capitalist economies and began the building of the new socialist order, modeled on the society that had already been in existence for 28 years in the Soviet Union. In the course of more than four decades, sociologists in these countries would study the new society, alternative to the capitalist one, would investigate the changes taking place in the course of its construction, and would provide information on the implementation of the large-scale program of socialism. Setting aside the question as to what type of society post-war East European sociology was situated in and studying, its social function appeared no different from the preceding traditional one. The mission of producing objectively valid, socially significant, and practically useful knowledge about society is something that characterizes the whole disciplinary history of sociology. In this sense, studying the new society and promoting its development by providing knowledge was a professional commitment of sociologists at that time. The questions we pose here concerns how this commitment was fulfilled under the new values orientation and against the background of society's new worldview; how sociologists fulfilled their professional vocation while being part not only of society, but of the ongoing historical time of society; how the ideas, ideals and values of the time nourished and modulated the scientific and social practice of sociology.

While the end of World War II marked a new start for all Europe and the whole world, for the countries of Central and Eastern Europe, it represented a political breakthrough that would soon assume the form of a new political model. The substitution of the pre-war and wartime undemocratic political regimes with coalition governments of the anti-fascist fronts opened the road to democratic governance[1] and nourished hopes for a better, more just and humane society. This general attitude of all East European nations was shared by

---

1 All historical studies have shown that until the end of the war democratic governance was almost non-existent in the countries of Central and Eastern Europe, with the exception of Poland (1918–1926), Hungary (October 1918-March 1919) and Czechoslovakia (the only democratic country before the war, but which was unable to oppose Nazi aggression).

© KONINKLIJKE BRILL NV, LEIDEN, 2018 | DOI 10.1163/9789004333635_015

sociologists as well. In their majority, the latter had leftist convictions and supported the social-political change; they undertook, in the framework of their profession, to work in support of this change. This description of the general post-war atmosphere in which sociology in these countries was placed is based on the lack of any contrary data and on the analysis of the ethos formed in Polish sociology immediately after the war. According to Jerzy Szacki (1998: 121),

> researchers, ideologically and scientifically moulded before the communists came to power, found themselves in a new political situation, whose nature and perspectives they were not yet able to appraise unequivocally. Moreover, the beliefs which most of them harbored, permeated with the faith in the need for a radical reconstruction of the Polish social world whose deficiencies sociology had been registering for decades, precluded any possibility of total refusal to participate in anything smelling of social revolution. Trusting in the practical utility of their knowledge, they believed that they were capable of influencing the ongoing changes in a positive way and that, without their scientific help, the changes would be left in the hands of amateurs.

Thus, Polish sociology started its post-war development "without revising its pre-war theoretical and methodological canon" (Ibid.: 118) and by applying knowledge "whose basic core was developed many years earlier, to new circumstances" (Ibid.: 120). In the practice of sociology, there was neither any "cognitive dissonance" nor any "basic value reorientation" (Szacki, 1993), inasmuch as the general feeling was that having been interrupted by the war, the development of sociology in its theoretical, methodological, and value orientations was being resumed.

As pointed out in Part 2.6, we refer to Polish sociology not in order to draw a general conclusion from a particular case regarding the post-war situation of sociology in all the countries under study. Being more advanced in cognitive and institutional terms than sociology in any other country in pre-war Central and Eastern Europe, Polish sociology made visible the fact that at this stage the new spirit of the times did not change the professional commitments of sociology. In the atmosphere of revived hopes for democracy, and amid the still continuing political pluralism, there was no conflict between the values of science (achieving valid and objective knowledge) and the other value orders (those related to a good, free, and just society). With the institutional revival of their activities, sociologists viewed the on-going social changes as a new object of research, and they mobilized their discipline's national tradition and theoretical-methodological heritage to study it. Sociology's vocation—firmly

established in history—to provide an objectively valid answer to the problems posed by social development continued to characterize the occupation
of sociologists, regardless of the various scales and tempos of the revival of the
discipline (due to the different degrees of pre-war institutional and cognitive
development of sociology in the various countries). However, when the dimensions of sociology's commitment began to be defined by factors external to the
professional sphere, then changes took place in the nature of this commitment
that presented challenges to the very production of sociological knowledge.
Here we argue that *changes in deontology lead to changes in the epistemology of
disciplinary practice*, and we stress the *mutual interweaving and metamorphoses of the scientific, political, and ethical imperatives when a single axiological
model is asserted in society.*

From the perspective of present-day researchers of the disciplinary past of
sociology in European Communist countries, we may easily relate the appearance of the new deontological model of sociological practice to the monopoly
on power established by the Communist parties in the late 1940s and to the
beginning Stalinization of social and political life. Here, we follow the methodological principle of irreducibility according to which the study of any historically defined stage in the development of a given discipline requires analyzing
the conditions of its emergence and waning; hence, we will discuss the process
of formation of a new value orientation in society and the establishment of a
new axiological model in science through the institutionalized state ideology
of Marxism and Communism.

What happened to these primal sources of the communist vision of the
world and its fundamental values when the self-declared carriers and guaran-
tors of this vision came to power?

After 1947–1948, an evident metamorphose took place in the publications
coming out in the scientific and mass press in all countries within the Soviet
zone of influence. The original ideas of the classics of Marxism (Marx, Engels,
and Lenin) started to be replaced with Stalin's interpretations of the classics.
The founding figures were present as an element of the argumentation only
insofar as their ideas were followed up, 'creatively' developed, and renewed in
their content by Stalin. The whole propaganda and style of scientific discourse
at that time presented Stalin as a "living classic of Marxism", a "creative genius
of Marxism", a master of the theory and practice of the Marxist-Leninist doctrine regarding the inevitable course of mankind from socialism to communism viewed as superior forms of social progress. No doubt, this propaganda
was both a product and an instrument of the "cult of personality" as a structural characteristic of society. Our focus here is on the impact of this trend for the
restructuring of the conceptual and value environment in the countries under

study. The Communist parties in these countries appropriated the project of 'people's democracy', and in implementing it, they took Stalin's version of socialism as an obligatory reference for understanding social processes but also as the sole source of the Marxist theoretical vision of the new society.

In the late 1940s and early 1950s, three texts coming from Moscow proved fundamental for the deontological, epistemological, and content-related construction of so-called Marxist-Leninist science[2] both in the Soviet Union and in its satellite countries. In chronological order, the first was a speech by Andrey Zhdanov, secretary of the Central Committee of the ACP(b),[3] entitled "The Situation and Tasks on the Philosophical Front" and given in June 1947 at a conference of Soviet philosophers; this was followed by Stalin's books *Marxism and Problems of Linguistics* (1950) and *Economic Problems of Socialism in USSR* (1951).

The discussion in 1947 was planned and conducted by decree of the CC of ACP(b), and headed by Zhdanov. The topic of the conference was the collective work *History of West European Philosophy* (1946) authored by a team headed by the philosopher G. F. Aleksandrov; the book had received a high state award and been recommended by the Ministry of Higher Education of USSR as a textbook in history of philosophy in the higher schools. Zhdanov's speech was not only an outright demonstration of party intervention in a sphere of scientific competence but also a blatant case of substituting the logic of historical development with a certain ideological vision of the world. Zhdanov asserted (cited from *Philosophska Misyl/Philosophical Thought*, 1947: 74)

> The scientific history of philosophy is the history of the birth, emergence and development of the scientific materialist worldview and its laws. Insofar as materialism grew and developed in struggle against idealist doctrines, the history of philosophy is also a history of materialism's fight with idealism.

---

2 In the expression 'Marxist-Leninist science' which referred to all scientific disciplines, the decisive element was the adjective which expresses the character, contents, goals and social role of scientific knowledge for all disciplines under the Communist regime. This adjective refers to knowledge based on dialectic materialism and the laws of historical progress leading to the inevitable future victory of communism. Due to the specificity of their objects of study, this politically sanctioned and socially institutionalized notion of science would have greater consequences for philosophy and the social and human sciences than for the natural sciences.

3 All-Union Communist Party (bolsheviks)—ACP(b)—was the name of the Communist Party of the Soviet Union until 1952.

This is why he defined Marxism as (Ibid.: 76)

> the beginning of a perfectly new period in the history of philosophy,
> when the latter became a scientific weapon in the hands of the proletar-
> ian masses fighting for their liberation from capitalism.

The subsequent discussions, Aleksandrov's self-criticism, and the articles published in the philosophical press of the other Communist countries about the
Soviet discussion and in the Soviet press about the tasks of philosophy were
all a public demonstration of the willingness of philosophers to accept a) the
party's political definition of their own field of study as 'Marxist-Leninist philosophy', meaning "*qualitatively* new, *qualitatively* different from all preceding
philosophies, having as its deepest foundation, criterion, and goal of cognition
the revolutionary and creative-constructive practice of the proletariat" (Pavlov, 1947: 111), and b) as proceeding from this definition, the new imperatives
and norms of cognitive activity which included the principles of 'partiinost'
[party-mindedness] in science, and of the "connection of morals, science, literature, philosophy, art, military ideology, etc. to politics".[4]

This view on Marxist-Leninist philosophy and its fundamental values was
methodologically buttressed by Stalin's formulations concerning the nature
of scientific knowledge (*Marxism and Problems of Linguistics*, 1950) and the
scientific laws of social development (*Economic Problems of Socialism in USSR*,
1951). While the former book explicitly formulates the political-ethical principles of scientific cognition (the connection of science to class-party principles,
the class and party character both of philosophy and of the particular sciences
and the arts, the class-party approach), the latter outlines the epistemological
principles of class-party cognition. The argumentation in both books leans on
Marx and Engels' theory of the proletariat's class struggle as the only road to
achieving the communist ideal—the supreme form of social progress. Outside
the class interests of the proletariat, there can be no objectively true knowledge of reality, such as would make possible its transformation according to

---

4   These principles were presented in the introductory article "Our Tasks" in the journal *Vopro-*
sui Philosophii/Questions of Philosophy (1948/2) in which Soviet philosophers described Zhdanov's speech as "an exceptionally important document" to which "they should constantly
turn" because "it gives the instructions of the Central Committee of […] the Party regarding
the character and direction of all […] philosophical science" (*Philosophska Misyl/Philosophi-*
cal Thought 1948/1: 3). The quotations are from the Bulgarian translation of the Soviet article immediately reprinted in the Bulgarian journal *Philosophska Misyl/Philosophical Thought*
(1948/1).

the social ideal; these class interests coincide with the the objective course of history and with the political aims of the Communist party which expresses and defends those interests.

Could such a political-ethical imperative fail to affect the epistemological requirements of scientific cognition? The impact is inevitable and almost direct, without intermediate transitions or links, due to the essentially activist principle on which Marxist theory is based but also because a single agent is identified as ensuring the connection between knowledge and its application.

Stalin's conception of the nature and action of economic laws under capitalism and socialism (1951) is a perfect example of methodological casuistry that reverses the epistemological vector of cognition, pointing it according to the teleological perspective of the political project. The ideas regarding development by leaps in nature and society, the forms of those leaps, the transitory nature of the law of value under socialism, the non-antagonistic nature of contradictions under socialism, the elimination of contradictions between city and village and between industry and agriculture—all these ideas are grounded by Stalin as objective laws that people can only (1952: 3)

> discover [...], become cognizant of, and by leaning on them, use in the interest of society, give a different direction to the destructive action of certain laws, limit the sphere of their action, open a wide space for other laws which break through; but they [people] cannot destroy or create new economic laws.

Given that the basic economic law of socialism is "the provision of maximum satisfaction of the constantly growing material and cultural needs of the whole society by means of the continuous growth and perfecting of socialist production based on the highest technology" (Stalin, 1952: 34); so the construction of socialist society is inevitably a materialization of this law.

Here, on the one hand, a society having little in common with real social life and economic practice is generated for political purposes; on the other hand, the logic of cognition is reversed. The effect of this procedure is to distort and block political action, the ideas underlying the project, and the forms of scientific cognition that rationalize the project. The holder of political power substitutes the actual functioning society with an ideological vision of society. Moreover, he turns that vision into a fetish, asserting it as the only reality, as the embodiment of objective truth, and thereby uses it as the ground of action, the aim of cognition, the criterion of truth, and the ideal in reference to which reality and cognition are assessed. At the epistemological level, the laws are not proven but presumed to be already discovered. The task of the particular sciences is to justify the existing practice by reference to the postulated regularities.

A new social imperative is addressed to Marxist-Leninist science: to prove the socially valid truth which means to reconfirm the ideologically projected reality endorsed by the holder of a monopoly on political power. Compared with the other sciences, this imperative proves to have the most serious consequences for sociology as the science of a society in which all actions—collective or individual—are guided and legitimated through the institutionalized social-political project. The problem for sociology under Communist regimes ensues not from the specific characteristic of the discipline's object of study,[5] but from the *specificity of the societal project institutionalized by the Communist party-state*, and from *the way the project functions*. Apart from that, the emergence and evolution of modern society has generally shown that it would be impossible without a certain idea of society that individuals and social groups strive to attain by mobilizing, organizing themselves, and opposing one another. A certain historically prevalent vision of society, politically sanctioned and institutionalized as an action program sets the framework of action and defines it as socially valid and admissible, so long as some new action program has not, in turn, taken shape and asserted itself. Democratic societies elaborate, modify, and amend their action programs through the work of multiple individual and collective actors. By contrast, the new society that the European Communist parties in power began to build had an action program that was predefined, without alternative and guaranteed by a single holder of political power. Not only was the goal of this program clearly defined, but the way to achieve that goal was traced in advance—there was only one possible future, and it was a bright one; the future and the efforts required to attain it were known beforehand, the roles of the social actors had been definitively assigned and where unchanging, the truth was postulated, and every action, knowledge,

---

5   This particular characteristic of society is perhaps one of the important premises of the link between politics and sociology, inasmuch as any societal project and sociology as a scientific project have society as their object. There is always a risk of mutual shifts, switches, displacements if the specific nature and principles of functioning of the two spheres of activity are violated. As Weber pointed out, in politics, there are norms, criteria of assessment, value orders, while in ontological terms, sociology has neither privileged perspectives for establishing a hierarchy of social life structures nor criteria of just and unjust, of good and evil with which to assess social phenomena. Any attempt on the part of sociology to pass judgments positions it in the role of politics and moves it away from its vocation of showing the conditions that make social action possible in a given socio-cultural context.

assessment was meant to confirm that truth as a guarantee for the historical longevity of the ideal, the idea and the project.

What does it mean to study a society that is not just to build a model, but should it embodies; a society in which the dominant social axiology not just permeates all spheres, but subordinates their specific professional ethics; a society in which what is politically defined as desirable becomes obligatory and universally significant?

The transition "from existence in theory to existence in reality", or the "deadly leap", as Pierre Bourdieu (1994: 27) calls it, *entails changes in the epistemological deontology of sociology*. How, why, and to what degree these changes are realized or not is one of the key issues of sociology under the Communist regimes; this is evident in the various modalities of disciplinary construction of this sociology. In a certain sense, the history of sociology in the European Communist countries is a history of the efforts to uphold the epistemological core of the discipline's scientific project, to uphold the way society is studied under prevailing preconditions for the replacement of sociological rationality by political or ideological rationality.

The study of the new society in the light of 'fundamental laws' deduced through an instrumental interpretation of the classics of Marxism (i.e., from the perspective of the practical goals of the ruling Communist party) amounts to merely establishing how well the ongoing processes match the prescribed laws, to pointing out errors made, to foreseeing possible deviations and overcoming them, rather than analyzing the society itself, much less assessing the validity of those laws.[6] Scientific and political rationalities overlap in their nature and purpose. Here, scientific reflection, similar to political reasoning, undertakes to point out the degree of correspondence between the socially real and the socially projected, instead of problematizing the implementation of the project in such a way as to provide knowledge that may be used for building new political and ideological programs.[7] The goal of both the political and the scientific form of rationalization of the world is to show that the new

---

6 That is why in the classical totalitarian phase of the Communist regimes (1948–1953), there were so many cases of criticism and self-criticism regarding both results in sectors of economic activity and research activity in philosophy and the social sciences.

7 In his large-scale study *L'idéologie ou l'origine des idées reçues*, Raymond Boudon (1986) presents a theoretical synthesis of key concepts of ideology, and reaches his own concept which he defines as a "limited" theory of ideology. Rejecting the radical contrasting of science vs. ideology typical of both Marxist and non-Marxist theoretical tradition, Boudon analyzes the "genetic" connection between ideas claiming to define the social order and guide political action, and their scientific justification.

society being built is the exact copy of the projected model, despite the deviations that might occur. There is a common algorithm for achieving the goal and a common source of that algorithm pointed out by the holder of power—the ruling party's version of Marxist theory which underlies the communist ideal.[8] All that needs to be done to achieve the ideal practically and cognitively is to proceed from the basic principles of historical materialism, to apply the dialectical materialist method, and to follow the envisaged roads to communist society. There is no tension between social reality and theory, because the truth about society is foretold through knowledge of the basic contradictions, the dependencies, the mechanisms of integration, and the impelling conflicts which irreversibly lead to "the advancing homogenization of socialist society", "the elimination of all antagonistic and non-antagonistic contradictions", "the growth of public goods", etc. The criteria for the validity and credibility of the produced knowledge are found in 'Marxism-Leninism' which has been politically recognized as the doctrine that provides "the most enlightened", "the most incisive", and "the most coherent" reading of today's and tomorrow's society. Hence, argumentation becomes exegetic; it is based on the authority of Marx, Engels, Lenin, Stalin, and their followers in each country; it consists in interpreting their formulations. Science is meant to study, and assist the achievement of a society to which the future inevitably belongs, a society projected in the communist ideal. Hence, science is assigned a specific social function—to make a *critical scientific assessment imbued with communist class-based party-mindedness*. The communist judgment is both an element of the ethics of argumentation and the criterion of scientific quality.

How and why is an element external to science integrated into scientific argumentation? Moreover, this element is considered a necessary condition for truth and validity of the produced knowledge. What are the reasons for the axiological and argumentative isomorphism between the political-ideological and the scientific forms of rationalization of society at that time?

Let us return to the logic of the Marxist cognitive process. The fact that Marx's theory was turned into the foundation both of communist political pragmatics and of Marxist-Leninist science requires an explanation. Setting aside the various historical contexts of the creation and use of Marx's theory, we may focus our attention on those elements of the theory that make it

---

8   Though self-evident, this specification of the version of Marxism in question is important because this is the kind of Marxism that would be turned into a state ideology by the Communist party-state and would serve as the general fund of ideals and as the axiological measure for any reflection (political, scientific or pertaining to everyday life) and any action during the whole time of the Communist regimes in Europe.

applicable under different social-political conditions. Or conversely, by examining these conditions only in their epistemological dimension, as a context of discovery and a context of legitimatization of a given theory, we may identify the points of intersection of the construction and the functioning of that theory.

The theoretical system Marx used to explicate 19th century capitalism takes as privileged the viewpoint of the proletariat presented as the most truthful one, because it derives from the specific social position of the proletariat. This position is such that it defines the proletariat as the only factor of the fulfillment of the future free development of man and society, and hence makes the particular viewpoint of the proletariat potentially universal. What Marx criticized in the whole philosophy of his time—namely the generalization of a particular viewpoint—was not overcome in his own analytic approach. Having taken the position of the working class which he theoretically discovers to be the embodiment of new social relations, Marx constantly seeks to tie the explanation of capitalist society to the goal of its transformation. In this effort, he will be successfully aided by the existing "indissoluble link between the theoretical and value judgment" (Goldmann, 1970: 165), a link which flows from Marx's conception of human activity as essentially practical activity to which knowledge is internally proper, and also from his epistemological approach which seeks the truth in a symbiosis of "cognition-action" achieved through the gradual deconstruction of the aggregate of social relations in which the acting subject enters. In other words, the privileged position of the working class's purposes which become a perspective of thought and action is the axis around which Marx's whole conceptual system turns. From here on, it is not important whether the system will be used as an instrument for legitimating political action or as a means for scientific explanation, insofar as the system's social teleology remains the deepest foundation and the measure both of political and of cognitive action. Of course, we must also take into consideration the structural constraints that Marxism-Leninism—when institutionalized by the ruling Communist parties—exerts on scientific activity. However, these constraints do not exclude the ideology-generating elements in Marx's own theory, which invariably appear when scientific analysis is assigned the intentions and functions of political reflection and action.

So, without being specific to sociology, Marxist-Leninist deontological epistemology was formed in the first years of the establishment of the Communist regimes. At this stage, Marxist-Leninist philosophy played a central cognitive role for all sciences, not only for sociology; it impelled the rethinking of their tasks and functions in the new social-political reality, and was also the 'legislator' of the scientific deontology corresponding to this reality. Sociology found itself in an institutional timelessness, or in the first cycle of institutional mimicry discussed in Part 2. This alone was a sufficient reason why it could not take part in formulating new epistemological rules. Yet those new rules would continue to determine sociology's cognitive development during the following institutional cycles as well. It could be hypothetically expected that, given the two constant factors—the Communist party-state as the one giving the order for and controlling sociological research, and Marxism-Leninism as the dominant theoretical and axiological paradigm—the amalgamation of political, ethical, and scientific imperatives would be the pattern by which, or against which sociology in the European Communist countries would develop. As any other scientific practice, the practice of sociology proved richer than the theoretical presumptions about it. The following chapter will be devoted to the ways in which the national sociologies in the European Communist countries managed, or failed, to dissolve the amalgamation of the political-ethical, social, and scientific principles and norms of the dominant ethos during the various institutional cycles.

CHAPTER 14

Multifaceted Sociology: Modalities of Knowledge Production

> All formations arose along a natural path, only the socialist formation arose in a counter-natural way, through the organized actions of the masses. Is this not where our problems stem from? This is what we should think about.
>
> ALEXEY RUMYANTSEV (1999)

> [...] sociology becomes a science only to the extent that, irrespective of the intentions and sympathies of its researchers, it gets results which, after appropriate interpretation, may be used by anyone who feels obliged to reckon with the facts.
>
> JERZY SZACKI (1998)

> Historical scholarship provides a means by which we can reflect on the origins and nature of our own standards and intellectual preferences, including the standards and intellectual preferences that we apply in order to make these judgements.
>
> STEPHEN TURNER (1998)

After 1956, in all the countries under study, sociology returned to the sphere of science and to society as a 'Marxist' science, and such would be its official image in both the East and the West of Europe until the collapse of the Communist regimes in the end of the 1980s. This self-identification and stereotypes about sociology under Communist governance would start being questioned after 1989 in different forms of attempted sociological self-reflection (in scholarly publications, national discussions, interviews with sociologists). In retrospect, the things emphasized foremost by these sociologists would be discursive tricks, editorial and publication strategies, escapes into politically neutral problem fields, practices of self-censorship, etc., where the cognitive results retained their Marxist facade, but were obtained by familiar means drawn from the theoretical and methodological corpus of sociology at that time. The fact of 'playing' with the context of scientific knowledge production (a device that was a modus vivendi of sociological practice in Communist-type totalitarian societies) does not eliminate questions regarding the production per se of knowledge about a society that, in the course of its development, increasingly

© KONINKLIJKE BRILL NV, LEIDEN, 2018 | DOI 10.1163/9789004333635_016

becomes aware of itself as differing from the proclaimed social ideal and from the path to its achievement. Nor does it eliminate questions regarding the role of the produced knowledge for the growth of society's self-understanding that it differs from the politically maintained ideological vision of it.

Given two independent epistemological variables—the communist vision of the world as axiological horizon, and Marxism-Leninism in its dual status as state ideology and dominant scientific paradigm—sociologists practiced discipline in ways that give grounds to identify different modalities of knowledge production in the then society. Here we will define those modalities by analyzing the *changes in thematic structure*, the *ways of problematization*, and the *models of argumentation that went on in the context of an unchanging syncretic epistemological deontology*. The fact that the same modalities of knowledge production occurred in different institutional cycles directs our attention to the conditions that made these modes possible in terms of a dynamic combination of socially-determined organizational forms, professional principles, and social commitments of sociologists themselves.

Regardless of the different national particularities of sociology's path back to the family of the 'legitimate' sciences in the post-Stalinist Central and Eastern Europe,[1] the first generation of sociologists found themselves in the same social and cognitive situation. In all these countries, the disciplinary emancipation of sociology was justified in terms of professional competence (and capacity), and by the social commitment to produce empirically verifiable scientific knowledge relevant for the implementation of the reformed political project of socialism. This connection between the cognitive and the social function of sociology, already evident in the practice of Polish sociologists in the first post-war years, displays the relatedness—typical for the very genesis of the social sciences—between the researchers' cognitive goals and tasks, and society's moral expectations regarding "the true, the just, and the good" (Caillé, 1986). As Jacques Coenen-Huther points out (1997: 138),

> Since the age of the founders, sociology has always combined, in different proportions, scientific aspirations with ethical commitments. In fact, oftentimes precisely the moral concerns formed the motive of scientific research.

---

1 With reference to the pre-war development of sociology, we may say there was a restoration, or comeback of sociology in Poland and Czechoslovakia, a new start in Bulgaria and Hungary, and a return to the 'victorious' theory (i.e., historical materialism as a building component of Marxism-Leninism) in the Soviet Union (see Part 2.8 and Koleva, 2002b).

He gives Durkheim as an example, for whom (Ibid.)

> the moral element [...] had a direct impact on the analytical procedures.
> How else can we explain the tying of the logic of causal analysis to the
> logic of functional analysis when studying the process of social diversifi-
> cation leading from mechanical to organic solidarity [...]? The argumen-
> tation based on function would seem unnecessary after causal sequence
> is revealed, if the intention were purely analytic. But Durkheim cannot
> be content with the idea that the division of labour is a neutral mecha-
> nism [...]. It is necessary for him to ground the emergence of new forms
> of solidarity, carriers of a new value system. And this, in some sense, [...]
> is the latent function of his functional analysis.

Hence, viewing the discipline's tradition in a historical perspective, we may
assume that it is not the intentionality and value orientation as such of modernity that create a problem for the cognitive development of post-1956
sociology under Communism, but the way in which the practice of sociology
integrates into itself and assimilates this intentionality and orientation. However, we must not forget that the (re)appearance of sociology in the second
half of the 1950s came about in the context of an already forged deontological
and epistemological model of Marxist-Leninist science. This model comprised
not only the social aspirations for freedom, equality, truth, justice, but also the
political project for their achievement and its ideological rationalization. That
is why the tension between social cause and scientific truth—which is typical
for any sociological practice—became a pitfall here, as it imposed not a double
standard of sociological reflection but a syncretic standard. The nature of the
latter was displayed not in the formula "scientific + party-minded" but in the
formulation of their mutual determination, and hence of the common, single
source and criterion of truth. As Zhivko Oshavkov points out (1960: 43),

> Marxist-Leninist sociological studies [...] have a proletarian, socialist, and
> class-party character, and that is precisely why they are scientific, have a
> scientific methodological basis. Their party-mindedness not only does
> not contradict but fully coincides with their scientific quality; it grounds
> their scientific quality, since the interests of the proletariat under capital-
> ism and the interests of socialist society require scientific knowledge of
> society, of the objective laws of society's development.

Such statements can be found both during the first cycle of institutional
expansion (1956–1968) and during the second cycle of institutional mimicry

(1968–1980). Were they a matter of inner conviction or just camouflage rhetoric in keeping with the 'spirit of the times'? This we cannot say from a present-day perspective. The important thing was that *this norm was postulated as the criterion of scientific truth.* The sociologically significant question concerns the changes that the disciplinary project of sociology underwent when confronted with imperatives of a different order, and in view of the substitution of scientific principles with political-ideological principles of research activity. The only way to identify the impact of the norm upon the various components of the cognitive process is by analyzing the practice of sociology under the changing conditions of political-ideological and scientific control over the application of the norm. This would show that the norms of scientific rationality were not unrelated to the social structures (as classical epistemology and classical sociology of knowledge would claim), nor dissolved in them (according to some modern currents of sociology). If we maintain the view that sociological knowledge is an active element of the constituting of reality, then its specific epistemological characteristics (truth, objectivity, validity) appear as "a particular form of existence of social relations between the object and the subject of cognition" (Slavov, 1989: 15) and are upheld, both in the construction of knowledge and in the course of its social functioning.

Viewed through the prism of this postulate—that construction and functioning of scientific knowledge are mutually connected—the cognitive development of sociology under the Communist regimes displays certain specific features that outline different modalities of disciplinary construction of sociology.

14.1   Sociological Practice Between Theory Deficit and Methodological Rigor

From 1956 to 1989, the development of sociology in European Communist countries was marked by a constant contradiction between theory and methodology. Sociology grew under conditions of a deficit of theory, but complied with the methodology of sociological cognition. This statement may seem paradoxical as a whole and in its separate parts. Is it possible to achieve objective and valid knowledge on society only by applying the scientific rules and norms of empirical study, and in the absence of an adequate theoretical model? Can we say there was a deficit of theory given that, during the entire period of Communist governance, Marxism-Leninism retained the status of a dominant theoretical and axiological paradigm both for science and for society? Is this statement not a faulty generalization, in view of the fact that various processes

and phenomena in those societies were analyzed using borrowed Western theoretical models and research methods, and with certain conceptual innovations, especially introduced in the 1980s? If the 'rules of sociological method'
were strictly followed, why did the sociologists in these Communist countries
fail to disclose the structure-determining principle of their society, much less
foresee its collapse (a failure they themselves readily admit, and for which they
are reproached by co-nationals from other scientific disciplines and by their
Western colleagues)?

A comprehensive answer to these questions which concern all aspects of sociological epistemology, theory, and methodology can hardly be hoped for. In
asking them, we only mean to anticipate the idea we reached in our analysis of
part of the pre-1989 sociological production in the countries under study, and
of the post-1989 assessment of that production (including self-assessments)
made by the sociologists themselves in their writings and in interviews. If the
theoretical deficit is viewed as a discrepancy between the specificity of the
object of science and the analytical perspective of the study of that object, and
if methodological rigor is taken as consisting in an adequate correspondence
between the contextualized research problem and the approach to its study
(an approach that leads to objectively valid, precise and demonstrable knowledge), then the practice of sociology under the Communist regimes appears
as a *constant overcoming of the contradiction between absence of a sociological
theory about the new society* (a theory of socialist society as a specific object of
study) and *its study as a historical specific phenomenon by using of methods and
techniques established in the course of history of sociology*. The types of connections that sociologists established between the observed facts and empirically
found regularities on the one hand, and the explanation and interpretation of
these on the other hand, determined the forms of sociological conceptualization of that society and the modalities of knowledge production.

Thus, in keeping with the disciplinary tradition, the knowledge produced
in the former Communist countries was subjected to the double control of
theory and empirical experience. But unlike the sociological practice in pluralist societies, here Marxism-Leninism exerted a contradictory pressure on
the cognitive process and its results due not only to the *isomorphism of its
cognitive status* in the scientific and ideological reflection on society[2] and its
monopoly position in both forms of rationalization of the world. Marx's social
theory built upon critique of bourgeois society places social development in

---

2 Marxism was the common reference, interpretative and explanatory framework both in the
   political doctrine of the ruling Communist parties and in the conceptual model of sociology.

a teleological perspective and outlines a new society, but does not explain it. This society—built in the perspective of the ideal, and in which the confusion between that which is and that which ought to be is maintained politically and guaranteed by institutions—proves to be the greatest challenge for its study by sociology—a study that represents an effort to know society on the basis of the collective experience of its construction, and not with reference to a pre-assumed, pre-established model of its future.

14.1.1   *From Marxist to Post-Marxist Sociology: The Gradual Cognitive Diversification and Professionalization of Sociological Practice*

Faced with a qualitatively new society, the sociologists in the Communist Central and Eastern Europe did not raise the question as to the manner of studying it and the designing of theoretical-methodological tools adequate to its specificity. The social-historical context in which sociology legitimated itself after 1956 was such that arguments of a different order were required. Given the hegemony of Marxist-Leninist philosophy, respectively, of historical materialism with regard to the scientific study of the new political project, and given the supreme position of the Communist party as the only legislator and decision-maker in society, sociologists had to display the Marxist content of their sociological research 'program' and the Marxist methodological foundation of that program (Bulgaria, Hungary), to fit the new social knowledge into the thematic structure of Marxism (USSR), and to engage sociology in the new social functions of Marxist science (Poland).

Viewed in the historical perspective of the general disciplinary tradition, Marxist sociology was justified through a *dual epistemological break*: one, away from the world history of sociology as an autonomous discipline (apart from Marx, the other classics of world sociology were mentioned either sporadically or in order to be condemned as exponents of idealistic, non-scientific knowledge about society) and, two, away from the pre-war national sociological tradition in each country. Even in Poland, Florian Znaniecki—with his unquestionable contribution to the advance in sociology in the 1930s, and his training of students who *de facto* restored sociology after the war—was "forgotten"[3] and rediscovered as late as the 1970s under the influence of a new interest in

---

3   In fact, the ban on Znaniecki began in the early 1950s in the form of oblivion and denunciation of his school, at the time when the Stalinist regime and dogmatic Marxism-Leninism were was being firmly established in Poland (Chałasiński, 1959). In 1955, Adam Schaff, a leading figure of Marxist-Leninist philosophy at that time, published a book in which he described Znaniecki's legacy as the "main source of idealism in Polish historiography" (quoted from Chałasiński, 1959: 141).

American humanistic sociology. In the case of Polish sociology, Jerzy Szacki identifies two main reasons for this discontinuity (Szacki, 1993, 1998). On the one hand, the achievements of world sociology, accumulated during the years of 'banning' and isolation in Poland, applied a language, theoretical models and research methods that were unfamiliar (alien) and hardly comprehensible to the renascent Polish sociology. On the other hand, experts in the so-called social sciences trained during the period of stagnation were not familiar with pre- and post-war Polish sociology; thus when they took up sociology *en masse* after 1956, they turned to the latest Western publications in the discipline and criticized them, or they turned directly to Marx, rather than to the national tradition in sociology. Even the pre-war Polish Marxist tradition represented by Krzywicki and Czarnowski was ignored. "In a way, breaking away from tradition was essential scientifically and psychologically" (Szacki, 1993: 171).

Breaking away from the pre-war international and national disciplinary tradition (in different ways—by passing it over in silence, eliminating, ignoring, rejecting it) proved to be a common strategy practiced even by those who had been educated in that tradition and were certainly familiar with it. Why was this so? The explanation may be sought by looking, once again, at the "context of argumentation", at the audience that this discourse addressed (Perelman, Olbrechts-Tyteca, 1970). In an epistemic environment dominated by orthodox Marxism and the powerful positions of the upholders of historical materialism both in science and in the party structures, the effective strategy for the emancipation of particular social sciences would have to be pursued on the home turf of the opponents of this emancipation. Of course, the cognitive structure and logic of Marxist-Leninist science was the scientifically valid and socially legitimate field of argumentation, because Marxism functioned as the official doctrine of the ruling power and as the theoretical and axiological framework of any interpretation and understanding of society. The mutual transformation and 'reincarnation' of the social and logical conditions of cognition that Bourdieu (1980) refers to are displayed here with the utmost clarity. The research structures established in all the countries under study in the 1960s, as well as the educational ones (especially those in Poland), were a sign that disciplinary autonomy was being won; these structures provided institutional conditions for the further cognitive development of sociology. From here on, *what kind of sociological knowledge about society is produced would depend on how far sociologists would succeed in revealing the structural truth about that society by complying with the principles and norms of empirical sociology.* The wish to make the research results audible in a politically modeled and ideologically controlled society affected sociological discourse. In any case, the clash between empirical social reality as the object and context of sociological practice, and the way in which sociologists saw the social mission of scientific knowledge, determined the *various forms of sociological rationalization of society*—forms situated at various levels and at various distances from the politically sanctioned model of scientific knowledge and the orthodox version of the dominant Marxist paradigm.

Taking as examples the conducted sociological research on the social structure of societies at that time, we will show, on the one hand, the *internal segmentation of the Marxist epistemic area* which began from the very start of empirical research on social reality, and, on the other hand, the *emergence of what may be called a post-Marxist epistemic space*—sociological conceptions that subjected the theoretical postulates of original Marx's ideas to empirical testing or sought analytical solutions outside it, thereby moving to a distance from the dogmatic Marxist doctrine and ideological approach.

It is not by accident that we choose social stratification research as a special case that may explain the cognitive diversification of sociology in the Communist countries. Abolishing inequality and building an egalitarian society was the declared major goal by which the Communist party-state legitimated itself during the whole time of its existence. Hence, the social structure of society was an object of intense ideological propaganda and constant social engineering. Here the clichés of orthodox Marxism were most stable, so that the ruptures of the political-ideological image of socialist society (an image based on the official Marxist-Leninist *two-class-one stratum* model) would have particularly serious consequences for social science, for the self-awareness of society, and for social management. As pointed out by the Hungarian sociologist Tamás Kolosi, one of the world-renowned specialists in stratification studies (interview with Tamás Kolosi conducted on 28 March 2001, Budapest, personal archive),

> social stratification was much more important for us than for Western sociologists because the social inequality or social equality, the position of social classes, the relation between classes and power, these were really the main important legitimization question of socialism. [...] It was not very difficult to get money for studying these questions.

Social structure was a common topic of interest both for the ruling power and for sociologists; it also proved to be the area of a shared ordeal when political expectations and sociological results began to diverge. Then became evident the whole complexity involved in the scientific and social practice of sociology, a complexity ranging from the justification of obtained results before the professional community to making those results public; from upholding them before the political power that had ordered the research (and had a specific interest in the results) to countering the risk the findings might be used against the sociological community; from defending the results as a scientific fact to instrumentalizing them as expert knowledge. As for the ruling class (Kolosi, Szelényi, 1993: 148)

> For some time, sociology proved to be a useful tool for [...] reform-communists, although eventually it turned into a double-edged sword. It was successful in de-mystifying the apologetic character of the orthodox Marxist theory of socialist social structure, but, at the same time, it started to discover those social contradictions which were difficult to manage within the framework of state socialism.

As early as 1956, at the Third World Congress of ISA in Amsterdam, the Polish sociologist Stanisław Ossowski elaborated the idea of occupational stratification as a characteristic of socialist societies where private ownership had been eliminated; he set the start of sociological reflection emancipated from the dogmatic variant of the Stalinist interpretation of Marxism. His study on *Class Structure in Social Consciousness* (1957) laid the foundations of an original analytical approach to class structure, social stratification, and their dimensions in social consciousness. Ossowski demonstrated not only the complexity of the stratified socialist society, but also the need to take into account the motivation of individuals and social groups when explaining how society functions. Borrowing conceptual solutions from different theoretical schools (behavioristic, Marxist, functional, socio-psychological) and using the achievements of empirical, mainly American, sociology, Ossowski's followers Andrzej Malewski (1961, 1964) and Stefan Nowak (1962, 1969) succeeded in developing this approach further, extending the field of possible hypotheses about individual and group behavior under Communism and enriching the category apparatus with concepts possessing a greater differentiating potential which were later used by their colleagues in the other Communist countries.

The influence of Ossowski's ideas was felt first, and perceptibly, among Hungarian sociologists, who, proceeding from the general theoretical framework of Marxism as revised by Georg Lukács,[4] came to revealing a "realistic picture of social inequalities and conflicts under actually existing socialism" (Kolosi, Szelényi, 1993: 150). Zsuzsa Ferge (Hungarian Central Statistical Office) and András Hegedüs (Institute of Sociology, Hungarian Academy of Sciences) were among the first researchers of the social structure of Hungarian society

---

4   According to Lukács, this was a "return to the original values of Marxism and to the respect of reality" (quoted from Kolosi, Szelényi, 1993: 147).

to defend and empirically confirm the hypothesis regarding the existence of social inequalities based not on property rights but on differences stemming from the division of labour (Ferge, 1966, 1969; Hegedüs, 1964, 1966). Recalling the start of her research, Zsuzsa Ferge points out (interview with Zsuzsa Ferge conducted on 28 March 2001, Budapest, personal archive):

> Working at the Hungarian Central Statistical Office, I came across data that did not indicate an egalitarian, unstratified society which was the dominant idea in the late 1950s and early 1960s. We managed to convince the director at that time of the Central Statistical Office, György Péter, father of the economic reform, of independent economic thought, that we should conduct a survey on inequalities and social stratification. [...] This survey, which was carried out neither at the order of the Party nor according to the Party's directives, but certainly in respecting the political limits, [...] indicated the unequal distribution by income, inequalities between men and women, inequalities between social classes and strata. And when sociology was officially institutionalized under the leadership of András Hegedüs, the question of social stratification was the first issue raised, this time not in statistical terms but theoretically.

Thus, the first empirical surveys and analyses showed that, although the socialist society being built had overcome class divisions, it remained stratum unequal due to the differences in the division of labor and the existence of a social hierarchy, with high-level bureaucrats and professionals at its peak and unskilled and agricultural workers at its bottom. However, occupational differences were explained as being the products of backwardness or as a heritage of the capitalist past. Thus, while in empirical terms the picture of Hungarian society was at a distance from the ideological claims regarding a "worker's state", the theoretical sociological explanation did not represent a serious threat to the guardians of the propaganda image.

A trend of empirically based revision of the orthodox Marxist paradigm regarding the social structure of socialist society went on in Czechoslovakia as well in the 1960s. Emblematic in this respect was the social survey *Vertical Social Differentiation and Mobility* headed by Pavel Machonin from the Institute of Sociology in Prague.[5] The most general framework of this study was a historical-materialist conception of social reality, but free of economic and class reductionism. In it, the forces of production were present under the term

---

5   In fact, this was the first nation-wide sample survey on social stratification in Czechoslovak society. As Pavel Machonin explains, the name of the survey "was not intentional, because

"primal culture", and the relations of production figured under the concept of "secondary culture". The social structure, which in the Marxist conception is built on the basis of class relations, was described here in two aspects: social integration and social differentiation. The object of the study—social differentiation—was viewed in terms of its objective elements (the character of labour, qualification, wage level, participation in government and management) and its subjective dimensions (social-professional prestige, self-assessment, etc.) deriving from the connections between the objective elements. Each dimension underlies a separate status the variations of which designate different positions of the surveyed person. The interconnection between these statuses forms the so-called synthetic status composed of five indicators (complexity of labour and professional status; way of life—cultural level, recreation, consumption; education and qualification; income and standard of living; participation in political power and in management). Viewed in terms of the empirically measured indicators of synthetic status, society seemed to be composed of multiple strata. The most significant factors of social differentiation appeared to be the character of labour, qualification, and way of life. The differences in terms of income and power, although having some importance for stratification, were not among the influential and determining independent variables. The egalitarian trend in income distribution ran counter to the trend of growing differentiation of the educational and social-professional level. The last-mentioned trend occurred concurrently with the shift from bureaucratic to technocratic organization of social relations. From a macro-social viewpoint, Czechoslovak socialist society in the late 1960s was a "variant of the industrial society based on evaluation of labor, on *achievement*, [...] a differentiated and [...] stratified society—even though the stratification was not fully crystallized— consequently [...] a diversified society in terms of the interests, opinions, and representations of its members" (Machonin et al., 1969: 165).

Based on the operationalization of the Marxist theoretical postulates, the borrowing of concepts from the American sociological tradition (such as

we were not sure that the society was really stratified. This was the result" (interview with Pavel Machonin conducted on 10 November 2000, Prague, personal archive). The survey was conducted in 1967 with a sample of 13,215 persons. Information was collected about 24,466 members of the respondents' families. The research results were published in 1969 under title *Ceskoslovenska spolecnost—Sociologicka analyza socialni stratifikace/Czechoslovak society: Sociological analysis of social stratification*; in 1972, these results were discussed by two other Czechoslovak sociologists, Zdeněk Strmiska and Blanka Vaváková, in *Revue Française de Sociologie*, where the authors assessed it as "the largest-scale, most documented and [...] most significant work" on the social structure of Czechoslovak society at the end of the 1960s (1972: 213). The survey was published in full for the first time in 1992 (Machonin, 1992).

"status incongruence")[6] and the conducting of empirical surveys, Polish sociologists of a Marxist orientation likewise described Polish society in the 1960s as a stratified society (Bauman, 1964; Hochfeld, 1963; Wesołowski, 1966, 1970; Wiatr, 1962). Unlike their non-Marxist colleagues, and similar to Hungarian sociologists, they interpreted the registered social differences as due to yet unsurmounted remnants of the class structure of the previous, capitalist society, and as resulting from the growing division of labour. The empirically registered inconsistency between the three dimensions of social status (education, income and prestige) was not perceived as a symptom of increasing social inequalities but as a possibility for overcoming the feeling of social injustice and as a resource for a social policy that might, through appropriate impact, compensate for the low values of one of the status measures (for instance, smaller income) by high values of another dimension (for instance, higher prestige).

Sociological research on social structure continued in the 1970s under the contrary conditions of increased political-administrative control and of undiminished state financial support for sociology, which characterized the second cycle of institutional mimicry (see Part 2.9). Sociologists not only confirmed the existence of social differences in the socialist societies but also sought their causes in the very principles of functioning of the socialist economy. Hungarian researchers went furthest of all in their interpretation of social inequalities evident in housing allocation (Szelényi, Konrád, 1969; Szelényi, 1972), the working class (Kemény, 1972), the industrial firm (Héthy, Makó, 1978). Socialist society was not equal, not because it had inherited inequalities from the previous, capitalist system, but because it produced inequalities itself through its own system of economic reproduction and redistribution. The differentiated and hierarchic functioning of socialist society could be explained not by the functionalist stratification theory, but by the theory of class structure that emphasizes the process of expropriation of surplus (Kolosi, 1974). At the top of this society's social hierarchy are the redistributors of the whole society's surplus, i.e., the professionals with a higher education, and at the bottom are the "producers of surplus", the low-skilled industrial and agricultural workers and workers without professional qualification (Konrád, Szelényi, 1974). According to this view, *socialist society creates a new type of class structure, dominated*

---

6   The concept was first introduced into Polish sociology by Andrzej Malewski (1964) and later
    used by Włodzimierz Wesołowski, head of the Laboratory for Research on Social Structures
    at the Institute of Philosophy and Sociology of Polish Academy of Sciences. Wesołowski was
    also a member of the Central Committee of the Polish United Workers' Party and closely
    connected to Edward Gierek's government; he had at his disposal considerable funds for so-
    ciological research on social differentiation and mobility.

by a new class—the technocratic intelligentsia, so that the study of this society requires a new critical class theory of socialism (Szelényi, 1978).

Beginning from the late 1970s and throughout the 1980s, i.e., during the cycle of second institutional expansion (see Part 2.10), there was intensive circulation of techniques, methods, concepts, indicators, conceptual models among sociologists of the separate Communist countries of Europe; expansion of scientific exchange and cooperation in the framework of the Communist camp but also between West and East[7]; unconcealed borrowing of research techniques from Western sociology; and, not least, expansion of the public presence of East European sociology on the international sociological stage through publications in the specialized Western press (Andorka, Kolosi, 1984; Kolosi, Wnuk-Lipinski, 1983; Kolosi 1988) and participation in the leading organs of the ISA. The society of the 1980s, quickly changing under the influence of social-economic crises and political attempts to save socialism, was studied from different theoretical perspectives, ranging from occupational categories (Andorka, 1982; Ferge, 1979) through the concept of status inconsistencies and multi-dimensional analysis of inequalities (Bokor, 1985; Wesolowski, Slomczynski, 1978) to dual social structures and processes of class formation (Kolosi, 1984; Szelényi, 1986–1987). The assimilation of American and West European conceptual and methodological tools for social stratification studies moved from Hungary and Poland to Bulgaria and the Soviet Union. Czechoslovakia held a specific place in this conceptual transfer; here, sociologists who in the 1960s had been creators of analytical tools in the field of social stratification turned into

---

7   Here we will point out only a few key events in the cognitive evolution of the research field of social structure in the 1980s, events that are relevant for all the countries under study. 1) At the initiative of the Problem Commission for Multilateral Scientific Cooperation between the Academies of Sciences of the COMECON member states—"Evolution of the Social Structure of Socialist Society. Social Planning and Prognostication"—an international comparative survey was conducted, entitled "Influence of Higher Education and Reproduction of the Social Structure of Socialist Society" (1977–1981). The total survey sample of all countries was 29,113 persons. The survey coordinators were the Institute for Sociological Studies of the AS of USSR and the Scientific Research Institute on Youth (SRIY) in Bulgaria. The president of the International Coordinating Council was Petar-Emil Mitev, then director of SRIY (Mitev, 1982; Mitev, Filipov, 1982; Filipov, Mitev, 1983). 2) In 1983, the Second Session of the International Varna Sociological School was devoted to "The Sociological Legacy of Karl Marx and the Study of Social Structure and of the Contemporary Way of Life". 3) The TÁRKI Joint Social Research Center in Hungary, a national center by origin and location, created in 1985 and headed by Tamás Kolosi, soon became a research reference for sociologists of social stratification from other Communist countries, and a transmission center for international research thanks to its membership in the International Federation of Data Organizations (see Part 2.10).

bricoleurs of methods during the "normalization", remaining in a grey zone of unofficial research practices (Spalová, 2006). If the concepts of 'stratum', 'status', 'mobility' were present in the professional vocabulary of Polish, Hungarian, Czechoslovak sociologists already in the 1960s, these terms started to make a path for themselves in Bulgaria in the late 1970s (Kyuranov, 1977) and acquired scientific legitimacy only in the 1980s in Bulgaria (Kyuranov, 1982; Tilkidjiev, 1987) and the Soviet Union, although they were applied there within the horizon of meanings set by these concepts. As Vladimir Yadov points out (interview with Vladimir Yadov conducted on 17 May 2000, Moscow, personal archive):

> We talked not about social mobility but about social advancement, not about stratification but about social layering ... Shkaratan conducted a survey on the social structure of workers in Tatar and obtained many stratification groups by combining qualification, education, nature of work, etc., but they were called layers of the working class and movement between these layers.[8] Shubkin conducted a survey on life plans and aspirations of schoolchildren, but this was in fact a survey on social differentiation.[9] And what did he obtain? A perfectly clear picture of social inequality, because he found that youths from families of the intelligentsia, party officials, economic managers enrolled in whichever higher schools they wanted, while the children of ordinary workers did not enroll. The share of those who could continue their education in a higher school proved to be related to the social position of the parents.

Presenting the sociological truth in politically correct forms that would not endanger scientific activity proved to be a constant concern for sociologists in all European Communist countries during the whole history of the discipline under Communist regimes. Whatever the cycle of institutional development, the actual mismatch with the proclaimed model of a conflict-free equal society—a mismatch established as a result of methodologically precise work—was presented in terms such as "objective interest intrinsic to every class" (Hochfield), "structural non-antagonistic conflict," "socioeconomic wage" (Wesołowski), "low-income categories" (Ferge), "bureaucratic equal system" (Machonin), "social minimum" (Kyuranov). Even in the 1980s in Hungary, under conditions of economic reform, a relatively liberal political atmosphere, and the use of multiple paradigms by researchers in the field of social stratification, the language

---

8   See Shkaratan (1970, 1973, 1985).
9   The research results were published in Konstantinovsky and Shubkin (1977). See also Cherednichenko, Shubkin (1985).

of sociology avoided direct confrontation with the concepts of political ideology. Tamás Kolosi notes (quoted interview):

> We wanted to measure the seven most important dimensions of inequality—from career inequality to occupation inequality, from culture inequality to life-style inequality. And, of course, one of the most important dimensions of inequality was the power. But we didn't call it power inequality but inequality in how people are able to realize their interests. Everybody knew that this dimension was the power dimension but in the official publications, in my book too, we spoke about 'interest realization dimension'. What is 'interest realization'? It is the power dimension of inequality. That is only a little example showing that there were some taboos.

• • •

Positioned within the institutional history of East European sociology, the surveys on social structure of socialist society serve as a sort of key to the cognitive evolution of a sociology that has placed itself, or has been placed, in the theoretical and methodological framework of Marxism. During all the periods, from the first institutional expansion (1956–1968) through the second institutional mimicry (1968–1980) and to the end of the second cycle of institutional expansion (1980–1989), sociological research on social structure invariably touched on ideologically sensitive issues and developed on a field mined with political expectations and control, and dominated by dogmatic Marxism with its postulates about a just, equitable, and conflict-free society. That is why the evolution of the thematic, theoretical and argumentative structure of this research area of sociology brings out in relief the role of various factors (internal to science, social, and institutional) of the development of sociological cognition.

Proceeding from the postulate of an egalitarian society, and studying the social groups of working class, peasants, and intelligentsia (the groups traditionally defined and sanctioned by Marxist-Leninist theory and Communist ideology), as early as the 1960s, sociologists found a discrepancy between the prescribed model of social relations in the new society and the actual structure and functioning of society. The ideologically proclaimed existence of egalitarian social relations was not confirmed by the empirical findings. Moreover, sociologists found that the new society, in the course of its development, produces differences, inequalities, status incompatibilities, and proves to be socially multifaceted, unequal, differentiated, charged with potential social conflicts. In the invariable context of the cognitive, political and axiological monopoly of Marxism, the possibility of formulating and empirically verifying and grounding such a view derived from the *logic of cognitive construction and argumentation* characterizing sociology as a science.

Proceeding from the Marxist postulate regarding the primacy of economy in society, all research teams sought the roots of social differentiation in the sphere of production, reproduction, and distribution in socialist society, and obtained relatively similar results concerning social differentiation. But they pointed to different factors as the cause of the social differences (division of labour, professional qualification, the ways in which the results of labour are (re)distributed among the members of society) and proposed different interpretations of the differentiation and heterogenization of the supposedly egalitarian socialist society.

The valid empirical results of all the studies were obtained thanks to the methodological rigor of the research process. All the procedures that distinguish sociology as an empirical science were strictly observed by researchers of the social composition and structure of their society, including construction of a theoretical model of the object of study; formulation of research hypotheses; operationalization of the basic concepts and the designing of indicators; and selection of appropriate methods and techniques for gathering and processing information. While these procedures ensured the 'technical' validity of the empirical results, the scientific value of the produced knowledge about society stemmed from the argumentative logic of sociological analysis. The comparison of the collected data with the initial postulates made visible the discrepancy between the projected image of society and the actual functioning of that society. Argumentation in sociology involves a constant tension between, on the one hand, the formulation of terms (by means of a combination of analytic schemas, data construction models, comparisons of the theoretical and the empirical) and, on the other hand, the justification of the deduced correlations (Berthelot, 1996). In the case under discussion, these procedures led to a conceptualization of the social structure of socialist society in terms of hierarchic, unequal, opposed and mutually opposing social groups. Taking the Marxist paradigm as their reference framework, the researchers of social stratification sought an explanation of the observed and registered social differences by turning to functionalist stratification theory; they proposed a revision of Marx's classical theory of class, and came to new thematic perspectives on the same research object (Strmiska, Vaváková, 1972).[10]

The study of the social tensions and differences which occurred under conditions of a growing economic crisis (in the case of Poland) and of a gradual liberalization of the socialist economy (first in Hungary and later in the other

---

10   Strmska and Vaváková, following the argumentation logic of Machonin's survey, raise
        questions related to the pertinence of including lifestyle in a system that consists only of

countries) led to new conceptualizations of inequalities (Ferge, 1986; Manchin, Szelényi, 1987) and of social conflicts (Staniszkis, 1984) under state socialism. The zone of tabooed topics was gradually reduced, though at a different pace and to different degrees in the different countries. While in Hungary the formerly sensitive issue of poverty had been studied since the late 1970s (Bokor, 1985), by the end of the Communist regimes it was researched in the other countries as well, albeit under the conceptual disguise of "social minimum" (Kyuranov, 1977; Tymowski, 1976). An overview of sociological literature in the separate countries and the opinions of the interviewed sociologists outline a trend of decreasing limitation on research topics to the point where only the Communist party's position, taken for granted, remained more or less 'off-limits' to sociological analysis. It is through thematic restrictions the role of the institutional context stands out most clearly. The questions of the inner structure and mode of functioning of the ruling party, of the "apparatchiki" and the privileged groups, of the state of the political class and the recruitment of elites, of the dissidents and the political opposition among intellectuals were discussed either in national underground publications or in the official Western press supported by legal institutions and organizations.[11] However, in both contexts—domestic and emigré—the specialized scholarly public and

---

vertical indicators; revealing the true role of political status as one of the most powerful factors of social differentiation in socialist society; the need to study social differences in the social-psychological aspect; and the influence of institutionalized values on social differentiation in socialist societies. By these questions, they outline a new problematization of the same topic—the social differences proper to socialism.

11   Some of the more important editions outside of the Communist European countries were: the Paris-based Polish emigré monthly *Kultura* established in 1946; *Problems of Communism* (*Problems of Post-Communism* since 1992) published by the United States Information Agency since 1952; *Survey: A Journal of East & West Studies* founded in 1955 as a journal of the International Association for Cultural Freedom (which, in 1967, inherited the Congress for Cultural Freedom after it became known that the CIA had taken part in the creation of the latter in 1950) and published in association with the Institute for European Defense & Strategic Studies (created in 1979); *Index on Censorship*, a quarterly magazine published in London since 1972. Both in the Czechoslovak samizdat journal *Sociologický obzor/Sociological Horizon* (1987–1989) published in Czechoslovakia (Nešpor, 2014; Spalová, 2006), and in the legal Western journals, sociologists often published their works under pseudonyms. For instance, Jakub Karpiński's analysis of "The New Regime" was published in *Survey: A Journal of East & West Studies* under the name Marek Tarniewski (Tarniewski, 1980). The connection between the political orientation of these publications and the sociological conceptualization of the problems they analyzed could be the topic of a separate study.

the non-scholarly public had only limited access to such publications, which restricted their impact on the development of knowledge and self-awareness of society at that time.

As for the choice of ways of interpreting the research results and of publicizing them in scientific circles and in society (the subversive or, on the contrary, stabilizing tone of the results depended on these ways), here the researchers' value orientations, social commitments, political and institutional ties proved more directly influential than they were in the course of knowledge production. Commenting on the interpretation given by Wesołowski who saw the status inconsistencies observed in the 1960s "as a positive sign that the society is moving towards Socialism because [...] people who have less income are compensated by higher prestige and vice versa", Wiatr defines it as "ideology stabilizing rationalization. [...] this is something which goes beyond the censorship of political interference. I think that we ourselves probably tended to see the reality in a better light" (interview with Jerzy Wiatr conducted on 29 March 2000, Warsaw, personal archive).

Kolosi and Szelényi who personally participated in the efforts of Hungarian researchers to study social structure in the 1960s and 1970s give a different assessment. Viewed at the level of sociology-power, "Hungarian sociology travelled a long way from the apologetical orthodox Marxist two-class-one-stratum model via the semi-critical, semi-apologetic stratification theory to a new critical class theory of socialism" (Kolosi, Szelényi, 1993: 152).

These assessments of their colleagues' achievements were made by sociologists with different institutional and professional trajectories, from a distance in time, on various occasions, and after certain evolutions of relations with those colleagues in the course of time.[12] The assessments illustrate to what

---

12   Wiatr's assessment on Wesołowski was made in an interview given in the framework of the research project *Sociology in Central and Eastern Europe from the mid-50s to 1989: The Road to the Challenges of the 90s* conducted with the financial assistance of the Research Support Scheme of the Open Society Foundation (1999–2001). Both before and after 1989, Wiatr remained connected to the paradigm of a revised Marxism in which Wesołowski also worked. Kolosi's and Szelényi's evaluation of the Hungarian research tradition in the field of stratification studies is based on these authors' analysis in the book *Sociology in Europe. In Search of Identity* (Nedelmann, Sztompka, 1993). Their own conceptual stances evolved over the years, and their distance from Hungarian sociology was both institutional and spatial. After publishing *The Intellectuals on the Road to Class Power* (1974, 1978), Szelényi was forced to emigrate and in the early 1990s became a professor of sociology at University of California, Los Angeles. Tamás Kolosi was the founder of TÁRKI Joint Social Research Center in 1985 and its director for many years, including the 1990s; from 1987 he is a professor of sociology at Budapest University (ELTE).

extent the interpretation of past cognitive results depends on the stakes of the present day and the chosen prism of analysis, but also on the set of professional, civic, and political stances of the person making the evaluation. But the very existence of a variety of assessments proves that the times are past when scientific discussions and commentaries were consciously avoided for fear of being used politically against the sociologists (see Part 2.9). Let us hope those times are gone forever.

And so, in the course of approximately ten years, sociologists working in different institutional phases (in terms of nature and degree of intellectual freedom and professional autonomy), and in countries with different degrees of political and ideological control, attained research approaches that, though compatible with the Marxist perspective and conceptualization of society,[13] did not confine themselves to this perspective. *While the monopoly of ideological Marxism was preserved, Marxism as an approach and scientific system was set on different paths of development.* In the form of 'open Marxism', 'revisionist Marxism', sociologists assimilated, integrated, and developed concepts, ideas, approaches that enabled them to describe and explain the changing socialist society with greater precision. Regardless of whether the causes of this were tactical or based on deep intellectual convictions, the fact was that since the start of the first cycle of institutional expansion (1956–1968), dogmatic Marxism began to lose its monopoly position and no longer held a monolithic epistemic space. Not that orthodox Marxism had disappeared, but it ceased to legislate in research practice and to define the content of sociological analyses. This situation continued both in the second cycle of institutional mimicry (1968–1980) and in the second cycle of institutional expansion (1980–1989).

At the same time, the development of the research topics of social stratification in these Communist countries reveals another particularity of sociological practice—a feature that persisted, although under changing forms, through all the different institutional cycles. While extending "the limits of the possible" with regard to the social problems they studied, and placing these limits within a sociologically relevant methodological framework, the sociologists of social structure and inequalities were always working under conditions of a kind of theoretical deficit. The problems posed by this qualitatively new society could not find a theoretical solution either in classical Marxism or in the theories based on the societal experience of democratic and economically free societies. This question—which was first formulated in the late 1980s by the sociologists

---

13   The compatibility of structural functionalism with Marxism has been pointed out by nearly all interviewed sociologists.

of these countries (Giza-Poleszczuk, 1989) but remained unresolved because of the historical end of Communism there—still retains its theoretical and methodological importance due to the universal nature of the problem.

14.1.2 *"Empirical" Sociology: From Methodological Rigor to Theoretic Eclecticism*

> There is no more virtue in empirical inquiry as such than in reading as such. The purpose of empirical inquiry is to settle disagreements and doubts about facts, and thus to make agreements more fruitful by basing all sides more substantively. Facts discipline reason; but reason is the advance guard in any field of learning
>   CHARLES WRIGHT MILLS (1959)

It was no accident that "empirical" sociology became a separate modality of knowledge production in all its methodological, theoretical, institutional and social preconditions and implications. Throughout the whole "Communist" history of the countries under study, empirical social research remained one of the most efficacious means for the cognitive and institutional legitimation of sociology and for the upholding of its disciplinary identity within the epistemic field of "Marxist-Leninist" science. At the same time, under the Communist regimes (as throughout the whole disciplinary history of sociology), empirical sociological research was the area where the influence of extra-scientific factors (in terms of political intrusion, the particular funding institution, the source of orders, etc.) was most perceptibly exerted in terms of the choice and definition of research problem and the interpretation and public presentation of research results. Hence, the way in which sociologists fulfilled the empirical component inherent to their work was not a merely procedural or technical aspect of sociological practice. Viewed as a process of constructing knowledge, the empirical sociological survey is situated between the epistemic and the social, and its evolution permits seeing the logic underlying the construction of sociology as a discipline studying social reality and developing within the limits defined by social reality.

The empirical study of the historically new society with which sociology began its institutional expansion after 1956 in the Communist countries was a professional challenge for researchers, whether they were sociology graduates or novices in their profession. The shared conviction among the emerging community of sociologists was that survey research based on mathematical and statistical methods provided objective and valid empirical information. Assimilating survey methodology and methods became the primary task of sociologists, on which the scientific value of the results and the social and cognitive legitimation of sociology depended. It would not be mistaken to claim that, except for Poland, the specialists coming from other professions and shifting to sociology acquired their first specialized sociological knowledge precisely in the field of quantitative research methods. This knowledge was obtained through self-study (especially in the case of Soviet sociologists),[14] or in specialized courses organized in educational institutions not specialized in sociology,[15] or in universities.[16]

The quickly developing empirical research's practice in the European Communist countries during the 1960s reflected two tendencies. One was a general scientific trend related to the dominant positivistic philosophy and methodology of science which imposed the model of physical science as the ideal of scientific cognition (Sułek, 1992); the other, which had its specific national

---

14   See the interviews with Vladimir Yadov, Yurii Levada, Tatyana Zaslavskaya in *Russian Sociology of the 1960s* (1999).

15   A telling example is the first six-month course in sociology at the Higher Party School in Sofia which trained cadres for Party, non-Party and government organs in Bulgaria. Veska Kozhuharova, a graduate in philology, and later a professor of rural sociology at the Institute of Sociology at Bulgarian Academy of Sciences, recalls: "It is hard for me now to say what I knew about sociology before taking [that] course [...] which began somewhere around the middle of 1968. [...] The idea of the course was to give, in six months of a stable load of 6–8 hours daily, six days a week, a minimum of knowledge in sociology—in history of sociology, theory and methodology of sociological cognition and methods of concrete (that was what they were called then) empirical sociological surveys. At the end of the course, each of us had to defend a course project. [...] I have often thought about the conception used in organizing that course which made it possible in a short term to obtain that needed minimum of knowledge and practical skills, so one could after all take one's first steps in sociology. Some of the first people appointed at the Institute of Sociology attended the lectures together with us" (*Sociology in Bulgaria...,* 2012: 159–160). Stefan Donchev has a different viewpoint on this period of extensive formation of sociologists through several-month-long courses between 1968 and 1970. A philosopher by education, he is a professor of sociology of enterprises and sociology of organizations at the Institute of Sociology of Bulgarian Academy of Sciences, and belongs to the same first post-war generation of Bulgarian sociologists, but he did not attend those courses. He pointed out: "there was no sociology as a specialty in the universities, and yet sociologists had to be formed. [...] Many of those who [completed those courses], were of very low quality, they had no mentality for scientific work. [...] That was the fact and there was awareness of it" (Ibid: 150).

16   One of the first departments of sociology in USSR was the Department of Methods of Concrete Social Studies at Moscow State University founded in 1969 under the leadership of Galina Andreeva who had defended a doctoral thesis on "Methodological Problems of the Empirical Social Survey" in 1965.

variants in the region, resulted from the efforts of researchers who identified themselves as sociologists in order to oppose the "dogmatic mumbo-jumbo" of orthodox Marxism (Mokrzycki, 1974; Urbanek, 1994), or to the contrary, was the result of the strategy of historical materialism proponents to push the emerging sociologists out of the area of theory and into the field of empirical research.[17] Whatever the political context, "the leitmotif of that time to make sociology 'scientific', alias 'empirical'" (Mokrzycki, 1974: 50) was the common goal of scientific practice both in the East and West of Europe. The production of objective, empirically verifiable knowledge about society (meant to serve the scientific management of social processes) was a common feature of both the scientific and non-scientific (political, technocratic) understanding of the social purpose of sociology. Also, the methodology of empirical research was the first field of communication between the 'Marxist' sociologists of Eastern Europe and the 'bourgeois' sociologists of the West, due to what both sides assumed to be the political neutrality of this field. International scientific conferences on social research methods were held in Moscow and in Warsaw already at the end of the 1950s and the beginning of the 1960s.[18]

The first large-scale surveys in all the countries under study (see Part 2.8) were unanimously recognized to be a school for methodology. This is meant in a double sense. On the one hand, the first post-1956 generation of sociologists was educated in conducting them; on the other hand, they became a model of methodological rigor for the following generations of sociologists (*Russian Sociology of the 1960s*, 1999; *Sociology in Bulgaria...*, 2012; Sułek, 1992). The people trained by Vladimir Yadov in the 1970s point out the "minute methodological precision" in research as an invariable distinguishing feature of the so-called Leningrad School (interview with Vladimir Kostyushev conducted on 20 May 2000, Saint Petersburg, personal archive). Sociology in Novosibirsk, born under a "mathematical guise", won a similarly high reputation for itself (Ryvkina in *Russian Sociology of the 1960s*, 1999: 270). Since it became an institutional structure in the Institute of Economics and Organization of Industrial

---

17   This view on the emergence of post-Stalin Soviet sociology is shared both by sociologists of the 1960s generation (Boris Firsov, Igor Kon, Rozalina Ryvkina, Vladimir Yadov) and the following generation (Gennady Batygin). See *Russian Sociology of the 1960s in Memoirs and Documents* (1999).

18   In January 1958, an International Conference of Sociologists was held in Moscow with the participation of Raymond Aron, Tom Bottomore, Georges Friedmann, Everett Hughes, T. H. Marshall, Helmut Shelsky (Batygin, Deviatko, 1994: 17). In 1966, an International Seminar of Methodology of Social Research was held in Warsaw under the sponsoring of UNESCO.

Production of the Siberian Branch of the Academy of Sciences of USSR, at the initiative of Abel Agambegyan and under the leadership of Tatyana Zaslavskaya, the Novosibirsk school developed with a close link to economics and economic mathematical models.[19]

During the discipline's first cycle of institutional expansion, in response to the needs of research, there was a growing number of publications on methodology and methods of empirical research. This part of sociological knowledge enlarged its presence through translations from Western authors or from sociologists of the other Communist countries[20] and through publications by the sociologists in each of the countries under study. The national scientific production comprised critical analyses of 'bourgeois' empirical sociology (Andreeva, 1965), as well as systematized presentations—meant for purely educational purposes—of the methods and techniques of quantitative research (Andreeva, 1971, 1972; Nowak, 1965; Oshavkov, 1960; Tzonev, 1958; Yadov, 1968, 1972[21]; Zdravomyslov, 1969). With the growth of national research experience, a growing number of publications presented research findings in different fields (Grushin, 1967; Zdravomyslov, Yadov, Rozhin, 1967), or discussed various methodological aspects of the sociologist's empirical work arising in the course of research (Venedikov, 1969). Sociological reflection followed two lines. On the one hand, sociologists strove to conceptualize the new society on the basis of the gathered data; in this way, they not only continued to affirm the importance of their science within the specific scientific and social context of each country, but also opposed "the doubts often expressed in the West

---

19   According to Martine Mespoulet (2007b), the close link between sociology and economy was characteristic not only of Novosibirsk sociology but of all Soviet sociology. This was due to the political conception launched by the Communist regime, and taken up by researchers, regarding the joint study of the economic and social dimensions of building socialist society.

20   Some of the translations were typewritten and disseminated in the sociological structures within institutions without being officially published. However, this cannot be considered illegal dissemination of sociological literature but rather self-organized activity on the part of sociologists as an informal response to the urgent need for specialized knowledge on the methods and technology of empirical surveys. Some examples are the Russian translation, made by Novosibirsk sociologists, of the West German *Manual in Empirical Sociology* edited by Rene Koenig, and of Jan Szczepański's book *Elementary Concepts of Sociology* which was officially published in 1969 and was used by Bulgarian sociologists as well (Maslova, Tolstova, 1998).

21   Yadov's book *Sociological Survey: Methodology, Program, Methods* was published for the first time as a rotary printing edition in the University of Tartu (Estonia) in 1968 (Maslova, Tolstova, 1998).

as to the possibility of deriving an empirical sociology from the theoretical principles of historical materialism" (*Empirical Sociology in Poland*, 1966: 3). On the other hand, there were critiques of the practice of empirical research which had different epistemological meaning depending on the author's assumptions. Even within a single national sociology, critical stances towards "empirical" sociology had different backgrounds and expressed different views on the nature of sociological practice. While Stanisław Ossowski and Jan Szczepański saw the excessive, unreflective use of empirical surveys as holding a risk for the theoretical development of sociology and its mission to promote society's self-awareness (Mokrzycki, 1974),[22] Adam Schaff attacked "polling mania" as being a form of "subjectivistic distortion of sociology" (1962), and thereby continued his political critique of 'bourgeois' sociology from a kind of Marxist stance that had been typical for the period of Stalinism: "Bourgeois sociology used various methods, but all of them led to one result; to pseudo-scientific falsification of reality, i.e., to the distortion of science in the name of bourgeois interests" (1951: 42). Also ideologically based were the reproaches made against the use of mathematical methods and models in Soviet sociology which was quickly taking its first steps in the 1960s. "Fetishization of numbers", "mathematical methods in sociology: the Trojan horse of bourgeois ideology" were some of the formulations whereby the proponents of the historical materialism paradigm rejected the mathematical sociology emerging in Soviet scientific circles (Maslova, Tolstova, 1998).

From the perspective of the disciplinary project of sociology viewed as a perpetual, never completed process of its self-construction,[23] the proliferation of

---

22   J. Kapr and M. Petrusek support a similar opinion on empirical sociology in Czechoslovakia in *Topical Problems of Czechoslovak Sociology* (1969).

23   The disciplinary project was connected with the production, development and use of scientific knowledge and related to the body of theoretic, methodological, and epistemological components typical for every science, as well as their cognitive institutionalization, social embeddedness, and legitimation in a given social-historical context. In this research plan for studying sociology in Central and Eastern Europe in the period 1945–1989 through the prism of the discipline's scientific tradition, the concept 'disciplinary project' guards us from two extremes: viewing European sociology under the Communist regimes as derived from an external project, translated and effective who knows how and why within the national epistemic space of the countries under study, or contrastingly, as an original local product in an isolated cognitive and social environment. Thus, sociology in the geo-political space-time of the European Communist regimes appears in its multi-situated forms of knowledge shaped by "contexts, regions and their histories, spaces and their geographies, States and their political regimes" (Roulleau-Berger, 2016: 181).

social surveys in Communist countries in the 1960s highlights the mobile bor-derline between presences and absences that Thierry Hentsch refers to (2006), a borderline that indicates, or at least reminds us of, the aporias of sociological cognition. Being simultaneously a product and a condition of the develop-ment of sociology, social surveys were carried out within sociology's official institutional structures in the European Communist countries just coming out of Stalinism but still remaining within the official ideology and theoretical par-adigm of Marxism. As significant as the political liberalization may have been, all institutions continued to function upon the ideological foundation and on the political-administrative principles of the Communist party-state. In their empirical study of the new society, sociologists found themselves placed be-tween the general theoretical framework of Marxism and the methodologi-cal requirements of their discipline. At this stage, the connection between the two was not explicitly problematized. Under a theory whose postulates are assumed to be axiomatic truths, efforts were aimed at strict compliance with, and precise application of, the norms, methods, procedures, stages of research that ensured valid empirical knowledge of society. Looking back from the dis-tance of time, we may define *methodological rigor as the outstanding feature of sociological practice* in the 1960s, and indicate *an epistemological aporia* that would accompany the work of sociologists in these countries almost until the end of the Communist regimes. The disconnection between theory and em-pirical research, between theoretical and empirical levels of knowledge was the trap in which sociologists found themselves when working under the syn-cretism of Marxist scientific, political, and ideological normativity. This dis-connection grew over the years and assumed different forms that demonstrate how sociologists developed their discipline in studying their national societies.

After the first institutional expansion, sociology became victim to its suc-cess. The risk that sociological research findings held for the ruling power drove the authorities to undertake action for the political disciplining of sociology, while continuing to fund institutions providing sociological information on the processes and trends taking place in society. During the 1970s, "empirical" sociology was the most widespread form of practice of this discipline both in academic and in applied research institutions in all the countries under study. As for the unofficial area of sociological practice (which emerged as a result of the political sanctions and restrictions imposed after the dramatic year 1968), it too was typically involved in doing empirical research. Wherever and by whomever they were conducted, the empirical surveys in this period were marked by a few common and some specific features related to methodology.

First, the borrowing of methods and techniques from Western sociology continued: researchers were convinced that the universal qualities of these methods ensured the scientific validity of research results even when applied to the study of socialist society. Quantitative methods continued to be primary, but some qualitative methods began to find a place in non-academic institutions of a sociological or non-sociological orientation and in institutions outside the sphere of science (factories, hospitals). An example of this were the studies conducted by the Center for Sociological Research on Youth in Bulgaria[24] and by Czech sociologists who had been forced to work outside scientific institutes or universities because of "normalization" measures (Havlová, Sedláček, 2004; Spalová, 2006). The difference between the two cases lay in the way the qualitative methods, new for these countries, were assimilated and applied; it was a difference stemming from the specific organizational environment of the sociologists themselves. In the above-mentioned Bulgarian institute, which although not academic, had high academic standards, researchers worked in an environment of open methodological discussions, and with a strictly demanding scientific council (Koleva, 2005; *Sociology in Bulgaria...*, 2012). For the marginalized Czechoslovak sociologists, the use of qualitative methods (biographical method, verbal history, interviews, narrative procedures, et.) was a form of "personal, institutional, paradigmatic or methodological opposition" and was done in the form of sociological bricolage (Spalová, 2006: 112).

Secondly, the study of various aspects of applied mathematics and statistics in sociology (sample design, measurement, scaling, typologies, modeling)

---

24   In fact, from the very start of its activity, in the first nation-wide representative survey *Potential Migration of Rural Youth to the City* (1967–1968) which was one of the model surveys in Bulgarian sociology, the Center conducted *interviews* with experts regarding the objective characteristics of the village, and with youth activists regarding the rural youth environment (Semov, 1982). The studies conducted in the 1970s used *time budget observation with chronochart* (*Leisure of Youths under Conditions of Five-day Work Week*, 1969–1971), *document analysis* (for the first time, in the same study; Doynov, 1975), *in-depth interviews and associative experiment* (for the first time in the study *Youth and Books* 1970–1971; Mitev, Yaneva, 1972), *critical situations method* (observations on the behavior of youths under conditions of an artificially created critical situation, in the study *Willingness of 16–18-year-old Male and Female Youths to Defend the Fatherland*, 1971–1972; Yolov, 1973, 1975), *semi-structured interviews* with administrative managers and leaders of amateur artistic groups (in the study *The Interest of Youths in Amateur Artistic Activity*, 1974–1975). I am especially grateful to Professor Petar-Emil Mitev, Director of the Scientific Research Institute on Youth in Bulgaria (1972–1988), for providing comprehensive information on the qualitative methods used by the Institute which was founded under the designation Center for Sociological Research on Youth (1968), transformed into Center for Research on Youth (1974), and still later, into Scientific Research Institute on Youth (1979).

and the instruments and methods of the social survey became established as a separate branch of sociology (Maslova, Tolstova, 1998; Mihailov, 1979). The fact that under Communist regimes sociologists worked on social surveys' methodology and methods has been interpreted post factum by those same researchers as a way of escape into fields of science that were unfamiliar and esoteric for the holders of political power. Apart from social-scientific deontological considerations, the theory of empirical sociological survey, viewed in the epistemological aspect, is presented purely as the logic and methodology of the research process, as something unrelated to the historical particularity of the society in which it is applied. However, this feature of sociology in the European Communist countries is not something specific to it. In Western literature on social survey methodology from that period, it would be hard to find any publications addressing the issue of the social origin of the research instruments or of the epistemological consequences of disregarding the context of research activity. David Bloor's "strong programme" (1976) had already appeared, but it would give impetus to a new sociology of sciences that, since the 1980s, in its various currents, has enhanced relativism in scientific cognition and deconstructs scientific rationality (Dubois, 2001).

Thirdly, the wide use of survey methods and the proliferation of applied sociology impeded strict control over the methodological instruments and research procedures, and as a result, the empirical survey models from the 1960s were not only ignored, but also seldom applied as a methodological standard (Mokrzycki, 1974; interview with Vladimir Yadov conducted on 17 May 2000, Moscow, personal archive). There was a double paradox in this situation of methodological laxity and increased political-ideological control. On the one hand, the empirical findings corresponded much closer to the expectations of those ordering them. It sufficed to formulate the questions, use the methods, select the data, in such a way that the final result would show, for instance, that "people devote more time to reading, to culture" (quoted interview with Yadov). On the other hand, the more the empirical results failed to correspond to the dominant ideological paradigm, the more they were in need of ideological cover. In both cases, this form of applied sociology turned into "ancillary", "official", "servile" sociology (Gennady Batygin, Edmund Mokrzycki, Boris Grushin, Soňa Szomolányi, Antoni Sułek, Nikolai Tilkidjiev, Vladimir Yadov),[25] though at various costs. For the sake of professional survival, either

---

25   The fact that, almost 30 years later, sociologists from a different national tradition would
      define in the same way part of the sociological practice in their own countries during the
      1970s justifies our referring to a common profile of the practice of this discipline during
      this period of the Communist regimes.

the methodological or the interpretative rigor of knowledge production had to be sacrificed.

Fourthly, at the same time the 1960s mathematical ideal of scientific validity transformed into methodological rigidity. The uncritical acceptance of the heuristic possibilities of mathematics led to a dictate of mathematical methods for assessing factor influences (chi-square analysis, dispersion, regression, and correlation analysis) which reached caricature forms. As Stefan Donchev points out (*Sociology in Bulgaria...*, 2012: 150),

> Mathematics was perceived as the cure-all of science. The important thing was to do it with precision, and what if the task was incorrect ... We would joke—establishing correlations between the number of teeth in a mouth and, say, the attitude towards China, political moods. [...] Correlation analysis had been brought to that degree.

Taken from the 1960s, the idea of objectively attaining the real measurability of the social world by means of social indicators and mathematical formulas turned into a scientific obsession in the 1970s.

Fifthly, between methodological laxity and methodological rigidity, "empirical" sociology continued to incorporate conceptual models that were theoretically and methodologically compatible with Marxism (such as Parsonian structural functionalism with its basic ideas of order and stability, functionalist stratification theories, neo-Marxist theories, human relations in industry), without attaining new conceptualizations of the studied social processes and phenomena despite the accumulated empirical information.[26] This was also the case in the sociological subdisciplines developing during this period, such as sociology of labor, sociology of enterprises, sociology of education, rural sociology. Researchers specializing in these fields were able to become familiar with the leading Western conceptions through books supplied to the national libraries in all the countries, or through translations (even if provided "for official use only"), or during specializations or ISA congresses.[27] Under the conditions of a kind of theoretical eclecticism, and with their accumulated

---

26   This particularity is especially characteristic for applied empirical sociology whose research questions correspond to social orders, and are not derived from the discipline's internal cognitive logic.

27   We do not have at our disposal any comprehensive data about the number of East European sociologists who specialized in Western Europe and the US in the 1970s or took part in the ISA congresses (Toronto, 1974; Uppsala, 1978), but on the basis of data indicated in separate publications and interviews, we may assert that, with the exception of Czech and

empirical experience, sociologists succeeded in transforming part of the politically imposed topics into a scientifically construed problem of sociological
reflection,[28] but they did not overcome the tabooed topics tacitly present in all
countries ever since the 1960s. The issues of the Communist party's leading
role, of the Communist nomenklatura and its privileges, and of relations with
the Communist Party of the Soviet Union, i.e., of political power—the fundamental principle of the structure of Communist society—remained off-limits
issues for sociologists in all countries under consideration. Varying in frequen-
cy and sustainability from country to country, the politically risky research
topics included the questions of the nation, of religion (Poland, Slovakia), of
the Gypsies (Hungary), and of social pathology (the Soviet Union, Bulgaria).
Sociologists opted for micro-, rather than macro-social problems, and this
choice was based on cognitive influences (for instance, the individualist model
of American sociology which made its way into the other Communist countries via Poland), as well as ideological considerations (taking refuge in more
or less politically neutral zones). Choosing research topics at the meso- and
micro-levels of society (for instance, family research) and the psychologization
of social issues (for instance, study of the personality and self-consciousness,
of the socio-psychological aspects of conflicts in the enterprise) were among
the frequently used stratagems for avoiding ideological control.

•••

It has been pointed out that the major merit of "empirical" sociology among
the various sociological subdisciplines is that it provided a "social photograph
of the life of people", even though "interpretation may lag behind". Continuing
with the case of Soviet sociology (where, of all national sociologies, the political project of socialism always had the greatest importance for the formation
of professional practice),[29] we will examine the specific manifestation of the

---

Slovak sociologists, the participation of sociologists from Communist countries in various
forms of international contacts was greater in this period than in the preceding ones.

28   Most indicative in this respect are Ivo Možný's seminars in Brno on "The Socialist Way
of Life as Social Reality" and the continuing work on Boris Grushin's mammoth Tagan
rog project on "Functioning of Public Opinion and Activity of State Institutions in Urban
Conditions" launched as early as 1966 (Rimachevskaïa, Prokofieva, 2007).

29   This does not mean that other national sociologies in the region under study developed
without connection to the political project of communism and independently of its evolution over the years. Unlike them, however, Soviet sociology, even in its most critical
forms, did not cease to think of the development of society in an economic, political

contradiction between theory and methodology in the empirical study of the historically new type of society.

Nearly a decade after the breakdown of the Soviet Union, the country in which their professional careers had developed, some Russian researchers gave various assessments of the achievements and failures of Soviet sociology in the 1970s.[30] According to Vladimir Yadov, the important thing was "that when you look at the numbers, the invoice is not false, because the level of methodology was good". Yurii Davidov, who is of the same generation as Yadov, does not accept the positivist quantitative methods of study of Soviet society because of their underlying uncritical assimilation of Western sociology. In his view, Western sociology was "employed to refine the analysis of our reality". Leonid Ionin, of the next generation of sociologists, also believes that, during that period of Soviet sociology, "functionalism predominated in theory, and positivism—in empirical research. Both [trends] were brought over from the West, mostly uncritically and unreflectively, and taken together, were called Marxist sociology" (Ionin, 2007: 5). In his self-reflection on his own research practice, Gennady Batygin, who received his formation in the 1970s, shares,

> I had to write a book on the topic of 'Entering the Worldviews Maturity'. I conducted a social survey using a methodology that, in my opinion, was not falsified beforehand. But when reality is falsified, the sociological method of mass-scale polling cannot fail to be falsified as well. [...] I did not write the book.

Nina Naumova—one of the first associates in the Department of research on new forms of labor and everyday life at the Institute of Philosophy of the Academy of Sciences of USSR (1955–1968)—is also critical in her assessment (*Russian Sociology of the 1960s*, 1999: 304–306).

> We had to start from some modern level. And we reached such a level only through American sociology. [...] But the reality that American

---

and social perspective outlined by the initial project, and ultimately, to "assist" or "serve" that project. Even this distinction between assisting and serving drawn by Boris Grushin (quoted interview), does not contradict that serving the political project of building a new society continued to be a function that structured Soviet scientific ethos and, hence, was not subject to revision.

30   All quotations, except those from Leonid Ionin and Nina Naumova, are drawn from the author's interviews with Soviet sociologists conducted in May 2000 at Moscow and Saint Petersburg.

sociology studies is the most distant from our social reality. The European realities are closer to us, but we knew nothing [about the European
sociologies]. [...] And the result was [...] this one-sidedness in the study
of sociology! Regardless of whether we understood it or not, the schema
that we assimilated and absorbed did not permit us to orient ourselves in
the society in which we lived. It was hardly suited to it [our society] and
not particularly effective. It turned out that we began to develop sociology, we worked hard, having available a not particularly suitable instrument. Where it could really be applied, there some results were achieved,
and where it was not suitable ... [...] It is perfectly clear [now] that this
was a dead-end situation in terms of science.

We have purposely selected these viewpoints so as to illustrate not the diversity of assessments but the complexity of sociological practice which always
goes on within a dynamic configuration of different orders of elements (cognitive, methodological, discursive, institutional, social, etc.). Beyond the various professional trajectories and standpoints they express, these assessments
highlight the sociological experience of studying 'socialist' society with the
inherited and new contradictions of this experience. After more than a decade of research expansion in the 1970s, using professionally assimilated and
applied methods and techniques, sociology succeeded in giving a precise picture of the society that was building socialism. Although every 'photograph'
involves the standpoint from which it was made, at that stage it was important
for professionals to take the photo using perfectly mastered techniques. The
epistemological discrepancy between the theoretical and empirical level of
knowledge—which had already been evident in the 1960s and was now growing greater—was evident in three modalities: as a discrepancy a) between the
general theoretical Marxist framework and the middle-range theories used in
the special sub-disciplines and borrowed from the world sociological tradition;
b) between, on the one hand, the methodology and instruments of empirical
research with their historically produced rationality, and, on the other hand,
the specific type of society to which they were being applied; c) between the
theoretical postulates, the empirical results, and the interpretation of the tension that existed between the socially prescribed/ projected, the scientifically
hypothetical, and the empirically found.

   This discrepancy, in its three modalities, became the major pitfall for this
type of "empirical" sociology in the 1970s. Except for the extreme case of
Czechoslovak sociology, where the discrepancy assumed the form of a literal
division of sociological work into empirical and theoretical, sociologists in the
other countries were inevitably caught in this trap, no matter what cognitive

moves they made in the course of research per se. Borrowing conceptual models from the Western research tradition in order to build the theoretical model of empirical research, sociologists in the Communist countries under study reverted to Marxism when the time came to draw conclusions and present their findings. The need to interpret the obtained empirically credible knowledge in terms of the axiological framework of Marxism—in which the real and the desired were closely intertwined—led to selecting the kind of data that would depict a desired image rather than the reality. In the cases in which surveys remained coherent with the original non-Marxist theoretical model—ranging from the definition of the research object to its empirical study and analysis of collected data—the conclusions did not represent an alternative to the official "synthesis" of Marxist theory of society; they only supplemented, modernized or beautified the latter (Szacki, 1998: 127).

Thus, while at the analytical level sociology remained confined to the intellectual and axiological horizon approved by Marxism, the theory and methodology of the empirical sociological survey failed to resolve the contradictions within its own research practice. The effort to overcome the theoretical-methodological contradiction proper to sociology in the European Communist countries since its disciplinary expansion in the 1960s began in the 1980s, when sociologists ceased to take the System as a given.

14.1.3   *From Theoretical Escapes to Conceptual Innovations; From Loaned Methodologies to Methodological Creativity*

The whole development of sociology under the Communist regimes in Europe was situated between the monopoly of Marxist theory and the disciplinary polyparadigmatic perspectives; between ideological requirements and scientific imperatives; between the historical specificity of the research object and the adequacy of methods used for its studying. Did the sociologists in these countries succeed in overcoming the discrepancy between the empirical reality which contradicted official Marxist theory and the theories that were incapable of explaining that reality? Did they create conceptions, concepts, methods based on the specific social reality in each of these countries? The development of the disciplinary project of sociology in the societies ruled and shaped by the Communist party-state can be defined as a *movement from theoretical escapes toward conceptual innovations; from borrowed methodologies to methodological creativity*? This movement went on amid continuous interaction between sociology and society in which society not only exerted influence on sociology but was in turn subject to influence by the latter, and sociology not only studied society but learned things from the changing society.

14.1.3.1   Theoretical Escapes *from*, Theoretical Escapes *to*

In the course of the institutional history of sociology in the European Communist countries, the search for intellectual horizons outside the predominant Marxism-Leninism assumed different forms. In the 1960s, the striving to escape from orthodox Marxism took the form of 'critique of bourgeois sociology' (Aseev, Kon, 1961; *Critique of Contemporary Bourgeois Philosophy and Sociology*, 1961, 1963; *Critique of Contemporary Bourgeois Sociology*, 1976; *Critique of Contemporary Bourgeois Theoretical Sociology*, 1977; Osipov, 1964)—a characteristic trend in the national sociologies that continued until the end of the 1980s. The field was gradually renamed 'critique of Western sociology' and 'critical commentary on sociological texts',[31] and flowed into the more general discipline 'history of sociology' (*From the History of Bourgeois Sociology, 19ᵗʰ—20ᵗʰ Century*, 1968; *History of Bourgeois Sociology 19ᵗʰ—Early 20ᵗʰ Century*, 1979; Kon, 1964; Szacki, 1979), attracting the new generation of researchers in the 1970s by the possibility it offered to expand the theoretical boundaries of sociological thought and to place the 'young' Marx in dialogue with 20ᵗʰ century thinkers. Thus, this area of sociological knowledge authorized by the party and science nomenklatura in view of its prescribed function to serve as an arm against the ideological enemy was transformed over the years into a) a means of transmission of the world heritage and latest achievements in sociology; b) a school for acquiring high theoretical culture[32]; c) a laboratory for conceptual syntheses. As pointed out by Igor Kon—founder of the ISA Research Committee on history of sociology at the Seventh World Congress in Varna, 1970, and chairman or vice chairman of the committee for 20 years (*Russian Sociology of the 1960s*, 1999: 116),

---

31   As pointed out in Part 2.10, starting from the first 1984 issue of the Bulgarian academic journal *Sociological Problems*, the rubric "Critique of Bourgeois Sociology" was substituted with the rubric "Sociological Texts with Critical Commentary".

32   In the early 1990s, a research team from EHESS headed by Rose–Marie Lagrave undertook a prospecting trip in the countries of Central and Eastern Europe in response to the program of the French Ministry of Foreign Affairs to assist the restructuring of social sciences after the fall of the Communist regimes. In an interview conducted in October 2009 (in the framework of the research project *Circulation and Internationalization of Knowledge through Sociological Exchange between France and Bulgaria/Circulation et internationalisation des savoirs à travers les échanges sociologiques entre la France et la Bulgarie*, project No 21468 under the Convention for Scientific Cooperation between CNRS and BAS, 2008–2010), Rose–Marie Lagrave admits her whole team had been surprised at the rich sociological culture and erudition displayed by East European researchers at the first meeting held before the creation of the social science research training workshops (see also Lagrave, 1998).

Judging by the designation [critique of bourgeois philosophy and sociol-
ogy], it seemed to be a hundred percent ideology. In fact, it often was.
But under the guise of critique of "alien theories", we could familiarize
the Soviet readers with them [the theories] and discuss problems that
were new to them. For the Soviet intelligentsia, "critique" was a substitute
for inaccessible sources [...]. In fact [...] this was camouflaged enlightenment. Later, when censorship grew weaker, "critical critique" turned
into positive elaboration of the respective problem field or into normal
history of philosophy and science.

The separation of history of sociology into an individual field in academic institutes of sociology and into a discipline in university curricula in all
of the countries in question provided a possibility to study sociology by its
own measure. Of course, it depended on the researchers and teachers themselves whether the classical heritage was taught and analyzed in terms of the
discipline's own internal logic or in terms of extra-scientific imperatives. The
important thing was that as early as the end of the 1960s and beginning of
the 1970s, the institutional conditions for this subject were created, and by
the late 1980s, analyses of the classics of sociology (Fotev, 1979, 1982; Genov,
1982; Sztompka, 1984b) or of theoretical currents and schools (Szacki, 1979;
Sztompka, 1979, 1984a) were published in the national literatures of each of
the countries. Among the generation of sociologists born in the 1950s and
trained in the 1970s in the institutional, social, and cognitive environment
created by their elders,[33] interests were turned towards ethnomethodology,

---

33   The Bulgarian sociologists whose professional careers began in the 1970s emphasize
      they had found themselves in a specific environment. Their generation was lucky to be
      working amid a professional ethos of freedom of thought that had been established and
      defended by their teachers, the founders of some of the first sociological institutions in
      the country after 1956. "They did not so much organize our searches as allow them, in-
      spire them, and assist them" (Andrey Raychev in *Sociology in Bulgaria...*, 2012: 308). In
      the same publication, see the interviews with Andrey Bundzhulov, Deyan Deyanov, Lili-
      ana Deyanova, Georgi Dimitrov, Petya Kabakchieva. Igor Kon, a Soviet sociologist from
      the generation that had paved the way for sociology in the USSR in the 1960s, also talks
      about potential dissidence. "My generation was subjected to weaker social and mental
      pressure than were people in the 1930s; students in the 1960s found it hard to under-
      stand certain situations of decades-long pressure, and for youths today, the 1970s seem
      a time of strange pusillanimity and lack of principle. But how can you be proud of hav-
      ing been born in a different, more liberal time? Your liberal-mindedness was partially
      paid for by the silence those who came before you had to keep" (*Russian Sociology of the
      1960s*, 1999: 114).

phenomenology, comprehensive sociology (Golosenko, Ionin, 1978; Koev, 1981, 1982). Of course, the escape from dogmatic Marxism towards new theoretical horizons could be useful for expanding the perspective of sociology and developing critical scientific thinking only on condition that the analyses of non-Marxist theories and conceptions were of high quality and not based on ideological postulates or conspicuous axiological assumptions.

Translations of relevant literature also played an important role for the formation of a broad academic sociological culture. Starting from the early 1960s, translations of books by Western authors were officially published in the Soviet Union—authors whose works contained historical analyses of sociology or presentations of the recent state of separate theoretical currents (*American Sociology*, 1972;[34] Becker, Boskoff, 1961; *New Directions in Sociological Theory*, 1987; Smelser, 1965; Turner, 1985). Their translation into Russian also made them accessible to sociologists in other Communist countries, where people had knowledge of the Russian language—a mandatory subject in basic, secondary and higher education until 1989.

Another means of overcoming the scientific dogmatism of Marxism-Leninism was in-depth study of the logic and methodology of Marxian thought (Mamardashvili, 1968), the study of Marx in terms of the dialectics of his own method and in the perspective of the historical construction of sociological cognition,[35] scientific reflection on Marx's entire legacy, a return to classical Marxism in order to draw its real potential for social critique (Mitev, 1984), "stressing the humanistic, anthropological aspects of Marxism, in addition to the concept of 'objective human practice' and the dialectical method" (Urbanek, 1994: 84). The sociological practice shows other modes of escape from the dictate of Marxism-Leninism, contrary to those mentioned above, such as avoiding "discussions about Marxism and its relationship to other theoretical orientations" (Kwasniewicz, 1994: 30); a preference for empirical interpretation over theoretical explanation, or what has ironically been called "neutralization through operationalization" (Mokrzycki, 1989: 115). This strategy, often applied in "empirical" sociology, arrested both the development of sociological knowledge and the growth of social self-consciousness, as it diverted attention away from socially important problems.

---

34   This collection primarily contains translations of Talcott Parsons.

35   The discipline "Sociological Problems in the Works of the Classics of Marxism-Leninism"—taught by Petar-Emil Mitev as part of the mandatory curriculum in sociology at Sofia University in the 1980s—was one of the most interesting lecture courses; it educated critical thinking in sociology students in those years (*Sociology in Bulgaria...*, 2012).

14.1.3.2   Towards Conceptual Innovations

Conceptual creativity in the national sociologies of the countries under study was a feature of their development starting from the first institutional expansion of the discipline (1956–1968) through the second institutional mimicry (1968–1980) and to the end of the second institutional expansion (1980–1989). While in the 1960s and 1970s the new concepts served to designate politically unacceptable facts in a politically acceptable form,[36] in the 1980s the new concepts expressed new conceptualizations of the society of that time whose growing economic and political crises shed light on the nature and structural principles of the 'socialist society' that had been under construction for several decades.

The efforts to achieve a scientific understanding of 'socialist' reality in the 1980s went on at a different pace and on different scales in the various national sociological communities depending on the depth and forms of crisis processes in each country, on the mobility of political limits set to possible activity, including cognitive activity, on the acquired research experience and extent of participation of sociologists in international scientific contacts. In any case, in the course of what would prove to be the last decade of the Communist regimes, the production of sociological knowledge *in* and *about* these societies went on in two basic forms. First, independently of one another, sociologists in the different countries attained similar conceptualizations of socialist society. Second, as a result of joint work with colleagues from the other Communist countries and from countries outside the 'Socialist Bloc', researchers developed original conceptions about the trends and processes common to societies regardless of their type of social formation.

In both cases, the attempts to comprehend one of the most important societal "experiments" of the 20th century contributed to overcoming the theoretical deficit of sociology as a whole, a deficit that accompanied the realization of that experiment.

Discrepancies and contradictions between the project of socialism (buttressed by ideological assertions and political reforms) and the actual functioning of society had accumulated over the years and became the object of intense reflection during the last decade of the Communist regimes. The efforts to explain and interpret the specificities of the dysfunctions, cleavages, and paradoxes of those societies gave birth to some original concepts.

---

36   The terminological inventiveness of East European sociologists was especially keen when they were researching social differences and inequalities in socialist society—a society that, according to ideology, should be, and was politically declared to be, without class inequalities (see Part 3.14.1.1).

In Poland, Stanisław Ossowski elaborated the conception of *three types of social order*: the first of these is defined as related to collective representations where the social system is determined by the pressure of traditional patterns; the second is polycentric when social equilibrium is created by spontaneous interactions; the third is monocentric when social organization is regulated by the state and its institutions, as in the case of state socialism (Ossowski, 1983: 82). Based on the findings of his own social surveys, Stefan Nowak formulated the concept of the *social vacuum* to designate the missing link (civil society in Poland under state socialism) between the micro-level of the family and other primary groups and the macro-level of the state. According to him, the structure of Polish society during those decades resembled a "federation of primary groups united psychologically in an abstract national Gemeinschaft with very weak bonds between these two levels" (Nowak, 1979: 128).

In Czechoslovakia, the Slovak sociologist Róbert Roško elaborated the theory of the "social working circle" and the "home working circle", using it to explain the dualism in the functioning of socialist economy. Labor—he pointed out—was performed both in the state "socialist sphere" and in the non-socialist, "domestic sphere" (Roško, 1984).

The duality of the socialist system also attracted the attention of Bulgarian sociologists of the 1970s generation. The system of personal connections and "pulling strings" in which everyone was involved as participant or victim was conceptualized by Andrey Raychev[37] under the term "second network" (Raychev, 1984).[38] This network is engendered by two deficits that were proper to

---

37   Andrey Raychev points out that the term "second network" was first introduced by Petar-Emil Mitev in the early 1980s (Raychev, Stoychev, 2008) and the idea itself was discussed and shared by Deyan Deyanov and Andrey Bundzhulov, sociologists of the same generation; however, their ideas regarding the "networks" developed in different directions after 1989 (Bundzhulov, 2003; Deaynov, 2003). In an interview given by Petar-Emil Mitev to Nina Nikolova, he specifies: "Already starting from the 1960s, an important step was taken towards a theoretical grasp of the 'networks'. I well recall conversations with Dr Nedyalka Mihova. In the newspaper *Narodna mladezh/People's Youth*, I was in charge of a rubric in which I published her article that carried precisely that title, 'The Second Network'" (*Sotziologicheski problemi/Sociological Problems*, 2003: 139).

38   The concept itself was publicized for the first time in the book *Youth and "the Small Justice"* (Raychev, 1984). In an interview in 2002, Raychev talks about "the camouflage elements, meaning they had put an idiotic title of the type 'the Little Justice' [...]. Now, it's true, the title, my title, was 'the Second Network'. [...] 'The Small Justice' was a quote from Todor Zhivkov. In that way they wanted to camouflage it using a thesis by Todor Zhivkov. So big deal! They didn't touch a single word in the content" (*Sociology in Bulgaria...*, 2012: 314).

socialism: an economic deficit (of goods) and a power deficit (of real economic and political power). Essentially, the "second network" represents an exchange of statuses (that provided power in different spheres of society) and commodities in three basic directions: a) statuses in exchange for commodities, b) commodities for commodities, and c) statuses for statuses. Thus, through exchange of these two kinds of "goods", the second network compensated for the structural defects of the system.[39]

The dualistic mode of functioning in economy, politics, culture evident in late Communism was also studied and conceptualized by many Hungarian researchers, who designated it as a "second (secondary) economy" (Gábor, 1978), a "shadow society" or a "second Hungary" (Forintos, 1982), "disguised political platforms" (Pokol, 1983), a "hidden dimension" (Bogár, 1983), or a "latent", or "hidden" sphere (Bruszt, 1984). The sociologist Elemér Hankiss made a theoretical synthesis of these ideas in his conception of the "second society" (1988).[40] On the basis of the findings of his colleagues, he formulated nine criteria used to distinguish between the first and the second society in Hungary in the 1980s: homogeneity versus differentiation and integration; vertical versus horizontal organization; descendance versus ascendance; statization versus non-statization; centralization versus non-centralization; political versus socio-economic dominance; ideology versus non ideology; visibility versus invisibility; acceptance (legitimate, ideologically and politically accepted sphere) versus non-acceptance (ambiguous legitimacy or illegitimacy). Applying these criteria to the study of various "second" areas in Hungarian society (second economy, second public, second culture, second social consciousness, second sphere of socio-political interaction, etc.), Hankiss reconsidered "the first-versus-second society dichotomy" and outlined "a hypothetical alternative society opposed to the now dominant first society and that the 'second society' lies somewhere between the two as an intermediate sphere" (1988: 39). In other words, Hankiss's analysis showed that whereas the "second society" is characterized by the absence of the main features of the first society, the "second society" had not yet fully developed the characteristics that were contrary to those of the "first society". The hypothetical alternative society would be marked by "fully developed opposite characteristics: horizontal organization, upward

---

39   In publications and debates after 1989 related to the historical sociology of socialism in Bulgaria (see *Sociological Problems*, 2003), Andrey Raychev argues that the "second network" was a form of civil society within the framework of the socialist state.

40   See also Kemény (1987) who presented the evolution of ideas and concepts of "second society" in Hungarian social sciences.

flow of power, predominance of non-state ownership, autonomy of social and economic actors, and differentiation cum integration" (Ibid.).

Hankiss had completed his text in English in 1986, but it was disseminated through samizdat in Hungary, Poland, Czechoslovakia, and other countries (Skilling, 1989)[41] before being officially publication in *Social Research* in 1988. This shows once again that, even in the second half of the 1980s, and under one of the most liberal Communist regimes, a sociological conceptualization of society that refuted the official political version could not be freely disseminated. Politically defined limits were set to the possibility of sociology to publicize its findings, especially when these findings showed the limits of the system's political unsoundness. As for the conceptualization of that society, the general sociological theory of Hankiss (similar in vision and coinciding in the time of its appearance with concepts elaborated by sociologists in the other countries regarding the various forms of dualism of structures and ambivalence of processes in socialist society) enables us to notice an important particularity of sociological knowledge production. Made in different places by sociologists who were neither in direct nor in virtual (through publications) communication between themselves, the interpretation of socialism in terms of "three types of social order" (Ossowski), "social vacuum" (Nowak), "two working circles" (Roško), "second network" (Raychev), "second society" (Hankiss) unfolded as a "co-production and co-construction of common knowledge" (Roulleau-Berger, 2016: 2).[42] It was not accidental that similar conceptions appeared in the different European Communist countries after 30 years of construction of socialism. Those were years in which the proclaimed new society was able to objectify itself in practices that displayed systematic paradoxes and contrasts at the level of everyday life and provoked people's concealed resistance, evident indifference, daily inventiveness and deceitfulness towards the System.

---

41   The first, typescript, version of the text was entitled "The 'Second Society'. The Reduplication of the Social Paradigm in Contemporary Societies: The Case of Hungary"; the second revised version was entitled "The 'Second Society': Is There a Second Special Paradigm Working in Contemporary Hungary?" (for details, see Skilling, 1989: 269). In the interviews, some Polish and Slovak sociologists pointed out the influence Hankiss's conception had exerted on studies of "second society" phenomena in their countries.

42   That is how Laurence Roulleau-Berger defines the "post-Western space of knowledge" (2016). Although the concept of Post-Western Sociology refers to the sociological study of today's global world, its revolutionary heuristic potential lies in the possibility of setting sociological practices from the recent past in "relationships of equivalence" and to seeing them in the multiplicity of their connections and disconnections, exchanges and lack of exchanges, unequal development and common challenges.

The 1980s also led to conceptual innovations that, based on international research experience, explained certain trends and phenomena common to the world at that time. Sociology of youth was a sub-discipline whose research object—perhaps more than that of any other sociological discipline—confronted sociologists coming from different national traditions, contexts and social-political systems with common theoretical challenges and with the need to overcome their personal ideological, political, cultural preferences and attitudes. In the 1960s, youth came out on the stage of various societies that differed by their degree of development and their economic and political order; in the next decades, youth asserted itself as a specific social actor whose presence could not be disregarded by societies striving for both stability and dynamic development. The changing position, role and status of youth in all types of societies gradually turned, from a topic of interest for researchers in separate countries, into a focus of collective international sociological efforts which were institutionalized in 1975 in ISA Research Committee 34 Sociology of Youth, at the initiative of the Rumanian sociologist Ovidiu Bădina. Petar-Emil Mitev, chairman of this research committee from 1982 to 1986, points out (Mitev, 2016:128)

> People who made a special contribution to international collaboration in the 1970s and 1980s were scholars like Prof. Ovidiu Bădina (Rumania), Dr Rudi Meyer (FRG), Prof. Jürgen Hartman (Sweden), Prof. Peter Hexel (Austria), Dr Sibylle Hübner-Funk (FRG), Prof. Vladimir Shubkin (USSR), Prof. Walter Friedrich (GDR), Prof. Arthur Meier (GDR), Prof. Vladimir Lisovsky (USSR), Prof. Władysław Adamski (Poland), Dr Zoltán Békés (Hungary), Prof. Yedla Simhardi (India), Assistant Prof. Antonín Matějovský (Czechoslovakia), Prof. Ladislav Macháček (Czechoslovakia).

From a present-day perspective, we could say that the specific manifestations of common regularities in the development of youth throughout the world engendered a kind of international consortium that crossed the geo-political borders of the Cold War. The joint work on empirical study of youth led to at least three achievements as regards the conceptual tools of sociology of youth and the theoretical treatment of youth problems. Firstly, scholars demonstrated the need for *complex* study of youth problems, which was designated as "juventology" (Gospodinov, 1980; Mahler, 1983). This new concept was not invented out of academic eccentricity but reflected the search for the most adequate way (through interaction between sociology and other disciplines) to identify, study, and explain the topic in its complexity, mobility, homogeneity and diversity. Secondly, the concept of "juventization" was created by which scholars designated not only the specific impact of youth on society but also the changes taking place in society as a result of the development and activity of youth. In other words, the term conceptualized the whole process of transformation of youth from an object of socialization into a subject of activities whose effects penetrate the entire society. Together with this, both sides of the process—socialization and juventization—were viewed as mutually determining. From its first appearance in 1975 in an article by Konstantin Gospodinov (dealing with the methodology of research on the effects of different types of education) and to Petar-Emil Mitev's elaboration and consistent enlargement of a sociological theory of juventization (1980, 1982, 1983, 1988), the concept was affirmed in sociology of youth as an analytical instrument for understanding the nature and importance of youth activity, and for operationalizing the manifestations of this activity (Hartman, Trnka, 1984; Hartman, Stefanov, 1984; Grootings, Stefanov, 1986; Pavelka, Stefanov, 1986; Velev, 1985). Thirdly, the study of youth in a historical and comparative perspective led to its conceptualization as a socio-biological group. It was seen as a product of the accelerated social development in the second half of the 20th century, and in this sense, as a "comparatively new historical phenomenon" which both expresses and generates changes in social relations, and is characterized by its homogeneity in terms of age but also by its inner differentiation. This conception of youth, presented by Petar-Emil Mitev at the 11th World Congress of ISA in New Delhi in 1986 when he completed his mandate as chairperson of RC 34 Sociology of Youth, proves convincingly that the development of scientific knowledge, including sociological, is possible only through the interaction of collective efforts and individual contributions. As for the cognitive value, heuristic potential, and incisiveness of this idea, the strongest proof of these are the data and research results that, 30 years after the text was first published, confirm the conceptualization of youth as a socio-biological group and of its main trends of development (Mitev, 2016).

The reader would be justified in asking why the theoretical achievements of sociology in the European Communist countries are discussed here in the field of a single sociological sub-discipline to which Bulgarian researchers have made a contribution generally acknowledged by the international community. Given the nationality of the author, the argument that we are again applying the procedure whereby a given practice (national, institutional, cognitive, etc.) is taken as a concentrated expression of certain characteristics, and serves to highlight these, would probably not be sufficient. We owe the reader an additional explanation—though not because of the author's nationality. It is certainly true that the historical sociological study of any sociological sub-discipline should present national achievements as well as contributions coming from beyond national borders, affiliations and biases. The case of sociology of youth is important not only and not so much in its theoretical achievements as with regard to the collective way they were made and by the fact that all colleagues have acknowledged the individual contribution of each researcher.

14.1.3.3   From Borrowed Methodologies to Methodological Creativity

The analysis of sociological production, of the interviews made in the framework of the author's research project, as well as of the other sociologists' projects, lead to a firm conclusion. The knowledge, assimilation and application of methods, techniques and instruments of sociological research were an integral part of sociological practice in the European Communist countries throughout the whole time of Communist rule. The pace at which new sociological instruments were assimilated and the scale on which they were applied in the different countries varied depending on different factors, including the pre-war disciplinary tradition, the degree of post-war participation of the national sociological community in international scientific cooperation, and the social urgency of the research problems in each country. Moreover, sociologists from different countries made methodological innovations, starting from the very first nation-wide sample surveys. Was this due to their scientific isolation at that time, to the specificity of the research topic, to the professional profiles of the first sociologists, or to all of these factors? It would be hard to give a categorical answer; the important thing is that researchers were determined to find an adequate instrument for studying a specific problem in a specific context.

In her analysis of "Sociology in the First Decade of Socialist Poland", Nina Kraśko (1998) has shown that one of the problems discussed by Polish sociologists at the time when Marxist-Leninist science was being firmly established (1948–1956) was related to the use of traditional methods of fieldwork for the study of the new society, of the socialist nation, of the processes of social transformation. Although, with the advance of dogmatic Marxism, political and ideological considerations intervened in the discussion, the question of the adequacy of the research tools to the topic of study was a purely scientific, epistemological problem. Regardless of the variety of viewpoints, and the ideological pathos of some of them, the Polish sociologists, who were formed before the war and had started the revival of the discipline immediately after the war, united around the stance of Jan Szczepański that "it was possible to utilize all the methods which were later used by sociologists: direct observation, official statistics, interviews and even personal documents" (Kraśko, 1998: 192). Ironically, under the conditions of a more democratic regime and the restart of sociology as an autonomous discipline (1956–1968), sociology's typical qualitative research methods and techniques were abandoned, quantitative methods gained ground and found a permanent place, and epistemological questions were forgotten. This was true not only for Polish sociology which had the greatest pre-war experience, but likewise for the other reviving or almost first emerging national sociologies in the other countries east of the Iron Curtain. This curtain proved permeable for methodologies. After World War II, American sociology exported its research experience and pragmatic orientation both West and East (Pollak, 1993; Sułek, 1998), and the methods of quantitative research became a common language between specialists from the two sides of the politically and ideologically divided world. Moreover, perfectionism in the assimilation and application of these methods became a condition for the affirmation of sociology as an independent research field and profession, for the legitimation of its influence on society, and for international recognition by the professional community (see Part 2.8; Part 3.14.1.2).

However, already in the period of extensive growth of social surveys, some new features appeared in fieldwork and in the processing of empirical data. Two social surveys that became emblematic for Bulgarian sociology—"Religiousness of the Population in Bulgaria" (1962) and "Potential Migration of Rural Youth to Cities" (1967)—displayed methodological creativity as an essential element of research, regardless of the context, or due to the context. There are several reasons why these surveys are selected here to illustrate the search for methodological solutions to specific research problems. They were conducted in a period when sociology was proving itself before the scientific community and society, and in a country that had small research experience compared with the national sociologies in the other European Communist countries. They were conducted by two research teams from two different kinds of institutions (an academic and a non-academic),[43] and by "researchers"

---

43   The study on religiousness in Bulgaria was conducted as part of the official research plan of the Department of Historical Materialism at the Institute of Philosophy of Bulgarian Academy of Sciences (BAS) according to the conception and under the leadership of Zhivko Oshavkov who would be the first director of the Institute of Sociology at BAS founded in 1968. The idea of the study on the migration potential of rural youth to cities was born in the structures of the printed organs of the Bulgarian Komsomol (Communist Youth League) and enjoyed the support of one state institution (the Ministry of Agriculture) and one political organization (the Komsomol). While participants in the former study were research associates from an academic institute, the latter was conducted by people working in the Komsomol structures and its publication units. In this sense, it is a case of non-academic research practice from which one of the ablest and most authoritative non-academic institutions for social research would grow in 1968: the Center for Sociological Research on Youth at the Central Committee of the Communist Youth League, subsequently transformed into the Center for Youth Studies in 1974, and into the Scientific Research Institute on Youth in 1979 (Semov, 1982: 104–106).

without a professional education in sociology. Despite this lack which is a shortcoming from a present-day viewpoint, both teams carried out studies that proved to be exemplary for Bulgarian sociology in their methodological precision. Moreover, the research innovations they contained received international acknowledgement in publications in the foreign scientific press (Mihailov, 1967; Oshavkov, 1966a; 1966b).

Two new methods for gathering data were used for the religiousness survey: indirect questionnaire (collecting information about the surveyed person from people surrounding him/her without the persons' knowledge) and direct questionnaire with a questionnaire box (all respondents fill in the questionnaire simultaneously in the same room and drop the filled-in questionnaires in a box). While the invention of the indirect questionnaire was motivated by the desire to obtain the most precise possible information about the religious attitudes and practice of the surveyed person by comparing the information he/she gives with the opinions of other people about him/her, the direct questionnaire with box was mostly used for technical reasons: the limited number of interviewers and difficult access to the homes of respondents. The comparison of the data obtained from the two types of questionnaires is favorable to their heuristic value, but disagreement has been voiced by some regarding the ethical aspect of obtaining information both *from* and *about* the respondent. Venetz Tzonev, a statistician who designed the survey sample and the model for statistical processing of the data, categorically rejects the scientific value and ethical soundness of a method that involves a lack of forthrightness towards the respondent, and hence discredits the surveys themselves (interview with Venetz Tzonev conducted on 28 October 1999, Sofia, personal archive).

In the study on the potential migration of rural youth to cities, the research team also made innovations in conceptualizing migration, measuring it, and in the data collection methods.[44] In studying the migration factors, the researchers sought the connection between the objective characteristics of villages and the desire of rural youth to migrate—a connection that had not been considered previously. In order to study factor influences, Yordan Venedikov and Angel Venedikov elaborated a coefficient for ranking factors by their significance which gained international recognition. This coefficient which in itself was from the sphere of statistics owes its heuristic value to the analytic approach used to define factor traits and the "result phenomenon". The approach combines sociologically grounded views concerning the "factorial traits on which

---

44   Besides questionnaire surveys, researchers also used the interview method (see
      Part 3.14.1.2, footnote 24).

the migration desires of rural youth *might depend*" (Venedikov, 1969: 246) with a statistically argued disclosure of the logical inconsistencies in the previously used methods for seeking a connection between the resultative phenomenon and the supposed factors. Thus, the researchers obtained a new approach that was "adequate to solving the task of investigating factorial influences" (Ibid.: 251). With this approach, "the resultative phenomenon is studied on the basis of the varieties of the factorial trait (instead of studying the factorial phenomenon on the basis of the varieties of the resultative trait)" (Ibid.: 253).

Methodological loans and innovations continued during the 1970s and 1980s, as well as innovative adaptation and application of methods from world research practice used here to study various social phenomena in the 'socialist reality' of the separate countries. The methodological work and reflection of the East European sociologists in this period was marked by several common particularities. There was an expanding use of qualitative methods in the academic and non-academic structures of sociology, and in the unofficial (enterprises and non-sociological institutions where the Czech and Slovak sociologists dismissed from the academic sphere were working) and illegal (the Solidarity research centers) zones of sociological practice. Whereas in the period of extensive growth of research activity (the 1960s), quantitative methods were more or less directly applied without epistemological analysis of the transfer process,[45] in the 1970s and 1980s the use of qualitative methods in research was combined more often with theoretical reflection on the context of their application and their real cognitive potential (Lutyńska, 1976; Mitev, 1976) and with exchange of research experience (the international symposium "Non-questionnaire Methods and Their Application to Research on Youth", Primorsko, Bulgaria, 1975). During these two decades, the sociologists from the countries under study integrated into their work nearly all the then-known qualitative methods for empirical data collection and data analysis (content analysis, semi-structured interviews, observation, biographical method, associative tests, psychological tests, social experiment) and often used them combined with one another or with quantitative methods. Moreover, depending on the social situation they were in when studying a given problem, researchers

---

45   Of course, during the 1960s in each national sociology, there were studies showing the application of the normative model (that uses mathematics and statistics) of empirical sociology to specific research fields. Our claim regarding a lack of epistemological analysis relevant to the transfer of methods and techniques refers to the lack of reflection on the difference between the context in which the methods were designed and the context in which they were now being applied, and on the connection between object and method of study, as discussed in Part 3.14.1.2.

developed their methodology in several directions: a) they assimilated methods they had not used before; b) they transformed already used methods; c) or they devised specific new methods.

In Poland, the 1980s began with a new sociological practice—the so-called "events sociology". In his analysis of Polish sociology of the period 1944–1989 made in post-Communist Poland nearly ten years after the end of the regime, Jerzy Szacki points out (1998: 129)

> The first symptom of change was surely the fact that the events of a dozen or so months in 1980 and 1981 were immediately submitted to sociological observation, description and reflection. It is in this immediate response to the events that I am willing to detect the origins of the fundamental change in the very nature of Polish sociology.

With regard to research topics, not only did the focus of interest change (Polish sociologists began studying collective action, social movements, political interactions, social conflicts), but thematic taboos practically fell away. With regard to methodology, "sociologists now began to resign from routine surveys and discover new methodological perspectives" (Ibid.). "Event sociology" actually enhanced the empirical nature of the discipline by integrating methods and techniques that enriched its empirical basis. In studying what was happening to and in connection with Solidarity, some of the Polish sociologists engaged as experts or keeping at a distance turned to methods previously rarely used in their practice, such as

> participation in social movements, sociological intervention *à la* Touraine, observation of real interactions or the analysis of their stenographic, audio, or film records, statistical research of the composition of the social groups, analysis of the biographies of political elites, and so on (Sułek, 1992: 376).

Some of these methods were also used in studying various alternative groups and movements related to religion, culture, arts, or lifestyle that were emerging in Polish society in the 1980s.

Sociological practice in the other European Communist countries—which was developing in the last decade of Communism in a less dramatic social context than in Poland—was also marked by a much wider use of qualitative methods compared with previous periods. Viewing this practice in a broader, international perspective, beyond geo-political borderlines, we see that the intensive use of qualitative methods in the 1980s was far more the result of the logic of development and interaction of scientific disciplines than of the logic of social development. The social context from which research activity is inseparable exerted an influence mostly on the pace of assimilation and ways of application of scientific methods—not disregarding, of course, the sociological imagination and inventiveness of the researchers themselves. Thus, besides "participant observation", Bulgarian sociologists of youth also used the "implanted lexicon" method. The latter was first applied in the survey "Behavior of Young Persons in Informal Contacts" (1976–1978). When a high school student participating in the survey gives his "lexicon" to be filled in by his peers and friends, in it are included several "specific" questions related to the research goals (Nikolova, 1976). Participant observation was also used in Soviet sociology in the late 1960s and in the 1970s to study "man in actual production relationships",[46] but in the middle of the 1980s, Andrey Alekseev, a "sociologist-worker" studying labour interrelations, would designate his own experience by the term "observant participation"; in the next decades he would conceptualize this as "dramatic sociology" (Alekseev, 1997; 2003).

> Observant participation implies investigating social situations through targeted activity of the subject [the sociologist] who makes of his own behavior a kind of instrument and a controllable factor of the study. [...] In contrast with the well-known examples of social experiment, in the case of observant participation the new factors come not 'from outside' the situation but 'from inside'. Their inclusion can be improvised at times and is not amenable to a strict procedure (Alekseev, 2003: 14).

Published nearly 15 years after the study, Alekseev's "dramatic sociology" seems similar to Erving Goffman's dramaturgical approach, but differs from the latter in scope (as it refers only to the play aspects in the researcher's behavior); it also recalls Alain Touraine's sociology of action and sociological intervention, but differs from these insofar as they have the educational aim of "introducing the quality of consciousness in spontaneous movement" (interview with Andrey Alekseev conducted on 21 May 2000, Saint Petersburg, personal archive). It would not be wrong to say that this was his own original approach to the process of research and to the process of sociological knowledge production

---

46   Vadim Olshanskiy—who began a doctoral dissertation in the Research Department "New forms of labor and daily life" at the Institute of Philosophy of the Academy of Sciences of USSR—explored interpersonal relations at work using the method of participant observation: he was employed as a locksmith in an industrial plant. He tells about this experience in *Russian Sociology of the 1960s* (1999: 180–184).

taken as interconnected. According to Alekseev's method, the researcher is not only part of the object of study but is an element of the dynamics of that object; and cognition comes equally from observation of the object of study and from observation of the effects of the researcher's behavior upon the object. Study and self-reflection go hand in hand during the whole cognitive process, and the self-reflection always concerns not only the research procedures but also the connection between the "sociologist participating in the process under study" and the dynamics of the process in which he/she is participating. The originality of the approach appears even more striking in view of the fact that until the mid-1990s, the inventor of "observant participation", as he admits in several interviews, was not familiar with Goffman's approach. Beyond the possible assessments of Alekseev's work that can be made from various viewpoints, it will be remembered for its results and for the individual and collective courage shown in upholding these results despite political penalties and discontinuance of the study.[47]

14.1.3.4   "Reinventing the Wheel and/or Setting the Wheel in Motion?"
The post-1989 self-assessments by sociologists regarding the achievements of their national sociologies under the Communist regimes are, overall, self-critical. Neither generational differences nor the past or present affiliation of people to different research traditions result in any difference in their tone of judgments. It is not that the sociologists fail to acknowledge the empirical and theoretical achievements of their own national practice. To the contrary, on this point opinions are almost unanimous. The minor realism in their judgment begins when these achievements are put in a comparative perspective—either compared with their own national sociological tradition from the time before the Communist regime, or with other sciences in their own country ("We had theoretical achievements, but they did not attain the class of Erdei, Lukács, Polanyi", Julia Szalai believes), or with the achievements of sociologists in other countries (Czech and Slovak sociologists often give their Polish colleagues as an example; the Poles admit they were late to start studying the problems of poverty compared with the Hungarians; the Hungarians point out that Czech,

---

[47]   In 1980–1988, Andrey Alekseev, a research associate at the Institute of Social-Economic Problems in Leningrad, worked consecutively as a fitter and locksmith at the Leningrad Polygraph Machine Factory where he studied actual work relations. Although his research was coordinated with the Leningrad Municipal Committee of the CPSU, at the very start (1981) he became the target of political accusations. He was expelled from the Party, had to temporarily stop work on his research as he was sentenced to jail, and had his notes confiscated. His Party membership was restored in 1988.

and especially Polish, sociology were "exceptional" during the first half of the 20th century),[48] or with the world level of sociology (this reference point occurs most often among the Soviet/Russian sociologists).

We do not deny that the so-called "national character or habitus" (Elias, 1973, 1976, 1996), the "national attitude" (Lepenies, 2006) influences the different measures sociologists use to assess their own national practice; but here we are interested in the measure per se. Since it is a way of looking at the national variants of disciplinary development, the measure permits us to see the logic of disciplinary development in the separate countries.

> We reached new conceptualizations, new ideas, but they appeared sporadically, outside the context of world sociology. These were cases of reinventing the wheel, at times completely fantastic, at times brilliant. And there were people who invented brilliant wheels, very precisely, without knowing the traditions of world sociology.

(interview with Vladimir Kostyushev conducted on 20 May 2000, Saint Petersburg, personal archive)

> People succeeded in creating something significant only when [...] they deviated from everything they knew and created something by themselves from scratch. Overall, everything in our country is a homemade product. Yadov's conception is a genuine scientific achievement, but it is a homemade product too. In what sense? He does not fit into what already exists in this field, particularly in American sociology. Not because he does not know where to fit in, and not because his theory is poor. The reality is different. In order to fit in somewhere, our reality needed a theoretical sociology of its own. (Nina Naumova in *Russian Sociology of the 1960s*, 1999: 306)

Here, representatives of two different generations of researchers present their extreme assessments and paradoxical judgments, and this extremeness fully displays the inwardly contradictory logic of the cognitive development of sociology. Though sociology is possible only as practiced in multiple national contexts, it represents in each of these contexts "the contingent new beginning of the same contingent process using other data" (Deleuze, Guattari, 1991: 94); in other words, it is production of knowledge about society with reference to the established sociological principles and norms. Thus, in the specific

---

48   See Kolosi, Szelényi (1993: 141).

historical development of every national sociological tradition, cases of "discovering or reinventing the wheel" are almost inevitable. The important thing is to set that wheel in motion and, through its motion, to study and explain the specific social reality in a scientifically credible and valid way.

14.2   Sociological Practice in the Continuity of Engagements-Detachments

> Sociology [...] is not only knowledge about society but is itself a social activity. It loses its meaning without public realization, or changes it if this realization does not correspond to scientific credibility.
> PETAR-EMIL MITEV (2016)

During the first decade after 1989, sociologists often described the forms of national sociologies under the Communist regimes as "social movement", "critical" sociology, "alternative" sociology, "activist" sociology, engaged sociology, ideologized sociology, official sociology, "sociology of the grey zone", "a useless occupation", "sociology of the establishment", etc. These definitions which indicate that sociology had been practiced in a variety of ways are all based on the same criterion—the divide between political power and sociology—and refer to the different social roles that sociology fulfilled at different times of its development; moreover, they implicitly assume the absence of opposition between sociology and society. "In the service of society or in the service of the regime?"—is one of the traumatic questions that permeates the critical self-reflection of these national sociologies on their own Communist past—even if, at times, it is stated only to be rejected as a question that reduces social reality and thus restricts the scope of analysis on the issue (Szacki, 1998).

Here, our interest in sociology as a social activity, and in sociologists as social actors possessing specific professional competence (with regard to building life in society in the Communist countries), is focused on the relation science—politics—ethics and the variety of forms in which it was displayed in sociological practice. We view this relation in terms of the coupled concepts 'engagements-detachments'—not in the sense of Elias' (1956) distinction between involvement and detachment, and the epistemological implications he attaches to the concepts, nor in terms of the interpretation of the social role of the intellectual elaborated in the French tradition. We use the notions 'engagements' and 'detachments' in the plural in order to reveal the dynamic configuration of professional practices within the coordinate system formed by the disciplinary project of sociology and the political project of socialism.

Taken together, the various forms of disciplinary memory (scientific analyses and personal testimonies, memoirs and retrospective assessments) depict a far more complex reality than that defined by the binary relations *us-them, inside-outside, integration-marginalization*. In this sense, the engagements and detachments we refer to do not represent the two opposite poles between which sociological practice was pursued, but are forms of articulation of the various values (scientific, political, ethical) which intertwined in the sociologist's work, i.e. forms of professional and social behavior that had various effects both on sociology and on society itself.

Perhaps more than any other historically and socially situated practice of sociology, its practice under conditions of undemocratic regimes raises the question of the boundaries between science, politics, and ethics. In countries where a given political doctrine and its ideology sets the framework in which social problems are defined, and outline the axiological perspective in which solutions are sought, the question arises: what are the limits of sociology as a whole and the limits within sociology? With respect to what, and to whom, do sociologists set limits in a society where everything is politics, but in which there is nothing political, in Arendt's sense of the term[49]? What kind of a limit is sociology, and for whom, given that the party-state has imposed a social profile of truth? What is the limit of compromise for the sociologist in a situation of constant hiatus between the declared humanism and the actual politics? Not least, what were the stakes involved in the different limits, in their dynamics and interrelations for the sociology as a cognitive and social practice?

In sociological practice in the European Communist countries, the political project of socialism was only one of the points of intersection of these limits. Depending on how sociologists perceived, studied, and conceptualized the societal project of socialism, they found themselves in various postures of engagement or detachment—in the cognitive and social aspect. Hence, the sociology they produced varied with respect to its scientific content and presence in society; and there were practically countless combinations of scientific cogency, social usefulness and moral value in this science.

49   In her political philosophy, Arendt makes a distinction between *politics* and the *political*. Politics is invariably linked to the existence of a state structure and formal institutions, while the political refers to what free people do (*praxis*) and express (*lexis*) in their relations with other people. In this sense, the political is not reducible to action imposed by and stemming from a state structure per se but neither does it exclude such a structure (Arendt, 1958).

14.2.1   *From the Political Project of Socialism as a Goal and Ideal of Society, to the Empirical Reality of Socialism*

Although the first decade of the practice of socialism as a new society and a geo-political system was marked by political arbitrariness, repression and violence both within the countries in the Soviet zone of influence and on the part of the Soviet Union towards those countries, socialism remained their common goal of development. In all of them, the institutionalization and cognitive (re)legitimation and expansion of sociology was linked to de-Stalinization of governance, to political promises, and social expectations for an end to the deformities connected with the "cult of personality", for a restoration of the authentic values of the social project and the overcoming of ideological dogmatism.[50] In order to achieve the social ideal, efforts began on the part of sociologists to win an epistemic space for themselves from the dominant dogmatic Marxism-Leninism, as well as a space in the institutional structures of society whose center of gravity was in the Communist party-state.

The strongest argument of the 'revivers' of sociology in all these countries was the empirical study of society according to the discipline's 'rules of method' which are capable of providing precise and reliable information on social processes and their management. It is not accidental that Russian sociologists describe the appearance of their science in the de-Stalinizing Soviet society as a "social movement" (Novikov, 1994; *Russian Sociology of the 1960s*, 1999). In the way it emerged, was formed and unfolded, sociology made a breakthrough both in the triadic disciplinary structure of Marxist-Leninist philosophy (dialectical materialism, historical materialism, scientific communism) and in the political practice of the Communist party-state. Sociology claimed the right to exist thanks to its already completed studies which were unquestionably engaged with topical social problems, but formulated in ways that differed from the official idiom, and studied by means of scientific methods. The fact that the decision to institutionalize sociology was made by the party structures confirms the basic principle of functioning of Soviet society, but does not exclude the agency of the researchers who identified themselves as sociologists.

---

50   As we showed in Part 2.8, the post-Stalin course of democratization in the separate countries was uneven, non-linear and reversible (e.g., the relapse to the use of violence in Poland and especially in Hungary) depending on the ratio of Stalinists and reformers in the Communist parties and on the capacity of social groups for resistance and for bringing about reform. These conditions also had an influence on when the institutionalization of sociology began and at what pace it advanced.

Once it acquired institutional status, sociology assumed different faces depending on the different professional behavior of the individual researchers. In all the countries under study, nearly until the end of the Communist regimes, there were *forms of sociological practice that directly served the ruling power*. These had various epistemic profiles which evolved over the years. In the 1960s, their primary form was laudatory publications about socialist society that parroted the official view on society and were confined to a most general abstract level of reasoning. Reminiscent in their style of 1950s orthodox Marxism, they viewed the social functions and role of sociology for solving problems of building socialist society through the lens of political programs and decisions. Whether they dealt with the tasks of the discipline's scientific practice (the discussed problems were related to the theoretical and methodological level of general sociological cognition and of the particular sociological disciplines) or with the application of cognitive results to various areas of social life, these publications represented self-legitimation of a *quasi-sociological practice* in the perspective of the official political and ideological view on socialist society. In the 1970s and 1980s, the kind of sociology that served the ruling power found expression in professionally conducted studies whose interpretation of data remained bound to the ideologically decreed image of society. These studies provided *practically relevant knowledge* about various social communities, groups and institutions, thus contributing to the *social and political engineering* of the Communist party-state. Czech and Polish sociologists most often mention a specific form of sociological service to the ruling power, evident in the 1970s in the context of the Czechoslovakian "normalization" and the Polish "stabilization": this was the sociological practice in which the directives of Communist Party congresses were immediately transformed into research projects. Sociological problematization duplicated the ways in which social problems were identified and argued by the Communist Party leaderships, and the process of scientific work sought solutions to problems in ways that were outlined beforehand as desirable by the respective political program. Unlike the *quasi-sociology* of the 1960s, this type of sociological practice produced a quasi-reality in order to cover up the real problems; hence, it may be described as a sociology *of substitution*. This substitution of genuine social problems with a political view of those problems is described by Miloslav Petrusek in his article "The Two Renaissances of Czechoslovak Sociology" (1992). Research on the three main topics in the 1960s—social structure, leisure time, and civilizational aspects of the scientific and technological revolution—degenerated respectively into a study of the pseudo-realities of the supposedly closing gap between the working class and the intelligentsia in 'developed socialism', of the 'socialist' way of life, and of the acceleration of scientific and technological development; in other words, into a study of problems formulated by the Communist Party as a new social program.[51] In this *ideologized* and *regime-serving sociology*, the engagement in the politically decreed model of socialism and its carrier was effected at the cost of scientific validity but using the methods of science. The substitution of sociological rationality with political expediency was done by researchers belonging to various institutional locations of professional practice—in the educational and research structures of the party and in academic institutes and universities.

Apart from this, the politically defined topics could be researched in a professional sociological way. Research on the 'socialist way of life' which had political support and funding resulted in some original conceptualizations of socialist society (Možný, 2003) and paved the way for new sociological problematizations of everyday life and for the use of phenomenological and ethno-methodological approaches to this field. Such is the case of the teaching and research activity of Lyuben Nikolov, the founder and first head of the first department of sociology created in Sofia University in 1976. The research project he led entitled "Youth on Itself" (1974–1977), his lecture course on Sociology of Personality, his article "Everyday Situations and Value Orientations of the Personality" (1975) were pointed out by his former students—who would later become researchers of everyday life—as a decisive influence on their research interest and approach to the problems in the framework of the topic of 'socialist way of life' ideologically endorsed at a plenum of the Central Committee of the Bulgarian Communist Party (see Andrey Bundzhulov, Liliana Deyanova in *Sociology in Bulgaria...*, 2012; Deyanova, 2010).

However, the general features of these official institutions of sociological activity were defined by scientific principles and the professional rules and procedures of the sociological study of social reality. Starting from the first empirical studies in the 1960s, the strict application of these rules and procedures led to disclosing the discrepancies between proclaimed goals and sociological facts. The social-critical potential of sociology and the risk that potential carried became visible both to the sociologists and to the ruling authorities. From there on, the specific way in which sociologists assumed professional responsibility for the social risk that the results of their work carried depended both on the ethos of the professional community and on the ethical principles of each researcher. The need to make compromises appeared primarily at the

---

51   Such metamorphoses in the construction of the object of sociological research were observed in the other Socialist countries as well.

stage when results were to be published. Here, the main regulating mechanism was the ideological model of society upheld by the ruling political power and protected by its professional guardians—the censors; this model functioned as a broad "context of argumentation" (Perelman, Olbrechts-Tyteca, 1970). The applied strategies varied from passing over certain results in silence and over-looking them, to reformulating the conclusions and camouflaging them by re-ferring to the politically untouchable trio Marx-Engels-Lenin or to the latest party documents.[52] Inasmuch as the aim was to bring the produced knowledge to the attention of society, the search for a politically admissible form of pub-licizing was something that engaged sociology both as a scientific and a social practice.

In a purely social aspect, this *critical sociology* was displayed in various forms of behavior on the part of researchers. In the 1960s, scientific critique and social activism went hand in hand, insofar as there was still no disso-nance between the call for scientifically based management of society and the belief in the transformative power of scientific cognition (a belief made all the stronger by Marx's legacy). Gradually, in the 1970s, the clash between, on the one hand, the periodically renewed calls for reforming the System and, on the other hand, the response of the party to the unpleasant findings of so-ciological research and the subsequent administrative measures taken against individual sociologists or whole research teams, led to two basic kinds of meta-morphose of the strongly activist stance. Some of the sociologists withdrew from activism and worked strictly in the field of science where they continued to study, describe, explain the then society without making compromises with the theoretical-methodological principles of sociology. Enclosing themselves in pure cognitive activity meant they did not produce expert knowledge for the needs of governance, but it also meant non-participation in scientific dia-logue with colleagues for fear that differences in scientific standpoints could be used for political accusations, as discussed in Part 2.9. Other sociologists continued their efforts to reform and "humanize" the system from within by using the high positions they held in the party or science hierarchy to propose societal solutions based on professionally made sociological analyses. Beyond individual choices to 'join in' or 'withdraw from' the real system of power, the scholars practicing this *critical sociology* of the real functioning socialist soci-ety remained loyal to an identical professional and social ethos. Until the very end of the System's existence, they continuously attempted "to push back the

---

52   In all the interviews, sociologists mentioned various forms of a sort of self-censorship applied when publishing research results.

'walls' of the possible as far as possible"[53] (interview with Zsuzsa Ferge conducted on 28 March 2001, Budapest, personal archive).

14.2.2   From Studying the Empirical Reality of Socialism
to Doubting the System of Socialism

Starting from the moment when not only the "walls" but also the social system within these walls were seen as a problem, sociology entered a new phase of conceptualization of society and a new phase of social engagements with social development, or of detachments from the System. The 1980s witnessed new forms of connection between social activism and social criticism. These forms—designated as *sociology of engagement*—first appeared in Polish sociology. Polish society which ever since 1953 had periodically been reacting in various ways against the regime, in 1980, with the workers' strikes and the creation of the first legal independent trade union in the history of any Communist country, provided a historical chance for sociology of engagement. The Polish sociologists engaged with Solidarity acted concurrently as experts, researchers, and citizens. This 'sociology in action' was reminiscent of 'action through sociology'—the stance of the critically minded and reform-inclined sociologists of the 1960s and 1970s. The difference here lay in the attitude towards the object of sociological critique and, hence, in the mode of reformist action. The start of the 1980s set a dividing line between thinking *about change within the framework established by the System* and thinking *about changing the System itself.* This was not the first time that a discrepancy appeared between the official viewpoint on society (how the Communist Party politically and ideologically rationalized the societal project of socialism) and the sociologist's viewpoint on that society. The illegal sociology existing since the 1970s had in fact always been mobilizing sociological resources to reveal the unsoundness of a society built on the total power of a single party, even if this was a party expressing the interests of the "class that carries social progress" (*Between East and West: Writings from "Kultura"*, 1990). Being opposed to the System, this sociology was handicapped by two structural defects of that very System. First, as long as they were situated in the unofficial, "grey" zone of public structures, these sociologists could not intervene in the on-going social developments, unlike those sociologists who, while critically minded, were integrated in legitimate sociological, political, and professional institutions. Secondly, until the early 1980s, the social-political conditions did not

---

53   Here, Zsuzsa Ferge explicitly refers to *The Walls/Falók* (1968), a film by the movie director
      András Kovács that depicts "the attempts to expand public space, the space of the possible, the space of public discourse" (Ibid.).

permit action based on the knowledge acquired *by* illegal sociology critical of the System. By contrast, in the 1980s sociologists involved in opposing the status quo, even if working in illegal sociology, had a real basis for applying their sociological knowledge.

•••

Of course, the above-described forms of sociological practice under the Communist regimes were embodied in countless specific situations and professional trajectories. These specificities lend substance but also add nuances to the typologies, and thus safeguard the researcher from confusing or switching their components. The forms of engagements and detachments, and the level of professionalism in the activity of each sociologist belonged to different value orders, so that

> one must not confuse political evaluations with scientific ones. Even if subservience to the regime had a negative effect on the outcomes of scientific research (and everything suggests that it did), the fact that one has proclaimed oneself in favor of the opposite side does not automatically lead to positive outcomes (Szacki, 1998: 131).

At the same time, however, the individual sociologists were responsible for their choice of the cause and social values to which they commit the sociological knowledge, produced by them in conformity with scientific norms and standards.

Viewed through the eyes of sociologists themselves, the collective history of every national sociology brings into relief a particularity related to the social applicability of research results. Beyond the concrete cases of government decisions that took into account the facts and conclusions provided by sociological research in each country, the retrospective assessments made by sociologists after 1989 leave the impression of the uselessness of their work under the Communist regime. Russian sociologists have formulated this feeling most eloquently. Boris Grushin talks about "the bitter taste of uselessness". Igor Kon, describing the hardships undergone by the Institute for Concrete Social Studies in Moscow, admits that from its creation and until its breakup, "we always raised the same toast—'to the success of our hopeless work'" (*Russian Sociology of the 1960s*, 1999: 127). As regards the nature and principles of functioning of that society, the failure to apply and utilize the sociological results in society reveals and confirms a *paradoxical deficit of social rationality amid super-production of ideological messages*. However, viewed in the historical perspective of events, the results of sociological efforts under the Communist regimes not only seem useless in the concrete pragmatic aspect, but were made pointless by history in the theoretical aspect as well. In his assessment of the development of Polish sociology, Antoni Sułek emphasizes the role of the new generation of Polish sociologists in the 1980s which did a sociology that was alternative in its scientific and social practice[54] (interview with Antoni Sułek conducted on 24 March, Warsaw, 2000, personal archive):

> They were opposition-minded and theoretically equipped, and they were not cabinet thinkers but studied society. They managed to create an excellent theory of real socialism, an excellent, very interesting theory of real socialism. Actually, they only laid the foundations of this theory and they started to develop this theory. And as they were developing this theory, the object of this theory collapsed. Their intellectual tools became useless and they had to start from the beginning.

Theoretically most advanced attempt to understand and explain the then society, the "critical sociology of real socialism" provides what is perhaps the strongest instance of fragility of the results and of the purpose of cognitive efforts.

---

54   Antoni Sułek has in mind the theoretical analyses by Jadwiga Staniszkis, Edmund Wnuk-Lipiński, Mirosława Marody, Andrzej Rychard who were of the generation of talented Polish sociologists appearing in the 1980s.

CHAPTER 15

Summing-up. Production of Scientific Knowledge about the 'Socialist Society': Surmounting the Paradoxes

The development of sociology in the Communist countries of Central and Eastern Europe began with a cognitive paradox and went on with a continuous surmounting of paradoxes. Sociology sought its scientific self-legitimation in the study of society the truth about it was previously defined, already known, and institutionally safeguarded in such a way that any deviation from that truth was penalized. Having been institutionally recognized within the disciplinary system of 'Marxist-Leninist science', sociology found itself in a theoretical and deontological framework where scientific truth was tied to political goals and subject to ideological criteria. From then on, and until the collapse of the Communist regimes, sociological practice went on in the context of the syncretism of the epistemological, political, and ideological normativity of institutionalized Marxism-Leninism. The production of objectively valid and reliable knowledge about the new type of society necessary for that society's development on the road to the historical goal required not only the devising of adequate theoretical-methodological instruments, but also the social legitimation of sociological knowledge under conditions of a politically modelled and structured society, and politically sanctioned and controlled knowledge.

The rejection of the principle of a priori truth postulated by orthodox Marxism was a first step towards sociology's cognitive emancipation in the countries where the Communist Party had established its power and imposed its ideological vision of society. The claim to study society as it is, so that it may attain what it wants to be, confronted sociology with still other paradoxes, but placed it definitively in the field of scientific rationality. Sociology was part of a society in which political and ideological rationality held an institutional monopoly, so the sphere of sociological cognition had to be built through perpetual surmounting of non-scientific criteria regarding the perception and description of society and the profile of truth about society defined by those criteria.

The search for sociological truth about society in the course of that society's development passed through a series of cognitive paradoxes deriving from the discipline's historically new research object and new context of practice, and also from the state of social science at that time. The Cold War context in which sociologists in Communist countries were studying the new socialist society enhanced the cognitive paradoxes and delayed their surmounting inasmuch as the geo-political division was translated to scientific communication as well. The extent to which the theoretical-methodological paradoxes of sociological practice under the Communist regimes were resolved determined the scientific soundness and social importance of the research results.

Our analysis of the logic of construction and production of sociological knowledge about the new type of society has shown several epistemological paradoxes.

First, conceptual deficit was something that continued to characterize East European sociological practice as long as it was building the problematization of phenomena upon theories meant to explain a different social-historical reality than that of socialist society. Whether it was the classical Marxian social theory or the current conceptions of Western authors, the scientific categories and the analytic perspective defined by them referred to a different historical experience. This mismatch was overcome when the researchers confronted the empirical data with the chosen theoretical model and thereby achieved thematizations and concepts that were able to explain the specificity of the phenomena under study.

Secondly, the excessive value attached to methodology—reduced to strict application of research methods and techniques—resulted in the reduction of sociological research to a technical procedure capable of producing data but not meanings. Reflecting on the adequacy of how research instruments are applied, and on the limits of their cognitive capacities, begins at the point when empirical information, though correctly produced in terms of methodology, no longer serves as a key to understanding the phenomena under study.

Thirdly, the epistemological cleavage between the theoretical and empirical level of sociological cognition led to the creation of mutually discrepant cognitive worlds—a situation that impeded not only sociological reflection on society but also the building of adequate scientific foundations for social action.

Fourthly, as long as it functioned in harmony with the surrounding context of argumentation (Coenen-Huther, 1997), sociology was able to guarantee its own existence and that of the System of which it was a part. As soon as it put in question the System as the guarantor of the dominant social order, sociology began to reveal the structural truth about society: that it was a society born in the name of the utopian ideal of "free development of each as a condition for the free development of all", but which in the course of its development had reached the anti-utopian reality of real socialism. The historical collapse of socialist societies in Central and Eastern Europe confirmed the heuristic value of the conceptions that had revealed the structural principles and dysfunctions of the Communist-type totalitarian regimes, but it brought about a new paradox. The object of those theories disappeared into the historical past, and the societies that were starting on the road to democracy and market economy needed a new theory.

The entire post-war history of sociology in the Communist countries to the very end of their political system shows that, despite the paradoxes inherent to the conditions under which it was practiced, it succeeded in maintaining scientific standards in the production of knowledge. Its efforts to do so found expression in different modalities of knowledge production within which the separate components and stages of the cognitive process had various potential capacities for protecting the production of knowledge from the dominant political and ideological schemas of explanation and perception of the world. In sum, the analysis of these modalities of sociology indicates that its chances for producing objective knowledge on society decreased in proportion as the representatives of this science a) interiorized the prohibitions and coercions currently in effect and turned them into thematic restrictions for the discipline, thereby narrowing down both their own problem field and the horizon of society's self-knowledge; b) forgot the fundamental Weber's distinction between sociology and politics, and instead of problematizing the very implementation of a given socio-political project (which is the foremost intellectual purpose of science), undertook, similarly to 'political reason', to establish the degree of correspondence between the socially real and the socially desired, omitting to even display the political ferments of the normative cognition they were producing; c) narrowed down the possibility of society's development to the vision endorsed by a single political power and thus restricted not only the intellectual horizon of the discipline but the possibility of society to think of itself in alternative perspectives.

By its obstacles, errors, failures, and achievements, East European sociology in the period 1945–1989 has taught us that to develop scholarly professionalism without also cultivating civic responsibility is just as dangerous for the discipline and for society as to fuel hopes in the power of science without applying a critical spirit to reality and produced knowledge about it. It has taught us that science is more than the 'rules of the method' but nevertheless can turn into something other than science if these rules are violated, silenced, sacrificed or substituted. In other words, science can only exist when—despite coercions, compromises, and concessions—the practice of scientific reason remains loyal to its own order of values whose supreme principle is the freedom of thought and the search for truth despite the 'truth' imposed by power.

Conclusion: "A Legacy Without a Testament"

Whereas the end of a text represents a new beginning, or at least a return to the beginning, the text—between its conception and its completion—is situated as upon a screen where we may see projected the things left unsaid and unachieved.

Our aim in this book has been to understand the development of sociology according to its own measure in societies marked by various forms and metamorphoses of totalitarian experience in 20th century Europe, i.e., in societies where, according to normative sociology, it is impossible to achieve objective and valid knowledge about the social. Our initial theoretical premise based on empirical experience was different. Departing from the idea of sociology as a rational and methodical answer to problems that occur 'here and now', and that coexisting individuals encounter in their common experience, we have examined the development of the discipline in post-war Communist Central and Eastern Europe, viewing it as inseparable from that common experience, as an activity of constant problematization both of the experience in question and of the ways in which we come to know it. In other words, for us, sociological practice in these countries was a rationalization of the experience in a non-democratic totalitarian-type society—a rationalization that was part of the specific organization of that society, or in Aldo Giorgio Gardani's words, it was a "structuring of the common experience" (Gardani, 2013). In order to understand sociological practice in its disciplinary universality and historical specificity, we have analyzed the national sociologies in six countries of Central and Eastern Europe that, after the end of World War II and until the end of 1989, lived under Soviet-type Communist regimes. Two basic questions have been at the center of our attention. First, how did sociology defend and develop its disciplinary project becoming an institution that was both a component of the structure of the Communist party-state and an element of the disciplinary structure of 'Marxist-Leninist science'? And secondly, how was sociological knowledge produced *in* and *for* the Communist society that concurrently represented a new research object, a new context of disciplinary practice, and a new value model? What kind of knowledge was being produced, and what was its cognitive and social value? In other words, how did sociology—functioning *within* and *as* part of a totalitarian type of society—defend its scientific identity as objective and valid knowledge on society, knowledge produced according to the currently operating models of control and verification of cognitive results?

© KONINKLIJKE BRILL NV, LEIDEN, 2018 | DOI 10.1163/9789004333635_018

In seeking answers to these questions, we have chosen not retrospection, not reconstruction of the history of sociology but the *self-description* of the disciplinary construction of each national sociology at the successive stages of its institutional and cognitive development through analyses and self-reflection of its representatives. As forms of disciplinary memory, the scientific production before and after 1989 related primarily to self-legitimation and reflection on sociology's development, and the interviews we conducted with representatives of different generations of sociologists from the countries under study, have enabled us to capture the *traces of self-understanding of the discipline at given moments of time*. Thus valuable with chronotopes, i.e., by their relatedness to a specific time of the professional experience and institutional position of the interviewee or the author of a text, publications and interviews have helped trace *the history of these scholars' reflection on the evolution of their discipline*.

We now have the advantage of a distance in time—25 years after the end of the Communist regimes and 15 years after the research project was completed. We have tried to use this advantage to trace the national discussions about the totalitarian past of sociology with their thematic emphases, passions, and assessments, and to thereby complement the picture of the discipline's self-reflection. In the course of the presentation, we have purposely left as they were the different ways in which sociology defined the society of that time, and itself, at their various stages of development. We hope this will not lead to terminological confusion and will permit seeing the process of self-identification of sociology and of the society it was studying.

We have endeavored to reveal the *institutional* and *cognitive logic of the disciplinary construction of sociology* in the course of development of its object and context, as well as the connection and interweaving of these two types of logic. Two concepts have guided us in this research: *institutional cycles* and *modalities of knowledge production*.

'Institutional cycle' designates relatively similar positions of sociology (as science and social practice) under specific configurations of relationships between actors in and outside science within separate periods of time. This concept has enabled us to identify the zones of organizational autonomy of sociology (legitimate and illegal, official and unofficial, formal and informal) and the role of these zones for the cognitive development of the science. The analysis of the genesis of different organizational forms of sociological activity has shown they were a product *not* of the monopoly-holding political subject but of the activity, the 'agency' of the sociologists themselves. The Communist Party endorsed already commenced processes of professional self-organization, of research, educational, and publication activity; depending on political expediency, the Party created, closed down, restructured, or transformed institutions that had already appeared.

By means of 'modalities of knowledge production' where the emphasis falls on the discipline's scientific problematization and argumentation, we have retraced several cognitive trends and their occurrence in different institutional cycles in the context of the monopoly of Marxism-Leninsm as institutionalized theory and state ideology. The movement from the monoparadigmality of Marxism to post-Marxian polyparadigmality was effectuated through the meticulous empirical study of social reality and the search for models of explanation and interpretation of the registered social facts. In cases when the obtainment of quantitative data was detached from the overall cognitive process and came to be viewed as the 'pure effect' of method, then methodological rigor turned into methodological rigidity. Two extreme cases of sociological practice under Communism, two extreme cases—the illegal work of Solidarity research centers versus the official sociology done in state institutions—suggest that just as the scientific 'purity' of each component of the research process is not a separate epistemic quality but is achieved by coordinating research goals, research methods, and social conditions for the production of sociological knowledge, so too must professionalism and scientific ethics be upheld at every stage of the research process beyond its organizational forms, institutional imperatives, and the social expectations it addresses. As scholars gradually distanced themselves from the assumption that socialist society is a superior formation, the development of this society served as the most powerful catalyst for the development of social science; as a result, researchers achieved conceptions capable of explaining the historical specificity of society in their times.

In this book, we have not always been able to explicitly state and demonstrate that

- the institutional and cognitive development of sociology are mutually connected without being identical or isomorphous;
- just as institutional expansion does not in itself result in better quality, so too, institutional isolation does not imply less professionalism; high academic standards will continue to define professional ethos as long as there are researchers for whom those standards are a matter of professional duty, even though institutions might violate them;
- civic engagement is not synonymous with scientific rigor, just as political commitment is not synonymous with ideologization of cognition; yet the sociologist's commitment to political action and social values has ethical and political implications for his/her professional activity;

- every national sociology had its emblematic heroes and anti-heroes; the former succeeded in putting time at the service of sociology, the latter took advantage of time and sociology for personal benefit;
- regardless of the context, we may always allow ourselves the freedom of thinking independently of 'truth' imposed by power;
- sociology is both a professional commitment and a social responsibility, and these two characteristics remain compatible and mutually enhancing as long as the sociologist defines him/herself through his/her professional autonomy—no matter how relative this might be; thus, by referring itself to universality, scientific knowledge transcends the determinants of its own society and enables individuals and society to transform the conditions that determine their history.

Apart from that, "a text can exist only in the presence of a reader" (Hentsch, 2006: 22). This text invites the reader to a meeting with the disciplinary past of sociology under the conditions of the Communist regimes as collective work involving past, present and future generations, as a prospective dialogue, as "a work on the elaboration of what is not yet" (Collin, 1986). While the greatest achievement of the sociologists who worked in the European Communist countries was the disciplinary institutional and cognitive legacy they left (with all its "brilliant ideas or brilliant errors"),[1] the transmission and assimilation of this legacy, and the way it will be used, depend on the coming generations. As would say René Char, Hannah Arendt, and Françoise Collin,[2] sociology in the Communist time-space of Europe has left "a legacy that comes to us without a testament".

---

1 See Hankiss (2002).
2 René Char's idea that "our inheritance is not preceded by any kind of testament" (Char, 1946), was later taken up, further developed, and conceptualized, by Hannah Arendt (Arendt, 1961) and Françoise Collin (Collin, 1986).

Appendix

Questionnaire: Sociology in Central and Eastern Europe, 1945–1989

1   *Personal Trajectory in Sociology*

What provoked your interest in sociology; why did sociology appeal to you; why did you become sociologist? When you got involved with it, what was sociology in your country like as an academic discipline and an institutional structure? When did you first become involved with sociology?

Who were your teachers in sociology? Who are the people you consider your teachers in sociology?

2   *Main periods, Principal Sociological Schools, Key-figures, Theoretical and Empirical Achievements in the Development of Sociology in your Country from the mid-1940s to 1989*

Periods

In your view, what periods were there in the development of sociology in your country? On the basis of what criteria do you personally make this periodization? Is it possible to distinguish between purely cognitive factors and social factors of the development of sociology in your country?

Schools

During these 45 years, were separate sociological schools established? Did they differ from one another? In what way did they differ?

Was there any competition between the different schools of sociology in your country? What forms of competition were there?

- In the field of research projects;
- In terms of the positions sociologists held within the field of sociology;
- In terms of the positions sociologists held in the State structures.

Was there any theoretical orientation or paradigm that predominated during certain periods? Did the followers (adherents) of this paradigm enjoy any privileges in their career or with regard to funding? Why did certain trends or paradigms predominate? Was it due to certain trends in world sociology? Was it by the influence of the leading person promoting this conception and his/her institutional position?

Key-figures

Who were the key-figures in the development of sociology in your country after 1944 and, at theoretical and institutional level, what was their contribution to research, etc.?

In your opinion, what were the greatest theoretical and empirical achievements of the sociologists of your country? Did they formulate any theories, concepts, methods inspired by the specific social realities in the country? Did sociologists from other countries later use these concepts?

3   *The Role of Marxism in the Development of Sociology in the Country*
What was the role of Marxism in the development of sociology in your country?

Was the adjective "Marxist" synonymous with scientific quality, validity and objectivity of sociological knowledge and of sociological findings (as it was in Bulgaria)?

How did Marxism as a theory and Marxism as an ideology coexist in sociology? Was the debate between Marxist and non-Marxist sociologists theoretical or ideological, given that the borderline between Marxist argumentation and ideological conventions was barely discernible?

What were the relations between the Marxist and non-Marxist sociologists? Did the fact of being a Marxist provide greater chances or advantages in a person's professional career? Did a person's Marxist theoretical orientation involve his/her Party membership and vice versa? Did Party membership provide more chances and advantages in a person's professional career?

4   *Mode of Sociological Problematization, Criteria of Scientific Truth and*
       Methodological Requirements for Seeking it, Cognitive and Deontological
       Patterns of Sociology in your Country
In each society, independently of its political and economic model, there exists a link between sociological problems and the crucial problems of society during that period of its development. Knowing the model of functioning of the totalitarian-type society, do you think that, in your country, this parallel or correlation assumed specific dimensions and was subject to specific rules or mechanisms? Was it driven by specific regulations or mechanisms?

Can you assess the mutual influence between sociology and politics and the extent to which sociological knowledge could be transformed into political directives? Also, is it possible to estimate how the political projects could serve as a basis of sociological investigation?

What was the interaction between sociologists in your country and the Party authorities in defining of sociological problems? Were sociologists in your country used for political purposes?

Looking back to that time, can we say there were different cognitive patterns for a sociological study? For example:

- studies in which researchers confirm, or do their utmost to confirm, a truth that is already prescribed by the ideological model;
- studies in which sociologists legitimize or model the political and economic practices of the totalitarian society;
- studies in which sociologists reject or undermine these practices.

Having in mind the double-faced character of the Communist society of that time, did sociology in your country produce original cognitive results and specific forms of scientific reflection and discourse? Under the conditions of ideological control, did sociologists have to promote the truth through channels of their own or in roundabout ways?

How did sociologists in your country protect their discipline from ideology? In what way did Marxist ideology influence the development of sociology?

5   *Relations between Sociology and Power*
What were the relations between sociology and power?

Were there any taboo subjects?

What was the reaction of the State-Party authorities when the findings of sociological surveys and analyses were not favorable for the regime? Was the dissemination of this information put under a ban?

6   *Relations between Sociology and Society*

What role did sociology in your country play for the development of your society? How do you assess this role? Did sociology in your country contribute to shedding light on the problems of society or rather to placing those problems in the limelight of attention? Was sociology in your country ahead of the times, did it anticipate events or follow events? Did sociology in your country make mistakes during that period? Did it miss any chances?

What problems did sociology in your country conceal during these years? What did sociology fail to say (reveal) and why? What problems was sociology in your country reluctant to declare, and why?

In the intellectual history of sociology in your country, can you distinguish between its known and its unknown parts? Was there anything in the development of that sociology that has remained hidden, or unknown to the sociological community of your country?

7   *Relations between Sociologists in your Country and Sociologists from Eastern and Western Europe*

What were the relationships between the sociologists of your country and of the other Communist countries at the time? What kinds of contact were there? Was there any sort of hierarchy, including subordination and domination, in these relations? Did relations lead to joint research projects?

Which sociologists from other Communist countries did you keep in touch with and on what occasion?

What were your relationships with Western sociologists? Did you carry out any joint research projects?

8   *National Sociology after 1989—State and Trends*

In your opinion, what are the landmarks in the development of sociology in your country after 1989?

Bibliography

Adorno, Th. W. 1959. Zum gegenwärtigen Stand der deutschen Soziologie. *Kölner Zeitschrift für Soziologie und Sozialpsychologie.* 11 (Jg): 257–270 [On the Current State of German Sociology. *Cologne Journal of Sociology and Social Psychology*].

Alekseev, A. N. 1997. *Dramaturgical Sociology (A Sociologist-Worker's Experiment).* Vol. 1–2. Moscow: Institute of Sociology, Russian Academy of Sciences [Алексеев, А. Н. 1997. *Драматическая социология (эксперимент социолога-рабочего).* Кн. 1–2. Москва: Института социологии РАН].

Alekseev, A. N. 2003. *Dramaturgical Sociology and Sociological Self-reflection.* Vol. 3. Saint Petersburg: Norma [Алексеев, А. Н. 2003. *Драматическая социология и социологическая ауторефлексия.* Том 3. Санкт-Петербург: Норма].

Alexander, J. 1995. How "National" is Social Theory? *Revue Suisse de Sociologie (Swiss Journal of Sociology).* Vol. 21 (3): 541–546.

American Sociology. 1972. Edited by G. V. Osipov. Moscow: Progress [*Американская социология.* 1972. Ред. и вступ. ст. Г. В. Осипова. Москва: Прогресс].

Andorka, R. 1982. *A társadalmi mobilitás változásai Magyarországon.* Budapest: Gondolat Kiadó [*Changes in Social Mobility in Hungary*].

Andorka, R., T. Kolosi (eds.). 1984. *Stratification and Inequality.* Budapest: Institute for Social Sciences.

Andreeva, G. M. 1965. *Contemporary Bourgeois Empirical Sociology.* Moscow: Mysl [Андреева, Г. М. 1965. *Современная буржуазная эмпирическая социология.* Москва: Мысль].

Andreeva, G. M. (ed.). 1971. *Topical Problems of the Development of Concrete Social Surveys.* Moscow [Андреева, Г. М. 1971. *Актуальные проблемы развития конкретных социальных исследований.* Москва].

Andreeva, G. M. (ed.). 1972. *Lectures on Methods of Concrete Social Surveys.* Moscow: Moscow State University Press [Андреева, Г. М. 1972. *Лекции по методике конкретных социальных исследований.* Москва: Изд-во МГУ].

Arendt, H. 1979 [1951]. *The Origins of Totalitarianism.* San Diego, New York, London: A Harvest Book, Harcourt Brace & Company.

Arendt, H. 1958. *The Human Condition.* Chicago: University of Chicago Press.

Arendt, H. 1961. *Between Past and Future.* New York: The Viking Press.

Aron, R. 1965. *Démocratie et totalitarisme.* Paris: Gallimard [*Democracy and Totalitarianism*].

Aseev, Y. A., I. S. Kon. 1961. *Main Directions in 20th Century Bourgeois Philosophy and Sociology.* Leningrad: Leningrad University Press [Асеев, Ю. А., И. С. Кон. 1961. *Основные направления буржуазной философии и социологии XX века.* Ленинград: ЛГУ].

Avramov, R. 2003. Socialism in Bulgaria's XXth Century. *Sotziologicheski Problemi/Sociological Problems*. *1–2*: 131–135 [Аврамов, Р. 2003. Социализмът в стопанския XX век на България. *Социологически проблеми*].

Bachelard, G. 1934. *Le nouvel esprit scientifique*. Paris: PUF [*The New Scientific Spirit*].

Bad, M. 1986. Les limites du dicible. *Actes de la recherche en sciences sociales*. *61(1)*: 52–54.

Baeva, I. 1995. *Eastern Europe after Stalin 1953–1956. Poland, Hungary, Czechoslovakia and Bulgaria*. Sofia: Sofia University Press [Баева, И. 1995. *Източна Европа след Сталин 1953–1956. Полша, Унгария, Чехословакия и България*. София: Университетско издателство "Св. Климент Охридски"].

Baeva, I. 1998. "When the 'Iron Curtain' Was Falling (1944–1949): Poland, Czechoslovakia and Hungary". In *Before and after the "Iron Curtain"*. Edited by M. Radeva. Sofia: Tilia, pp. 132–176 [Баева, И. 1998. "Когато се спускаше "Желязната завеса" (1944–1949): Полша, Чехословакия и Унгария". В *Преди и след "Желязната завеса"*. М. Радева (съст.). София: Тилиа].

Baeva, I. 2010. *Eastern Europe through the XXth Century. Ideas, Conflicts, Myths*. Sofia: Paradigma [Баева, И. 2010. *Източна Европа през XX век. Идеи, конфликти, митове*. София: Парадигма].

Barbano, F. 1961. *Sociologia della politica: concetti, metodi e campo di ricerca*. Milano: A. Giuffrè [*Sociology of Politics: Concepts, Methods and Research Field*].

Batygin, G. 1998. "Continuity of the Russian Sociological Tradition". In *Sociology in Russia*. Edited by V. A. Yadov. Moscow: Institute of Sociology, Russian Academy of Sciences, pp. 23–44 [Батыгин, Г. 1998. "Преемственность российской социологической традиции". В *Социология в России*. Под редакцией В. А. Ядова. Москва: Издательство Института социологии РАН].

Batygin, G., I. Deviatko. 1994. "The Metamorphoses of Russian Sociology". In *Eastern Europe in Transformation. The Impact on Sociology*. Edited by M. F. Keen, J. Mucha. Connecticut & London: Greenwood Press, Westport, pp. 11–23.

Bauman, Z. 1964. *Zakys marksistowskiej teorii społeczeństwa*. Warszawa: Państwowe Wydawnictwo Naukowe.

Becker, H., A. Boskoff. 1961. *Modern Sociological Theory*. Moscow: Innostrannaya literatura [Беккер Г., А. Босков. 1961. *Современная социологическая теория*. Москва: Иностранная литература, translation from English to Russian].

Becskehazi, A., T. Kuczi. 1994. "The Sociology of Reformist Socialism: The Hungarian Model". In *Eastern Europe in Transformation. The Impact on Sociology*. Edited by M. F. Keen, J. Mucha. Connecticut & London: Greenwood Press, Westport, pp. 39–52.

Berger, P. L. 1963. *Invitation to Sociology. A Humanistic Perspective*. New York: Anchor Books, Doubley & Company, Inc.

Berger, P. L., T. Luckmann. 1966. *The Social Construction of Reality: A Treatise in the Sociology of Knowledge*. Garden City, New York: Doubleday.

Berthelot, J.-M. 1996. *Les vertus de l'incertitude. Le travail de l'analyse dans les sciences sociales*. Paris: PUF [*The Virtues of Incertainty. The Work of Analysis in the Social Sciences*].

Berthelot, J.-M. 1998. Les nouveaux défis épistémologiques de la sociologie. *Sociologie et sociétés*. Vol. *30* (1): 23–38 [The New Epistemological Challenges of Sociology. *Sociology and Societies*].

Berthelot, J.-M. 2001. *Epistémologie des sciences sociales*. Paris: PUF. [*An Epistemology of Social Sciences*].

Between East and West: Writings from "Kultura". 1990. Edited by R. Kostrzewa. New York: Hill & Wang.

Birnbaum, N. 1993. "Circus at Varna". In *Searching for the Light. Essays on Thought and Culture*. New York, Oxford: Oxford University Press, pp. 5–15.

Bloor, D. 1976. *Knowledge and Social Imagery*. London: Routledge & Kegan Paul.

Bogár, L. 1983. *A fejlődés ára. Gazdasagi nehézségek főbb okainak tőrteneti aspektusa.* Budapest: Közgazdasági és Jogi Könyvkiadó. [*The Price of Development. Historical Aspects of the Major Causes of Our Economic Difficulties*].

Bokor, Á. 1985. *Depriváció és szegénység. Rétegződés-modell vizsgálat VI*. Budapest: Társadalomtudományi Intézet [*Deprivation and Poverty. Examination of Stratification Models VI*].

Boltanski, L. 1979. Les systèmes de représentation d'un groupe social: les « cadres ». *Revue française de sociologie*. Vol. *20* (4): 631–668. [Systems of Representation of a Social Group: the 'Cadres'].

Borges, J. L., O. Ferrari. 2014. *Conversations,* Vol. *1.* Seagull Books.

Boucheron, P. 2015. *La magistrale leçon inaugurale au Collège de France*, 17.12.2015. Accessed April 5, 2016. http://www.telerama.fr/idees/au-college-de-france-la-magistrale-lecon-inaugurale-de-l-historien-patrick-boucheron,135840.php [*The Inaugural Lecture at Collège de France*].

Boudon, R. 1986. *L'idéologie ou l'origine des idées reçues*. Paris: Fayard [*The Ideology, or the Origin of Received Ideas*].

Boudon, R. 2000. *Etudes sur les sociologues classiques II*. Paris: PUF [*Studies on Classical Sociologists II*].

Bourdieu, P. 1975. La spécificité du champ scientifique et les conditions sociales du progrès de la raison. *Sociologie et sociétés*. Vol. *7* (1): 91–118 [The Specificity of Scientific Field and the Social Conditions of the Progress of Reason].

Bourdicu, P. 1980. *Le sens pratique*. Paris. Les Editions de Minuit [*The Practical Sense*].

Bourdieu, P. 1994. *Raisons pratiques. Sur la théorie de l'action*. Paris: Seuil, Coll. Essais [*Practical Reason. On the Theory of Action*].

Bourdieu, P. 2001. *Science de la science et réflexivité*. Paris: Editions Raisons d'agir [*Science of Science and Reflexivity*].

Bourdieu, P., J.-Cl. Passeron. 1970. *La Reproduction. Eléments pour une théorie du sys- tème d'enseignement*. Paris: Les Editions de Minuit [*The Reproduction. Elements for a Theory of Education System*].

Bourgeois Sociology in Search of a Theory. 1966. Moscow: Znanie [*Буржуазная социология в поисках теории*. 1966. Москва: Знание].

Boyadjieva, P. 2010. "Shooting at a Moving Target: Rediscovering Sociology in Bulgaria". In *The ISA Handbook of Diverse Sociological Traditions*. Edited by S. Patel. Los Ange- les, London, New Delhi, Singapore, Washington DS: Sage, pp. 163–174.

Bruszt, L. 1984. *Informális társadalom és legitimatás*. Budapest: Társadalomtudományi Intézet [*Informal Society and Legitimacy. Research Reports*].

Brzezinski, Z. K. 1989. *The Grand Failure: The Birth and Death of Communism in the Twentieth Century*. New York: Charles Scribner's Sons.

Bukharin, N. I. 1921. *Theory of Historical Materialism: A Popular Textbook of Marxist So- ciology*. Moscow: Gosizdat [Бухарин. Н. И. *Теория исторического материализма. Популярный учебник марксистской социологии*. Москва: Госиздат].

Bundzhulov, A. 1995. Lenin, "The State and the Revolution": Archetypes of Communist Discourse. *Sotziologicheski Problemi/Sociological Problems*. *3*: 27–39 [Бунджулов, А. 1995. Ленин, "Държавата и революцията": архетипи на комунистическия дискурс. *Социологически проблеми*].

Bundzhulov, A. 2002. The Scholar and the Power. *Sotziologicheski Problemi/Sociologi- cal Problems*. *1–2*: 48–61 [Бунджулов, А. 2002. Ученият и властта. *Социологически проблеми*].

Bundzhulov, A. 2003. What Appears in Place Of? Artificial Joints and Networks in So- cialism. *Sotziologicheski Problemi/Sociological Problems*. *1–2*: 87–105. [Бунджулов, А. 2003. Какво възниква на мястото на? Изкуствените стави и мрежи при социализма. *Социологически проблеми*].

Busino, G. 1992. *La sociologie sens dessus dessous*. Genève: Librairie Droz [*Sociology Turned Upside Down*].

Caillé, A. 1986. *Splendeurs et misères des sciences sociales*. Genève, Paris: Librairie Droz [*Splendor and Misery of Social Sciences*].

Castel, R. 1995. *La métamorphose de la question sociale: une chronique du salariat*. Paris: Fayard [*The Metamorphosis of the Social Question: A Chronicle of the Wage Labor*].

Chałasiński, J. 1948. Trzydzieści lat socjologii polskiej, 1918 do 1947. *Przegląd Socjologic- zny*. Vol. *10*: 1–54 [Thirty Years of Polish Sociology, 1918–1947. *Przegląd Socjologiczny/ The Sociological Review*].

Chałasiński, J. 1959. "Sociology and Social Mythology in Post–War Poland". In *Transac- tions of the Fourth World Congress of Sociology*. Vol. *1*. Milan and Stresa, 8–15 Septem- ber 1959, pp. 139–146.

Chapoulie, J.-M. 2005. Un cadre d'analyse pour l'histoire des sciences sociales. *Revue d'histoire des sciences humaines*. *13* (2): 99–126 [An Analytical Framework for the History of Social Sciences].

Char, R. 1946. *Feuillets d'Hypnos*. Paris: Gallimard, Coll. Espoir [*Leaves of Hypnos*].

Cherednichenko, G. A., V. N. Shubkin. 1985. *Youth Entering Life (Sociological Studies of the Problem of Choosing a Profession and Finding Employment)*. Moscow: Mysl [Чередниченко, Г. А., В. Н. Шубкин. 1985. *Молодежь вступает в жизнь (социологические исследования проблем выбора профессии и трудоустройства)*. Москва: Мысль].

Chichovska, V. 1981. "State Cultural Institutions in Bulgaria (1944–1948)". In *Bulgaria 1300. Institutions and State Traditions*. Sofia: Sofia University Press, pp. 459–482 [Чичовска, В. 1981. "Държавни културни институции в България (1944–1948)". В *България 1300. Институции и държавни традиции*. т. 1. София: СУ "Климент Охридски"].

Coenen-Huther, J. 1996. Sociology between Universalism and Diversity: Some Remarks on the Alexander-Munch Debate. *Revue Suisse de Sociologie (Swiss Journal of Sociology)*. Vol. 22 (3): 501–506.

Coenen-Huther, J. 1997. Diversité de la sociologie et styles d'argumentation. *Revue européenne des sciences sociales*. Vol. *35* (107): 137–142 [Diversity of Sociology and Styles of Argumentation].

Coenen-Huther, J. 2002. La sociologie des sciences entre positivisme et sociologisme. *Revue européenne des sciences sociales*. Vol. *XL* (124): 219–231 [Sociology of Science between Positivism and Sociologism].

Collin, F. 1986. Un héritage sans testament. *Les Cahiers du GRIF*. Vol. *34* (1): 81–92. [A Legacy without a Testament].

Critique of Contemporary Bourgeois Philosophy and Sociology. 1961. Moscow: Higher Party School and Academy of Social Sciences at CC of CPSU Publishers [*Критика современной буржуазной философии и социологии*. 1961. Москва: Изд-во ВПШ и АОН при ЦК КПСС].

Critique of Contemporary Bourgeois Philosophy and Sociology. 1963. Moscow: Higher Party School and Academy of Social Sciences at CC of CPSU Publishers [Критика современной буржуазной философии и социологии. 1963. Москва: Изд-во ВПШ и АОН при ЦК КПСС].

Critique of Contemporary Bourgeois Sociology. 1976. Vol. *1–2*. Moscow: Institute of Sociologicial Studies, Academy of Sciences of URSS Publishers [*Критики современной буржуазной социологии*. 1976. Т. 1–2. Москва: ИСИ АН СССР].

Critique of Contemporary Bourgeois Theoretical Sociology. 1977. Edited by G. V. Osipov. Moscow: Nauka [*Критика современной буржуазной теоретической социологии*. 1977. Отв. ред. Г. В. Осипов. Москва: Наука].

Decision, Statutes, Governing Organs of the Soviet Sociological Association. 1977. Moscow: Academy of Sciences of USSR [*Решение, устав, руководящие органы Советской социологической ассоциации.* 1977. Москва: АН СССР, ССА].

Deleuze, G., F. Guattari. 1991. *Qu'est-ce que la philosophie?* Paris: Les Editions de Minuit [*What is Philosophy?*].

Deyanov, D. 2003. The Society of Networks and the Socio-analysis of the Gift (Pierre Bourdieu and Ivo Možný). *Sotziologicheski Problemi/Sociological Problems.* 1–2: 72–86 [Деянов, Д. 2003. Обществото на мрежите и социоанализата на дара (Пиер Бурдийо и Иво Можни). *Социологически проблеми*].

Deyanova, L. 2001. Micro-history as Trace. *Kritika i Humanism/Critique and Humanism.* 2 (11): 36–49 [Деянова, Л. 2001. Микро-историята като следа. *Критика и хуманизъм*].

Deyanova, L. 2003. The Everydaylife of Communism. Book Review on Sandrine Kott. *Le communisme au quotidien. Les entreprises d'Etat dans la société est-allemande.* 2001. Paris: Belin. *Sotziologicheski Problemi/Sociological Problems.* 1–2: 307–309 [Деянова, Л. 2003. Всекидневието на комунизма. Рецензия на книгата на Sandrine Kott. *Le communisme au quotidien. Les entreprises d'Etat dans la société est-allemande.* 2001. Paris: Belin. *Социологически проблеми*].

Deyanova, L. 2008. "SocRealism and RealSocialism. Towards the Methodology of Socialism Studies". In *Socialist Realism: New Studies.* Edited by P. Doynov. Sofia: NBU [Деянова, Л. 2008. "Соцреализъм и реалсоциализъм. Към методологията на изследването на социалистическата епоха". В: П. Дойнов (съст.). *Социалистическият реализъм: нови изследвания.* София: НБУ].

Deyanova, L. 2009. Scientific Archives after the Scientific Front, Disciplinary Memory and Interdisciplinary History. *Kritika i Humanism/Critique and Humanism.* 2 (29): 193–210 [Деянова, Л. 2009. Научните архиви след научния фронт, дисциплинарна памет и интердисциплинарна история. *Критика и хуманизъм*].

Deyanova, L. 2010. "Les sciences sociales socialistes à l'epreuve de la consommation élargie. Le double tournant à l'Est". In *Vie quoitidienne et pouvoir sous le socialisme. Consommer à l'Est.* Edited by N. Ragaru, A. Capelle-Pogacean. Paris: Karthala & CERI, pp. 52–81 ["Socialist Social Sciences Facing the Challenge of Enlarged Consumption. The Double Turn in Eastern Europe". In *Daily Life and Power under Socialism. Consumption in Eastern Europe*].

Deyanova, L. 2015. Social Sciences in the State Security Archives. *Sotziologicheski Problemi/Sociological Problems* 1–2: 134–153 [Деянова, Л. 2015. Социалните науки в архивите на Държавна сигурност. *Социологически проблеми*].

Dictionnaire des Sciences Humaines. 1990. Paris: Nathan [*Dictionary of Human Sciences*].

Đilas, M. 1983 [1957]. *The New Class: An Analysis of the Communist System.* San Diego: Harcourt Brace Jovanovich.

Dimitrov, G. 1995. *Bulgaria in the Orbits of Modernization*. Sofia: University Press St. Kliment Ohridski [Димитров, Г. 1995. *България в орбитите на модернизацията*. София: Университетско издателство "Св. Климент Охридски"].

Doellinger, D. 2013. *Turning Prayers into Protests. Religious–based Activism and its Challenge to State Power in Socialist Slovakia and East Germany*. Budapest: Central European University Press.

Doynov, St. 1975. "Youth and Its Leisure". In *Sociology Facing Youth Problems*. Sofia: CSRY Publishers [Дойнов, Ст. 1975. "Младежта и нейното свободно време". В *Социологията пред проблемите на младежта*. София: ЦНИМ].

Draganov, M. 1993. Zhivko Oshavkov—need new reading. *Sotziologicheski problemi/Sociological Problems*. *3*: 134–141 [Драганов, М. 1993. Живко Ошавков— необходимост от нов прочит. *Социологически проблеми*].

Dubois, M. 2001. *La nouvelle sociologie des sciences*. Paris: PUF, coll. "Sociologies". [*New Sociology of Sciences*].

Eastern Europe in Russian Archive Documents, 1944–1953. 1998. *Vol. II. 1949–1953*. Moscow, Novosibirsk: Siberian Chronograph [*Восточная Европа в документах российских архивов, 1944–1953 гг*. 1998. *Т. II. 1949–1953*. Москва, Новосибирск: Сибирский хронограф].

Elias, N. 1956. Problems of Involvement and Detachment. *British Journal of Sociology*. *7* (3): 226–252.

Elias, N. 1973 [1939]. *La civilisation des moeurs*. Paris: Calman-Lévy [Published in English as *The Civilizing Process*, Vol. *I. The History of Manners*. 1969. Oxford: Blackwell, and *The Civilizing Process*, Vol. *II. State Formation and Civilization*. 1982. Oxford: Blackwell].

Elias, N. 1976. *La dynamique de l'Occident*. Paris: Calman-Lévy [*Dynamics of the West*].

Elias, N. 1996. *The Germans: Power Struggles and the Development of Habitus in the Nineteenth and Twentieth Centuries*. Cambridge: Policy Press.

Empirical Sociology in Poland. 1966. Warsaw: PWN (Polish Scientific Publishers).

Fabiani, J.-L. 1993. Métaphysique, morale, sociologie. Durkheim et le retour à la philosophie. *Revue de métaphysique et de morale*. *1*: 175–191 [Metaphysics, Morals, Sociology. Durkheim and the Return to Philosophy].

Fabiani, J.-L. 1994. Epistémologie régionale ou épistémologie franciscaine? La théorie de la connaissance sociologique face à la pluralité des modes de conceptualisation dans les sciences sociales. *Revue européenne des sciences sociales*. Vol. *32* (99): 123–146 [Regional Epistemology, or Franciscan Epistemology? The Theory of Action in front of the Plurality of Modes of Conceptualization in Social Sciences].

Falt'an, L. 1995. The Institute of Sociology—five Years in Existence. *Sociológia/Slovak Sociological Review*. Vol. *27* (3): 162–170.

Farrugia, F. 2000. *La reconstruction de la sociologie française (1945–1965)*. Paris: L'Harmattan [*Reconstruction of French Sociology (1945–1965)*].

Fear, Ch. 2013. The question-and-answer logic of historical context. *History of the Human Sciences. July* (26): 68–81.

Fecteau, J.-M. 2002. La dynamique sociale du catholicisme québécois au XIXe siècle. Eléments pour une réflexion sur les frontières et les conditions historiques de possibilité du social. *Histoire sociale.* Vol. *35* (70): 497–515 [Social Dynamics of Quebec Catholicism in the 19th century. Elements for a Reflection on the Boundaries and the Historical Conditions of Possibility of the Social].

Ferge, Z. 1966. Társadalmunk rétegződés Magyarországon. *Valóság/Reality. 10*: 23–36 [Social Stratification in Hungary].

Ferge, Z. 1969. *Társadalmunk rétegződés.* Budapest: Közgazdasági és Jogi Könyvkiadó [*Social Stratification*].

Ferge, Z. 1979. *A Society in the Making.* White Plains: Sharpe.

Ferge, Z. 1986. Zsörtölődő megjegyzések Szelényi Iván és Manchin Róbert tanulmányához. *Medvetánc. 2–3*: 113–126 [Critical Comment on the Szelényi-Manchin's Article].

Filipov, F. R., P.-E. Mitev (eds.). 1983. *Youth and Higher Education.* Moscow [Филиппов, Ф. Р., П.-Э. Митев (сост.). 1983. *Молодёж и высшее образование.* Москва].

Forintos, I. 1982. Honunk a hazában. *Valóság/Reality. 25* (1): 8–20 [Our Home in our Country].

Forest, M., G. Mink 2004. *Post-communisme: les sciences sociales à l'épreuve.* Paris: L'Harmattan, Coll. "Pays de l'Est" [*Post-Communism: The Challenge for Social Sciences*].

Fotev, G. 1979. *The Sociological Theories of E. Durkheim, M. Weber, and V. Pareto. A Critical Comparative Analysis.* Sofia: Nauka i Izkustvo [Фотев, Г. 1979. *Социологическите теории на Е. Дюркем, В. Парето, М. Вебер.* София: Наука и изкуство].

Fotev, G. 1982. *Principles of Positivist Sociology.* Sofia: Bulgarian Academy of Sciences Publishers. [Фотев, Г. 1982. *Принципите на позитивистката социология.* София: Българска академия на науките].

Fotev, G. 1993. *History of Sociology.* Vol. *1.* Sofia: University Press St. Kliment Ohridski [Фотев, Г. 1993. *История на социологията.* Том първи. София: Университетско издателство "Св. Климент Охридски"].

Fotev, G. 2006. *Disciplinary Structure of Sociology.* Sofia: Printing House "East-West" [Фотев, Г. 2006. *Дисциплинарна структура на социологията.* София: Издателство "Изток-Запад"].

Friedrich, C. J. 1954. *Totalitarianism: Proceedings of a Conference Held at the American Academy of Arts and Sciences.* Cambridge: Harvard University Press.

Friedrich, C. J. 1957. *Totalitäre Diktatur.* Stuttgart: Kohlhammer [*The Totalitarian Dictatorship*].

Friedrich, C. J., Z. Brzezinski. 1956. *Totalitarian Dictatorship and Autocracy.* Cambridge: Harvard University Press.

From the History of Bourgeois Sociology, 19th—20th Century. 1968. Moscow: Moscow University Press [*Из истории буржуазной социологии XIX—XX вв*. 1968. Москва: Издательство МГУ].

Gábor, I. 1978. The Second (Secondary) Economy. *Acta Oeconomica*. 22: 291–311.

Gardani, A. G. 2013. *Le savoir sans fondements. La conduite intellectuelle de l'expérience commune*. Paris: Éditions Vrin [*Knowledge without Foundations. Intellectual Conduct of the Common Experience*].

Geiger, Th. 1949. *Aufgaben und Stellung der Intelligenz in der Gesellschaft*. Stuttgart: Enke Verlag [*Tasks and Position of Intelligentsia in Society*].

Genov, N. 1982. *Talcott Parsons and Theoretical Sociology*. Sofia: Bulgarian Academy of Sciences Publishers [Генов, Н. 1982. *Толкът Парсънз и теоретичната социология*. София: БАН].

Genov, N. (ed.). 1989. *National Traditions in Sociology*. London: Sage.

Genov, N. 1994. "Sociology as Promise and Reality: The Bulgarian Experience". In *Eastern Europe in Transformation. The Impact on Sociology*. Edited by M. F. Keen, J. Mucha. Connecticut & London: Greenwood Press, Westport, pp. 53–67.

Genov, N. 2002. "Sociology-Bulgaria". In *Three Social Science Disciplines in Central and Eastern Europe. Handbook of Economics, Political Science and Sociology (1989–2001)*. Edited by M. Kaase, V. Sparschuh, A. Wenninger. Bonn/Berlin, Budapest: Social Science Information Centre/Collegium Budapest, pp. 386–404.

Genov, N., U. Becker (eds.). 2001. *Social Science in Southeastern Europe*. Paris, Bonn, Berlin: International Social Science Council.

Giddens, A. 1984. *The Constitution of Society*. Cambridge: Polity Press.

Giddens, A. 1995. *Politics, Sociology and Social Theory*. Stanford: Stanford University Press.

Giza-Poleszczuk, A. 1989. Sociology and Social Life. *Sotziologicheski Problemi/Sociological Problems*. 5: 71–76 [Гиза-Полешчук, А. 1989. Социология и обществен живот. *Социологически проблеми*].

Glezerman, T. E., V. Z. Kelle, N. V. Pilipenko. 1972. Historical Materialism: Theory and Methodology of Scientific Cognition and Revolutionary Action. *Kommunist*. 4 [Глезерман Т. Е., В. Ж. Келле, Н. В. Пилипенко. 1972. Исторический материализм—теория и методология научного познания и революционного действия. *Коммунист*. 4].

Goldmann, L. 1970. *Marxisme et sciences humaines*. Paris: Gallimard [*Marxism and Human Sciences*].

Golenkova, Z. T., N. P. Narbut. 2010. *History of Sociological Thought in the Countries of Central and Eastern Europe*. Moscow: Russian University Peoples's Friendship [Голенкова, З. Т., Н. П. Нарбут. 2010. *История социологической мысли в странах Центральной и Восточной Европы*. Москва: Российский Университет Дружбы народов].

Golosenko, I. A., V. V. Kozlovskiy. 1995. *History of Russian Sociology 19th–20th Centu-ry.* Moscow: Onega [Голосенко, И. А., В. В. Козловский, 1995. *История русской социологии XIX-XX вв.* Москва: Онега].

Gorbachev, M. S. 1987 [1986]. *Perestroika: New Thinking for Our Country and the World.* New York: Harper Collins.

Gospodinov, K. 1975. Methodology and Abstract Models for Studying the Effects of the Type of 'Education'. *Problems of Youth. 15* [Господинов, К. 1975. Методоло-гия и абстрактни модели за изследване на ефектите от типа "възпитание" и процесите от типа "възпитаване". *Проблеми на младежта.* 15].

Gospodinov, K. 1980. Philosophical Introduction to Juventology. *Philosophska Mi-syl/Philosophical Thought. 8* [Господинов, К. 1980. Философски увод към ювентологията. *Философска мисъл.* 8].

Grootings, P., M. Stefanov (eds.). 1986. *Transition from School to Work.* Sofia: Sofia: IYS.

Grushin, B. A. 1967. *Opinions on the World and the World of Opinions: Problems of the Methodology of Public Opinion Survey.* Moscow: Politizdat [Грушин, Б. А. 1967. Мнения о мире и мир мнений: Проблемы методологии исследования общественного мнения. Москва: Политиздат].

Guidebook for Internal Use. 1981. Praha: Czechoslovak Academy of Sciences Press.

Habermas, J. 1997 [1980]. "Modernity: An Unfinished Project". In *Habermas and the Un-finished Project of Modernity. Critical Essays on the Philosophical Discourse of Moder-nity.* Edited by M. Passerin d'Entrèves, S. Benhabib. Cambridge, Massachusetts: The M.I.T. Press, pp. 38–55.

Habermas, J. 1987. *Logique des sciences sociales.* Paris: PUF [*Logic of Social Sciences*].

Hankiss, E. 1988. The Second Society: is there an Alternative Social Model Emerging in Contemporary Hungary? *Social Research.* Vol. 55 (1–2): 13–42.

Hankiss, E. 2002. "Brilliant Ideas or Brilliant Errors?". In *Three Social Science Disciplines in Central and Eastern Europe. Handbook of Economics, Political Science and Sociolo-gy (1989–2001).* Edited by M. Kaase, V. Sparschuh, A. Wenninger. Bonn/Berlin, Buda-pest: Social Science Information Centre/Collegium Budapest, pp. 17–24.

Hartman, J., M. Stefanov (eds.). 1984. *Youth in Europe. Integration through Participation.* Sofia: IYS.

Hartman, J., S. Trnka (eds.). 1984. *Integration of Youth into Society.* Upssala: Upssala Uni-versity.

Hartog, F. 2003. *Régimes d'historicité. Présentisme et expérience du temps.* Paris: Seuil, La librairie du XX siècle [*Regimes of Historicity. Presentism and Experience of Time*].

Havlová, J., O. Sedláček. 2004. Sociologie práce a průmyslu v letech 1965–1989. *Sociolog-ický časopis/Czech Sociological Review.* Vol. 40 (5): 651–664 [The Sociology of Work and Industry 1965–1989].

Hegedüs, A. 1964. A szocialista társadalom strukturális modellje és a társadalmi réteg-ződés. *Valóság/Reality.* *5*: 1–15 [Structural Model of Socialist Society and Social Strat-ification].

Hegedüs, A. 1966. *A szocialista társadalom struktúrájáról.* Budapest: Akadémiai Kiadó [*On the Structure of Socialist Society*].

Heilbron, J. 2008. Qu'est-ce qu'une tradition nationale en sciences sociales? *Revue d'histoire des sciences humaines.* Vol. *18* (1): 3–16 [What is a National Tradition in Social Sciences?].

Hentsch, Th. 2006. *La mer, la limite.* Montréal: Héliotrope [*The Sea, the Limit*].

Héthy, L., C. Makó. 1978. *Munkások, érdekek, érdekegyeztetés.* Budapest: Közgazdasági és Jogi Könyvkiadó [*Workers, Interests, Bargaining*].

History of Bourgeois Sociology 19th*—Early 20th Century.* 1979. Moscow: Nauka [История буржуазной социологии конца XIX—начала XX веков. 1979. Москва: Наука].

History of the Development of Sociology in Russia. 1989. Moscow: Press of the Institute of Sociology, Academy of Sciences of USSR [*История развития социологии в России.* 1989. Москва: Институт социологии, АН СССР].

History of the Emergence of Soviet Sociological Science 1920s–1930s. 1989. Moscow: In-stitute of Sociology of URSS [*История становления советской социологической науки 20–30-е гг.* 1989. Москва: Институт социологии АН СССР].

Hochfeld, J. 1963. *Studia o marksowskiej teorii społeczeństwa.* Warszawa: PWN [*Study on the Marx's Theory of Society*].

Illner, M. 2002. "Sociology—Czech Republic". In *Three Social Science Disciplines in Central and Eastern Europe. Handbook of Economics, Political Science and Sociology (1989–2001).* Edited by M. Kaase, V. Sparschuh, A. Wenninger. Bonn/Berlin, Buda-pest: Social Science Information Centre/Collegium Budapest, pp. 405–424.

Innerarity, D. 2009 [2001]. *Éthique de l'hospitalité.* Québec: Les Presses de l'Université Laval [*Ethics of Hospitality*].

International Varna Sociological School. 1980. *Statutes.*

Ionin, L. G. 1978. *Comprehensive Sociology: A Historical-Critical Analysis.* Moscow: Nau-ka [Ионин, Л. Г. 1978. *Понимающая социология: Историко-критический анализ.* Москва: Наука].

Ionin, L. G. 2007. "One Needs to Agree with One's Own Choice". *"Telescope": Journal of Sociological and Marketing Research.* *3*: 1–27 [Ионин, Л. Г. 2007. "Надо соглашаться с собственым выбором". *"Телескоп": журнал социологических и маркетинговых исследований.* 3: 1–27].

Isusov, M. 1978. *Political Parties in Bulgaria 1944–1948.* Sofia: Nauka i Izkustvo [Исусов, М. 1978. *Политическите партии в България 1944–1948.* София: Издателство "Наука и изкуство"].

Kaase, M., V. Sparschuh, A. Wenninger (eds.). 2002. *Three Social Science Disciplines in Central and Eastern Europe. Handbook of Economics, Political Science and Sociology (1989–2001)*. Bonn/Berlin, Budapest: Social Science Information Centre/Collegium Budapest.

Kabakchieva, P. 2016. *Communist Modernities. The Bulgarian Case*. Sofia: University Press St. Kliment Ohridski [Кабакчиева, П. 2016. *Комунистическите модерности. Българският случай*. София: Университетско издателство "Св. Климент Охридски"].

Keen, M. F., J. Mucha (eds.). 1994. *Eastern Europe in Transformation. The Impact on Sociology*. Westport, Connecticut & London: Greenwood Press.

Keen, M. F., J. Mucha (eds.). 2003. *Sociology in Central and Eastern Europe. Transformations at the Dawn of a New Millennium*. Westport, Connecticut & London: Praeger.

Keen, M. F., J. L. Mucha (eds.). 2006. *Autobiographies of Transformation. Lives in Central and Eastern Europe*. London, New York: Routledge, Taylor & Francis Group.

Kelle, W. 1994. Über eine lang zurückliegende Polemik. In *Zeitgenosse Jürgen Kuczynski*. Berlin: Elefanten Press [*Overcoming Polemics*].

Kemény, I. 1972. A magyar munkásosztály rétegződése. *Szociológia*. *1*: 36–48 [The Stratification of the Hungarian Working Class].

Kemény, I. 1987. Hongrie: économie et société civile. *L'Autre Europe*. *13*: 38–59 [Hungary: Economy and Civil Society. *The Other Europe*].

Klobucký, R. 2009. Forty Years of Journal Sociológia/Slovak Sociological Review. *Sociológia/Slovak Sociological Review*. Vol. *41* (1): 52–82.

Knorr Cetina, K. 1995. Epistemic Cultures: Forms of Reason in Science. *Sotziologicheski Problemi/Sociological Problems*. *2*: 54–68 [Кнор Сетина, К. 1995. Епистемичните култури: форми на разум в науката. *Социологически проблеми*].

Knorr Cetina, K. 1998. Les épistémès de la société: l'enclavement du savoir dans les structures sociales. *Sociologie et sociétés*. Vol. *30* (1): 39–54 [The Epistemes of Society: the Enclosing of Knowledge within Social Structures].

Koev, K. 1981. *Phenomenological Sociology of Everyday Life: Alfred Schütz*. Unpublished PhD thesis. Sofia [Коев, К. 1981. *Феноменологичната социология на всекидневието: Алфред Шютц*. Непубликувана дисертация. София].

Koev, K. 1982. The Problem 'Everyday Life—Science' in the Phenomenological Sociology of A. Schütz. *Sotziologicheski Problemi/Sociological Problems*. *4*: 74–82 [Коев, К. 1982. Проблемът 'всекидневие—наука' във феноменологичната социология на А. Шютц. *Социологически проблеми*].

Koev, K. 1992. Masks and Faces: Bulgarian Sociology in Search of Itself. *International Sociology*. Vol. *7* (1): 102–109.

Kolaja, J. Th., M. S. Das (eds.). 1990. *Glimpses of Sociology in Eastern Europe*. New Delhi: C.L. Gupta Prints India.

Koleva, S. 1998. La sociologie et la société dans les pays de l'Est: bilan d'une coexistence tourmentée. *Cahiers du GERIS,* Université du Québec à Hull. *5* [Sociology and Society in the East European Countries: the Assessment of a Troubled Coexistence].

Koleva, S. 2002a. Sociology in Central and Eastern Europe after the WW2 till 1989: Institutional Cycles and Prospects for Development. *Sotziologicheski Problemi/Sociological Problems. 1–2*: 62–77 [Колева, С. 2002. Социологията в Централна и Източна Европа след Втората световна война до 1989 г.: Институционална цикличност и шансове за развитие. *Социологически проблеми*].

Koleva, S. 2002b. The Disciplinary Identity of Sociology: Profiles of Construction (Sociology in Poland, Russia and Bulgaria in the 1950s and 1960s). *Sociological Problems.* Special Issue: 74–91.

Koleva, S. 2002c. "Unwritten History of the Contemporary Bulgarian Sociology". In *Sociological Perspectives.* Edited by N. Tilkidjiev, S. Donchev. Sofia: BAS's Press, pp. 11–24 [Колева, С. 2002. "Неписаната история на съвременната българска социология". В: Тилкиджиев, Н., Дончев, С. (съст.). *Социологически перспективи*. София: Академично издателство "Проф. Марин Дринов"].

Koleva, S. 2005. *Sociology as a Project. Scientific Identity and Social Challenges in Bulgaria, 1945–1989.* Sofia: Pensoft [Колева, С. 2005. *Социологията като проект. Научна идентичност и социални изпитания в България, 1945–1989.* София: Пенсофт].

Koleva, S. 2011. "Le marxisme comme idéologie d'État versus le projet politique du socialisme". In *Les deux faces de Janus. Essais sur le libéralisme et le socialisme.* Edited by B. Coutu, H. Forcier. Montréal: Éditions libres du Carré Rouge, pp. 307–321 ["Marxism as a State Ideology and Socialisme's Political Project". In *The Two Faces of Janus. On Liberalism and Socialism*].

Kołomejczyk, N., A. Koseski. 1977. *Europejskie państwa socjalistyczne 1948–1960: zarys historii politycznej.* Warszawa: Wiedza Powszechna [*European Socialist Countries 1948–1960: An outline of Political History*].

Kolosi, T. 1974. *Társadalmi struktúra és szocializmus.* Budapest: Kossuth Könyvkiadó [*Social Structure and Socialism*].

Kolosi, T. 1984. *Státusz és réteg. Rétegződés-modell-vizsgálat III.* Budapest: Társadalomtudományi Intézet [*Status and Strata. Examinations of Stratification Models III*].

Kolosi, T. 1988. Stratification and Social Structure in Hungary. *Annual Review of Sociology. 14*: 405–419.

Kolosi, T., I. Szelényi. 1993. "Social Change and Research on Social Structure in Hungary". In *Sociology in Europe. In Search of Identity.* Edited by B. Nedelmann, P. Sztompka. Berlin, New York: Walter de Gruyter, pp. 141–163.

Kolosi, T., E. Wnuk-Lipinski. 1983. *Equality and Inequality under Socialism: Poland and Hungary Compared.* London: Sage.

Kon, I. 1964. *Positivism in Sociology. A Historical Outline*. Leningrad: Leningrad University Press [Кон, И. 1964. *Позитивизм в социологии. Исторический очерк.* Ленинград: ЛГУ].

Konrád, G., I. Szelényi. 1978 [1974]. *The Intellectual on the Road to Class Power*. Bern: Európai Protestáns Magyar Szabadegyetem.

Konstantinovsky, D. L., V. N. Shubkin. 1977. *Youth and Education*. Moscow: Nauka [Константиновский, Д. Л., В. Н. Шубкин. 1977. *Молодежь и образование*. Москва: Наука].

Kornai, J. 1992. *The Socialist System: The Political Economy of Communism*. Princeton: Princeton University Press & Oxford: Oxford University Press.

Kostov, G. 1993. The Bulgarian Sociological School and the Contemporaneity. *Sotziologitcheski Problemi/Sociological Problems*. 3: 133–134 [Костов, Г. 1993. Българска та социологическа школа и съвременността. *Социологически проблеми*].

Kott, S. 2001. *Le communisme au quotidien. Les entreprises d'Etat dans la société est-allemande*. Paris: Belin [*Communism in Everyday Life. State Entreprises in the East German Society*].

Koudelka, F. 2004. Česká sociologie na Palackého univerzitě v Olomouci v letech 1962–1970. *Sociologický časopis/Czech Sociological review*. Vol. *40* (5): 623–630 [Czech Sociology at Palacký University in Olomouc in the Years 1962–1970].

Kraśko, N. 1997. "Historia Polskiego Towarzystwa Socjologicznego, 1957–1994". In *Z dziejow Polskiego Towarzystwa Socjologicznego. Wspomnenia i materiały*. Edited by E. Tarkowska. Vol. *1*, Warsaw: PTS, pp. 32–75 ["A History of the Polish Sociological Association, 1957–1994". In *From the History of Polish Sociological Association. Memoirs and Materials*].

Kraśko, N. 1998. Sociology in the First Decade of Socialist Poland. *Polish Sociological Review*. Vol. *122* (2): 177–195.

Kubiak, H. 1996. Hopes, Illusions and Deceptions: Half a Century of Political Sociology in Poland. *Current Sociology*. Vol. *44* (3): 21–39.

Kuczynski, J. 1957. The Sociological Laws. *Voprosui Philosophii/Questions of Philosophy*. *5* [Кучински, Ю. 1957. Социологические законы. *Вопросы философии*].

Kuhn, T. 1962. *The Structure of Scientific Revolutions*. Chicago: University of Chicago Press.

Kusá, Z., B. Búzik, L. Turčan, R. Klobucký. 2002. "Sociology—Slovakia". In *Three Social Science Disciplines in Central and Eastern Europe. Handbook of Economics, Political Science and Sociology (1989–2001)*. Edited by M. Kaase, V. Sparschuh, A. Wenninger. Bonn/Berlin, Budapest: Social Science Information Centre/Collegium Budapest, pp. 518–535.

Kyuranov, Ch. 1977. *Social Classes and Social Stratification*. Sofia: Nauka i Izkustvo [Кюранов, Ч. 1977. *Социални класи и социална стратификация*. София: Наука и изкуство].

Kyuranov, Ch. 1982. *Human Communities*. Sofia: Nauka i Izkustvo [Кюранов, Ч. 1982. *Човешките общности*. София: Наука и изкуство].

Kwasniewicz, W. 1993. "Between Universal and Native: The Case of Polish Sociology". In *Sociology in Europe. In Search of Identity*. Edited by B. Nedelmann, P. Sztompka. Berlin, New York: Walter de Gruyter, pp. 165–187.

Kwasniewicz, W. 1994. "Dialectics of Systematic Constaint and Academic Freedom: Polish Sociology under Socialist Regime". In *Eastern Europe in Transformation. The Impact on Sociology*. Edited by M. F. Keen, J. Mucha. Connecticut & London: Greenwood Press, Westport, pp. 25–38.

Lagrave, R.-M. 1998. *Voyage aux pays d'une utopie déchue. Plaidoyer pour l'Europe centrale*. Paris: PUF [*Voyage to the Lands of a Fallen Utopia. A Plea for Central Europe*].

Laiferova, E. 1998. "Up and Down of Slovak Sociology during the 20ᵗʰ Century". In *Čarnijev zbornik (1931–1996). Zbornik mednarodnih dru žboslovnih in humanisti čnih razprav*. Ljubljana: Faculty of Arts, Department of Sociology, pp. 354–365 [*A Festschrift for Ludvik Čarni (1931–1996). Studies in Humanities and Social Sciences*].

Lakatos, I. 1970. "Falsification and the Methodology of Scientific Research Programmes". In *Criticism and the Growth of Knowledge*. Edited by I. Lakatos, A. Musgrave. Cambridge: Cambridge University Press.

Laudan, L. 1977. *Progress and its Problems*. Berkeley: University of California Press.

L'Autre Europe. 1987. *Sociologies à l'Est*. Paris: L'Age d'Homme. *13*. [*The Other Europe. Est European Sociologies*].

Lavabre, M.-Cl. 1994. *Le fil rouge. Sociologie de la mémoire communiste*. Paris: PFNSP. [*The Red Wire. Sociology of Communist Memory*].

Le Moigne, J.-L. 1995. *Les épistémologies constructivistes*. Paris: PUF, Coll. « Que sais-je ? » [*Constructivist Epistemologies*].

Lenin, V. I. 1977. *Selected Works in five volumes*. Sofia: Partizdat [Ленин, В. И. 1977. Избрани произведения в пет тома. София: Партиздат].

Lepenies, W. 1997. *Benimm und Erkenntnis*. Frankfurt am Main: Suhrkamp [*Behavior and Knowledge*].

Lepenies, W. 2006. *The Seduction of Culture in German History*. Princeton: Princeton University Press.

Levada, Y. 1969. Lectures on Sociology. *Information Bulletin*, issues 20–21 [Левада, Ю. А. 1969. Лекции по социологии. *Информационный бюллетень*. Серия: Методические пособия, 20–21. Москва: ИКСИ АН СССР].

Linhart, J., M. Petrusek, A. Vodáková, H. Maříková. 1996. *Velký sociologický slovník*. Praha: Karolinum [*Great Sociological Dictionary*].

Lipset, S. M. 1959. Some Social Requisites of Democracy: Economic Development and Political Legitimacy. *The American Political Science Review*. Vol. *53* (1): 69–105.

Lutyńska, K. 1976. Relevance Analysis of Responds' Answer Obtained in an In-depth Pilot Study. *Quality and Quantity*. Vol. *10* (3): 209–233.

Lutyński, J. 1998. The Development of Polish Sociology: Some Determinants and their Consequences. *Polish Sociological Review*. Vol. *122* (2): 151–163.

Macháček, L. 2000. Rozhovor s Róbertom Roškom o sociológii a sociológoch na Slovensku pri príležitosti milénia. *Sociológia/Slovak Sociological Review*. Vol. *32* (1): 5–30 [Millenium interview with R. Roško about Slovak sociology and sociologist].

Macháček, L. 2004. Slovenské aspekty rozvoja sociológie v Československu. *Sociologický časopis/Czech Sociological Review*. Vol. *40* (5): 631–642 [Slovak Aspects of the Development of Sociology in Czechoslovakia].

Machacek, L. 2006. "From totality to pluralistic democracy: a sociologist and sociology in the course of social change in Slovakia". In *Autobiographies of Transformation. Lives in Central and Eastern Europe*. Edited by M. F. Keen, J. L. Mucha. London, New York: Routledge, Taylor & Francis Group, pp. 70–85.

Machonin, P. et al. 1969. *Československá společnost. Sociologická analýza sociální stratifikace*. Bratislava: Epocha [*Czechoslovak Society—Sociological Analysis of the Social Stratification*].

Machonin, P. 1992. *Sociální struktura Československa v předvečer Pražského jara 1968*. Praha: Karolinum [*The Social Structure of Czechoslovakia on the Eve of the Prague Spring of 1968*].

Machonin, P. 2004. K sociologii v období normalizace. *Sociologický časopis/Czech Sociological Review*. Vol. *40* (5): 643–650 [Sociology during the Period of Normalization].

Macků, J. 1996. "Sociologie česká do r. 1948". In *Velký sociologický slovník*. Edited by J. Linhart, M. Petrusek, A. Vodáková, H. Maříková. Praha: Karolinum, pp. 1041–1043 ["Czech Sociology until 1948". In *Great Sociological Dictionary*].

Mahler, F. 1983. *Introducere in Juventologie*. Bucuresti: Ed. ştiintifică şi enciclopedică [*Introduction to Juventology*].

Malewski, A. 1961. Dwa modele socjologii. *Studia Socjologiczne/The Polish Sociological Bulletin*, 3–4. [Two Models of Sociology].

Malewski, A. 1964. *O zastosowaniach teorii zachowania*. Warszawa: PWN [*About the Applications of the Theory of Behavior*].

Mamardashvili, M. 1968. *Form and Content of Thought (to the Critique of Hegel's Doctrine of the Forms of Knowledge)*. Moscow: Vuishaya shkola [*Формы и содержание мышления (К критике гегелевского учения о формах познания)*. Москва: Высшая школа].

Manchin, R., I. Szelényi. 1987. "Social Policy under State Socialism". In *Stagnation and Renewal in Social Policy*. Edited by G. Esping-Anderson, L. Rainwater, M. Rein. White Plains: Sharpe, pp. 102–139.

Mandeville, L. 1989. La sociologie en URSS. Réalisme sociologique ou terrain privilégié de la politique d'ouverture. *Revue française de sociologie*. V. *30* (1): 137–154 [Sociology in USSR. Sociological Realism, or a Privileged Field of Political Openness].

Markiewicz, W. 1970. Socjologia polska: 1919–1969. *Studia Socjiologiczne*. *1* (36): 5–38. [Polish Sociology: 1919–1969].

Martuccelli, D. 2014. *Les sociétés et l'impossible*. Paris: Armand Colin. [*Societies and the Impossible*].

Martuccelli, D. 2016 . La société et les régimes de réalité. *Les Cahiers de recherche sociologique*. *59–60*: 99–112 [Society and Regimes of Reality].

Marx, K. 1843–1844. "German-French Yearbooks". In: Marx, K. *Early Writings*. 1971. London: Penguin Books, pp. 199–210.

Marx, K. 1844. *Economic and Philosophic Manuscripts of 1844*. Accessed March 7, 2016. https://www.marxists.org/archive/marx/works/download/pdf/Economic -Philosophic-Manuscripts-1844.pdf.

Marx, K. 1845–1846. *The German Ideology*. Accessed March 7, 2016. https://www.marxists .org/archive/marx/works/1845/german-ideology/.

Marx, K. 1845. *Theses on Feuerbach*. Accessed March 7, 2016. https://www.marxists.org/ archive/marx/works/1845/theses/.

Marx, K., F. Engels. 1848. *Manifesto of the Communist Party*. Accessed March 7, 2016. https://www.marxists.org/archive/marx/works/download/pdf/Manifesto.pdf.

Maslov, K. 2015. 'Neither Class, nor Party': Paradoxes and Transformations of the Russian and Soviet Scientific Intelligentsia. *History of the Human Sciences*. *April* (28): 111–127.

Maslova, O., Y. Tolstova. 1998. "Methodology and Methods". In *Sociology in Russia*. Edited by V. A. Yadov. Moscow: Institute of Sociology Russian Academy of Sciences [Маслова, О., Ю. Толстова. 1998. "Методология и методы". В *Социология в России*. Под ред. В. А. Ядова. Москва: Издательство Института социологии РАН].

Matalon, B. 1993. "Réponse à Angelo Maria Petron". In *Le relativisme est-il résistible? Regards sur la sociologie des sciences*. Edited by R. Boudon, M. Clavelin. Paris: PUF, pp. 126–129 ["Answer to Angelo Maria Petron". In *Is Relativism Resistible? Insights into the Sociology of Science*].

Merton, R. 1973 [1938]. "Science and the Social Order". In *The Sociology of Science. Theoretical and Empirical Investigations*. Edited by R. Merton. Chicago, London: The University of Chicago Press, pp. 254–266.

Merton, R., A. Wolfe. 1995. The Cultural and Social Incorporation of Sociological Knowledge. *The American Sociologist*. Vol. *26* (3): 15–39.

Mespoulet, M. 2007a. Quelle sociologie derrière le « rideau de fer » ?—1950–1989. *Revue d'histoire des sciences humaines*. *16* (1): 3–10 [What Sociology behind the 'Iron Curtain'?—1950–1989].

Mespoulet, M. 2007b. La « renaissance » de la sociologie en URSS (1958–1972). Une voie étroite entre matérialisme historique et « recherches sociologiques concrètes ». *Revue d'histoire des sciences humaines*. *16* (1): 57–86 [The 'Revival' of Sociology in the

USSR (1958–1972). A Narrow Path between Historical Materialism and 'Concrete Sociological Research'].

Michéa, J.-Cl. 2007. *L'Empire du moindre mal: Essai sur la civilisation libérale*. Paris: Climats [*The Empire of the Lesser Evil: An Essay on Liberal Civilization*].

Mihailov, St. 1966. The Indirect Questionnaire as a Tool for Sociological Research. *Mens en maatchappij*. Rotterdam, November-December.

Mihailov, St. 1973. *Empirical Sociological Survey*. Sofia: Partizdat [Михайлов, Ст. 1973. *Емпиричното социологическо изследване*. София: Партиздат].

Mihailov, St. 2003. *Sociology in Bulgaria after the Second World War*. Sofia: M-8-M [Михайлов, Ст. 2003. *Социологията в България след Втората световна война*. София: M-8-M].

Mihailov, St. 2010. *The Sociological System*. Sofia: M-8-M [Михайлов, Ст. *Социологическата система*. София: M-8-M].

Mills, Ch. W. 1959. *The Sociological Imagination*. New York: Oxford University Press.

Mink, G. 1982. Compte-rendu du VIe congrès national de sociologie polonaise (Łódź: 9–12 septembre 1981). *Revue d'Etudes Comparatives Est-Ouest*. Vol. 13 (1): 157–164 [Report on the Sixth National Congress of Polish Sociology (Łódź: 9–12 September 1981)].

Mink, G. 1987. Une autre sociologie? *L'Autre Europe*. 13: 6–22 [Another Sociology? *The Other Europe*].

Migev, Vl. 1981. "Milestones in the development of Bulgarian socialist state". In *Bulgaria 1300. Institutions and State Traditions*. V. 1. Sofia: Sofia University Press, pp. 391–414 [Мигев, Вл. 1981. "Основни етапи в развитието на българската социалистическа държава". В *България 1300. Институции и държавни традиции*. София: СУ "Климент Охридски"].

Mitev, P.-E. 1976. Subordination of Questionnaire and Non-questionnaire Methods Used in Scientific Research on Youth. *Problems of Youth*. 5 [Митев, П.-Э. 1976. Субординация анкетных и неанкетных методов, используемых в научных исследованиях молодежи. *Проблемы молодежи*].

Mitev, P.-E. 1980. *The Modern Youth. Specific Moral Traits*. Sofia: Narodna Mladezh [Митев, П.-Е. 1980. *Съвременният млад човек. Специфични нравствени черти*. София: Народна младеж].

Mitev, P.-E. 1982. *Sociology facing the Problems of Youth*. Sofia: IYS.

Mitev, P.-E. 1983. Jugend und Arbeit. In *Ausbildung und Arbeitsplatzrisiko Jugendlicher*. München: DJI Verlag Deutsches Jugendinstitut [Youth and Work. In *Education and Risks of Finding Jobs by Youth*].

Mitev, P.-E. 1984. *From the Social Problem to Worldview Discoveries*. Sofia: Nauka i Izkustvo [Митев, П.-Е. 1984. *От социалния проблем към светогледни открития*. София: Наука и изкуство].

Mitev, P.-E. 1986. "Youth and Socio-bilogical Stratification of Society". Paper presented at the XI World Congress of Sociology, New Delhi, India.

Mitev, P.-E. 1988. *Youth and Social Change.* Sofia: Narodna Mladezh [Митев, П.-Е. 1988. *Младежта и социалната промяна.* София: Издателство "Народна младеж"].

Mitev, P.-E. 2016. *Bulgarians: Sociological Insights.* Sofia: East-West [Митев, П.-Е. *Българите: Социологически погледи.* София: Изток-Запад].

Mitev, P.-E., F. Filipov (eds.). 1982. *Youth and Higher Education.* Sofia: Institute of Youth Studies, Bulgarian Sociological Association.

Mitev, P.-E., V. Yaneva. 1972. Reading under Conditions of Audio-visual Attack. *Septemvri/September. 12* [Митев, П.-Е., В. Янева. 1972. Четенето в условията на аудиовизуална атака. *Септември*].

Mokrzycki, E. 1974. From Social Knowledge to Social Reseach: The Case of Polish Sociology. *Acta Sociologica.* Vol. *17* (1): 48–54.

Mokrzycki, E. 1989. "Polish Sociology in the Eighties: Theoretical Orientations, Methods, Main Research Trends". In *Sozialwissenschaften in der Volksrepublik Polen.* Edited by R. Scharff. Erlangen: Institut fuer Gesellschaft und Wissenschaft, pp. 91–124.

Možný, I. 1996. "Sociologie ceska, v. 1. 1948–1994". In *Velký sociologický slovník.* Edited by J. Linhart, M. Petrusek, A. Vodáková, H. Maříková. Praha: Karolinum, pp. 1043–1046 ["Czeck Sociology, 1948–1994". In *Great Sociological Dictionary*].

Možný, I. 2003. *Why so easy ... About some familial reasons for the Velvet Revolution.* Sofia: East-West [Можни, И. 2003. *Защо толкова лесно ... Някои семейни основания за нежната революция.* София: Изток-Запад].

Možný, I. 2004. Brněnská anomálie? Brněnská sociologie 1963 až 1989—subjektivní historie. *Sociologický časopis/Czech Sociological review.* Vol. *40* (5): 609–622 [The Brno Anomaly? Sociology in Brno 1963–1989—A Subjective History].

Mucha, J., P. Załęcki. 2002. "Sociology—Poland". In *Three Social Science Disciplines in Central and Eastern Europe. Handbook of Economics, Political Science and Sociology (1989–2001).* Edited by M. Kaase, V. Sparschuh, A. Wenninger. Bonn/ Berlin, Budapest: Social Science Information Centre/Collegium Budapest, pp. 484–501.

Münch, R. 1995. Geopolitics in the Guise of Universalistic Rethoric. *Revue Suisse de Sociologie (Swiss Journal of Sociology).* Vol. *21* (3): 547–555.

Musil, J. 2004. Poznámky o české sociologii za komunistického režimu. *Sociologický časopis/Czech Sociological review.* Vol. *40* (5): 573–595 [Comments on Czech Sociology under the Communist Regime].

Nedelmann, B., P. Sztompka (eds.). 1993. *Sociology in Europe. In Search of Identity.* Berlin & New York: Walter de Gruyter.

Nemchinov, V. S. 1955. Sociology and Statistics. *Voprosui Philosophii/Questions of Philos-ophy*. 6 [Немчинов, В. С. 1955. Социология и статистика. *Вопросы философии*].

Némedi, D. 2010. "Traditions and Ruptures in Hungarian Sociology 1900–2000". In *The ISA Handbook of Diverse Sociological Traditions*. Edited by S. Patel. Los Angeles, London, New Delhi, Singapore, Washington DC: Sage, pp. 152–162.

Némedi, D., P. Róbert. 2002. "Sociology—Hungary". In *Three Social Science Disciplines in Central and Eastern Europe. Handbook of Economics, Political Science and Sociology (1989–2001)*. Edited by M. Kaase, V. Sparschuh, A. Wenninger. Bonn/Berlin, Budapest: Social Science Information Centre/Collegium Budapest, pp. 437–451.

Nešpor, Z. R. 2013. Čeští sociologové vpočátcích slovenské sociologie. *Sociológia/Slovak Sociological Review*. 45: 27–47 [Czech Sociologists in the Beginnings of Slovak Sociology].

Nešpor, Z. R. 2014. Miloslav Petrusek ve světle své publikační činnosti v samizdatovém Sociologickém obzoru. *Sociologický časopis/Czech Sociological Review*. Vol. 50 (2): 189–210 [Miloslav Petrusek and the Samizdat Sociologický obzor: (New) Insight into a Sociological Thinker].

New Directions in Sociological Theory. 1987 [1978]. Translated from English into Russian by L. G. Ionin. Edited by G. V. Ossipov. Moscow: Progress [*Новые направления в социологической теории*. 1987. Пер. с англ. Л. Г. Ионина. Под ред. Г. В. Осипова. Москва: Прогресс].

Nickolov, L. 1992. Sociologists in Bulgaria Today. *International Sociology*. Vol. 7 (1): 99–102.

Nikolov, L. 1975. "Everyday Situations and Value Orientations of the Personality". In *Sociology of Personality*. Edited by L. Nikolov. Sofia: Sofi-R, pp. 224–249 [Николов, Л. 2001 [1975]. "Всекидневни ситуации и ценностни ориентации на личността". В: Николов, Л. *Социология на личността*. София: Софи-Р].

Nikolova, V. 1976. The Implanted Lexicon: A New Method of Sociological Research. *Problems of Youth*. 5 [Николова, В. 1976. Внедренный лексикон—новый метод социологического исследования. *Проблемы молодежи*].

Novikov, N. 1982. The Sociological Movement in the USSR (1960–1970) and the Institutionalization of Soviet Sociology. *Studies in Soviet Though*. Vol. 23 (2): 95–118.

Novikova, S. S. 1996. *History of the Development of Sociology in Russia*. Moscow, Voronetz: Institute of Practical Psychology Publishers [Новикова, С. С. 1996. *История развития социологии в России*. Москва-Воронеж: Издательство Институт практической психологии, МОДЕК].

Nowak, S. 1962. Środowiskowe determinanty ideologii społecznej studentów Warszawy. *Studia Socjologiczne/The Polish Sociological Bulletin*. 2: 91–103 [Social Attitudes of Warsaw Students].

Nowak, S. 1965. *Studia z metodologii nauk społecznych*. Warszawa: Państwowe Wydawnictwo Naukowe [*Essays in the Methodology of Social Sciences*].

Nowak, S. 1969. "Changes of Social Structure in Social Consciousness". In *Structured Social Inequalities*. Edited by C. S. Heller. New York: MacMillan, pp. 235–247.

Nowak, S. 1979. "Przekonania i odczucia współczesnych". In *Polaków portret własny*. Kraków: Wydawnictwo Literackie, pp. 122–145 ["Convictions and Feelings of Contemporaries". In *Polish Self-Portrait*].

Oates-Indruchová, L. 2007. Reporting or Story-telling?: Qualitative Research on Censorship in Czech Social Sciences, 1968–1989. *Sotziologicheski Problemi/Sociological Problems*. Vol. *39* (1–2): 288–301 [Оутс-Индрухова, Л. 2007. Доклад или разказ? Качествено изследване на цензурата в социалните науки в Чехия, 1968–1989 г. *Социологически проблеми*].

Oshavkov, Zh. 1956. The Process of Differentiation of Philosophy and the Non-philosophic Sciences as Specific Forms of Cognition. *Philosophska Misyl/Philosophical Thought*. 4:34–51 [Ошавков, Ж. 1956. Процесът на обособяване на философията и нефилософските науки като специфични форми на познанието. *Философска мисъл*].

Oshavkov, Zh. 1957. On the Object of Philosophy and the Non-philosophic Sciences. *Philosophska Misyl/Philosophical Thought*. 4: 24–48 [Ошавков, Ж. 1957. За предмета на философията и нефилософските науки. *Философска мисъл*].

Oshavkov, Zh. 1958. *Historical Materialism and Sociology*. Sofia: Bulgarian Academy of Sciences Publishers [Ошавков, Ж. *Историческият материализъм и социологията*. София: Издателство на БАН].

Oshavkov, Zh. 1960. *On the Nature, Methodology, and Methods of Sociological Surveys*. Sofia: Bulgarian Academy of Sciences Publishers [Ошавков, Ж. 1960. *За характера, методологията и методиката на социологическите изследвания*. София: Издателство на БАН].

Oshavkov, Zh. 1965. On Sociological Surveys at a Modern Scientific Level. *Novo vreme*. *11*: 29–44 [Ошавков, Ж. 1965. За социологическите изследвания на съвременно научно равнище. *Ново време*].

Oshavkov, Zh. 1966a. Les problèmes méthodologiques d'une étude de la religiosité en Bulgarie. *Archives de sociologie des religions*. *21* [Methodological Problems of a Research on Religiosity in Bulgaria].

Oshavkov, Zh. 1966b. Les résultats d'une étude sociologique de la religiosité en Bulgarie. *Revue française de sociologie*. *4* [The Results of a Sociological Study on Religiosity in Bulgaria].

Osipov, G. V. 1964. *Contemporary Bourgeois Sociology (A Critical Outline)*. Moscow: Nauka [Осипов, Г. В. 1964. *Современная буржуазная социология (Критический очерк)*. Москва: Наука].

Osipov, G. V. 1979. *Theory and Practice of Sociological Studies in USSR*. Moscow: Nauka [Осипов, Г. В. 1979. *Теория и практика социологических исследований в СССР*. Москва: Наука].

Osipov, G. V., L. N. Moskvichev. 2008. *Sociology and Power (How Things Really Were)*. Moscow: Economy [Осипов, Г. В., Л. Н. Москвичев. 2008. *Социология и власть (как это было на самом деле)*. Москва: Экономика].

Ossowski, S. 1963 [1957]. *Social Stucture in Social Consciousness*. London: Routledge and Kegan Paul; New York: Free Press.

Ossowski, S. 1983. *O osobliwościach nauk społecznych*. Warszawa: PWN [*On the Peculiarities of Social Sciences*].

Padovan, D. 1999. "Comments on Sociology in Italy". In *Yearbook of Sociology*. Institut for Sosiologi og Samfunnsgeografi dell'Università di Oslo—Norvegia. *1*: 213–223.

Padovan, D. 2006. Le scienze sociali e la costruzione dello spazio pubblico: il caso del razzismo fascista. *Rassegna italiana di sociologia*. *2*: 225–268 [Social Sciences and Construction of Public Space: the Case of Fascist Racism].

Pašiak, J. 2009. Reminiscences on the Origins of Journal Sociológia. *Sociológia/Slovak Sociological Review*. Vol. *41* (1): 5–13.

Pasiak, J., L. Machacek. 1994. "Sociology in Slovakia: Fiction and Reality". In *Eastern Europe in Transformation. The Impact on Sociology*. Edited by M. F. Keen, J. Mucha. Connecticut & London: Greenwood Press, Westport, pp. 89–99.

Passeron, J.-Cl. 1991. *Le raisonnement sociologique. L'espace non poppérien du raisonnement naturel*. Paris: Nathan. [*Sociological Reasoning. The non-Popperian Space of Natural Reasoning*].

Patel, S. (ed.). 2010. *The ISA Handbook of Diverse Sociological Traditions*. London: Sage.

Pavelka, F., M. Stefanov (eds.). 1986. *Rural Youth—Yesterday, Today, Tomorrow*. Sofia: IYS.

Pavlov, T. 1947. The Philosophical Discussion in URSS. *Philosophska Misyl/Philosophical Thought*. *3–4*: 100–130 [Павлов, Т. Философската дискусия в СССР. *Философска мисъл*].

Perelman, Ch. 1970. *Le champ de l'argumentation*. Bruxelles: Presses Universitaires de Bruxelles [*The Field of Argumentation*].

Perelman, Ch., L. Olbrechts-Tyteca. 1970. *Traité de l'argumentation. La nouvelle réthorique*. Bruxelles: Editions de l'Institut de Sociologie [*Treaty of Argumentation. The New Rhetoric*].

Petrusek, M. 1992. Dvoji renesance ceskoslovenské sociologie. *S-obzor*. *2*: 6–14 [Two Rebirths of the Czechoslovak Sociology].

Petrusek, M. 1995. Dekonstruovaný "Informátor" a sociální konstrukce českého národa. *Sociologický časopis/Czech Sociological Review*. *31* (2): 245–252 [Deconstructed 'Informátor' and Social Construction of the Czech Nation].

Petrusek, M. 2004. Výuka sociologie v čase tání a v časech normalizace (1964–1989) (Kapitola o vztahu vědění a moci, vědy a politiky, reality a mýtotvorby). *Sociologický časopis/Czech Sociological review*. Vol. *40* (5): 597–607 [Teaching Sociology in the

Periods before and during Normalization (1964–1989) (The Relationship between Knowledge and Power, Science and Politics, and Reality and Myth)].

Philosophska misyl/Philosophical Thought. 1947. *3–4* [Философска мисъл].

Philosophska misyl/Philosophical Thought. 1948. *1* [Философска мисъл].

Pinto, L. 1986. Un regard sur la sociologie en Hongrie. *Actes de la recherche en sciences sociales. 61*: 48–51 [A Look at Sociology in Hungary].

Piron. A Sofia Electronic Publication for Art and Culture. 2013–2014. *The Academic (Under)Ground 1981–1989. 8* [*Пирон.* Софийско електронно издание за изкуства и култура. 2013–2014. Академичният (Under)Ground 1981–1989].

Plekhanov, G. V. 1974. *Selected Philosophical Works.* Vol. *1.* "Socialism and the Political Struggle" [1883]; "Our Differences" [1885]. Moscow: Progress Publishers.

Pollak, M. 1993. *Une identité blessée, études de sociologie et d'histoire.* Paris: Métaillié [*An Injured Identity, Sociology and History Studies*].

Pokol, B. 1983. *Az érdekképviseleti szervek és a politikai rendszer reformlehetőségei.* Budapest: Institute of Social Sciences, Workshop Papers [*Representative Institutions and the Reform Potentials of the Political System*].

Potůček, M. (ed.). 1995. *Normalizace ve společenských vědách, můj život v normalizaci.* Praha: ISS FSV UK [*Normalization in the Social Sciences, my Life in Normalization*].

Purkrábek, M. 1995. "Normalizace ve společenských vědách—můj život v normalizaci". In *Normalizace ve společenských vědách, můj život v normalizaci.* Edited by M. Potůček. Praha: ISS FSV UK, pp. 36–40 [*Normalization in the Social Sciences, my Life in Normalization*].

Quéré, L. 2002. "Pour un calme examen des faits de société". In *A quoi sert la sociologie?* Edited by B. Lahire. Paris: La Découverte, pp. 79–94 ["For a Calm Examination of the Society's Facts". In *What is Sociology about?*].

Ragouet, P. 1994. D'une critique sociologique des épistémologies positives à l'abandon du projet sociologique. *Revue Suisse de sociologie* (*Swiss Journal of Sociology*). Vol. *20* (2): 487–503 [From a Sociological Critique of Positive Epistemologies to the Abandonment of the Sociological Project].

Raychev, A. 1984. *Youth and "the Small Justice".* Sofia: Narodna Mladezh. [Райчев, А. 1984. *Младият човек и "малката правда".* София: Народна младеж].

Raychev, A., K. Stoychev. 2004. *What Happened? A Narrative about the Transition in Bulgaria 1984–2004.* Sofia: East-West [Райчев, А., К. Стойчев. 2004. *Какво се случи? Разказ за прехода в България 1984–2004.* София: Изток-Запад].

Remington, R. A. (ed.). 1969. *Winter in Prague. Documents on Czechoslovak Communism in Crisis.* Cambridge, Massachusetts: The M.I.T. Press.

Revel, J. 2001. "Les sciences historiques". In *Epistémologie des sciences sociales.* Edited by J.-M. Berthelot. Paris: PUF, pp. 21–76. ["Sciences of History". In *Epistemology of Social Sciences*].

Revue d'Histoire des Sciences Humaines/Review of History of Human Sciences. 2005. Nouveaux travaux en histoire de la sociologie. Vol. *13* (2) [New Works in History of Sociology].

Revue d'Histoire des Sciences Humaines/Review of History of Human Sciences. 2007. Quelle sociologie derrière le "rideau de fer"? 1950—1989. Vol. *16* (1). [What Sociology behind the 'Iron Curtain'? 1950–1989].

Revue d'Histoire des Sciences Humaines/Review of History of Human Sciences. 2008. Traditions nationales en sciences sociales. Vol. *18* (1). [National Traditions in the Social Sciences].

Rimachevskaïa, N., L. Prokofieva. Entretien: L'enquête de Taganrog. *Revue d'histoire des sciences humaines*. Vol. *16* (1): 95–112 [Interview: Taganrog's Investigation].

Rimachevskaïa, N., L. Prokofieva. 2007. L'enquête de Taganrog. Le début de la sociologie du niveau de vie en URSS. *Revue d'histoire des sciences humaines*. Vol. *16* (1): 87–94 [Taganrog's Investigation. The Beginning of the Sociology of the Living Standard in the USSR].

Roško, R. 1984. Privlastňovací aspekt materiálnych podmienok života v zbližovaní robotníkov a inteligencie za socializmu. *Sociológia/Slovak Sociological Review*. Vol. *15* (6): 618–631 [Possession and Material Living Condition in Bridging the Gap between Workers and Intelligentsia in Socialism].

Roško, R. 1995. Thirty Years Ago. *Sociológia/Slovak Sociological Review*. Vol. *27* (3): 154–158.

Roulleau-Berger, L. 2016. *Post-Western Revolution in Sociology. From China to Europe*. Leiden, Boston: Brill.

Russian Sociology of the 1960s in Memoirs and Documents. 1999. St. Peterburg: Russian Christian and Human Institute. [*Российская социология шестидесятых годов в воспоминаниях и документах*. 1999. Санкт-Петербург: Российский Християнский гуманитарный институт].

Schaff, A. 1951. Zadania frontu filozoficznego w świetle uchwał i Kongresu Nauki Polskiej. *Myśl Filozoficzna/Philosophical Thought*. 1–2: 35–36 [Philosophical Front Tasks in the Light of the Congress of Polish Science' Resolution].

Schaff, A. 1962. Ankietomania czyli o drogach rozwoju polskiej socjologii. *Polytika*. 16: 2–3 [Polling Mania, or the Paths of Development of Polish Sociology].

Semov, M. 1982. *The Youth during the 60s. Changes and Problems*. Sofia: Narodna Mladezh [Семов, М. 1982. *Младежта през 60-те години. Промени и проблеми*. София: Народна младеж].

Shkaratan, O. I. 1970. *Problems of the Social Structure of the Working Class in USSR (A Historical-Sociological Study)*. Moscow: Mysl [Шкаратан, О. И. 1970. *Проблемы социальной структуры рабочего класса СССР (историко-социологическое исследование)*. Москва: Мысль].

Shkaratan, O. 1973. *Scientific-technological Revolution, the Working Class, the In-telligentsia.* Moscow: Politizdat [Шкаратан, О. И. 1973. *НТР, рабочий класс, интеллигенция.* Москва: Политиздат].

Shkaratan, O. 1985. *Worker and Engineer. Social Factors of the Efficiency of Labor.* Moscow: Mysl [Шкаратан, О. И. 1985. *Рабочий и инженер: социальные факторы эффективности труда.* Москва: Мысль].

Šiklová, J. 2004. Nelegální výzkum veřejného mínění v období normalizace. *Sociologický časopis/Czech Sociological Review.* Vol. *40* (5): 673–679 [Illegal Public Opinion Research during the Period of Normalization].

Simmel, G. 1987. [1900]. *Philosophie de l'argent.* Paris: PUF [*Philosophy of Money*].

Simon, P.-J. 2001. *Eloge de la sociologie ou la fécondité du néant.* Paris: PUF [*In Praise of Sociology, or the Fecundity of Nothingness*].

Simon, D., V. Sparschuh. 1994. "East German Sociology: Between the Production of Weltanschauung, Ideological Adaptation, and Empirical Social Research". In *Eastern Europe in Transformation. The Impact on Sociology.* Edited by M. F. Keen, J. Mucha. Connecticut & London: Greenwood Press, Westport, pp. 101–111.

Skilling, H.G. 1989. *Samizdat and an Independent Society in Central and Eastern Europe.* London: The MacMillan Press Ltd.

Slavov, Sv. 1989. Social Functions and Cognitive Characteristic of the Social Theory. *Sotziologicheski Problemi/Sociological Problems.* *5*: 14–21 [Славов, Св. 1989. Социални функции и познавателни характеристики на социалната теория. *Социологически проблеми*].

Smelser, N. J. 1965 [1963]. *The Sociology of Economic Life.* Moscow: Progress. Translation from English into Russian [Смелзер, Н. 1965. *Социология экономической жизни.* Москва: Прогресс].

Sociológia/Slovak Sociological Review. 1998. Documents. Reflections and Self-Reflections of Slovak Sociology. Vol. *30* (1).

Sociológia/Slovak Sociological Review. 2000.

Sociologický časopis/Czech Sociological Review. 1995. Miloslav Petrusek's commentary on the jubilee assembly of Czech sociologists. Vol. *31* (2): 285–287.

Sociologický časopis/Czech Sociological Review. 2004. Česká sociologie v letech 1965–1989. Vol. *40* (5): 695–740 [Roundtable Czech Sociology 1965–1989].

Sotziologicheskie issledovaniya/Sociological Studies. 1988.

Sotziologicheski problemi/Sociological Problems. 2003. Historical Sociology of Social-ism. 1–2 [*Социологически проблеми. 2003. Историческа социология на социа-лизма*].

Sociology and Power. Collection 1. Documents 1953–1968. 1997. Edited by L. N. Moskvichev. Moscow: Academia [*Социология и власть. Сборник 1. Документы 1953–1968. 1997.* Под ред. Л. Н. Москвичева. Москва: Academia].

Sociology and Power. Collection 2. Documents 1969–1972. 2001. Edited by L. N. Moskvichev. Moscow: Academia [*Социология и власть. Сборник 2. Документы 1969–1972.* 2001. Под ред. Л. Н. Москвичева. Москва: Academia].

Sociology and Power. Collection 3. Documents 1973–1984. 2008. Edited by L. N. Moskvichev. Moscow: Academia [*Социология и власть. Сборник 3. Документы 1973–1984.* Под ред. Л. Н. Москвичева. Москва: Academia].

Sociology in Bulgaria through the Eyes of Generations (Interviews with Bulgarian Sociologists). 2012. Edited by S. Koleva, D. Nenkova, S. Treneva. Sofia: Pensoft [*Социологията в България през погледа на поколенията (интервюта с български социолози).* 2012. С. Колева, Д. Ненкова, С. Тренева (съст.). София: Пенсофт].

Sociology in Russia. 1998. Moscow: Institute of Sociology, Russian Academy of Sciences [*Социологии в России.* 1998. Москва: Институт социологии, РАН].

Spalová, B. 2006. La révolution de « velours » dans les sciences sociales tchèques. *Critique internationale.* Vol. *32* (3): 107–131 [The 'Velvet' Revolution in the Czech Social Sciences].

Spiro, H. J. 1968. *World Politics.* New York: Knopf.

Stalin, J. V. 1928. *About Opposition.* Moscow: Gosizdat [Сталин, Й. В. 1928. *Об оппозиции.* Москва: Госиздат].

Stalin, J. V. 1938. "On Dialectical and Historical Materialism". *Pod znamenem marksizma/Under the Banner of Marxism.* 9: 140–159 [Сталин, Й. В. "О диалектическом и историческом материализме". *Под знаменем марксизма*].

Stalin, J. V. 1950. "Marxism and Problems of Linguistics". *Pravda/Truth*, Moscow, June 20 [Сталин, Й. В. "Марксизм и вопросы языкознания". *Правда*, Москва, 20 июня].

Stalin, J. V. 1952 [1951]. *Economic Problems of Socialism in USSR* [Сталин, Й. В. [1951] 1952. Икономически проблеми на социализма в СССР. София: Издателство на БКП, translation from Russian into Bulgarian].

Staniszkis, J. 1984. *Poland's Self-Limiting Revolution.* Princeton: Princeton University Press.

Stengers, I. 1993. *L'invention des sciences modernes.* Paris: La Découverte [*The Invention of Modern Sciences*].

Stengers, I. 1997. *Sciences et Pouvoirs. Faut-il en avoir peur?* Bruxelles: Labor [*Sciences and Powers. Should We Be Afraid of It?*].

Strmiska, Z., B. Vaváková. 1972. La stratification sociale de la société socialiste. *Revue Française de Sociologie.* Vol. *13* (2): 213–257 [Social Stratification of the Socialist Society].

Sułek, A. 1992. The Rise and Decline of Survey Sociology in Poland. *Social Research.* Vol. *59* (2): 365–384.

Sułek, A. 1998. Paul Lazarsfeld and Polish Sociology: A Historical Record of Contact, Perception, and Impact. *Journal of the History of the Behavioral Sciences.* Vol. *34* (3): 367–380.

Sułek, A., N. Kraśko. 2002. The Multifarious and Changing Functions of the Polish Sociological Association. *International Sociology*. Vol. *17* (2): 213–231.

Szacki, J. 1979. *History of Sociological Thought*. Westport, CT: Greenwood Publishers.

Szacki, J. 1993. Sociology at the Turning-Points of Polish History. *Polish Sociological Review*. Vol. *3* (103): 167–175.

Szacki, J. 1998. Polish Sociology 1944–1989: In Service of Society or in Service of the Regime? *Polish Sociological Review*. Vol. *2* (122): 115–131.

Szakolczai, A. 1992. Weber et la méthode généalogique. *Magazine Littéraire*. 93–94 [Weber and Genealogical Method].

Szczepański, J. 1969. *Elementary Concepts of Sociology*. Moscow: Progress [Щепаньский, Я. 1969. *Элементарные понятия социологии*. Москва: Прогресс, translation from Polish into Russian].

Szelényi, I. 1972. Lakásrendszer és társadalmi struktura. *Szociológia*. *1*: 49–74 [Housing System and Social Structure].

Szelényi, I. 1978. Social Inequalities in State Socialist Redistributive Economies. *International Journal of Comparative Sociology*. *10*: 63–67.

Szelényi, I. 1986–1987. Prospects and Limits of the New Class Project in Eastern Europe. *Politics and Society*. *2*: 103–144.

Szelényi, I., G. Konrád. 1969. *Az új lakótelepek szociológiai problémái*. Budapest: Akadémia Kiadó [*Sociological Problems of Housing Developments*].

Szomolányi, S. 1995. Metareflexia histórie slovenskej sociológie. *Sociológia/Slovak Sociological Review*. Vol. *27* (3): 158–161 [Meta-Reflection on the History of Sociology in Slovakia].

Szomolányi, S. 2009. Metareflexia histórie slovenskej sociológie po dvadsiatich rokoch. *Sociológia/Slovak Sociological Review*. Vol. *41* (1): 15–28 [Meta-Reflection on the History of Slovak Sociology 20 Years after].

Sztompka, P. 1979. *Sociological Dilemmas: Toward a Dialectic Paradigm*. New York: Academic Press.

Sztompka, P. 1984a. *Masters of Polish Sociology*. Kraków: Polska Akademia Nauk.

Sztompka, P. 1984b. R. K. Merton's Constructive Destruction of the Sociology of Knowledge. *The Polish Sociological Bulletin*. *1–4*: 59–71.

Sztompka, P. 2004. "La condition de la sociologie en Europe centrale et orientale". In *Post-communisme: les sciences sociales à l'épreuve*. Edited by M. Forest, G. Mink. Paris: L'Harmattan, Coll. "Pays de l'Est", pp. 159–172 ["The Condition of Sociology in Central and Eastern Europe". In *Post-Communism: The Challenge for Social Sciences*].

Tabatchnikova, S. 2007. *Le cercle de méthodologie de Moscou (1954–1989). Une pensée, une pratique*. Paris: Editions de l'Ecole des hautes études en sciences sociales [*The Moscow Methodological Circle (1954–1989). A Thought, a Practice*].

Tabin, M. 1987. Pologne—sociologie clandestine. *L'Autre Europe*. *13*: 71–85 [Poland—Underground Sociology. *The Other Europe*].

Tarniweski, M. [pseudonym of Karpiński, J.]. 1980. The New Regime. *Survey. A Journal of East &West Studies*. Vol. *25* (1): 118–134.

The Russian Sociological Tradition of the 60s and the Contemporary World. 1994. Edited by V. A. Yadov. Moscow: Nauka [*Российская социологическая традиция 60-х годов и современность*. Под ред. В. А. Ядова].

Tilkidjiev, N. 1987. The Stratum Structure of Socialist Society. *Sotziologicheski Problemi/Sociological Problems. 3*: 11–42 [Тилкиджиев, Н. 1987. Слоевата структура на социалистическото общество. *Социологически проблеми*].

Tillion, G. 2009. *Fragments de vie*. Paris: Le Seuil [*Fragments of Life*].

Todorova, M. 2003. Conversion to Islam as a Trope in Bulgarian Historiography, Fiction and Film. *Eurozine*. www.eurozine.com.

Topalov, Ch. 2004. "Les usages stratégiques de l'histoire des disciplines. Le cas de l'"Ecole du Chicago" en sociologie". In *Pour une histoire des sciences sociales (Hommage à Pierre Bourdieu)*. Edited by J. Heilbron, R. Lenoir, G. Sapiro with the collaboration of P. Pargamin. Paris: Fayard, pp. 127–157 ["The Strategic Use of the History of Disciplines. The Case of 'Chicago Schooll' in Sociology". In *For a History of Social Sciences (Tribute to Pierre Bourdieu)*].

Transactions of the Seventh World Congress of Sociology. 1973. Vol. *5*. Sofia: Bulgarian Academy of Sciences Publishing House.

Turčan, Ľ. 2000. Podmienky rozvoja sociológia v tzv. malych krajinách strednej Európy—slovenská sociológia v 20. storoči. *Sociológia/Slovak Sociological Review*. Vol. *32* (6): 507–520 [The Circumstances of the Development of Sociology in Central European Countries—Slovak Sociology in the 20th Century].

Turčan, Ľ., E. Laiferová. 1997. Modernization and Continuity as Themes of Historians of Sociology. *Sociológia/Slovak Sociological Review*. Vol. *29* (1): 69–74.

Turner, J. H. 1974. *The Structure of Sociological Theory*. Chicago, Ill: The Dorsey Press.

Turner, J. H. 1985. *The Structure of Sociological Theory*. Edited by G. V. Osipov. Moscow: Progress [Тернер, Дж. 1985. Структура социологической теории (Общ. ред. Г. В. Осипова). Москва: Прогресс, translation from English to Russian].

Turner, St. 1998. Who's Afraid of the History of Sociology? *Revue Suisse de Sociologie (Swiss Journal of Sociology)*. Vol. *24* (1): 3–10.

Tymowski, A. 1976. "The Social Minimum as an Instrument for the Distribution of Consumption Funds in a Socialist Society". In *Grants and Exchange*. Edited by M. Pfaff. Amsterdam: North-Holland Publishing Co., pp. 467–477.

Tzonev, V. 1958. *Foundations of Representative Study*. Sofia: Nauka i Izkustvo [Цонев, В. 1958. *Основи на репрезентативното изучаване*. София: Наука и изкуство].

Urbanek, E. 1994. "Ups and Downs in Czech Sociology". In *Eastern Europe in Transformation. The Impact on Sociology*. Edited by M. F. Keen, J. Mucha. Connecticut & London: Greenwood Press, Westport, pp. 79–87.

Vaněk, A. 1986. *Slovník českých a slovenských sociálně politických myslitelů a sociologů 1848–1980*. Praha: Univerzita Karlova [*Dictionary of Czeck and Slovak Social-Political Thinkers and Sociologists, 1848–1980*].

Vasilev, R., M. Draganov, St. Mikhailov. 1990. "Sociology in Bulgaria". In *Glimpses of Sociology in Eastern Europe*. Edited by J. Th. Kolaja, M. S. Das. New Delhi: C.L. Gupta Prints India, pp. 29–42.

Velev, I. (ed.). 1985. *Social Indicators in Comparative Youth Studies*. Sofia: IYS, Bulgarian Sociological Association.

Venedikov, Y. 1969. "Logical Setting for Analysis, Statistical Methods, and Measuring Means in the Study of Factors of Migration of Rural Youth". In *Socialism and Youth*. Edited by I. Popov, M. Semov. Sofia: Narodna Mladezh, pp. 229–282 [Венедиков, Й. 1969. "Логическа постановка на анализа, статистически методи и измерители при проучването на факторите за миграция на селската младеж". В *Социализмът и младежта*. И. Попов, М. Семов (съст. и ред.). София: Издателство "Народна младеж"].

Vinck, D. 1995. *Sociologie des sciences*. Paris: Armand Colin [*Sociology of Sciences*].

Volokitina, T. V., G. P. Murashko, A. F. Noskova. 1993. *People's Democracy: Myth or Reality? Social-Political Processes in Eastern Europe 1944–1948*. Moscow: Nauka [Волокитина, Т. В., Г. П. Мурашко, А. Ф. Носкова. 1993. *Народная демократия: миф или реальность? Общественно-политические процессы* в Восточной Европе 1944–1948 гг. Москва: Наука].

Volokitina, T. V., G. P. Murashko, A. F. Noskova, T. A. Pokivailova. 2002. *Moscow and Eastern Europe. Formation of Political Regimes of the Soviet type: 1949–1953: A Short History*. Moscow: ROSSPEN [Волокитина, Т. В., Г. П. Мурашко, А. Ф. Носкова, Т. А. Покивайлова. 2002. *Москва и Восточная Европа. Становление политических режимов советского типа: 1949–1953: Очерки истории*. Москва: РОССПЭН].

Voprosui philosophii/Questions of Philosophy. 1948. 2.

Voříšek, M. 2008. Antagonist, Type, or Deviation? A Comparative View on Sociology in Post-War Soviet Europe. *Revue d'histoire des sciences humaines*. Vol. *18* (1): 85–113.

Wesołowski, W. 1966. *Klasy i warstwy i władza*. Warszawa: PWN [*Class, Strata and Power*].

Wesołowski, W. (ed.). 1970. *Struktura i dynamika społeczeństwa polskiego*. Warszawa: PWN [*Structure and Dynamics of Polish Society*].

Wesolowski, W., K. Slomczynski. 1978. Reduction of Social Inequalities and Status Inconsistency. In *Social Structure—Polish Sociology*. Edited by Polish Sociological Association. Warsaw: Ossolineum, pp. 103–121.

Wiatr, J. J. 1962. Uwarstwienie spoleczne a tendencje egalitarne. *Kultura i Społeczeństwo*. 2 [Wiatr, J. J. 1962. Social Stratification and Egalitarian Tendencies].

Wiatr, J. J. (ed.). 1971. *The State of Sociology in Eastern Europe Today*. Foreword by R. Herman. Lantz Carbondale and Edwardsville: Southern Illinois University Press.

Wiatr, J. J. 1973. *Past and Present in Polish Sociology*. Boston (mimeographed).

Yadov, V. 1968. *Sociological Survey. Methodology, Program, Methods*. Tartu: Tartu University Press [Ядов, В. 1968. *Социологическое исследование: Методология, программа, методы*. Тарту: ТГУ].

Yolov, G. 1973. *Critical Situations and Mass Psyche*. Sofia: Nauka i Izkustvo [Йолов, Г. 1973. *Критични ситуации и масова психика*. София: Наука и изкуство].

Yolov, G. 1975. *Personality and Critical Situations*. Sofia: Partizdat [Йолов, Г. 1975. *Личността и критичните ситуации*. София: Партиздат].

Yotov, St. 2001. Unconscious Normativism in 'Sciences of the Spirit'. *Kritika i Humanizam/Criticism and Humanism*. 2: 8–33 [Йотов, Ст. Неосъзнатият нормативизъм в "науките за духа". *Критика и хуманизъм*].

Žatkuliak, J. 1998. Slovakia in the Period of "Normalization" and Expectation of Changes (1969–1989). *Sociológia/Slovak Sociological Review*. Vol. *30* (3): 345–408.

Zdravomyslov, A. G. 1969. *Methodology and Procedures of Sociological Surveys*. Moscow: Mysl [Здравомыслов, А. Г. 1969. *Методология и процедура социологических исследований*. Москва: Мысль].

Zdravomyslov, A. G., V. A. Yadov, V. P. Rozhin (eds.). 1967. *Man and His Work (A Sociological Study)*. Moscow: Mysl [Здравомыслов, А. Г., В. А. Ядов, В. П. Рожин (под ред.). 1967. *Человек и его работа (социологическое исследование)*. Москва: Мысль].

Zdravomyslova, E. 2010. "What is Russian Sociological Tradition? Debates among Russian Sociologists". In *The ISA Handbook of Diverse Sociological Traditions*. Edited by S. Patel. Los Angeles, London, New Delhi, Singapore, Washington DS: Sage, pp. 140–151.

Zhelev, Zh. 1982. *Fascism. Documentary Exploration of German, Italian, Spanish Fascism*. Sofia: BZNS [Желев, Ж. 1982. *Фашизмът. Документално изследване на германския, италианския и испанския фашизъм*. София: Издателство на БЗНС].

Index of Names*

---

*   Certain names of authors are given in two different spellings. The first is the original (national)
     orthography, with accent strokes. The second is the spelling in English language-publications,
     without accents.

Index of Subjects